EMPIRE
OF
DEBT

EMPIRE

OF

DEBT

The Rise of an Epic Financial Crisis

William Bonner

and

Addison Wiggin

WILEY

John Wiley & Sons, Inc.

Published by John Wiley & Sons, Inc., Hoboken, New Jersey.
Published simultaneously in Canada.

Library of Congress Cataloging-in-Publication Data:

Bonner, William, 1948–
    Empire of debt : the rise of an epic financial crisis / Bill Bonner
and Addison Wiggin.
        p.   cm.
    Includes index.
    ISBN-13 978-0-471-73902-9 (cloth)
    ISBN-10 0-471-73902-2 (cloth)
    ISBN-13 978-0-471-98048-3 (paper)
    ISBN-10 0-471-98048-X (paper)
        1. Financial crises—United States.   2. Debt—United States.   3. United
States—Economic conditions—2001–   I. Wiggin, Addison.   II. Title.
    HB3722.B658   2006
    336.3'4'0973—dc22

                                                            2005023682

Printed in the United States of America.

10   9   8   7   6   5   4   3   2   1

Contents

Introduction: Slouching toward Empire   1

I. Imperia Absurda

1. Dead Men Talking   23
2. Empires of Dirt   39
3. How Empires Work   55
4. As We Go Marching   81

II. Woodrow Crosses the Rubicon

5. The Road to Hell   93
6. The Revolution of 1913 and the Great Depression   131
7. MacNamara's War   149
8. Nixon's the One   177

III. Evening in America

9. Reagan's Legacy   191
10. America's Glorious Empire of Debt   219
11. Modern Imperial Finance   247
12. Something Wicked This Way Comes   261

IV. The Essential Investor

13. Welcome to Squanderville 275

14. Still Turning Japanese 297

15. The Wall Street Fandango 305

16. Subversive Investing 317

Appendix: The Essentialist Glossary 335

Notes 341

Index 351

EMPIRE

OF

DEBT

Introduction:
Slouching toward Empire

The will of Zeus is moving toward its end.

—The Illiad

One day in early spring 2005, we traveled by train from Poitiers to Paris and found ourselves seated next to Robert Hue, head of the French Communist Party and a senator representing Val d'Oise. He sat down and pulled out a travel magazine, just as any other traveler would. Aside from one Bolshevik manqué who stopped by to say hello, no one paid any attention. A friend reports that he was on the same train a few months ago with then Prime Minister, Jean-Pierre Raffarin, who was accompanied by only a single aide.

Many years ago, when the United States was still a modest republic, American presidents were likewise available to almost anyone who wanted to shoot them. Thomas Jefferson went for a walk down Pennsylvania Avenue, alone, and spoke to anyone who came up to him. John Adams used to swim naked in the Potomac. A woman reporter got him to talk to her by sitting on his clothes and refusing to budge.

But now anyone who wants to see the president must have a background check and pass through a metal detector. The White House staff must approve reporters before they are allowed into press conferences. And when the U.S. head of state travels, he does so in imperial style; he moves around protected by hundreds of praetorian guards, sharpshooters on rooftops, and thousands of local centurions. When President Clinton went to China in 1998, he took with him his family, plus "5 Cabinet secretaries, 6 members of Congress, 86 senior aides, 150 civilian staff (doctors, lawyers, secretaries, valets, hairdressers, and so on), 150 military staff

1

(drivers, baggage handlers, snipers, and so on), 150 security personnel, several bomb-sniffing dogs, and many tons of equipment, including 10 armored limousines and the 'blue goose,' Clinton's bulletproof lectern."

Getting the presidential entourage and its armada of equipment to China and back, the Air Force flew 36 airlift missions on Boeing 747, C-141, and C-5 aircraft. The Pentagon's cost of the China trip was $14 million. Operating Air Force One alone costs over $34,000 an hour.

Today, the president cavalcades around Washington in an armored Cadillac. The limousine is fitted with bullet-proof windows, equally sturdy tires, and a self-contained ventilation system to ward off a biological or chemical attack.

The Secret Service—the agency charged with preserving the president among the living—employs over 5,000 people: 2,100 special agents, 1,200 Uniformed Division employees, and 1,700 technical and administrative wonks. Everywhere the president goes, his security is handled—by thousands of guards and aides, secure compounds, and carefully orchestrated movements. Security was so tight during a visit to Ottawa, Canada, in 2004 that some members of Parliament were refused entry into the building for lack of a special one-time security pass, an act apparently contradictory to the laws of Canada.

In late 2003, when Bush deigned to visit the British Isles, an additional 5,000 British police officers were deployed to the streets of London to protect him. Parks and streets were shut down. Snipers were visible on the royal rooftop.[1] After Bush's stay at Buckingham Palace in London, the Queen was horrified by the damage done to the Palace grounds. They were left looking like the parking lot at a Wal-Mart two-for-one sale.[2]

THE THEME OF THIS BOOK IN A NUTSHELL

Watching the news is a bit like watching a bad opera. You can tell from all the shrieking that something very important is supposed to be happening, but you don't quite know what it is. What you're missing is the plot.

Let us begin by noticing that this is a comic opera that seems as though it might veer into tragedy at any moment. The characters on stage are familiar to us—consumers, economists, politicians, investors, and businessmen. They are the same hustlers, clowns, rubes, and dumbbells that we always see before us. But in today's performance they are doing something extraordinary, they are the richest people on the planet, but they have come to rely on the savings of the world's poorest people just to pay their bills. They routinely spend more than they make—and think they can continue doing so indefinitely. They go deeper and deeper in debt, believing they will never have to settle up. They buy houses and then mortgage them out—room by room, until they have almost nothing left. They invade foreign countries in the belief that they are spreading freedom and democracy, and depend on lending from Communist China to pay for it.

But people come to believe whatever they must believe when they must believe it. All these conceits and illusions that we find so amusing in the Daily Reckoning (www.dailyreckoning.com), come not from thinking, but from circumstances. As they say on Wall Street, "markets make opinions," not the other way around. The circumstance that makes sense of this strange performance is that the United States is an empire— whether we like it or not. It must play a well-known role on the world stage, just as you and I must play our roles, not because we have thought our way to them, but simply because of who we are, where we are, and when we are. Primitive people play primitive roles. They are no less intelligent than the rest of us, but they would be out of character if they began doing calculus. They have their parts to play just as we do. Sophisticated people play sophisticated roles. They are no smarter than anyone else, but you still don't expect them to wear bones through their noses. We, citizens of the last great empire, have our roles to play too, and the empire itself, must do what an empire must do.

Institutions have a way of evolving over time—after a few years, they no longer resemble the originals. Early in the twenty-first century, the United States is no more like the America of 1776 than the Vatican under the Borgia popes was like Christianity at the time of the Last Supper, or Microsoft in 2005 is like the company Bill Gates started in his garage.

Still, while the institutions evolve, the ideas and theories about them tend to remain fixed; it is as if people hadn't noticed. In America, all the restraints, inhibitions, and modesty of the Old Republic have been blown away by the prevailing winds of the new empire. In their place has emerged a vainglorious system of conceit, deceit, debt, and delusion.

The United States Constitution is almost exactly the same document with exactly the same words it had when it was written, but the words that used to bind and chaff have been turned into soft elastic. The government that couldn't tax, couldn't spend, and couldn't regulate, can now do anything it wants. The executive has all the power he needs to do practically anything. Congress goes along, like a simpleminded stooge, insisting only that the spoils be spread around. The whole process works so well that a member of Congress has to be found in bed "with a live boy or a dead girl" before he risks losing public office.

American businesses are still capitalistic. They operate, as everyone knows, in the most dynamic, free, and open economy in the world. A recent press item reports, that General Motors will never be able to compete unless it ditches its crushing health care costs. Why does it not just cut the costs? It seems to lack either the nerve or the right, but the journalist proposed a solution: Nationalize health care! Meanwhile, CEO pay has soared to the point where the average chief executive in 2000 earned compensation equal to 500 times the average hourly wage. Stockholders, whose money was being squandered, barely said a word. They were still under the illusion that the companies were working for them. They had not noticed that the whole capitalist institution had been trussed up with so many chains, wires, red tape, and complications, it no longer functioned like the freewheeling, moneymaking corporations of the nineteenth century. Meanwhile, corporations in China—a communist country—had their hands and feet free to eat our lunches and kick our derrieres.

The entire homeland economy now depends on the savings of poor people on the periphery to keep it from falling apart. Americans consume more than they earn. The difference is made up by the kindness of strangers—thrifty Asians whose savings glut is recycled into granite countertops and flat-screen TVs all over the United States.

But these ironies, contradictions, and paradoxes hardly disturb the sleep of the imperial race. They have permitted themselves to believe so many absurd things that they will now believe anything. In the fall of 2001, people in Des Moines and Duluth were buying duct tape to protect themselves from terrorist "sleeper cells ready to attack the Midwest." In the fall of 2004, they believed the Chinese were manipulating their currency by pegging it to the dollar for nearly 10 years! Like Alice, they were expected to believe six impossible things before breakfast and another half dozen before tea: Real estate never goes down! You can get rich by spending! Savings don't matter! Deficits don't matter! Let them sweat, *we'll* think!

We can't help but wonder how it will turn out.

In this book, we turn once again to the dusty pages of history. We find ourselves often tracing the footsteps of the West's greatest empire—Rome—searching for clues. In Rome, too, the institutions evolved and degraded faster than people's ideas about them. Romans remembered their Old Republic with its rules and customs. They still thought that was the way the system was supposed to work long after a new system of *consuetudo fraudium*—habitual cheating—had taken hold.

Rome's system of imperial finance was far more solid than America's. Rome made its empire pay by exacting a tribute of about 10 percent of output from its vassal states. There were few illusions about how the system worked. Rome brought the benefits of *Pax Romana,* and subject peoples were expected to pay for it. Most paid without much prompting. In fact, the cost of running the empire was greatly reduced by the cooperation of citizens and subjects. Local notables, who benefited from imperial rule, but who were not directly on the emperor's payroll, performed many costly functions. Many functions were "privatized," says Ramsay Mac-Mullen in his *Corruption and the Decline of Rome.*

This was accomplished in a variety of ways. Many officials, and even the soldiers stationed in periphery areas, used their positions to extort money out of the locals. In this way, the cost of administration and protection was pushed more directly onto the private sector. *Commoda* was the word given to this practice, which apparently became more and more widespread as the empire aged.

MacMullen recalls a typical event:

> From Milan, a certain Palladius, tribune and notary, left for Carthage in 367. He was charged with investigating accusations of criminal negligence—"if you don't pay me, I won't help you"—brought against Romanus, military commandant in Africa. Because of Romanus's inaction, the area around Tripoli, had suffered attacks by local tribes, without defense from the empire. But the accused was ready for the inquisitor, and when Palladius arrived unexpectedly at military headquarters in the African capital—carrying the officers' pay—he was offered . . . under the table . . . a considerable bribe. Palladius . . . accepted it. But he continued his investigations, accompanied by two of the local notables whose complaints had launched the inquiry. He prepared his report to the emperor, telling him that the charges against Romanus were confirmed. But the latter threatened to reveal the bribes he had accepted. So Palladius reported to the emperor that

the accusations were pure inventions. Romanus was safe. The emperor ordered that the two accusers' tongues be torn out.[3]

As time went on, the empire came to resemble less and less the Old Republic that had given it birth. The old virtues were replaced with new vices. Gradually, the troops on the frontier had to depend more and more on their own devices for their support. They had to take up agriculture. "The effectiveness of the troops was diminished as they became part-time farmers," says MacMullen.

Gradually, the empire had fewer and fewer reliable troops. In Trajan's time, the emperor could count on hundreds of thousand of soldiers for his campaigns in Dacia. But by the fourth century, battles were fought with only a few thousand. By the fifth century, these few troops could no longer hold off the barbarians.

The corruption of the empire was complete.

If you deny that the United States is now an empire, you are as big a fool as we were. For a very long time we resisted the concept. We did not want the United States to be an empire. We thought it was a political choice. We liked the old republic of Jefferson, Washington, the U.S. Constitution . . . the humble nation of hard money and soft heads; we didn't want to give it up. We thought that if the United States acted as though it were an empire it was making an error.

What morons we were. We missed the point completely. It didn't matter what we wanted. There was no more choice in the matter than a caterpillar has a choice about whether to become a butterfly.

This was an important insight for us. Until then, all of the blustering and slapstick pratfalls on stage seemed like "mistakes." Why would the United States run such huge trade deficits, we wondered. It was obviously a bad idea, the nation was ruining itself. And why would it launch an invasion of Iraq or begin a war on terror—both of which were almost certain to be costly blunders. It was as if the United States wanted to destroy itself—first by bankrupting its economy, and second by creating enemies all over the globe.

Then, we realized, that of course, that is exactly what it must do.

We repeat, people come to believe what they need to believe when they need to believe it. America is an empire; its people must think like imperialists. In order to fulfill their mission, the homeland citizens had to become what George Orwell called "hollow dummies." An imperial people must believe that they deserve to be the imperial power—that is, they must believe they have the right to tell other people what to do. In order to do so, they must believe what isn't true—that their own culture, society, economy, political system, or they themselves are superior to others. It is a vain conceit, but it is so bright and so big it exercises a kind of gravitational pull over the entire society. Soon, it has set in motion a whole system of shiny vanities and illusions as distant from the truth as Pluto and as bizarre as Saturn. Americans believe they can get rich by spending someone else's money. They believe that foreign countries actually want to be invaded and taken over. They believe they can run up debt forever, and that their debt-laden houses are as good as money in the bank. That is what makes the study of contemporary economics so entertaining. We sit at our telescopes and laugh like a divorce lawyer looking at photos of a rich man in flagrante delicto; we know there's money to be made.

Things that are unusual usually return to normal. If they did not, there would be no "norma" to return to. That is why you can expect stocks to become more expensive when they are cheap and cheaper when they are expensive. Stocks today are expensive—they trade for an average of about 20 times earnings. Usually, they trade for only 12 to 15 times earnings, so you can expect them to get cheaper.

Houses are expensive too. They usually go up at a rate roughly equal to the rate of inflation, income, or GDP growth—no more. For the past 10 years, however, they've gone up three to five times as fast. House prices cannot grow faster than income for very long; people have to be able to pay the prices in order to live in them. So, you can expect houses to revert to their mean too. Prices will fall . . . or else stop rising.

These simple reversions to mean are hardly controversial. We don't know when they will happen or how, but that they will come about is practically guaranteed.

More interesting to us are the reversions to other, bigger means. An empire itself is a rare thing. It is normal, but unusual. Nature abhors a monopoly. An empire is a monopoly on force. Nature will tolerate it for a while, but sooner or later, the imperial people must revert to being normal people, and the preposterous beliefs that the imperial people cherish, also must pass away. They must go up to a kind of humbug heaven, where absurd ideas and idle flatteries strut around while the gods point, snicker, and collapse into mirth, rolling around clutching their stomachs as if the humor of it was going to kill them.

The dollar is an extraordinary thing too. Do you know what the long term mean value of paper currency is? Well, it is zero. That is what the average paper currency is worth most of the time . . . and it is the black hole into which all paper currencies in the past have gone. There could be something magic about the dollar that makes it unlike any paper currency in the past—that is, something that makes it non-mean reverting. But if anyone knows what it is he is not working on this book. For the last hundred years, the dollar has lost value faster than the decline of the Roman-era Dinarius after the reign of Nero. This is not surprising. Roman coins had silver or gold in them. In order to make the coins less valuable, they had to reduce the precious metal content. People didn't like it. The dollar, by contrast, contains no precious metal. Not even any base metal. It is just paper. It has no inherent value. There is nothing to take out, because there was never anything there in the first place. Over time, the dollar is almost certain to revert to its real value—which is as empty as deep space.

In the big picture of things, it is also unusual for one civilized nation to earn far more per capita than another. In the thousands of years of history, some groups were poor . . . others were rich. But extreme differences had a way of working themselves out—by trade, war, pestilence, and degeneracy. By the year 1700, a man in India, China, Arabie, or Europe had about the same standard of living, which was not very high anywhere. But along came the industrial revolution, which threw incomes out of balance and changed the way people think. Europe stole a march on the rest of the world's industries, with huge gains in output coming in a relatively short period of time. Soon, Europeans were the world's leading imperialists, convinced that they had its best economic system, its finest scholars, its highest morals, and its most splendiferous armies.

But if the world works the way we think it does, you can expect the incomes of Europeans—and their American cousins—to revert to their historic means. The process could take several generations. It could stall. There could be countertrends. But there is no reason to think a man's labor is inherently worth more in France than in Bangladesh, or that a plumber with stars and stripes on his overalls should earn more than one with a crescent moon.

If there is a mean, things will regress to it. You can expect, relatively speaking, Asian incomes to rise and American incomes to fall. That is, of course, just what is happening now. In India, for example, real incomes have more than doubled in the last 10 years. In America there is some dispute about the numbers, but if there has been any income growth at all it has been slight.

Just to introduce a gloomy remark, we note that we are personally and individually regressing to the mean. The mean for a human being is death—or non-existence. A person walks the earth for only three-score and 10, as it says in the Bible. The rest of the time, he is only a potential person . . . or a former person. For millions of years, he is either in the future . . . or in the grave.

You, dear reader, are enjoying that ever-so-brief period of exaggeration . . . of hyperbole . . . of extraordinary, mean-busting usualness we call "life." It is not for us to know the time or place when it comes to an end. But like all mean-reverting phenomena, only a fool would bet against it. (For our own part, we do not particularly care when or how we meet our end. We just wish to know where, so we can avoid the place.)

But betting against the end is just what most Americans are doing. They are borrowing and spending as if there were no tomorrow, and they are investing as though there were no yesterday. All they would have to do would be to look at the patterns of the past; they would see that it doesn't make sense to buy at high prices—you can't make money that way. The way people have always made money is by buying low and selling high. Doing it the other way around doesn't work. Nor does borrowing and spending make you rich. Tomorrow always comes—at least it always has up until now—and you have to pay your debts.

Over time, prices go up and down. Many other things ebb and flow as well, boom and bust or bloom and wither. All of these phenomena go through predictable cycles that can be roughly modeled. Analysts study the cycles to try to figure out where we are currently located in the habitual pattern. It is often frustrating work, because the patterns are rarely quite as regular and well-defined in the present as they appear to have been in the past. Still, it is a question worth asking: Where in the cycle are we?

One of the ways you can tell where you are in the cycle is to look at what your friends and neighbors believe. Markets make opinions.

We recall that you can tell where the market really is by looking at the opinions people have. When people you know are all of the opinion that stocks will rise 15 percent per year—for an indefinite amount of time— you can be sure you are nearer to a top than a bottom. When people believe the opposite—that stocks will never go up—most likely, you are near a bottom.

Beliefs give us a clue to the larger cycles as well. People must play the roles that have been thrust upon them. They are bullish near the end of a bull market; they are bearish near the end of the bear market. If it were otherwise, the market could never fully express itself. If investors grew suddenly cautious while nearing an epic bull market peak, they would sell their stocks, and the peak would never be reached. Or suppose that after several years of soaring house prices homeowners came to believe that housing prices would fall? How could you have a proper housing bubble? How can you have a rip-roaring party without anyone getting drunk, in other words? How can people make fools of themselves if they are unwilling to get up on the tables and dance?

These are deep philosophical questions. But they help us recognize where we may be in the cycle. As prices reach a loony excess, peoples' ideas grow loony too. Ergo, the loonier the ideas, the more likely it is that a turning point is near; the wilder the party, the more likely someone will call the gendarmes.

We also suspect that attitudes evolve similarly in an imperial cycle, during which a country's economic, financial, and military power runs up over several generations and then declines. At the peak, the imperial people come to believe that their system is superior, that their values are universal, and that their way of life will inevitably dominate the entire world.

Readers will recognize these attitudes in a famous article by Francis Fukayama, written after the fall of the Soviet Union, in which he suggested that the world may have reached the "End of History." It was the end of history because the American system had triumphed—no improvement seemed possible. Fukayama's idea was not original. Hegel and Marxist intellectuals had proposed the same thing more than a hundred years earlier. With the victory of the proletariat, no further advance could be made. History had to stop.

Hegel stopped ticking. Marx died, too. History continued.

But when people feel they are on top of the world, they begin to take things for granted that they previously thought absurd. As we mentioned earlier, Americans now depend on the savings of Communist China in order to pay for their lifestyles . . . and their wars to make the world safe for democracy. They do so without thinking. Subconsciously, they've come to believe what imperial people always seem to believe—that their society is so superior, that the rest of the world longs to be just like them or is inevitably drawn to become like them, whether they like it or not. That's the premise behind the billions of dollars Americans are investing in China. A few years ago if someone had suggested that they invest in a communist country they would have thought the person mad. China is still run by veterans of various "great leaps forward," but Americans are convinced that they're all leaping to become just like us—capitalists and democrats at heart! So vain are we that we can't imagine anyone wanting to be anything else.

Likewise, we were recently in Nicaragua. We have a house down there, and we buy more land whenever we get an opportunity. Prices have soared in the past five years. Someone bought a beach-front lot recently for $350,000, a price that would have been thought insane a few years ago. Nicaragua is, after all, a third-world country. It is also a country that was run by communists until a few years ago. One of the communists is now a leading candidate to become el presidente in the next election. And right now, the nation's politicians are debating a proposed law that would declare all land within 200 meters of high tide "public." In effect, we'd all lose our land, our houses, and the money we've invested down there. But none of us quite believe it will happen, because we're convinced that they all want to be just like us—and *we'd* never do such a thing.

And of course, the invasion of Iraq was based on the same sort of thinking: that even the grubby desert tribes want to be just like us. All we have to do is to get the dictator off their backs and the men will start building shopping malls and the women will all start dressing like Britney Spears.

Those are the sort of delusions you get at the top of an imperial cycle.

But cultures, political systems, and economies are never as universal and eternal as we think. Instead, everything evolves. Even in France, our closest cousins do not share our American attitudes. In the United States, we all seek to maximize our incomes. We work long hours. We start enterprises. We invest. In France, people do not seek to maximize their incomes. Instead, what they want to maximize is their leisure, and the quality of their lives. They spend more time talking about how to cook the bacon than they do about how to bring it home.

France once had a European Empire that reached from Spain to Moscow. Later, it had a worldwide empire, with subject countries and colonies in Africa, the West Indies, and the South Pacific. From the time of Richelieu to the time of Leon Blum, France had one of the most powerful armies on earth. Even at the beginning of World War II, France had the largest army in Europe—on paper. But there never was a cycle that didn't want to turn. And the imperial cycle turns along with the rest of them. For many generations, the French believed they had the finest culture, the best schools, the most advanced scientists, and the most dynamic builders in the world. France saw its mission as bringing the benefits of its civilization—of vin rouge and the Rights of Man—to the rest of the globe. But now it's our turn. It is we Americans who think we have the best culture, the best economy, the best government, and the best army the world has ever seen. Now, it is we who have the burden of the "mission civilisatrice." It is our duty to bring freedom and democracy to this tattered old ball; our president has said so.

How did America become an empire? We don't recall the question ever coming up. There was never a debate on the subject. There was never a national referendum. No presidential candidate ever suggested it. Nobody ever said, "Hey, let's be an empire!" People do not choose to have an empire; it chooses them. Gradually and unconsciously, their thoughts, beliefs, and institutions are refashioned to the imperial agenda.

While there has been no discussion of whether America should be an empire, there has been much public clucking on the specific points of the imperial agenda. Should we attack Iran or Iraq? Should we have national identity cards? Should we suspend the Bill of Rights in order to combat terrorists more effectively?

Many people wondered, including your author, what was the point of the war against Iraq. The country had no part in terrorist attacks. Au contraire, Saddam's Iraq was a bulwark of secular pragmatism in an area unsettled by religious fanaticism. It was the religious fanatics who posed a danger, said the papers, not the ruthless dictators who suppressed them. Others wondered if an attack on Iraq would make the world safer or more dangerous. Or if the United States had committed enough troops to get the job done.

But the big question had already been settled without ever having been raised. Why should Americans care what happened in the mideast? Or anywhere else? Did the Swiss wonder what kind of government Iraq should have? Did the Swiss try to make the rest of the world more like Switzerland, or allow themselves the vain fantasy of imagining that everyone on the planet secretly yearned to be more like the Swiss themselves?

While no one noticed, the imperial weed put down roots deep in the soil of North America. By the early twenty-first century, hardly anything else grew; it had completely crowded out the delicate flowers planted by the Founding Fathers. The debate surrounding the invasion of Iraq was an imperial debate—about means and methods, not about right and wrong or national interest. No one from either major political party bothered to suggest that the United States had no business nosing around in other peoples' business. Both parties recognized that Iraq was not a matter of national interest—it was a matter of imperial interest. No business, no where, was too small or too remote not to be of interest to the empire. From its military bases all over the globe, and its sensors orbiting the planet, the American imperium watched everyone, everywhere, all the time. In the year 2005, no sparrow falls anywhere in the world without triggering a monitoring device in the Pentagon.

This marks what may be the peak of a trend that began more than one hundred years ago. Just about the turn of the century, the United States became the world's largest economy—and its fastest growing one. Near the same time, Theodore Roosevelt began riding rough over small, poor nations. America's fat proto-imperialist rarely saw a fight he didn't want to get into. It was at his urging (he had threatened to raise his own army to do the job) that Wilson announced his readiness to join the war in Europe in 1917. Wilson said he was doing it to "make the world safe for democracy." This is the stated goal of nearly all U.S. foreign policy ever since: to improve the planet with more democracy. Of course, almost all empire builders think they are improving the planet. Even Alexander the Great thought he was doing it a favor by spreading Greek culture.

But when Wilson sent troops to Europe, people wondered then what the real point was. America had no interest in the war and no particular reason to favor one side over the other. But there too, they missed the point. America was quickly becoming an empire. Empires are almost always at war—for their role is to "make the world safe."

President Truman clarified the imperial modus operandus when he sent the United States into battle in Korea with no declaration of war. He didn't even tell Congress until after the army was engaged and Americans were dying. Then, President Johnson followed up with another war in a far-off place that made no difference to Americans—Vietnam. What was the point? The Swiss army was nowhere to be found. And where were the Belgians? Even the French had given up on Vietnam a decade before. But more than three million American soldiers went to Vietnam and many came back flat. And for what? Just another war on the periphery of the empire. None of these engagements made any sense for a humble nation that minded its own business. None would have made any sense for America until the first Roosevelt administration; but once the nation had become an empire—with a homeland and wide-ranging interests beyond it—almost all wars seemed appropriate.

Another landmark in the history of the American empire came on August 15, 1971. That was the day that Richard Nixon severed the link between the imperial currency and gold. Thitherto, empire or no, the United States had to settle its debts like other nations—in a currency it couldn't manufacture. Henceforth, the way was clear for a vast increase in empire spending . . . and debt.

Thus we arrive at the real problem for the American empire. It has by far the strongest military in the world. It has no serious challengers beyond its borders. Hence, it had to become its own worst enemy. All empires must pass away. All must find a way to destroy themselves. America found debt.

The traditional method of empire finance is so simple even a Mongol barbarian could master it. Nations are conquered and forced to pay tribute. The homeland is supposed to make a profit; it is supposed to grow richer compared to the vassal states. But here, America fell victim of its own scam. Pretending to make the world a better place, the United States could not very well require the poor nations it conquered to pay up. Instead, it had to borrow from them.

This was not a problem in the early days. Until the mid-1980s, U.S. industries were so robust they were able to take advantage of the pax dollarium to expand sales, jobs, and profits. But in the 1970s, the U.S. trade balance turned negative. By the year Alan Greenspan took over at the Fed, foreigners owned more U.S. assets than Americans owned foreign ones. American factories had grown old and expensive. American workers were paid too much. American businessmen invested too little in training and new capital equipment. The whole nation developed an attitude more in harmony with an empire on the decline than one that was still rising. The imperial people chose to spend rather than to save, and to hallucinate, rather than think hard. They demanded bread and circuses at home; let the Asians sweat abroad.

Empires are thought by many to be good things. They expand the area in which trade can take place. In modern parlance, they allow for increased "globalization." Generally, globalization is good for everyone. It permits people to specialize in what they do best, producing more and better things at lower costs. But it is more beneficial to some than to others. And currently, the Asians are getting the most out of it. There are three billion people in Asia. And almost every one of them is willing to work for a fraction of the average American wage. Not only that, they tend to save their money, rather than spend it. The savings rate in China, for example, is said to be nearly 25 percent. In America, it is near zero.

Globalization and artificially low interest rates in America have allowed Asian industries to flourish. But for every dollar earned by an Asian exporter, 6 cents in debt is added to America's heavy balance sheet.

Things happen that no one particularly wants or especially encourages, and the average man goes along with whatever humbug is popular—with no real idea where it leads or why he favors it.

Each person plays the role given to him; everyone believes what he needs to believe to play the part.

Alan Greenspan was famously against paper money that was not backed by gold when he was a libertarian intellectual. When he became a government functionary, his views conveniently changed. He came to believe what he had to believe in order to be the head of the American empire's central bank: the Federal Reserve. The empire needs almost unlimited amounts of credit to carry out its foreign wars, while making bread and circuses available at home. Alan Greenspan makes sure it gets it.

Expensive foreign wars, expensive bread, expensive circuses—these are, of course, what bankrupted almost every empire from Rome to London. But that is just the point: institutions play their roles, too. One grows; another decays. One is young and dynamic while another is old and decrepit. One has to die to make way for the new one to take its place. One has to ruin itself so that another may flourish.

Americans could cut their military budget by 75 percent and still have the biggest, most advanced army in the world. They could trim their household spending by half, and still live well. They could drive less in smaller cars, they could cease mortgaging their houses, they could "make do" with last year's clothes and yesterday's laptop, but how could they ruin themselves if they put on the brakes before getting to where they are going?

Alan Greenspan's easy money policies—the Fed has been lending money at a rate at or below the level of consumer price inflation for more than two years—do not merely lure Americans to borrow and spend, they also grease the skids of history, permitting one empire to slip away while another slides in to take its place. The main beneficiaries of the present gush of globalization are the Asians. As American consumers turn to Wal-Mart to buy more and more things at "Every-Day Low Prices," they find products from China and Malaysia on the shelves. Were it not for Greenspan's low lending rates, they would not have found it so tempting to borrow. Were it not for Greenspans low rates, they would not have found it so alluring to spend. Were it not for Greenspan's low rates, they would not have bought so much from Asian manufacturers, the Asians would have made less money and would have built fewer new factories and trained fewer new workers. Were it not for Greenspan's lending policies, in other words, Asia would not have grown so quickly and would not now pose such a competitive threat to the rest of the world's industries. And Americans would not owe Asians so much money. In today's paper for example, a headline tells the tale: "China joins global race for fastest computers: Beijing and Tokyo aim at a new barrier to overtake U.S. lead."[4]

Asians now own enough U.S. dollar assets to buy a controlling interest in every company on the Dow. They have enough T-bonds to destroy the U.S. economy on a whim. Their economic power is growing at three to five times the GDP rate of Western nations. So far, they have shown little interest in political power; that is for a later stage of the cycle, another role for another time.

None of these insights are new or original. Most Americans have heard these things. Longtime readers of our "Daily Reckoning" newsletter (www.dailyreckoning.com) have heard them so often they look for exits when they see your authors coming. But while people know these things to be true, they don't really believe them. They believe what they need to believe in this late, degenerate stage of the empire. That is, they believe in sloppy fantasies.

"The U.S. economy is still the most dynamic and flexible in the world," they tell each other. "We're the most creative, inventive people on the planet," they congratulate themselves. "We'll invent new businesses. We'll think of something!"

These vague expressions of faith are probably typical for an advanced empire. The Romans, even to the time of the last emperor, Romulus, when the Barbarians appeared before the city walls, most likely told each other: "We'll beat them again this time; we always do!"

You never know where you are in the cycle until it is too late to do anything about it. For all we know, we could be facing merely a temporary pullback in what is still a long-term bullish period for the American empire.

We have mentioned how present American attitudes seem more in keeping with the end of a great empire than the beginning of one. In addition to that, the math of it makes us think we are closer to the end than the debut. The United States pays the direct costs of globalization—a military budget greater than the combined military spending of all of the rest of the world combined. Plus, it bears the indirect costs of its own consumerist excesses—another $700 billion or so per year in trade deficit. Together, they represent a cost of empire of more than 10 percent of GDP . . . more than $1 trillion each year.

Instead of collecting tribute, the United States finances these costs by borrowing. Here, Alan Greenspan and the paper dollar were immensely helpful. There is no theoretical limit to the amount of debt that can be taken on. The problem is a practical one. The dollar must maintain a reasonable value or lenders will be unwilling to lend. Dollar loans must also pay a reasonable amount of interest. With $36 trillion in loans outstanding, even at 5 percent interest, that represents annual debt service payments of $1.8 trillion. Who's got that kind of money? Not Americans; they're already spending every penny. And the more they spend, the less money they have left to pay interest. All they can do is to refinance—taking on new debt in order to pay the interest on the old debt. We will not dwell on this, as it is obvious even to an economist that it can't go on for very long. Sooner or later people cannot continue to borrow and cannot continue to make their payments.

This reminds us of one of the delusions that has been especially fetching lately. Alan Greenspan tells us that as long as house prices rise in parallel with household debt there should be no problem. He must know that it is not true. Relative to his assets, he says, the U.S. consumer is not over indebted. This is a little like telling a man not to worry about drinking too much—as long as he is getting fatter at the same time! The price of a house is only of interest if he is going to sell out and live in a cave, or die. Otherwise, he has no way of realizing the inflated value of his house—except by borrowing against it, which only makes the situation worse.

Americans do not seem particularly concerned about their debts. They, like the economists who advise them, come to believe what they must. And just as they come to these beliefs as circumstances change—not by pure thinking—so do they give them up. They continue believing in these fantasies and conceits until they are crushed out of them. Then, and only then, do they take up new beliefs.

Currently, Americans still believe in stocks, even though they've made not a penny in them for more than six years. Based on past experience, the bear market that began in January 2000 will probably continue for another 10 years, taking prices down to six to eight times earnings. Then, their faith in stocks will finally be crushed out . . . at the very moment stocks are ready for another bull market.

Americans also believe that houses always go up in price. No cobwebs grow over a real estate office door. No mortgage lender sits by the phone waiting for it to ring. And yet, it is impossible for real estate prices to exceed the rate of GDP growth for very long. This belief will also have to be crushed out, by a long bear market in property. Prices in Rome began a downturn in the year AD 300 or so (this we do not know for a fact, it is just a good guess). They did not stop going down until 1,000 years later . . . in the Renaissance . . . or maybe later. Even as late as the eighteenth century, sheep were grazing where the Forum used to be.

The belief in the American empire—in American cultural, political, social, and economic superiority—must also be crushed out somehow. That is the likely next phase . . . the degenerate stage of empire . . . which could last one hundred years or more.

In summary, the theory we have been teasing out is that politics and markets follow similar cyclical patterns—boom, bust, bubble, and bamboozle. A handful of companies usually take a dominant position in the market; sometimes a single one does. So do a few countries dominate world politics . . . "empires" they are called. The difference between a regular nation and an empire is profound. A regular nation—such as Belgium or Bulgaria—tends its own affairs. An empire looks outward, taking on its shoulders the fate of much of the world. An empire is like a bull market. It grows, it develops . . . often it passes into a bubble phase, when people come to believe the most absurd things.

We don't know what stage the American empire has reached . . . but we look around and see so many degenerate and absurd things, we guess: We must be nearer the end than the beginning.

How will it end? What will happen next? We don't know, but we note that people do not give up their self-serving conceits and illusions readily. They hold on to them as long as possible. "America still has the greatest, most dynamic economy on earth," they tell themselves, even as the nation loses money (its income is less than its expenses). This kind of madness is hard not to like; it is like an aging woman who thinks she becomes more fetching with each passing year. The gap between perception and reality grows wider every day, until finally, the mirror cracks.

What will shatter America's confidence is probably a combination of financial crises. The dollar is vulnerable. So are Treasury bonds. So are stocks and house prices. Which one will crack the mirror is anyone's guess. Our guess is that house prices will stop rising, causing a cutback in consumer spending. This will send the U.S. economy into recession . . . probably a long, soft slump that will take down house prices and the stock market, but leave the dollar and bonds with little damage.

Long suffering readers will find this forecast familiar. It is the same one we made two years ago in another book with Addison Wiggin called *Financial Reckoning Day* (John Wiley, 2003). We thought then that the tech bubble would blow up, resulting in a long, soft slow slump, à la Japan. Whether we were wrong, or just early, only tomorrow's newspapers will tell. Instead of a real slump, the United States has had a 9-month phony recession (in which consumer debt actually expanded) and a phony boom since (in which consumer debt actually expanded). These two phony acts, we believe, set the stage for a real one—a not-so-soft, maybe not-so-slow, slump.

If we were sure of this forecast we would buy bonds. Since we are unsure, we buy gold. In the coming real slump, assets of all sorts are likely to be marked down—especially those with a debtor on the other side of the transaction. Gold is what people will buy when they start to wonder about the empire . . . and its money. We guess that they will begin to wonder more and more.

"I read in the Figaro that the American economy has become completely dependent on China," said a friend at a dinner party recently. "But I guess the Chinese have no choice. They need Americans to continue buying their products."

We are alarmed. Even chemists and shoe clerks have taken up macroeconomics. Everyone thinks he understands how the world economy works.

"Well, it is a little like that," we began to explain. "The Chinese do sell to the U.S. and they do lend money back to the U.S. But there's no law that says this has to continue.

"Imagine a shopkeeper whose biggest customer was having a hard time paying his bills. He extends credit . . . hoping the man will get his finances in order. But the more credit he gives him, the worse the man's finances are. It would be very nice if that could work out. But it rarely does. Instead, it eventually blows up. The customer has to stop buying and the shopkeeper has to stop lending. There's going to be hell to pay, in other words."

"What should an investor do to protect himself," our friend asked.

"Buy gold."

"Gold? What a strange idea. I haven't heard anyone mention gold in many years. It seems so out-of-date. I didn't think anyone bought gold anymore."

"That's why you should buy it."

I

IMPERIA
ABSURDA

Look back over the past with its changing empires that rose and fell and
you can foresee the changing future, too.

—Marcus Aurelius

1

Dead Men Talking

Tradition is the democracy of the dead.

—G. K. Chesterton

One of the nicest things about Europe's cities is that they are so full of dead people. In Paris, the cemeteries are so packed that the corpses are laid down like bricks, stacked one atop the other. Occasionally the bones are dug up and stored in underground ossuaries that are turned into tourist attractions. Thousands and thousands of skulls are on display in the catacombs; millions more must be spread all over the city.

In Venice, a dead man gets—or used to get—a send-off so gloriously sentimental he could hardly wait to die. There is barely room within the city walls for the living and none at all for the dead. Cadavers were loaded onto a magnificently morbid floating mariah—a richly decorated funeral gondola, painted in bright black with gold angels on her bow and stern. Then, as if crossing the river Styx, the boat was rowed across the lagoon to the island of San Michele by four gondoliers in black outfits with gold trim.

How American versifiers must have envied one of their own, Ezra Pound, when he took his last gondola ride in such fabulous style in 1972. And then, what luck! The former classical scholar, poet, and admirer of Benito Mussolini got one of the last empty holes on the cemetery island. Today, when Venetians reach room temperature, the best they can hope for is a damp spot on the mainland.

We do not hasten to join the dead, but we seek their counsel. When corpses whisper, we listen.

"Been there. Done that," they often seem to say.

Reading Margaret Wilson Oliphant's history of the dead dukes, or *doges*, in her classic book, *The Makers of Venice, Doges, Conquerors, Painters and Men of Letters*,[1] we felt as though someone should have sent a copy to George W. Bush. "Read this. Spare yourself some trouble," the author might have written on the accompanying note. But who reads anything but newspapers in the Capital City? Who reads at all? In the United States if it isn't on the evening news, it didn't happen. Ancient history is something that happened last week.

Too bad. For practically all the most preposterous ideas that emanate from the feverish swamps of the Potomac were tried out in the feverish swamps of Venice, hundreds of years ago.

LESSONS OF THE FOURTH CRUSADE

"Democracy! Empire! Freedom! Nation building!" The ideas are cast into the murky lagoon of human affairs as if the words were clarifying magic. Suddenly, wrong is as distinct from right, as day from night. Good from bad . . . success from failure . . . how clearly we see things in the crystal waters of our own delusions!

The United States congratulates itself as being the finest democracy the world has ever seen, but the system for ruling Venice eight centuries ago was also democratic. People voted for people who voted for other people, who then voted for yet more people who elected the doge. The whole idea was to allow ordinary people to believe that they ran the nation, while real authority remained in the hands of a few families—the Bushes, Kennedys, Gores, and Rockefellers of thirteenth-century Venice.

"So easy is it to deceive the multitude," says Mrs. Oliphant. "The sovereignty of Venice, under whatever system carried on, had always been in the hands of a certain number of families, who kept their place with almost dynastic regularity undisturbed by any intruders from below—the system of the *Consiglio Maggiore* was still professed to be a representative system of the widest kind; and it would seem at the first glance as if all honest men who were *da bene* and respected by their fellows must one time or other have been secure of gaining admission to that popular parliament."[2]

To Mrs. Oliphant's dictum on the multitude, we add a corollary: It is even easier to deceive oneself. Today, rare are the Americans who are not victims of their own scams. They mortgage their homes and think they are getting richer. They buy Wall Street's products as though they were gambling in Las Vegas and believe they are as clever as Warren Buffett. They went to the polling stations in November 2004 and believed they were selecting the government they wanted, when the choice had already been reduced to two men of the same class, same age, same schooling, same wealth, same secret club, same society, with more or less the same ideas about how things should be run.

In Washington, DC, the United States Senate meets in the same solemn deceit as the Consiglio Maggiore—pretending to do the public's business. While down the street, America's own doge, George W. Bush, takes up where the Michieli and the Dandolos left off: trying to hustle the East.

Making a very long story short, at the beginning of the thirteenth century, as at the beginning of the twenty-first, many people saw a clash of civilizations coming and sharpened their swords. They were, then as now, the same civilizations, clashing in about the same part of the world—the Middle East.

What was different back then was that the effort to make the world a better place (at least in this episode) was being prodded forward by the French, who were then an expanding, imperial power. St. Louis (King Louis IX) went on two crusades with a French army and failed both times.

Mrs. Oliphant's history tells of the arrival of six French knights in shining armor, who strode into San Marcos Piazza to ask the doge for help. They were putting together an alliance of civilized Western armies to reconquer Jerusalem, they explained—in the same spirit as King Louis centuries before.

They brought out all the usual arguments. But the Venetians were not so much convinced by the French as they convinced themselves. They were, they said to themselves (just as Madeleine Albright would repeat centuries later), the "indispensable nation." Without them, the effort would fail; therefore they must act. Yes, they could still fail, they ac-knowledged, but look what they had to gain! For not only would they being doing good, but they stood to do well, too—implanting trading posts and ports along the way.

And so a fleet of 50 galleys was assembled and set off, the old doge leading the way. Finding their French allies a bit worse for wear and tear,

the Venetians proposed a new deal: Instead of attacking the infidels forth-
with, they would warm up with an assault on Zara, a town on the Dal-
matian coast that had recently rebelled against its Venetian masters.

The French protested. They had come to make war against the enemies of Christ, not against other Christians. But since they needed the
Venetians' support, they had no choice.

In five days, the city of Zara surrendered; its defenses were no match
for the armies in front of them. And so the city was sacked and the booty
divided up. Soon after came a letter from Pope Innocent III, who wondered why they were killing fellow Christians; it was the pagans they
were meant to be killing, he reminded them. He commanded them to
leave Zara and proceed to Syria, "neither turning to the right hand nor to
the left."

The pope's letters greatly troubled the pious French, but the Venetians
seemed undisturbed. They ignored the letters and remained in Zara until
a new comic opportunity presented itself.

This time Constantinople was the unfortunate target. A young prince
from that city had come to them, asking support for a mission at once as
audacious as it was absurd. His father had been blinded and thrown in a
dungeon; the capital of Eastern Christendom was in the hands of men
who must have been ancestors of Saddam Hussein—evil usurpers, dictators whom the people detested. If the Venetians would come to his aid, he
promised, they would be rewarded generously. More than that, he and his
father would return the entire Eastern Empire back to the one true church
of St. Peter in Rome.

The Venetians couldn't resist. In April 1204, they set sail for Bosporus
Strait. And in a great battle that must have been an undertaker's dream,
they took the city. Historian Edward Gibbon describes the scene:

> The soldiers who leaped from the galleys on shore immediately as-
> cended their scaling ladders, while the large ships, advancing more
> slowing in the intervals and lowering a drawbridge, opened a way
> through the air from their masts to the rampart. In the midst of the
> conflict the doge's venerable and conspicuous form stood aloft in com-
> plete armor on the prow of his galley. The great standard of St. Mark
> was displayed before him; his threats, promises and exhortations urged
> the diligence of the rowers; this vessel was the first that struck; and
> Dandolo [the doge] was the first warrior on shore. The nations ad-
> mired the magnanimity of the blind old man . . .[3]

It proved, however, that the young prince on whose stories and promises the campaign was launched had been a bit frugal with the truth. Like the intelligence services' warnings of weapons of mass destruction in Iraq, his depiction of the circumstances prevailing in Constantinople at the time was inaccurate. Much of it seems to have been fanciful.

Though the initial conquest was fairly easy and glorious, subsequent events were less so. The local population rose up against the invaders. The city had to be retaken; this time, the battle was bloodier, and thousands of innocent citizens were put to the sword.

As near as historians can tell, the Venetians earned no lasting gain or benefit. Dandolo died in 1205, never having set foot in his homeland again. As for his compatriots, what was left of them eventually returned to Venice.

"But there still remains in Venice," adds Mrs. Oliphant, "one striking evidence of the splendid, disastrous expedition, the unexampled conquests and victories yet dismal end, of what is called the Fourth Crusade. And that is the four great bronze horses, curious, inappropriate, bizarre ornaments that stand above the doorways of San Marco. This was the blind doge's lasting piece of spoil."[4]

"Been there. Done that," whispers the old doge.

THE TYRANNY OF THE LIVING

Who cares? Each generation needs to be there to do that, too. Though happy to turn on an electric light invented by a dead man, the living—in love, war, and finance—believe nothing they haven't seen with their own eyes, except when they want to.

"Avoid foreign entanglements," cautioned the father of the country. But corpses have no voice and no vote, neither in markets nor in politics. George W. Bush is undoubtedly better informed than George Washington. He may have neither the wisdom of a Washington nor the brain, but at least he has a pulse.

Few people complain about this tyranny of the living. Most accept it as a fact of life. They would not want people to be excluded from the pleasures of life because of an accident of birth. But they are perfectly happy to have the oldest and wisest of our citizens systematically barred from the polling stations and the trading floors by the accident of death. The departed shut up forever, leaving behind them their car keys, their stocks, and their voter registrations—that is all there is to it. Goodbye and good riddance. It is as if they had learned nothing useful, noticed nothing, and had no ideas that might be worth preserving; as if each generation were smarter than the one that preceded it and every son's thoughts improved on those of his father.

Oh, progress! Thou art forever making things better, aren't thou? Throw out the sacred books—what are they, but the thoughts of dead imbeciles? Forget the old rules, old wives' tales, old traditions and habits of old generations, old-timers' superstitions, the old fuddy-duddies' doubts! We are the cleverest humans who have ever lived, right?

Maybe. But if we could convene a council from the spirit world and invite the dead to have their say, what would the corpses tell us?

Veni et vidi. Gaze on the dead, and learn their secrets.

No one seems to care about dead people. No stockbrokers ask for their business. No politicians pander for their votes. No one cares what they think or what they may have learned before they shucked their mortal shell. They get no respect, just a quick send-off, and then they are on their own.

What did the old-timers know of war? Of politics? Of love? Of money? If only we could ask!

Years ago, investors wanted more from a stock than just the hope that someone might come along who was willing to pay more for it. They wanted a stock that paid a dividend out of earnings. When heard about a stock, they asked: "How much does it pay?" That was what investing was all about.

But by the 1990s, the old-timers on Wall Street had almost all died off. Stock buyers no longer cared how much the company earned or how large a dividend it paid. All they cared about was that some greater fool would come along and take the stock off their hands at a higher price. And the fools rushed in. And now the market is full of greater and greater fools who think the stock market is there to make them rich. What would the old-timers think of them?

And what would our dead ancestors think of our mortgages? Most of them had small mortgages, if any at all, on their homes. And if they had them, they couldn't wait to get rid of them. (Even our own parents held little parties to celebrate finally paying off the mortgage on the family home.) What would our forebears think if they were to learn that the richest generation in American history has mortgaged a greater share of its homes than any in history? What would they think of no-money-down mortgages, minimum payment plans, and negative amortization schedules?

And what would the old-timers think of our government debt? The unpaid liabilities and obligations, expressed as though they had to be paid today, come to about $44 trillion, depending on the source you choose to believe.

And what do the generations of Republicans, now in their graves, who believed so strongly in balanced budgets for so many years, think of the *republicano* in the White House, who has proposed the most unbalanced budgets in history?

And what about the millions of dead Americans who immigrated to the United States to find freedom; what do they think of the country now? They came believing that if they minded their own business, they would be left alone to do what they wanted. But now, every pettifogging Pecksniff with a government service (GS) rating is on their grandchildren's case.

And what about those millions of dead people who scrimped and saved—who got by on almost nothing—so their children and grandchildren might live free, prosperous, and independent lives? What would they think of their descendants, so deep in debt and so dependent on Asian lenders that they can barely pass a Chinese restaurant without bending over and kissing the pavement?

Each generation seems to think they are the first to stand upright, that their mothers and fathers walked on four legs and howled at the moon! Even when the living feign admiration for same fallen forebear, it is usually without paying of the least attention to what the poor schmuck actually said or knew. The dead leave us their memoirs, their gospels, their histories, and their constitutions—for what is a constitution but a pact with the dead?—and we ignore them. We seem to believe that all that they suffered, all they went through, all the mistakes they made, hold no more interest for us than a comment by a sunstruck contestant in a TV survival show: "This is . . . like . . . weird . . ."

WISDOM OF THE FOUNDING FATHERS

A dead man, Edmund Randolph of Virginia, attended the Constitutional Convention in Philadelphia in 1789. He explained why America needed a constitution: "The general object was to produce a cure for the evils under which the United States labored; that in tracing these evils to their origins, every man had found it in the turbulence and follies of democracy."[5]

Another dead man, James Madison, made it even clearer: "Democracies," he wrote, "have ever been spectacles of turbulence and contention; have ever been found incompatible with personal security or the rights of property; and have in general been as short in their lives as they have been violent in their death."[6]

So, we leave you "a Republic, if you can keep it," added Ben Franklin.

Well, we couldn't keep it. Now, we have a curious empire, with a constitution as flexible as its money.

Everybody gets a vote in this new democratic Valhalla. Every half-wit's ballot is worth as much as George W. Bush's. Every fool and miscreant gets to have an opinion. Only the dead are left out. Excluded. Ignored. Forgotten.

It is as if only the living had opinions worth hearing, as if only the here and now counted for anything; as if the small, arrogant oligarchy of those who happen to be walking around had all the answers; as if the present generation had found the ultimate truth and reached the end of history.

Your authors have never killed anyone, but we read the obituaries with approval and interest. We look for the distilled wisdom of saint and sinner alike. (The editorial pages, by contrast, we read only for entertainment.) The trouble with the news is that it is impossible to know what is important when you must rely solely on the judgment of people who happen to be breathing. The living can imagine no problems more urgent than the ones they confront right now, and no opportunities greater than the ones right in front of them. We prefer the obituaries.

THE SECOND REICH

Germany's Third Reich is infamous. But what happened to the Second Reich? History never repeats itself perfectly. But what else can we study but history? The past may be imperfectly understood, but it is the only reference we have. Why not take a look at it? Why not shake the dust off a dead man and get his opinion? Why not venture into the land of the dead to ask some questions?

"The state's need of money increased rapidly," writes a dead man, Bresciani-Turoni, describing the scene in Germany 80 years ago. "Private banks, besieged by their clients, found it impossible to meet the demand for money."[7]

As the situation heated up in the summer of 1923, there were some old-timers who gave advice: "Less," they said.

But officials were in roughly the same situation as Ben Bernanke, Alan Greenspan, and George Bush today. "More," said they. They feared the economy might fall into trouble unless they made more cash and credit available.

One, named Helferrich, the finance minister in Germany's Weimar Republic, explained:

> To follow the good counsel of stopping the printing of notes would mean—as long as the causes which are upsetting the German exchange continue to operate—refusing to give economic life to the circulating medium necessary for transactions, payments of salaries and wages, and so on, it would mean that in a very short time the entire public, and above all the Reich, could no longer pay merchants, employees, or workers. In a few weeks, besides the printing of notes, factories, mines, railways and post office, national and local governments, in short, all national and economic life would be stopped.[8]

When an economy comes to depend on more and more credit, it must get more and more of it or that economy will come to a stop. A man who has borrowed heavily to finance a lifestyle he cannot afford must continue borrowing to keep up appearances. Or else he must stop. In market manias, love, politics, or war, people rarely stop until they are forced to.

In 1921, a dollar would buy 276 marks. By August 1923, it would buy 5 million of them. Middle-class savers were wiped out.

If only we could roust Herr Helferrich from his eternal sleep! We have some questions we would like to put to his wormy cadaver. (And here, we think not of praising the dead, but of tormenting them.) What fun it would be to show him what his policies—the same, by and large, as are now put forward by Greenspan, Bernanke, and Bush—provoked. How gratifying it would be to see the little kraut squirm under an intense interrogation: What was he thinking, after all? Why did he think that more of the dreadful printing press money would undo the harm that had already been done by too much? Bresciani-Turoni continues:

> The inflation retarded the crisis for some time, but this broke out later, throwing millions out of employment. At first inflation stimulated production . . . but later . . . it annihilated thrift; it made reform of the

national budget impossible for years; it obstructed the solution of the Reparations question; it destroyed incalculable moral and intellectual values. It provoked a serious revolution in social classes, a few people accumulating wealth and forming a class of usurpers of national property, whilst millions of individuals were thrown into poverty. It was a distressing preoccupation and constant torment of innumerable families; it poisoned the German people by spreading among all classes the spirit of speculation and by diverting them from proper and regular work, and it was the cause of incessant political and moral disturbance. It is indeed easy enough to understand why the record of the sad years 1919–1923 always weighs like a nightmare on the German people.[9]

Surely some special corner of Hell is reserved for central bankers. Ben Strong. John Law. They are probably all down there. Maybe Charles Ponzi is with them. What do they do down there? Play cards, perhaps.

Helferrich must be there too—roasting. For when he undermined the Germans' faith in their system, their money, and their culture, did he not also pave the way to Hell for millions of his fellow countrymen?

If only we could talk to them! Didn't they sacrifice their souls, and do they not now writhe in eternal torment? And for what? Why should God make a moral example out of them if no one pays attention?

Every central banker in the world has taken the devil's bait, creating money, out of thin air, as if no one were looking. As if it had not been tried before. As if they could get away with it and people really could get something for nothing! And yet, they all seem unable to do anything different—even with the threat of scorching their fat derrieres in the afterlife.

SECRETS OF THE NEAR DEAD

If the dead have secrets, what about those who are almost dead?

We read an interview with Sir John Templeton. The great old man said he thought shares and houses in America were too expensive and that the United States was cruising for trouble with its trade deficit and U.S. federal deficit. He said he anticipated a long bear market in shares, falling residential real estate prices and a serious slump in the economy. Implicitly, he advised investors to hold cash.[10]

The person who wrote the article then asked local analysts and stockbrokers what they thought of Templeton's opinion. One challenged Templeton's competence, saying that because of his advanced age (Templeton was 92), he might be "out of touch" with current thinking. Templeton was not even dead yet, and already they were shoveling the mud on his face. But being out of touch is precisely what made his opinions valuable.

We like old things. Old buildings. Old ideas. Old trees. Old rules. Old investors. The older the investor, the more confidence we have in him. He has seen good times and bad times. He has seen bulls and bears.

People who have been around for a long time have had an opportunity to see several cycles. An American born after 1960, on the other hand, barely came of age when the 1982 to 2002 boom began. He has never seen a sustained bear market or a period when the nation was downcast or desperate. Templeton was a young man when Wall Street crashed in 1929. He was an adult in the Great Depression. He recalls the dark days of World War II, when it looked as though the allies might lose. During his life span, there have been booms and busts, mass murders, the worst wars in history, famines, hyperinflation, and national bankruptcies. Dozens of currencies and at least five empires have gone defunct. Dozens of coups and revolutions have taken place. Ideologies have come and gone. Thousands of banks and businesses have gone bust. Prominent careers have been ruined and reputations lost.

A man who has seen so much and still has his wits about him is a great treasure. If he is still solvent, that is even better. Somehow, he must have avoided the bad ideas, bad investments, and bad advice.

Innovations are like genetic mutations. Most of them are mistakes. Most fail. Old people tend to reject new ideas, new styles, and new things. This is not simply because these dogs are too old to learn new tricks. What the oldsters know—from experience—is that the new tricks are probably not worth learning. What we have around us are only the innovations that succeeded. Companies, products, ideas, governments, clubs, styles—all that we see are the successful ones. The unsuccessful innovations—thousands and thousands of them—all disappeared.

Even wildly successful innovations, such as heavier-than-air flight, are not successful for everyone. Warren Buffett estimates that if you had owned the entire airline industry from the moment after Orville and Wilbur made the first flight, right up to the day the Concorde made its last flight, you scarcely would have made a dime. Many other industries are the same. There are companies quoted on Wall Street that make money in those industries. But they are the survivors. Many others failed long ago.

Nassim Nicholas Taleb explains it in his book, *Fooled by Randomness:*

> Mathematically, progress means that some new information is better than past information, not that the average of new information will supplant past information, which means that it is optimal for someone, when in doubt, to systematically reject the new idea, information, or method . . .

> The Saturday newspaper lists dozens of new patents of such items that can revolutionize our lives. People tend to infer that because some inventions have revolutionized our lives that inventions are good to endorse and we should favour the new over the old. I take the opposite view. The opportunity cost of missing a "new new thing" like the airplane and the automobile is minuscule compared to the toxicity of all the garbage one has to go through to get to these jewels (assuming these have brought some improvement to our lives, which I frequently doubt).[11]

A young man has access to information. With the Internet, he can get all he wants. What he lacks is the "high-proof" distilled information—the wisdom—that comes with age.

Mr. Taleb continues, "A preference for distilled thinking implies favoring old investors and traders, that is, investors who have been exposed to markets the longest, a matter that is counter to the Wall Street practice of preferring those that have been the most profitable and preferring the younger whenever possible . . ."[12]

Testing the proposition using a mathematical model, Taleb "found a significant advantage in selecting aged traders, using, as a selection criterion, their cumulative years of experience rather than their absolute success (conditional on their having survived without blowing up)."[13]

Distilled information tends to be expressed as moral interdictions. Don't steal. Don't lie. Don't buy expensive stocks or sell cheap ones. Don't expect to get something for nothing. Don't neglect your spouse. Don't forget St. Patrick's day. Don't spend too much. Don't eat too fast. Don't drink before 6 PM. Don't mess around with the boss's wife. Each *don't* represents lessons learned by previous generations. For every *don't*, there must be a million sorry souls burning in Hell.

Undistilled information, on the other hand, is nothing more than noise—newspaper headlines, TV babble, cocktail chatter, the latest innovation, the latest business secret, the latest fashion. It is public information, backed by no real experience or private insights. It is not useless. It is worse than useless, for it misleads people into thinking they know something.

DEAD PRESIDENTS

David M. Walker, Comptroller General of the United States, clarified America's debt situation in late 2004: "The Federal government's gross debt—the accumulation of its annual deficits—was about $7 trillion last September, which works out to about $24,000 for every man, woman, and child in the country," he announced. "But that number excludes items like the gap between the government's Social Security and Medicare commitments and the money put aside to pay for them. If these items are factored in, the burden for every American rises to well over $100,000."

We add to Walker's lament: As we will see, $7 trillion is chicken feed. The real debt is far higher. Plus, one out of every four dollars spent by the federal government is borrowed. And for every dollar that comes in the door from income taxes, the feds borrow another 80 cents. Economists used to worry about government using up the nation's savings. But now Americans have no more savings to use. Still, the nation that can't save a dime sets out to save the entire planet.

The cost is as monumental as the project. Taking out Social Security surpluses, federal deficits are expected to be about a half trillion dollars each year for the next 10 years—or $5 trillion in total (half of gross domestic product, or GDP). We put no exclamation point following that last sentence, because the numbers shriek without one. Still, America's economists are deaf to the problem, just as its policymakers are dumb to any solution. After all, in the words of Dick Cheney: "Deficits don't matter."

Meanwhile, the private sector also has been running up immense debts. In 2005, for every $19 Americans earned, they spent $20. This difference was recorded in the trade deficit figures, measuring the speed at which Americans raced down the road to ruin. Top speed as of this writing was $58.3 billion. That was the figure for January 2005 when the nation was clocked overspending at a rate of almost $2 billion per day. It was the difference between what Americans sold to foreigners in the month of

January and what they bought from them. It was a negative number. On a chart of the nation's accounts, it would be in red. Or in brackets. Or preceded by a minus sign.

If it were divided among the nation's families, it would come to about $600 for each one. This represents only a single month's trade deficit, so we should multiply it by 12 to get the measure of damage on an annual basis: $7,200 per family per year. Compared with the average family's income, it is such a big number that we wondered if we had done the arithmetic correctly. On a macroeconomic scale, the shortfall was rising to 6 percent of GDP.

In the old days of the gold standard, the nation on the plus side of this exchange would pile up its excess foreign currency and take it to the other nation's central bank. Gold was the common reference and an uncommon restraint. It was real money. If a nation ran out of gold, it ran out of money. It could no longer borrow. It could no longer run trade deficits, because when the foreign currencies were presented to it, it would have no means of settling up. It would have to declare bankruptcy, which happened from time to time.

But it has been 34 years since the United States settled its overseas obligations in gold. Since then, it has found it far easier to offer U.S. dollar-denominated Treasury bonds. Remarkably, the foreigners have accepted them as if they were as good as gold. More remarkably, for most of that time the bonds were not only as good as gold—they were better. Gold fell in price for two decades following Ronald Reagan's first presidential election. Overseas central bankers took the Treasury bonds and felt grateful, even lucky, to have them.

The United States was just too lucky. It could spend without really paying. It could borrow without ever really paying back. It could dig itself into such a deep hole of debt, it could find no easy way out.

Among the noisy headlines of 2005 was the remarkable information that China—a Third World nation—lends the United States $300 billion per year. Without Chinese support, the dollar would have already collapsed, bond yields would have soared, and the U.S. economy would be in a recession, if not a depression.

Where does the money come from? The Chinese get the dead presidents from selling products to live Americans, who seem ready to consume anything that comes their way. First, the dollars come rolling off U.S. printing presses, then they make their way into the hands of Chinese and other manufacturers, and finally, they are returned to their birth-place as loans.

China is fast becoming America's "company store," to whom we owe our standard of living and maybe even our soul. By the end of 2004, two central banks—Japan and China—held almost a trillion dollars' worth of U.S. Treasury bonds. On their willingness to save and to recycle savings into U.S. Treasury bonds stood the U.S consumer economy. A single word from either central bank could send the U.S. economy into a severe slump: sell.

And thus comes an even more remarkable curiosity:

"In an era of free trade," began a complaint from Treasury Secretary John Snow, "we should not have to confront the issue of countries distorting their currencies to gain unfair trade advantages."

The specific country to which Snow referred was China. The trade advantage the latter enjoyed was that it sold much more to the United States than the United States sold to it, by a ratio of 5 to 1. And the unfair distortion was that China pegged its own currency to the dollar. In the spring of 2005, the exchange was called "manipulation"; the United States demanded that China revalue by 10 percent.

How were the Chinese manipulating the yuan? By fixing it to the imperial currency! Oh, that was clever, wily, diabolical. The Chinese insisted on maintaining their 10-year-old policy of pegging the yuan to the dollar. The United States counts on a steady devaluation of its money. It buys from overseas and pays in dollars. Then, in effect, it prints up more dollars to replace those it has shipped overseas. The resulting inflation of the currency—reflected in the increase in prices of oil, gold, and other internationally traded goods—is a form of imperial tribute. It is America's only way of making the empire pay. As the dollar goes down, the trillions of dollars held in foreign accounts become less valuable. An "exorbitant privilege," said Charles de Gaulle.

But the Chinese refused to play along. As the dollar went down, so did their yuan. Instead of raising prices on Chinese goods and lowering the value of Chinese dollar holdings relative to its own currency, everything remained even. The Chinese weren't paying their tribute.

Americans were indignant. A Senate committee said it would rewrite the law of the land to make what the Chinese were doing qualify as currency manipulation. Bush administration officials gave the Chinese a deadline to shape up. In the summer of 2005, the Chinese finally announced that they were giving up the dollar peg, or at least widening "the channel" a little. But the problem was never caused by China.

An entire American generation has grown up being told that it could spend its way to prosperity. Snow, McTeer, Greenspan, Bernanke—they all still believe it. Debt is no problem, they say. Spend, spend, spend.

American spending created a boom in China, where the average person works in a sweatshop, lives in a hovel, and saves 25 percent of his earnings. Americans had come to believe there was something unfair about China's trade practices, that they must be stealing jobs with a distorted currency, instead of competing for them fair and square.

Meanwhile, in the United States, the average man lives in a house he can't pay for, drives a car he can't afford, and waits for the next shipment from Hong Kong for distractions he can't resist. He saves nothing and believes the Chinese will lend him money forever, on the same terms.

That this cannot go on forever hardly seems worth pointing out. Whether it will go on much longer, we cannot say. But that it will end badly seems a cinch.

We can barely wait to find out how it all turns out. Maybe a year from now. Maybe 2 . . . 5 . . . 10 years. We want to know the precise date on which the imperial consumer credit economy stops muddling through. For it must shake, rattle, and roll over some day. Everything does.

The day may come and go without notice. The world created in the pax dollarium era may end with scarcely a whimper and no bang whatsoever. But it will end. Then the dead will cluck: 'I told you so'.

2

Empires of Dirt

Long is the historical record of empires. Short is the list of common elements. There are "good" empires. And bad ones. There are ones in which the imperialists get rich and others in which they become very poor. There are some in which the imperium functions with the brute elegance of a guillotine; in others, the complexities and subtleties baffle historians. But among all the empires that have come and gone, the U.S. imperium stands out as the most absurd.

The absurdity arises at the most basic level. Seeking to deceive, the Ivy League Alexanders and the Plain State Caesars deceived themselves more than anyone. From the very beginning, they knew not what business they were in.

We can enjoy a superior chuckle at the screwball humbug of it. Historians of the future are likely to get cramps from laughing. But economists—when they finally come to their senses and realize what is happening—are the ones who will revel in the biggest joke. The only reason they are not palsied with mirth already is that they have missed the punch line. This is the funniest and most preposterous scheme of imperial finance the world has ever seen; when they finally get it, they will laugh till it hurts.

At the risk of spoiling a great joke, we will explain it. The typical program for imperial finance is simple. The imperial power, the *imperium*, provides—at its own initiative—a public good; it extends security and order. In return, the groups that benefit pay tribute. The imperium should not merely breakeven; it should make a profit. Living standards in the homeland should rise, compared with those in vassal states. Even the

Austro-Hungarians got that right, as a trip to Vienna will easily confirm. The city got rich in the nineteenth century.

America provides a *pax dollarium* for nearly the entire world. But the United States does not take direct tribute from its vassal states and dependent territories for providing this service. Instead, it borrows from them. Living standards rise in the United States. But they are rising on borrowed money, not on stolen money. The big difference is that America's vassal states can stop lending at any time. If they care to, they can even dump their current loans on the open market destroying the U.S. dollar and forcing interest rates so high that a recession—or depression—is practically guaranteed. What is worse, the longer the present system continues, the worse off Americans are.

The closer you look at it, the larger the absurdity becomes. In the first half of 2005, Americans got poorer, not richer—at the rate of $80 million per hour. Their system of imperial finance was impoverishing them. Even that is not the worst of it, because it also reduced their ability to compete in the modern economic world. While they were providing a public good—at a loss—their competitors were saving money, building capital and expertise, setting up factories, and taking market share away from them. Each year, Asians produce more of what Americans buy, and Americans produce less of what anyone buys.

Products leave Asia for North America. Money leaves North America for Asia. The money comes back to America within days. America's economists breathe easy. What is there to worry about, they ask, as long as it comes back to us. "It is a form of tribute," they claim; the empire works. But it works in a perverse way. The money that comes back is not the same as the money that left. It has been transformed: It goes out as an asset and comes back as a liability.

THE HUNS ARE COMING!

For many centuries, Europeans had nightmares. Periodically, barbarian invaders from the East came in waves from the steppes of Eurasia. Celtic tribes pushed out or exterminated whoever was there before them. Then, new groups came after them. Mounted on horseback, they came fast and hard. They so terrified the more settled communities that the tribes picked up and pushed to the west. Germanic tribes eventually pushed the Celts to the far corners of Europe and later sacked Rome.

The Huns were barbarians. They were ruthless, cunning, fearless, and were reported to be invincible in battle. What chance was there against them?

In market terms, this was a good time to be "short" Europe. A fund manager might say that he chose to "underweight" the Old World. It was a time when the expansion of the previous period was likely to be corrected. There would be wailing women and gnashing of teeth. It was a time when fear and despair would likely dominate. It was a sell signal for the growth of civilization and commerce, which tend to go hand in hand like a prisoner with his police escort.

Politics and war are not zero-sum games. For every winner there is not a loser. Nor is a dollar gained for every dollar that is lost. Instead, the destruction of war and the costs of politics make them net losing propositions always. Most people lose. Wealth disappears. As a whole, people are poorer.

But, as in a bear market, some people gain from war. Those who win the war feel like winners, even though they may be poorer and many of their comrades may be dead. A few contractors and speculators actually make money on war.

The barbarian invasions of Europe had their bright side. The barbarians were in their expansion phase—their bull market stage—with rising expectations and positive, bullish hopes. They were getting something, not for nothing, but for next to nothing. What was the effort of killing a man compared with the wealth it brought the killer? A small investment. A trifle really, and an enjoyable one for many people. But conquest was not without risk. There are no completely free lunches, even for thieves and murderers. The Huns took a risk. On the upside were booty, women, slaves—and the pure exhilaration of battle and the prestige of conquest. On the downside, they might be defeated and killed.

The Hun might have been a sell signal for civilization, but he was a buy signal for his own fortunes, his status, his group, his empire, and his genes. It was a time to be "long" politics: There is a time to plant, to reap, and to trade with others peaceably. And there is a time for force, for taking what you want without paying for it and for killing anyone who gets in your way, for the Hunnish invasions meant rape, not for sweet talk and courtship. They meant theft, looting, and pillage, not further elaboration of property rights or the division of labor. Things got simpler, more brutal, mean, and nasty; lives were shortened. It was not a time to be in the insurance business.

What caused the periodic invasions no one knows. Perhaps good weather out on the plains produced population explosions that caused the nomads to expand. Perhaps bad weather caused famine that sent hungry mouths in search of someone else's meat and grain. Historians don't know. But fear of the barbarians from the steppes has been a chronic theme of Western history—particularly among the Teutonic tribes that were most exposed to them.

THE GREAT KHAN

Perhaps the most successful empire builder of all time was a leader of one of these periods of barbarian expansion—Genghis Khan. Since the time of the Romans, it has been fashionable to put a civilized mask on your face when you put the imperial purple on your back. You are bringing religion to the heathen. You are bringing civilization to the indigenes. You are bringing culture, education, and technology. Even Alexander the Great thought he was doing the world a favor. Conquerors do not like to admit—even to themselves—that their instincts are no different from those of barbarians. They have better table manners. But they are subject to the same urges as Genghis or Attila. Bloodlust, prestige, power, status— who can deny that it would be a thrill to conquer a whole city or an entire nation? But empire builders typically put on the imperial purple like a set of angel's wings, leap off the balcony, and come down with a thud.

Genghis Khan needed no mask. The man showed his face as it really was. He united the Mongolian tribes in about 1129 and beginning with a series of attacks on northern China, he embarked on a spectacular epic of mass slaughter and rapine from which two empires were derived. One of them, the Ottoman Empire, lasted until the end of World War I. The Mongol hordes overran northern China, Tibet, Persia, nearly all of central Asia and the Caucasus, Korea, Burma, Vietnam, Anatolia, and much of Russia. They attacked India and eventually, in 1526, Babar, one of Genghis Khan's descendants, set himself up as emperor of the place. In China, too, Genghis's descendants founded the Yuan dynasty, which ruled until nearly the fifteenth century.

All empires have to pay, in one way or another. The Mongols made theirs pay in the most elemental, and probably most satisfying, way. From an evolutionary point of view, all human activity has a single purpose—to propagate one's genes. A man tries to get rich or get elected to demonstrate that he is the sort of fellow a woman would want to mate; he will produce offspring as capable as he is; and he has the resources to take care of them. In this sense, history records no more spectacular success than the great Genghis Khan.

At one point, Genghis was told by his generals that the sweetest pleasure in life was falconry. "No," the empire builder is said to have replied, "You are mistaken. Man's greatest good fortune is to chase and defeat his enemy, seize his total possessions, leave his married women weeping and wailing, ride his gelding and use the bodies of his women as a nightshirt and support."[1] Genghis was so successful that a recent DNA study of 2,123 men from across Asia permitted scientists to estimate that he may have as many as 16 million male descendants spread out from Manchuria to Afghanistan.

Genghis made the empire pay in another way, too. He imposed a rough income tax tribute on all his subject peoples. The rate was only 10 percent—considerably less barbaric than today's rates.

Now that Mongolia is free from Soviet rule, its citizens are beginning to take a renewed interest in the man so many of them can trace as an ancestor. "Within this rapidly changing world, Genghis Khan, if we acknowledge him without bias, can serve as a moral anchor. He can be Mongolia's root, its source of certainty at a time when many things are uncertain."[2]

We quote that passage from the *Harvard Asia Pacific Review* merely to embarrass Professor Tsetsenbileg, of the Mongolian Academy of Sciences, who said it. Genghis Khan may be popular in Mongolia, but it just raises questions about the Mongolians.

"All who surrender will be spared; whoever does not surrender but opposes with struggle and dissension, shall be annihilated,"[3] said Genghis before attacking the ancient cities of Bukhara and Samarkand. It has been estimated that his campaigns killed as many as 40 million people based on census data of the times:

> Genghis Khan preferred to offer opponents the chance to submit to his rule without a fight, but was merciless if he encountered any resistance.

Genghis Khan's conquests were characterized by wholesale destruction on unprecedented scale and radically changed the demographics in Asia. According to the works of Iranian historian *Rashid al-Din,* Mongols killed over 70,000 people in *Merv* and more than a million in *Nishapur.* China suffered a drastic decline in population. Before the Mongol invasion, China had about 100 million inhabitants; after the complete conquest in 1279, the census in 1300 showed it to have roughly 60 million people. How many of these deaths were attributable directly to Genghis and his forces is unclear.[4]

But those were also the days when a man lied to exaggerate his murders, rather than cover them up. Genghis Khan was proud of killing people. In a way, he should have been; he did it so well.

But how could so few have done so much to so many? The entire population of Mongolia could not have exceeded about 200,000 persons. Military historians argue that it was largely because the Mongols were so bloodthirsty, so merciless, so fanatical, so fast, and so lethal that they were hard to stop. They were superb horsemen, frequently without infantry support, who were able to move more quickly than their more sedentary enemies much like panzer divisions in World War II. Their *ghazi* was a forerunner of today's *jihad.* Their composite bows were like today's Kalashnikovs (a Russian-made rifle that can fire bullets continuously). And they had a sophisticated system of communications that included semaphorelike information exchange on the battlefield and a pony express relay of "arrow riders" shooting across the prairies. With these advantages, they took what they wanted and killed everyone who got in their way.

It was not a very polite way to run an empire, but it worked.

Genghis died in 1227. His son Ogedei was elected to succeed him. Those who think democracy deters state violence do not bother to talk to the dead: Mussolini, Hitler, and Ogedei Khan all won office, at least in part, thanks to the ballot box. After his election victory, Ogedei Khan continued his father's expansion. He pushed farther into northeastern Asia and conquered Korea and northern China. By the time of his sudden death in 1241, his armies were on the frontier of Egypt and present-day Poland. But democracy cut them off. Mongol law required that the new Khan be chosen by a new vote of Genghis's descendants. Were it not for this interruption, the Mongol armies might have pushed beyond the Rhine and thrown Europe into a new Dark Age. As it turned out, by the time the Mongols had chosen a new leader—Genghis's grandson, Mongka—the momentum in Europe had been lost.

In 1257, the Mongols turned toward Baghdad. Hulagu, another grandson of Genghis, demanded that the caliph of Baghdad, al-Muta'sim, receive him as his sovereign, just as he had done with the Seljuk Turks when they swept over the area. But the caliph of Baghdad was the 37th of the Abbasid dynasty and leader of Muslims throughout the Middle East. He believed that his people would come to his aid against the infidel. They did not, and Hulagu marched on Baghdad with an army of hundreds of thousands of cavalry, wiping out the old Assassin fortress at Alamut on his way.

The caliph realized his mistake. He offered Hulagu the title of "Sultan." Hulagu's name would be given at Friday prayers in all the mosques of Baghdad, he added. Later, the caliph went in person to see Hulagu. This time, he said his citizens would lay down their arms if the Mongols would spare their lives. But as soon as their swords and bows had been collected, the Muslim fighters were exterminated. Then the Mongols went to work on the civilians. Eighty thousand men, women, and children were massacred. The caliph was strangled.

The only people not killed in Baghdad were the Christians. Mongka Khan's mother was a Nestorian Christian. At one point, perhaps at her urging, the Mongols sent emissaries to the King of the Franks, who was then fighting their mutual enemies—the Muslims—in the Holy Lands. The Mongols offered to turn to Christ, but his suggestion seems to have been ignored so he turned East, instead of West. Mongka Khan died just as his armies were about to attack Cairo. The next Khan, Kublai, moved the Mongol court to Beijing and founded the Yuan dynasty.

Something about the Baghdad area must attract empire builders the way a beehive attracts bears. Only a few miles away is the site of ancient Ctesiphon—a city that was taken and retaken at least 36 times before it was finally destroyed after the Saracens took it in AD 637. The Romans took the place five times, three times in the second century alone. Before that, the Hittites, Akkadians, Persians, Parthians, Sassanids, Macedonians, and countless others had already left their sandalprints between the Tigris and Euphrates.

Emperor Trajan captured Ctesiphon in AD 116 and made it part of Rome. The next year, Hadrian gave it back to the Parthians in a peace settlement. In AD 164, it was again taken, by Roman general Avidius Cassius, but later abandoned. Then, Septimus Severus finally made the campaigns pay when he took the city in 197. He sold as many as 100,000 of the city's citizens into slavery.

A hundred years later, the city was again in the news. Emperor Galerius was defeated outside the city walls by an army of Persians. In 296, he sought a rematch and this time won the city, which he traded for Armenia. Much later, in 627, Heraclius, took the city. The Western Empire was already history, but Heraclius ruled briefly from Constantinople. He gave up the city soon after its capture. Ten years later, it fell to the Saracens and was soon in ruins. A British army was defeated by Ottoman forces in 1915, but regained title to the city in the Treaty of Versailles. Later, the British readily let go of Baghdad, after they realized how expensive it was to hold on to the place. It gained its independence along with other British imperial possessions in 1921. More recently, the city was once again taken by American forces.

WHERE HAVE ALL THE DEAD EMPIRES GONE?

Of all the silly things people said toward the end of the twentieth century, perhaps the silliest came out of the mouth of Francis Fukuyama. The man was so infatuated by the apparent success of the American imperium, he believed the "end of history" might have arrived. What is the history of this tattered ball but the record of the rise and fall of civilizations, of governments, of battles and heroes? But so perfect in Fukuyama's eyes was the new American empire, he thought it had risen beyond the tug of gravity. So, solidly launched was the rocket of democratic capitalism that he could not imagine that it would ever fall to earth. Nor could he fathom how anything could ever compete with it or take its place.[5]

Fukuyama did not seem to appreciate how history works. Politics, like markets and love affairs, often throws up periods of relative contentment, as well as sour periods of despair and bubbles of temporary insanity. If they last for more than a generation, people think they are permanent. In the case of bubbles, people believe that some new era has arrived and that things will never be as they were before. Bubble markets—such as the tech bubble in the late 1990s or the residential property bubble in certain areas of the United States in 2004 and 2005—come along from time to time. People take leave of their senses. They are willing to buy things at twice, three times, ten times prices they would have judged too high just a few years before. In the famous Tulip Bubble in Holland from 1634 to 1637, people paid up to 5,000 guilders for a single tulip bulb. In the South Sea Bubble in England, in 1711, speculators paid up to 1,000 pounds for stocks that were reduced to nothing by the latter half of 1720. In the Japanese Bubble of the late 1980s, investors paid such high prices for real estate in downtown Tokyo that the grounds of the Imperial Palace were said to be worth more than the entire state of California.

Investors pay extravagant prices because they are convinced that something fundamental has changed and that they will never again have an opportunity to buy at current prices, no matter how high they have become. They believe the world will never be the same, that the rules that govern human activity have been altered or suspended.

Markets make opinions, the old-timers say. It is an expression we return to several times in this book. As prices rise, people invent explanations for why they have gone up and they will continue. In the case of the tech bubble of the late 1990s, they told themselves that new developments in electronic communications had completely changed the ancient relationships. Thanks to computer-driven devices and the Internet, material progress was about to accelerate. Assets were about to get much more valuable. It did not bother them that the two propositions were contradictory. A society in which the future comes faster should logically depreciate the present more quickly. Factories, means of production, and capital assets should be expected to become obsolete sooner and thus should be worth less, not more. But no one thinks very hard when markets are rising. This is true of the real estate bubble on both coasts in 2004 and 2005. Houses in Southern California were increasing in value at four times the rate of gross domestic product (GDP) growth and an infinitely great multiple of real income growth—which was negative. It made no sense, but who mentioned it? Prices were rising; investors had no trouble coming up with reasons. It was a new era, they said; property would never again be worth what it used to be.

In politics, too, there are bubbles—times when the horizon is so clear and cloudless, people begin to think it will never rain again. The old principles—the wisdom of the dead and the virtues that brought them to where they are—no longer matter. It is a new era. They are the imperial power, the hegemon, the cock of the walk. They are on top of the world and are looking for reasons they will be there forever. But the reason comes to them readily. They look in the mirror, and there it is. Instead of their own faces, however, they see only the dull, puerile masks they have put on. It is as if they all have become candidates for president; they are "hollow dummies," to use Orwell's expression—vain imposters, pretending to be something even dimmer and less interesting than they actually are. They look in the mirror and think they see a race so clever, virtuous, sturdy, and industrious that they deserve to be on top of the world. Surely, they have created something that can never be matched. All of history has been marching toward this perfection. Time has stopped. History has come to an end; there is no need for any more of it. In 1989, American democratic imperialism triumphed unmistakably against its adversary— the Evil Empire. The Good Empire was the last one standing. God had shined his light on us and would never turn it off.

Many people said many dumb things in the twentieth century. Usually, they were only mistakes or lies. When Neville Chamberlain said we would have "peace in our time," he was making a prediction. He was wrong. But if you hung everyone who guessed wrong about the future, the lampposts and traffic lights of Wall Street would be full of bodies. And when Adolph Hitler said Germany needed *lebensraum,* he was merely covering up his desire for conquest by putting on a mask. But when, after the Berlin Wall fell and Francis Fukuyama declared the end of history, he must have made the gods chuckle. Here was a reflection so vain and imbecilic, it practically cracked mirrors.

It was as if Fukuyama never actually read any history. Empires are living things. They are born; they must die, too. No one conquers without eventually being conquered. No bubble expands without eventually blowing up. There are no exceptions. All empires die. Here, for amusement, we look at the gravestones (see Table 2.1). Only one, and that one of relatively recent naissance, still lives. But the grave and the tombstone are there, waiting for it.

Fukuyama's concept was that the desire for power, glory, conquest, revenge—all the dark forces of destruction and regression—had disappeared. They had been replaced by an evolving civilization of consensual, democratic government and market-driven material progress, led by an enlightened U.S. imperium. This is what America offered the world— peace and prosperity. But even a casual look at the historical record would show that neither empires nor democracy are any guarantee of peace or prosperity.

TABLE 2.1 EMPIRES THROUGHOUT HISTORY

Empires are living things with a logic of their own. They are born; they must die, too. No one conquers without eventually being conquered. No bubble expands without eventually blowing up. In history, there are no exceptions.

• Abyssinian Empire (1270–1974)	• Haitian Empire (1804–1806)
• Achaemenid Empire (*commonly known as the Persian Empire*) (c. 550–330 BC)	• Hittite Empire (c. 1460–1180 BC)
	• Holy Roman Empire (843–1806)
• Akkadian Empire (c. 2350–2150 BC)	• Inca Empire (1438–1533)
• American Empire (1917–)	• Ilkhanate (c. 1256–1338)
• Arabian Empire (c. 630–1258)	• Japanese Empire (1871–1945)
• Assyrian Empire (c. 900–612 BC)	• Khmer Empire (802–1462)
• Athenian Empire (c. 500–300 BC)	• Kongo Empire (c. 1230–1665)
• Austro-Hungarian Empire (1867–1918)	• Korean Empire (1897–1910)
• Austrian Empire (1804–1867)	• Macedonian Empire (circa 338 BC–309 BC)
• Aztec Empire (1375–1521)	• Mexican Empire (1822–1823, 1864–1867)
• Brazilian Empire (1822–1889)	• Mogul Empire (1526–1857)
• British Empire (circa 1583–)De jure*	• Mongol Empire (1206–1294)
• British Raj (1858–1947) (Imperial: 1877–1947)	• Old Babylonian Empire (c. 1900–1600 BC)
	• Ottoman Empire (1281–1923)
• Byzantine Empire (395–1453)	• Persian Empire (c. 648 BC–330 BC)
• Central African Empire (1977–1979)	• Portuguese Empire (1495–1975)
• Chinese Empire (221 BC–1912)	• Roman Empire (31 BC–AD 476)
• Dutch colonial empire (1627–1814)	• Russian Empire (1721–1917)
• Egyptian Empire (1550–1070 BC)	• Sassanian Empire (224–651)
• First French Empire (1804–1815)	• Seleucid Empire (323 BC–60 BC)
• Second French Empire (1853–1871)	• Seljuk Empire (c.1037 AD–1194 AD)
• French colonial empire (c. 1605–1960s)	• Spanish Empire (1492–1975)
• German Empire (1871–1918)	• Swedish Empire (1561–1878)
• German colonial empire (1884–1918)	• Timurid Empire (1401–1505)
• German Third Reich (1933–1945)	• Ur III Empire (c. 2100–2000 BC)
• Golden Horde (1378–1502)	• Vijayanagara Empire (c. 1350–1700)
• Greater East Asia Co-Prosperity Sphere (1940–1945)	

For proof that empires are hardly peaceful places, we turn to the history of Rome. And here we offer readers a history of the rise and fall of the world's greatest empire as brief as the latest Italian underpants.

THE ROMAN EMPIRE

In the eighth century BC, Rome was nothing more than a collection of villages along the Tiber, inhabited by several tribes, principally Latin, Sabine, and Etruscan. Gradually, these Romans grew in numbers and power, and went to war with almost everyone. They were already constructing an empire before the fifth century BC. In a celebrated early incident, perhaps only legendary, they invited their neighbors, the Sabines, to a feast and then stole their women. The Sabine men were not happy; they took offense and nursed a grudge. But there was hardly a tribe, kingdom, or empire in Europe, North Africa, or the Middle East with whom the Romans did not pick a fight. After the Sabine war, there were wars against the Albii, Etruscans, Volcii, Carthaginians, Etruscans again, the Latin League (and this is only a partial list), the Volsquii, Equii, Veieii, Gauls, Samnites, more Gauls, Epirians, Carthaginians again, and more Gauls, Macedonians, Syrians, Macedonians again, slaves in Sicily, Parthians—and even Romans in the civil wars. And we have not even arrived at Caesar's wars against the Gauls in 58 to 51 BC. Roman history has another 500 years of wars to go!

The civil wars in the first century BC put an end to the Republic. Then, Caesar crossed the Rubicon, and it was a new era in Rome. It was as if Tommy Franks had decided to move his army to Washington, DC, and make a regime change of his own. Some people would object, of course (the liberal papers would howl), but most people wouldn't care.

In ancient Rome, as in modern Washington, people chose their ideas the same way they chose their clothes—they wanted something that not only did the job, but was also fashionable. And at the time, it was à la mode for emperors and individuals alike to pretend they lived in a free republic that honored citizens' rights. But in practice, the government, and its leader, could get away with almost anything. And what they seemed to like doing was going out and making war against everyone they thought they could beat. That is what Empires do.

Back then, war was a paying proposition. When Emperor Trajan took Ctesiphon (near modern Baghdad), he captured 100,000 people who were sold into slavery. When Augustus took Egypt, he used the Nile's wheat harvest to feed the growing population of rabble in Rome.

But while some people came out ahead, in the aggregate, wars then—as now—were negative gain enterprises. And as the empire grew, the costs also mounted, to the point where both became grotesque and insupportable.

Octavian, under the name Augustus, was installed in 27 BC. The Romans only used pure gold and silver coins, but Augustus needed more money to finance his wars and domestic improvements. There were no government printing presses capable of running off a batch of $100s in a few seconds. Nor was there a global bond market, from which he could raise billions in loans overnight. All he could do was to order the government-owned mines in Spain and France to work overtime. Around the clock, miners dug out the precious metals. The money supply rose. As the supply of something rises relative to the supply of something else, the value of the former declines relative to the latter. Thus, did prices rise in Rome as more money chased the same quantity of consumer goods. Between the day Augustus came to power and the day Jesus Christ was born—a period of 27 years—consumer prices nearly doubled. Augustus, or his advisors, realized the problem. They cut back the money supply and prices stabilized.

Rome wasn't built in a day, nor was its money destroyed overnight. In AD 64, in Nero's reign, the aureus was reduced by 10 percent of its weight. Thereafter, whenever the Romans needed more money to finance their wars, their public improvements, their social welfare services and circuses, and their trade deficits, they reduced the metal content of the coins. By the time Odoacer deposed the last emperor in 476, the silver denarius contained only 0.02 percent silver.

THE INVINCIBLE ARMADA

The impulse to build up an empire seems to be as strong as the impulse to tear one down. To the question, when does a country aim for empire, comes the answer: whenever it can.

Every country in Europe has at one time or another reached for the imperial purple. Portugal and Spain discovered and conquered vast jungles, swamps, and pampas, and built empires for themselves. For Spain, the conquests were extremely profitable after they found huge quantities of gold and silver. But nothing ruins a nation faster than easy money. The money supply grew larger with every ship's return from the New World. People felt rich, but prices soon soared. Worse, the easy money from the new territories undermined honest industry. In the bubble economy of the early sixteenth century, Spain developed a trade deficit similar to that of the United States today. People took their money and bought goods from abroad. By the time the New World mines petered out, the Spanish were bankrupt. The Spanish government defaulted on its loans in 1557, 1575, 1607, 1627, and 1647. Not only was the damage severe, it was long-lasting. The Iberian Peninsula became the "sick man of Europe" and remained on bed rest until the 1980s.

If empires are to endure, they must pay. But if they pay too well, success ruins the homeland.

In the summer of 1588, the Invincible Armada of King Philip II of Spain headed toward the Low Countries. You and I, dear reader, can spot the error already. Philip would have done better to call his fleet the "Almost Invincible Armada," or perhaps even better, the "Best Little Armada We Could Put Together at the Time." Calling an armada *invincible* is like calling a WorldCom *unbeatable;* it is a challenge to the gods and an invitation to destruction.

The Armada's mission was simple, but not easy—to pick up soldiers in the Netherlands and transport them to England. It had been 500 years since anyone had attempted an invasion of England. The last assault, led by William, Duke of Normandy, had been a big success. Philip was ready to have a go at it again.

The reasons for the campaign were not so simple. In the jargon of today, he might have labeled his effort a "War on Terror," for English pirates had been terrorizing Spanish shipping for years. The pirates were not necessarily sponsored by the English crown. But they, literally, found safe harbor in English ports, similar to the way al-Qaida found Afghanistan hospitable.

Of course, there was more to it. Religion played a part. Just as George Bush's War on Terror has a subtext of religion, so did Philip of Spain's campaign against England. Henry VIII of England had rejected the authority of the pope and set himself up as head of the Church of England. When his daughter, Elizabeth, ordered the execution of her Catholic rival, Mary Queen of Scots, Philip (who had been king of England 30 years prior, when he was married to Mary I) thought the time had come for action.

By 1588, Spain had become a powerful empire—with colonies in the New World that had made them rich. Money poured into Spanish coffers during the sixteenth century—the country imported it the way the United States imports big-screen televisions, giving little in return. What a magnificent system of imperial finance. Ships went west with soldiers and came back with gold and silver. It was almost as good as America's system. In 2005, ships went west from Long Beach and Seattle almost empty. They came back full to the gunwales with Asian-made goods. And like America's system, Spain's trade was almost too good to be true.

Anything that must come to an end must come to an end somehow. Great empires look for ways to destroy themselves. They usually have little trouble finding them. In 1588, Spain found the English fleet—and the North Sea.

History records the Battle of Gravelines as one of the world's most important naval engagements. The Spanish ships were trapped against the Flemish coast. The Spanish commander, the Duke of Medina, decided to use a portion of his fleet to hold off the English, while the rest made their way to open water.[6]

The English engaged the defending Spanish ships with a 10-to-1 numerical advantage. Soon, three of the huge Spanish galleons were sunk, with 600 Spaniards killed and more than 800 others wounded. "The decks ran with their blood," said eyewitness accounts.[7]

Most of the English ships, having done their work and run out of ammunition, sought their ports. The Spanish, badly battered and realizing their cause was doomed, decided they could not fight their way back through the Channel. Instead, they sailed north intending to make their way around Scotland (though they had neglected to bring maps of the area) and thence back to Spain by the open Atlantic.

What the English began, the gods finished. On September 18, 1588, the Spaniards ran into one of the worst storms ever to smash into Scotland. In high seas off Cape Wrath, the Invincible Armada proved vincible; it broke up. Some ships sank; others ran out of food and water. In an effort to keep the leaky vessels above water, sailors manned the buckets day and night, but many soon ran out of energy or died of scurvy, dysentery, and fever.

The sun was never supposed to set on Philip's Spanish empire. But it sank along with the armada in 1588. Financially, Spanish fortunes had begun taking on water long before.

"The mines of Brazil were the ruin of Portugal, as those of Mexico and Peru had been of Spain; all manufacture fell into insane contempt . . ." explained Alfred Thayer Mahan in his opus, *The Influence of Sea Power upon History, 1660–1783,* "The tendency to trade, involving of necessity the production of something to trade with, is the national characteristic most important to the development of sea power."[8]

Prices rose sharply in the sixteenth century. As a result of the increase in the money supply caused by the gold and silver shipped in from the colonies, prices in all of Europe went up 400 percent. Then, when the mines and robberies eased off after 1580, the inflationary boom was over. A long depression began on the Iberian Peninsula. The Spanish and Portuguese were victims of their own good fortune.

3

How Empires Work

Nothing is born but from another living thing. No empire ever arose without some link to its predecessors. But the system of imperial finance in the United States bears little resemblance to its immediate predecessor, the British Empire. There are no colonies from which we buy raw materials at discount prices. And there are few U.S. factories for turning raw materials into salable products. Nor does the American imperium bear much likeness to the imperial finance systems of the Germans, the Austro-Hungarians, the Romans, the Greeks, or the Mongols. But there is a slight family resemblance in the Spanish colonial empire.

Ships went to the New World from Spanish and Portuguese ports armed with soldiers, provisions, and colonial administrators. They came back laden with gold and silver. Gold and silver was real money. It could not be easily replicated, counterfeited, or called into being with the stroke of a keyboard. Still, the increase in money—with no corresponding increase in productive output—was fatal to the Iberians. They spent without really earning. They consumed without producing. When the flow of easy money stopped, they found that real money had made them really poor, not rich.

America's impoverishment is even more ridiculous. She is sustained by foreign wealth, but without real money. It is merely paper money without the paper—electronic registration of units of paper money. It is a mirage—a chimeric representation of something that doesn't exist anywhere. For every additional dollar the U.S. Treasury calls into being, there is no extra dollar of savings, no extra dollar of profit, not even the paper dollar itself. At least the gold taken from Latin America is still around today and is still valuable. The dollars created by the Treasury are likely to disappear completely.

The United States entered the empire business in the late nineteenth century. She was able to straighten herself out for a few years but the lure of it later became irresistible. Between 1917 and 1971, the country was transformed from a simple republic that mostly minded its own business to a grandiose empire with imagined interests and real troops nearly everywhere.

In normal places at normal times, people go about their normal lives earning a living the best they can. But an empire changes the way people think. The common householder turns away from his humble house and his spouse and begins to think about the fair world beyond his kith, kin, and ken. He looks outward and sees how much better the world could be if he and his fellow citizens could run it their way. He sees that he must play a greater role in global affairs that he must walk on the world stage, not as a bit player, but as the main character—the hero. He must play the lead role.

Instead of sticking to their looms, fields, and factories, the imperial citizens begin to appreciate the financial logic of empire: They enjoy the loot that comes from the far edges of the imperial system. Gradually, they neglect their own commerce and depend on their subordinates, lackeys, and subject peoples to support them. While administrative commands, fashions, and proclamations flow from the center of the empire to the extremities, there also is an important flow in the other direction. Rome brought in its wheat from Egypt (Romans needed bread), its gladiators from the Balkans (Romans wanted circuses), its soldiers from Gaul, and its money from foreign treasuries and tax collectors from Judea to Britannia.

A modest republic pays its own way. In 1952, nearly 90 percent of the federal government's borrowings came from domestic investors. Americans saved their money and used some of it to support the programs of the Eisenhower administration. But the maturing empire of 2005 depends on a global debt market and the savings of foreigners. From less than 5 percent of Treasury bonds in overseas hands in 1952, the total now approaches 45 percent, while the percentage of lending coming from domestic sources has been cut in half.

Americans still grow their own wheat, but the trucks to move it may be manufactured in Europe or Asia, and the pans it cooks in are probably made in China. They get their electronic paraphernalia from Taiwan, clothes from Malaysia, and automobiles from Japan. They get scientists from India and classical musicians from Korea. And money comes from all over the Eastern Periphery to keep it all going.

THE HISTORY OF EMPIRES

Reading the history of empires, we learn that the central power tends to weaken as the peripheral states grow stronger. Eventually, the subordinate states get tired of supporting the imperium. They stop paying tribute and show up at the gates of Rome.

France and England built their own empires in the eighteenth and nineteenth centuries. Napoleon's conquests took less than a dozen years to complete, but the empire collapsed even faster. By the end of the nineteenth century, all that was left of the French empire were a few islands no one could find on a map and some godforsaken colonies in Africa that the French would soon regret ever having laid eyes on. Almost all were lost, forgotten, or surrendered by the 1960s with nothing much to show for them except what you find in the Louvre—and a population of African immigrants who now weigh heavily on France's social welfare budget.

England's empire was much grander, stretched further, and left more debris when it broke up. But the end result was about the same: The pound was degraded and the British were nearly bankrupt.

Germany lost its overseas colonies after World War I. It then created another empire—by conquest—in the late 1930s and early 1940s. The enterprise ran into Russia's empire in the East—resulting in history's largest and bloodiest land battles. In the end, thanks partly to American intervention on the side of the Russians, the German empire was destroyed. The Russians' empire collapsed under its own weight 44 years later.

• • •

While the Romans were still kicking Sabine derrieres, Athens was already a mini-empire. By 431 BC, Athens had become an empire, with subject states throughout the Aegean. In that year, on some pretext not worth recalling, the first Peloponnesian War began between Sparta and Athens and its allies.

Pericles decided that the best offense was a good defense. He brought the Athenians within the city's walls hoping that the enemy would exhaust itself in futile attacks.

But bubonic plague broke out in the besieged city and killed a quarter of the population—including Pericles. Thence, a nephew of Pericles, Alcibiades, stirred the Athenians to an offensive campaign. A great armada was assembled to attack Syracuse, a city in Sicily allied with Athens' foes.

The campaign was a complete disaster. The armada was destroyed and the army sold into slavery. Sensing a shift in the wind, other Greek city-states broke with Athens and went over to Sparta. In 405 BC, the remaining ships in the Athenian fleet were captured at the battle of Aegospotami. Not long after, Athens' walls were breached and the city became a vassal state to Sparta.

The Athenian empire was replaced by the Spartan empire, which was eventually supplanted by the Macedonian empire, which then became the empire of Alexander. When Alexander died in 323 BC, his empire died with him. The next great chapter of imperial history was written by the Romans, who defeated what was left of the Greeks at the Battle of Pydna in 168 BC.

One empire died. Another was born. Nature can't bear a vacuum and abhors a monopoly. A world without an empire is a world with a hole in it. An empire fills the empty spot. But Nature is a fickle mistress. No sooner has an empire been born than Nature hardens her face against it. An empire has a monopoly on the use of force, or attempts to have one. An empire claims for itself the exclusive right to use preemptive force against any power that may pose a challenge. Nature tolerates it for a while. But she nurtures rivals and encourages competitors. Sooner or later, they find their opportunity.

Athens ran the first recorded empire in the West. America runs the current one; it took over from Britain after World War I. For the first eight decades, Americans denied any imperial role or purple ambitions. But by the early twenty-first century, they were warming up to empire. In March 2004, the *New York Times* reported that it was now respectable to describe the United States as an empire. "Today," said the *NYT,* "America is no mere superpower or hegemon, but a full blown empire in the Roman and British sense."

"No country has been as dominant culturally, economically, technologically and militarily in the history of the world since the Roman Empire,"[1] added the columnist in the same paper.

Robert Kaplan's book, *Warrior Politics: Why Leadership Demands a Pagan Ethos,* gave this assessment:

> Our future leaders could do worse than be praised for their tenacity, their penetrating intellects and their ability to bring prosperity to distant part of the world under America's soft imperial influence. The more successful our foreign policy, the more leverage Americans will have in the world. Thus, the more likely that future historians will look back on the twenty-first century United States as an empire as well as a republic, however different from that of Roman and every other empire throughout history.[2]

The June 11, 2005, edition of *IHT* ran Roger Cohen's "Globalist" column, which contained this remark: "We guarantee the security of the world, protect our allies, keep critical sea lanes open and lead the war on terror," said Max Boot of the imperial burden. ". . . the Pax Americana in Asia, as in Europe, has been conducive to a half-century of growth, peace and prosperity."[3]

Paul Kennedy went further, pointing out that the imbalance is even greater than in the Roman era. "The Roman Empire stretched further afield," he notes, "but there was another great empire in Persia and a larger one in China."[4]

America had no rivals, he said. Militarily, China was no real competition; it was just another country on America's hit list.

Even after 227 years, America's stock continues to rise. That it had gotten high enough to vex Nature worries no one. That it might decline troubles no one's sleep. That being an empire is not necessarily an unadulterated blessing bothers neither the president nor his ministers.

The modest republic of 1776 has become the great power of 2005 with pretensions to empire that can no longer be denied. That its citizens will not be freer is understood and accepted. But will they be richer under an empire than they would have been under a humble republic? Will they be safer? Will they be happier?

If so, pity the poor Swiss. In their mountain fastnesses, they have only had themselves to boss around; only their own pastures, lakes, and peaks to amuse their eyes; and only their own industries to provide employment and sustenance. And their poor armed forces! Imagine the boredom, the tedious waiting for someone to attack. What glory is there in defense? Oh, for a foreign adventure! Thanks to their colonial empire, the sun never set on the

British. After the Napoleonic Wars, as many as a quarter of the world's population lived under British rule. Meanwhile, the sun set every single day on the Swiss Federation. But that didn't stop the Swiss franc from rising, almost daily, against the British pound. In 1815, a British pound could have been exchanged for 13 Swiss francs and a half-pound of cheese. Today, a pound brings you only 2.3 Swiss francs. And forget the cheese.

While the British economy grew sluggish in the twentieth century, the Swiss economy boomed. By the end of the century, gross domestic product (GDP) per person in Britain was only around $20,000. The Swiss, meanwhile, were producing $28,550 in GDP per capita.

But the poor yodelers never got the glory of empire. They never got to admire themselves on maps or in headlines. What Swiss president gets to send troops to remote hellholes, join a peace-keeping mission, or fight terrorists? How often do the Swiss get to cheer on their heroes and mourn their dead? Who even knows who the president of Switzerland is? Who cares? While Americans get to make a public spectacle of themselves, the Swiss have to make do with private life.

The Swiss have to mind their own business and watch the Sturm und Drang of the world pass them by. But would the Swiss really be better off if they too had an empire to run?

The available evidence from history is mixed and anecdotal. If the past is any guide, early military successes are inevitably followed by humiliating defeats. Financial progress is nearly always trailed by national bankruptcy and the destruction of the currency. And the good sense of a decent people is soon replaced by a malign megalomania that brings the whole population to complete ruin.

But who cares? It is not for us to know the future or to prescribe it. Instead, we get out our field glasses and prepare to watch the spectacle.

BACK TO THE FUTURE

A great empire is to the world of geopolitics what a great bubble is to the world of economics. It is attractive at the outset, but a catastrophe eventually. We know of no exceptions.

After the battle of Pydna, Rome became the leading empire of the Western world. (We continue our simplified narrative to show how things worked out.)

Augustus died in AD 14, leaving the empire in the hands of his stepson Tiberius, who had married Augustus' free-and-easy daughter, Julia. Tiberius *clipped* the coinage (reduced the precious metal content). This, and other prudent policies, greatly increased the amount of money in the treasury. By the time he was assassinated in AD 37, there were 700 million denarii in the treasury—far more than there had been at the time of Augustus's death.

Tiberius handed off the imperial purple to Caligula, who quickly spent all the savings and more. Rome suffered a series of mad and lavish rulers. To confiscate the money of wealthy Roman families, Caligula would falsely accuse them of plotting against him. He was succeeded by Claudius who, in turn, gave way to Nero. By this time, Rome was deeply in debt and running large trade deficits with its periphery states—similar to the condition of the United States today. Nero took the time-honored expedient of clipping the coins (taking out the gold and silver content) even more. In AD 64, he proclaimed that henceforth the aureus would be 10 percent lighter in weight. So, whereas in the past, 41 aurei had been minted from one pound of gold, the ratio now become 45 aurei to a pound.

Nero was deposed in AD 68. But the precedent was set. Maintaining order throughout the empire was expensive. Rome became dependent on imported capital, imported soldiers, and imported goods—just as America is today. But Rome had its own version of a central bank. Each new emergency was met with more phony cash just as it is today. By the time the barbarians sacked Rome, the currency, the denarius, still bore the ancient form with the images of dead emperors pressed on it. But the value had been taken out; the currency had lost 99.98 percent of its value. While this seems like a dreadful rate of inflation, it is not really as bad as the current U.S. example. In less than 100 years, the U.S. dollar has lost 95 percent of its value. If this rate continues for just another 150 years, the dollar will do in half the time what took the denarius almost 500 years.

Thomas Cahill describes the last days of Rome in his book, *How the Irish Saved Civilization:*

> . . . the changing character of the native population, brought about through unremarked pressures on porous borders; the creation of an increasingly unwieldy and rigid bureaucracy, whose own survival becomes its overriding goal; the despising of the military and the avoidance of its service by established families, while its offices present

unprecedented opportunity for marginal men to whom its ranks had once been closed; the lip service paid to values long dead; the pretense that we still are what we once were; the increasing concentrations of the populace into richer and poorer by way of a corrupt tax system, and the desperation that inevitably follows; the aggrandizement of executive power at the expense of the legislature; ineffectual legislation promulgated with great show; the moral vocation of the man at the top to maintain order at all costs, while growing blind to the cruel dilemmas of ordinary life . . .

Cahill continues:

. . . these are all themes with which our world is familiar, nor are they the God-given property of any party or political point of view, even though we often act as if they were. At least, the emperor could not heap his economic burdens on posterity by creating long-term public debt, for floating capital had not yet been conceptualized. The only kinds of wealth worth speaking of were the fruits of the earth.[5]

Finally, the cost so weakened the empire that the barbarians were at the gate.

"The thicker the grass, the more easily scythed," said Alaric, king of the Visigoths, from AD 395 to 410 He was speaking to the Roman envoys sent to shoo him away.

The Roman envoys had just told him that if he and his filthy band of barbarian buddies didn't go away, they would unleash legions of Roman warriors to crush him. They then asked him what it would take for him to turn around and go. He replied that his men would like to comb the city, take all the gold and silver plus everything else valuable that could be moved, plus all the barbarian slaves.

And what, said the envoys, would that leave us Romans? Replied Alaric, "your lives."[6]

Empires, like bubble markets, end up where they began. Rome began as a town on the Tiber, with sheep grazing on the hills. A bull market in Roman property lasted about 1,000 years—from 700 BC to about AD 300, when temples, monuments, and villas crowded the Palatine. Then, a bear market began that lasted at least another 1,000 years.

As late as the eighteenth century, Rome was once again a city on the Tiber with sheep grazing on the hillsides, amid broken marble columns and immense brick walls. They had been built for a reason, but no one could recall why.

IN PRAISE OF EMPIRES

It is said that empires provide an expanse of law and order under which trade, commerce, investment, and profit taking can flourish. Here, we will spot the empire builders and their apologists a point or two. Even the Mongol reign of terror was said to have permitted an uptick in trade. And why not? The imperialists levied a tribute on output. They had an interest in economic growth. Why shouldn't they make sure bills were paid and property was safe?

One of the leading proponents of the American empire is a man named Deepak Lal, who wrote a book entitled *In Praise of Empires.* "The Roman empire had through its Pax brought unprecedented prosperity to the inhabitants of the Mediterranean littoral for nearly a millennium," Lal writes.[7] He believes that empires are good things, because people are materially better off under imperial rule than other forms of government. We have no intention of trying to prove him wrong. The economic record is not complete enough to prove anything. How fat and happy might the residents of the Mediterranean littoral have been if the Romans had stayed in Rome? We don't know. Nor do we know much about the relative growth rates of groups not under Roman rule. So we cannot prove anything, except that Lal can't either. And for that we need to call only one witness to the stand, Lal himself.

In the 500 years preceding World War II, when the economic picture is more visible, the Holy Roman Empire—which, as Voltaire remarked, was neither holy, nor Roman, nor a real empire—was extinguished. In its place rose various sovereign nation-states, often with imperial ambitions and bubble-like excesses, but none able to assert itself over much of Europe or for very long. Europe, in other words, was nonimperial. China, India, and Anatolia/the Middle East, by contrast, were still run by the vestiges of the Mongol Empire and its successors. Which civilization was most successful economically? We have no figures for the Ottoman Empire, but the 500 years in China produced a net decline in GDP per person. In India, the rate of increase was negligible according to the figures that Lal presents; all the growth that there was came after the Mogul Empire had been replaced by the British. It wasn't imperial rule that gave the place a shot in the arm; it was British investment and know-how.

Lal makes the point decisively and then proceeds to ignore it:

> By creating order over a large economic space, empires have inevitably generated Smithian [as in Adam Smith's *Wealth of Nations*] growth. But given limited technological progress (except for the exceptional period under Sung China), Promethean intensive growth remains a European miracle of the anarchical system of nation-states established after the breakdown of the Roman empire.[8]

Actually, there are other instances of Promethean growth (e.g., Japan, Hong Kong, and Singapore after World War II). And currently, China is growing at 9 percent per year. Russia and India are growing at 7 percent. It could be argued that their growth is largely thanks to the shade provided by the Americans' imperial protection. But then you have to wonder why other places, similarly protected, enjoyed no such growth. You also have to wonder how other places, such as Switzerland and the Scandinavian countries got to be the wealthiest places in the world when they enjoyed no more imperial benefits than anywhere else and were largely indifferent to the imperial system. You also have to wonder how it is possible for China to register such high growth rates in the 1990s and 2000s when it is the very thing from which the American imperium offers protection. Apparently, an empire may increase growth rates even for its enemies.

The logic of Lal's "praise of empires" is no different from saying he likes chocolate cake. It is purely a matter of personal taste, nothing more. All we actually know about economic growth is that empire is neither a necessary nor a sufficient condition for it.

Empires come and go often, like stock markets. When they shoot up quickly, they generally fall sharply, too. And when they take centuries to build—as with the Romans—it takes centuries to take them back to where they began. By using carrier pigeons, the Mamelukes could have speedy news of all who come and go by sea or land, and thus escape surprise, since they live without defenses, and have neither walls nor fortresses. What finally destroyed the Mongols was the plague, which they picked up in the Far East, and gunpowder, which they also encountered in China. The first so reduced their numbers in the fourteenth and fifteenth centuries that they abandoned not only many of their conquests but also much of their own steppes; some of the best pastureland in Asia was effectively returned to nature. The second ended their attacks on more civilized people—who could now blow them out of the saddle. Their descendants in the Mogul Empire in India and the Ottoman Empire in Turkey were largely absorbed into the cultures where they had inserted themselves. And by the seventeenth and eighteenth centuries, the Mongols were once again tending herds of horses in the lonely and inhospitable wastes of Mongolia. By the nineteenth and twentieth centuries, they were paying their own tribute to Russian and Chinese empire builders.

Since the days of the great Khans, empires have become much more entertaining. This is not because they are less lethal. It is because they are much more delusional. They cannot bear the barbaric clarity of Genghis's imperial ambitions. They cannot put on the purple without putting on the masks. After a while their faces take the shape of the mask itself. Rather than follow their atavistic urges and give honest voice to their primitive instincts, they feel obliged to provide reasons that are often fatal to the believer and his victim, but hilarious to the distant observer.

Modern imperialists, like their distant ancestors, lust after the usual things—prestige, power, money, status—all proxies, perhaps, for genetic dispersement. These were the same urges that enticed the Khans and the Caesars. But today's imperialists feel ashamed to admit it. So, they pretend all manner of selfless and world-improving motives, everyone of which is either an obvious fraud or a monumental bamboozle. But that is what makes the whole thing so much more amusing and entertaining than either a modest republic or a primitive empire: Modern empire builders are such quacks and popinjays that they practically sprout tail feathers and grow webbed feet.

The gist of the modern empire builder's creed is that he has a duty to make the world a better place, and he can only do it by telling other people what to do. It is inconceivable to him that others might have their own ideas of what a better world would be like. Or that his own plans are nothing more than his own vain tastes and prejudices. It is as if he burst in on his neighbors to tell them what they were going to do on the weekend; it wouldn't bother him at all that they had their own plans. His are more important!

The charm in this is not in watching the empire builder make a mess of things, which he invariably does—usually a bloody mess. The charm is in the elaborate lies and imbecilities he spins to cover up what he is doing.

His real purpose is no different from those of any Mongol, Greek, or Roman—to feel important, to rule the world and boss other people around, to puff out his chest and pin medals on it, to have power over people and feel superior toward them. The logic of it is inescapable: He feels superior because he rules them. And why does he rule them? Because he is superior!

Since the days of Alexander, empire builders have developed elaborate and heroically absurd proofs for why they are superior. They have before them the evidence of their achievements; they have their neighbors under their heel and not the other way around. Fooled by the randomness of historical events, they look for a reason that explains their superiority and justifies their own rule.

Many are the daffy explanations and spurious proofs offered. Typically, a group believes it is given its right to rule directly from God. Jehovah delivered to the Jews title to the land of milk and honey. It didn't matter to them that there were other people who claimed title, too. "Slay them all," says their God. "And woe to you if you let any of them get away." The Jews thought they had a special covenant with God. But historians will search in vain for an imperial race whose gods opposed them. No matter what vile mischief they take up, people believe they have the gods' approval.

The European colonial empires in the New World, Africa, and Asia were justified on every imaginable pretext. The Spanish thought they had a duty to Christianize the heathen. The English saw their duty in bringing the benefits of Victorian morals and virtues, including clothing, to the naked savages:

> Take up the White man's burden—
> Send forth the best ye breed—
> Go, bind your sons to exile
> To serve your captives' need[9]
>   —Rudyard Kipling

The French, meanwhile, thought the natives should learn to like baguettes and French poets. Their culture was so superior, it was said, they wanted to share it with everyone. They were all successors to Cicero, who maintained that only under Roman imperial rule could civilization flourish.

It was obvious to them all that Europeans were superior to other peoples. Was it a matter of race? Religion? Culture? At one time or another, they put forward each of these hypotheses—sometimes all of them. Europeans were a superior race; therefore, they had evolved superior forms of religion, government, and culture.

And what accounted for their racial superiority? No delusion was too preposterous. When the Romans were on top of the world, they thought their mild climate must be responsible for creating the world's best humans. Two millennia later, when the center of empire had shifted to northern Europe, the rigors of European winters were credited with stiffening upper lips, backbones, and virtues. English ladies, traveling in the tropics, wore long-sleeved shirts and carried parasols, for fear that too much of the tropical sun might cause them to "go native."

The effect of all this self-deception is to turn the imperialists into a race of fools. They have to believe what isn't true—that they are, personally and collectively, better than the people they boss around. Constant dissembling has a corrosive effect on brains and a numbing effect on souls. European imperialists wondered if the Africans, East Indians, and Asians were fully human; often, they treated their subjects as though they thought they were not.

AUSTRO-HUNGARIANS

The impulse to imperial power is always the same, but there are many types of imperium. From the pure simplicity of the Mongols to the incomprehensible complexity of the Austro-Hungarians, you could make a go of almost any kind of empire. Whereas the Mongols got their empire by force, the Austro-Hungarian Empire (1867–1918) also known as the *dual monarchy* came into being largely because they couldn't think of anything better to do with it. Even its formal name—The Kingdoms and Lands Represented in the Imperial Council and the Lands of the Holy Hungarian Crown (of Stephen)—was a pileup of words on the information highway. Then, as now, no one knew how the empire worked—including the people who supposedly ran it.

But that it was an empire, we have no doubt. "A basic, consensus definition would be that an empire is a large political body which rules over territories outside its original borders," explains Stephen Howe in

Empire.[10] Austro-Hungary ruled over the Kingdom of Bohemia, the Kingdom of Dalmatia, the Kingdom of Galicia and Lodomeria, the Archduchy of Austria, the Duchy of Bukowina, the Duchy of Carinthia, the Duchy of Carniola, the Duchy of Salzburg, the Duchy of Upper Silesia and Lower Silesia, the Duchy of Styria, the Margraviate of Moravia, the Princely County of Tyrol (including the Land of Vorarlberg), the Coastal Land (including the Princely County of Gorizia and Gradisca, the City of Trieste, and the Margraviate of Istria).

And this was just on the Austrian side. On the Hungarian side were all the many obnoxious, quarreling peoples of central Europe and the Balkans—the Slovaks, Bohemians, Moravians, Italians, Poles, Ukrainians, Serbs, Albanians, Macedonians, Croats, Bosnians, Herzegovinians, Montegrans, Czechs, Magyars, and many others.

Each of these territories had its own language and customs. Many detested each other. All were jealous of power and how it was used. And at the top were some of the weakest and most confused and conflicted administrators who ever lived. Each had several layers of loyalties: to his own nation; his own class; his own religion; his own family, region, culture, and linguistic group; and his own aristocracy. How could you hope to govern such an empire?

The beauty of it was that you couldn't. There were two separate parliaments and two separate prime ministers along with a collection of archdukes of various talents and responsibilities. In theory, the one royal house—the Habsburgs—had absolute power over the central administration—particularly the military. In practice, they could do little or nothing; they had no money. Occasionally a forceful edict would issue from the government, such as the April 5, 1897, proclamation from the Austrian prime minister, Kasimir Felix Graf von Badeni that permitted the use of the Czech language, along with German, in Bohemia. The ordinance caused so much trouble that poor Badeni was tossed out and Czech was more suppressed than before. Henceforth, Czech newspapers would have to be printed in German!

Despite these annoyances, the empire was a modest success. It was largely peaceful and prosperous. Between 1870 and 1913, GDP per capita rose at an annual rate of 1.45 percent, which was faster than the rate in Britain or France, and almost as fast as in Germany.

But the imperial family had a bad habit of attracting trouble. Emperor Franz Josef's only son died under circumstances that are still considered mysterious. His brother had the bad judgment to meddle in the affairs of Mexico and died in front of a firing squad. And, finally, his nephew and heir, the Archduke Franz Ferdinand, had the misfortune to visit Sarajevo in 1914 at the very moment when Bosnian nationalists were gunning for him; he even wore a hat with a huge ostrich plume so they would be sure not to miss.

THE MAKING OF AN EMPIRE

When did Rome become an empire? Historians look for a particular moment, even a natural, physical boundary—such as when Caesar crossed the Rubicon—to mark the end of one period and the beginning of the next. No such simple marker exists, however, between empire and other forms of government. Nor does any precise boundary exist between democracy and, say, theocracy or dictatorship. Governments are categorized artificially and often arbitrarily on the basis of theories—usually fraudulent ones. It is often said that democracies depend on the consent of the governed, whereas dictatorships and monarchies do not. A moment's reflection, even by a professor of government, would reveal the lie. All systems of government depend on some measure of complicity.

"Given the very small number and insignificant presence of imperial agents and municipal officials to insure obedience to the state," explains Ramsay MacMullen in his *Corruption and the Decline of Rome*, "millionaires, magnates, and other local notables of all sorts must have cooperated, and from their own free will."[11] It doesn't matter whether you call a political society free, a democracy, a dictatorship, or an empire, it always involves a great amount of collusion and cooperation on the part of the population.

"[Imperial] administrators occupied only a minor place in the system. The emperor had only a handful of agents, whose means of reaching the people were few and rudimentary. The police were practically nonexistent. There were neither social workers nor prosecutors,"[12] MacMullen continues.

The people who actually ran things "had no official function, or if they had one, they had no need of it to make themselves heard. A huge number of decisions were taken each day and throughout the empire that conformed to their own desires more than to the law, the emperor, or his representatives. What's more, these decisions were those that counted, those that concerned property, movement, career choices, success on the farm, commerce or banking; sometimes even a person's physical safety."[13]

In business, as in empire, vast, complex, informal systems work largely on the basis of trust. People trust others to do more or less what they expect. The emperor could no more control what was done in Judea or Gaul than we can control what goes into our hamburgers. Still, we trust there is nothing too unsavory in them.

In the Roman Empire, order was transmitted through an extended web of personal connections, family ties, official functions, traditions, habits, and accepted ideas and procedures so that what happened was more or less what everyone expected. The emperor trusted not only his own functionaries to do what they were supposed to do, but also the local big shots with no official post or authority. The lowest slave responded to his overseer, who responded to his master, who responded to his landlord, who responded to his patron, who responded to his *potentiores, consuls, proconsuls, proteuntes, praetors,* and *quaestors,* on up the chain of command to the emperor himself.

Even prisons function with the cooperation and complicity of the convicts. In the Soviet gulag system, for example, a group of people—soldiers conscripted and sent to Siberia against their will—policed one group of prisoners who in turn policed a less fortunate group. Supposedly, the entire Soviet Union functioned as a vast slave society, in which everyone was told what to do and no one had any choice in the matter. But how could it be? If they were all in chains, who held the keys? And why did the jailers suddenly undo the locks in 1989?

We do not argue that the Soviet system was not wretched, but only that the border between its wretchedness and the misery inflicted by other systems of political organization is not nearly as well marked as we have been told. Always and everywhere, nuances and particularities trump the theories.

A dictator cannot rule a country on his own. He needs the help of henchmen and hangmen, soldiers and administrators, tax collectors, and spies. Depending on the size of the country, he might have millions of people all with a stake in his rule. Likewise, what monarch really ruled alone? Even the Sun King, Louis XIV, depended on a whole solar system . . . no, a galaxy . . . of supporters, agents, and factota. He had a vast web of private interests to which he was either beholden, in league, or at odds with: the clergy, the aristocracy, the bourgeoisie, the moneylenders, the armed forces, the tax farmers. There is no discreet line between empire and republic, or any other form of government for that matter. But that doesn't mean there is no difference. Sailing from the Caribbean to the North Atlantic, a voyager crosses no white line. Still, the weather in the two places is hardly the same.

A nation may have elections and yet not be a genuine democracy. It may have a king, but not be a genuine monarchy. It may even call itself an empire—such as the Central African Empire, which bullied several tribes in West Africa—but that doesn't mean it is one.

There is plenty of room for fraud and interpretation in political institutions, just as there is in the rest of life. Julius Caesar was accused of being a dictator. He was cut down by the old guard, who wanted to preserve the republic. But Rome had taken the path of empire long before Caesar was born. Like the United States today, it had troops spread far beyond the homeland. For five centuries, the Romans had been imposing themselves, first in what is now Italy and then the Cisalpine region, the Greek Isles, the coast of Anatolia, and down through the Middle East. Caesar himself made his reputation in his wars against the Gauls—people far from Rome who spoke a different language, with different customs, different traditions, different institutions, and different ideas about how things should be done. Caesar believed he was bringing the benefits of Romanization, which to him was one in the same as bringing civilization itself.

Octavian, Caesar's heir, did not call himself emperor or announce that henceforth Rome would be an empire. He did not need to. The term *imperator* meant "general." He was already an imperator. Nor was he particularly eager to stir up resentment among the republican partisans. He had seen what had happened to his uncle. Let the empire evolve; just don't mention it. Speaking to the senate, he was careful to play to the old sentiments: "And now I give back the Republic into your keeping. The laws, the troops, the treasury, the provinces are all restored to you. May you guard them worthily."[14]

But the old Republic existed only in their dreams and imaginations. No matter what they said, Rome was an empire. The senators crowned him Augustus, and forgot the old constitution.

"People do not easily change, but love their own ancient customs"; wrote Aristotle in his *Politics*. "And it is by small degrees only that one thing takes the place of another; so that the ancient laws will remain, while the power will be in the hands of those who have brought about a revolution in the state."[15] The revolution in Rome took centuries. In America, it took only 58 years (1913–1971). In both cases, most people hardly noticed. The changes were gradual and, generally, agreeable.

A republic, a monarchy, or even a dictatorship is a relatively modest undertaking. Its scope is limited, and controlled by leading citizens either through their influence on the autocrat or by shaping public opinion. An empire, on the other hand, steps onto the world stage and plays a role that is beyond the control of the citizens. Private life becomes auxiliary, moving to a supporting role while the grand public spectacle plays itself out. In the United States Constitution, it is expressly stated that the people are sovereign, not the government. Ultimately, what people want in their private lives is what is supposed to matter. But the idea passed away when the American Republic died and the empire was born. By 1960, John Kennedy was able to lecture voters to "ask not what the country can do for you; ask what you can do for your country." Suddenly, the government that was created by, for, and of the people was way out in front of them. They found themselves servants to it, no longer its masters.

They could, of course, still write letters to the editor and still vote, but the force of these expressions had gone out of them. The form had barely changed, but the meaning of it had turned around, like a word that had come to mean the opposite of what it once signified. *Virtually,* for example, once meant "truly." People would promise to be there "virtually" at noon. Over time, meaning follows practice; virtually slipped to mean not truly, almost, nearly, or sort of. So did the United States Congress come to be what it now is, something not-quite-what-it-was-meant-to-be.

Another important event of the revolution in American politics occurred on June 25, 1950. That is the day on which Harry Truman involved the United States in a war in Korea without authorization from Congress. The Constitution clearly states that the people's representatives alone have the power to determine when the nation's blood and treasure should be put at risk. But on that date, Truman sent U.S. troops to kill and die, without even informing Congress. Even though this happened while Congress was in session, members of the people's assemblies found out about it from reading the newspapers. For a week, Congress had little idea of what was going on, until the commander-in-chief decided to tell them.

As you might expect, a few members of Congress were cheesed off. But the majority went along. Like the senate in Rome, they had eaten of the imperial fruit and liked the taste of it. American forces had to react quickly, they were told. It was a "new era" in warfare, they believed. There was no time for discussion. Meanwhile, the Korean War went on for another 37 months—you would think that they might have found time to talk about it.

What had happened was not that the rest of the world had changed so much, but that America had changed. Truman's doctrine—that the United States would intervene anywhere in the world where it felt its interests were threatened—was not the doctrine of Monroe or Jefferson. It was an imperial doctrine. By then, the nation's focus had shifted away from the private desires and opinions of citizens, as expressed through their elected representatives, to the world outside America's borders. What the people thought no longer really counted for much. Public opinion was important, but it was merely part of the imperial burden—something to be carried around, manipulated, and managed. To that end, even in 1951, a huge propaganda apparatus was already set up—with confidential briefings, press leaks, public relations specialists, and enormous printing and publishing arms. Even then, the executive branch was spinning the news to appeal to the marginal voter.

They hardly had to bother. The average American reacted just as the average Roman had reacted. When the purple was hoisted, he stood up and saluted. It made him feel like a big shot. If Americans were bossing people around in Asia or the Middle East, it made him feel more important. His homeland team was winning all over the world. And if it did not always seem to be on the winning side, he knew he must support his troops and stand behind their commander-in-chief. No one wants to carp and criticize when soldiers take the field. It is unpatriotic. So, keep the soldiers in the field all the time!

While there is no precise DNA test that separates an empire from a ordinary country, there are certain telltale characteristics. A regular country has only its own territory. An empire has a "homeland" and various territorial interests beyond it. It may have subordinate states, protectorates, colonies, satellites, or other client states over whom it exercises a substantial authority. Sometimes it is not even mentioned; but the clients know that if they get out of line, the imperium will come down on them. Typically, the people in the homeland feel superior to the people in the periphery areas. As described, they develop reasons and explanations for their superiority, which are then used to justify further imperial expansion.

THE AMERICAN EMPIRE

America took its first awkward steps toward empire at the end of the nineteenth century, with Theodore Roosevelt intervening in various diarrhea countries for forgettable reasons and with regrettable results. Later, in April 1917, Woodrow Wilson took off at a trot with the fat Rough Rider still breathing down his neck. He urged Congress to declare war on a distant country with which it had no real beef and in which it had no genuine interest.

Twenty-three years later, the United States was in another major war. Few would argue that World War II was a case of needless intervention, since the U.S. fleet was attacked at Pearl Harbor. Still, had America wanted to stay out of it, she could have done so. Pearl Harbor was attacked because the U.S. Navy posed a threat to Japanese imperial ambitions. If the United States had not displayed imperial ambitions of her own and had no satellite state in the Philippines, she would have presented no danger to the Japanese imperial forces. Nor was there any particular reason to go to war against Germany. Though allied to Japan, there was no question of Germany intervening in the Pacific War.

After World War II, America stepped up the pace, engaging in 111 military actions between 1945 and 2005.

Today, the U.S. military divides the world into four regional commands, each given initials—PAC, EUR, CENT, and SOUTH. Each region has its own commander-in-chief (CINC), who is like a proconsul of the Roman Empire. American military bases can be found in 120 different countries, with strike forces ready to light out for almost any place on the planet at a moment's notice.

There is also a vast army of functionaries, intermediaries, consultants, advisors, scientists, engineers, contractors, and busybodies spread all over the globe. Trained in American universities, on the payroll of either the American government or oft-linked U.S. companies, these people provide a class of administrators to keep the imperial money and papers moving.

The work of these people was revealed in a marvelous book by John Perkins called *Confessions of an Economic Hit Man*. A supervisor explained to him:

There were two primary objectives of my work, First I was to justify huge international loans that would funnel money back to MAIN [the consulting firm for whom he labored] and other U.S. companies (such as Bechtel, Halliburton, Stone & Webster, and Brown & Root) through massive engineering and construction projects. Second, I would work to bankrupt the countries that received those loans (after they had paid MAIN and other U.S. contractors, of course) so that they would be forever beholden to their creditors and so they would present easy targets when we needed favors, including military bases, UN votes, or access to oil and other natural resources.

"Who can doubt that there is an American empire?" wrote Arthur Schlesinger Jr. "an informal empire, not colonial in polity, but still richly equipped with imperial paraphernalia: troops, ships, planes, bases, proconsuls, local collaborators, all spread around the luckless planet."[16]

America had mixed and confusing sentiments about empire from the get-go. Its founders were schooled in the history of Rome and determined to avoid what they saw as her mistakes. But at the same time, they couldn't help but lust for the grandeur of it. They longed for the imperial purple, perhaps, from the very beginning.

William Drayton, chief justice of the highest court in South Carolina, wrote in 1776:

> Empires have their zenith—and their declension and dissolution. . . . The British period is from the year 1758, when they victoriously pursued their Enemies into every Quarter of the Globe. . . . The Almighty . . . has made the choice of the present generation to erect the American Empire . . . and thus has suddenly arisen in the World, a new Empire, styled the United States of America. An Empire that as soon as started into Existence, attracts the attention of the Rest of the Universe; and bids fair by the blessing of God, to be the most glorious of any upon Record.[17]

John Quincy Adams, however, cautioned that while "she might become the dictatress of the world: she would be no longer ruler of her own spirit."[18] More than two centuries later, her spirit has run wild. She has soldiers garrisoned all over the world. She has interests in places few Americans have ever heard of and fewer still care about. There is no corner or dead-end street in the world that is not somehow patrolled by U.S. forces. At the end of this year, America is scheduled to spend more in a single year on defense than all the rest of the world combined.

Already, readers must be asking themselves questions: The United States is the world's only superpower; since the capitulation of the Soviet Union, she has no enemies capable of inflicting serious damage; what is she defending herself against? But that is just the point. The imperial spirit has gotten the best of her. She no longer plays a role that she can understand and control. Now, she is an imperial power; she must read from the script that has been thrust in her hands. She must provide security for the entire world. She must provide the public good of law and order. Someone has to do it. Who else could, but America? It is her turn to wear the purple, whether she wants to do so or not. Thus, did she become dictatress of the world; but no longer ruler of her own spirit—or her own finances.

We stop a moment to reflect. The urge to empire is as irresistible as a free lunch. The male of the species cannot pass up a chance to strut around feeling superior. Scarlet tunics and ostrich feathers have gone out of style, but the men who wore them are the same as those who sacked Rome with Alaric, laid waste to Albi with the Duke de Montfort, and entered Baghdad with the Third Army. The uniforms change, but men are the same grasping, vaunting, humbugging dudes they always have been.

There is nothing quite so amusing as watching another man make a fool of himself. That is what makes history so entertaining. And what makes the history of empires particularly entertaining is watching the great emperors: the Napoleons, Alexanders, Caesars, Attilas, and Adolphs—with all their pretensions and sordid butchers—put on the red tunics and burnished helmets, mount their white chargers, and ride right into a stone wall.

While leaders make fools of themselves, the mass man is tanned by the reflected glory of empire. His chin grows stronger as he admires the stalwart troops. His chest swells with every victory. He grows so tall he almost hits his head at the top of doorjambs. We literary economists, on the other hand, can barely suppress a laugh. It is obvious that the poor man has become delusional; but no one appreciates our saying so. Still, we also feel superior, for we cannot help but notice what numskulls they are.

Evolutionary biologists reduce the whole impulse to empire to nothing more than genes and math. After a man has enough to eat, his genes—and by command, his thoughts and emotions—want nothing more than to spread his seed as widely as possible. Genes are only interested in replication, according to the hypothesis. All the trappings of wealth and power—including the urge to lord it over others—are merely proxies and substitutes for sexual attractiveness. A great ruler conquers a city much for the same reason a middle-aged lawyer buys an expensive sports car, a peacock spreads his tail feathers, or a moral philosopher writes a popular book. It indicates to females that he has good genes. The entertainment comes in when the great ruler is defeated and hung from a meat hook, when the peacock is taken by a fox, and when the red sports car gets the boot. (The prospect of finding this book on the remainder table is not entertaining!)

President Wilson got America's self-deception off to a running start early in the twentieth century: "I believe that God planted in us visions of liberty," he said, seeking the Democratic nomination in 1912, "that we are chosen and prominently chosen to show the way to the nations of the world how they shall walk in the path of liberty."

So worthy was the mission that there seemed no need to figure out how to pay for it. If God had set us on the trail of Empire, He could jolly well figure out how to pay for it. Neither then, nor now, have Americans bothered to understand how the business of empire works. They think they are doing the world a favor. That deception alone would not be so grave, but they totally miss the point: Nearly every imperial power has claimed to act for the good of others, but they all found a way to make it pay. When it stops paying, they are out of business.

Like the Mafia, the United States runs a protection business. Under the protection of the imperial pax dollarium, trade and commerce can flourish. People get rich. They should be grateful and happy to pay for the service. The imperial power must charge for that service; otherwise, what would be the point?

But America has so cleverly deceived itself that it believes it gets its immediate tribute from global commerce and its thanks in Heaven. We have no way of knowing what awaits it in Heaven, but we look around and notice that the tribute America gets is so perverse that we're glad she does not get more. Instead of getting paid for providing protection, the United States is on the receiving end of loans from its tributary states and trading partners. The whole idea is mad and preposterous. An imperial power is supposed to control lesser states and exploit them for its own selfish ends. Of course, it does not admit it. Truthfulness is as much a disappointment in politics as it is in marriage or poker. The idea is to pretend to do good, while you do well. In America's absurd version, she does badly for herself and good for others. That is the theme of this book: to call America an imperial power is flattery. In her bizarre version of empire, it is the subordinate powers that control her. They can stop paying tribute whenever they want.

"Will China be setting U.S. rates?" asked an article in a May 2005 edition of the *International Herald Tribune*.[19] The writer, Floyd Norris, had noticed the perverse logic of American imperial finance. What he hadn't realized was that China was already setting U.S. interest rates. By the end of 2004, China owned $120 billion of U.S. Treasury obligations—or 10 percent of the total in foreign hands, which itself was 25 percent of the total outstanding.[20] Had it not bought those bonds, or had it decided to sell them, there would have been significantly less demand for U.S. debt. Or, looked at from a more traditional perspective, there would have been fewer people willing to lend to the United States. Either way, the almost certain result of Chinese lending was to lower the price of lent money, that is, to lower interest rates. Thanks to Asian lending, the United States was able to drop its interest rates below the rate of inflation and keep them there for 22 months.[21]

"The way things work now," Norris explained, "China sells to the world most everything the world wants. China then uses the dollars it receives to buy Treasury securities. That helps to hold down U.S. interest rates and stimulates consumer spending, enabling Americans to buy more from China."[22]

This put China in a commanding position. As Americans spent, China built its productive capacity. China got rich, selling gewgaws, electronic knickknacks, and assorted consumer goods. The imperial consumers, on the other hand, got poorer. In 2004, alone, wealth equivalent to 1 percent of the value of all the assets in the United States passed out of Americans' hands.

The idea of imperial finance is that the central, imperial power gets rich at its vassals' expense. America found a way to do it in reverse; it grew poorer, relatively and absolutely, every day. GDP growth during the five years—2000 to 2005—averaged only 4.4 percent per annum in nominal terms.[23] Meanwhile, net operating losses—the difference between what she earned on overseas sales and what she spent on imports far outpaced GDP, growing in 2004 by 24 percent.[24] And the cost of maintaining her imperial role—the military budget—was 3.3 percent of GDP.[25] The whole thing was a losing proposition. America had found a way to make empire pay—but only for its rivals and enemies.

To make matters worse, the periphery powers, which were supposed to be subordinate, were capable of ruining the central imperium. If the Chinese and other major holders of U.S. Treasury bonds were to sell, there would be hell to pay in the United States. Interest rates would rise. The housing boom would turn into a housing bust. The imperium would have to beg its subordinate states for more credit.

"The U.S. suffers from . . . structural deficits that will limit the effectiveness and duration of its crypto-imperial role in the world," explains Niall Ferguson. "The first is the nation's growing dependence on foreign capital to finance excessive private and public consumption. It is difficult to recall any empire that has long endured after becoming so dependent on lending from abroad."[26]

What kind of odd empire is this? We have had a long line of U.S. leaders strutting across the world stage—the buffoonish Theodore Roosevelt, the weaselly Wilson, the other Roosevelt, Truman, Kennedy, Johnson, Reagan, Bush (both of them)—but none of them seems to have understood how to make an empire pay.

One of the most riveting features is the remarkable way the masses rush not only to their own ruin, but to the elimination of the institutions they claim to cherish. In America, they claim to love freedom but at the first imperial trumpet blow—the war to make the world safe for democracy, the Cold War to contain the red menace, or the War on Terror—they line up to get registered, inspected, searched, probed, approved, and certified. There seems to be no violation of their liberty so great that they would protest nor any violation of anyone else's that they wouldn't applaud, and no expenditure of funds so extravagant that they would bother to ask questions. In 1989, America's post-World War II rival empire—the Soviet Union—threw in the towel. Not only had it had enough of military competition with the United States, but in one of the great turnarounds of history, it simply renounced its whole ideology. It was almost as if the Jews had tossed aside the Torah, thrown off their yarmulkes, and decided to become Rosicrucians or Jehovah's Witnesses. But even more astonishing was what happened next. For the first time in 16 centuries, and perhaps the first time in history, the world faced almost no serious military crisis. America had no military competition. No serious threats. There were no nations on earth who could do serious damage to the United States. That did not mean that Americans were guaranteed safe. In addition to the harm they did to each other, they might be kidnapped or killed by any number of freelance gangs or revolutionary groups. But the government of the United States had no reason to worry. No nation posed a worthy challenge. So what happened in America? Military expenditures rose!

The absurdity can be illustrated by the United States' attack on Iraq. Like so many imperial powers before it, American forces took Baghdad. But where was the payoff? Were slaves sold? Was oil stolen? Were women carried off, or at least violated on location? Was Iraq made to pay tribute? No. America seems to have missed the whole point. It invaded Iraq and now pays tribute to the Iraqis! It sends in engineers, medical people, food, contractors, administrators—at a cost of $1 billion per week—to try to keep the Iraqis from disliking them. They would be a lot better off, financially, if the Iraqis had beaten them off. But Americans have worn the mask of their good intentions for so long, their faces have grown in to it. They look in the mirror and see an imperialist who wants only good things for the world—democracy, freedom, harmony. They are all set to ban cigarettes and require seat belts all over the world.

They think they can be a "good" empire—killing people neither for glory nor for money, but to make the world a better place.

We have to rub our eyes and shake our heads to believe it.

4

As We Go Marching

The Germans occupy a special place in recent world history. "Give a German a gun and he heads for France," was a common expression in the past century. "The Hun is either at your throat or at your feet," was another.

People wondered what it was about the Germans that had made them so ready to go to war and so willing to go along with ghastly deeds on a national scale. Was it something in their blood, in their culture, or in their water?

Now, of course, the Hun has been tamed and has become a pacifist. America urged him to join the war against Iraq, but he demurred; he has had his fill of war. And so the question is more puzzling than ever. Has his blood changed? His culture? Or his economy?

A marvelous little book by John T. Flynn, *As We Go Marching*,[1] was written during World War II and provides some insights. Flynn argues that fascism had no particular connection to the Germans themselves nor was there anything in the Teuton spirit that made them especially susceptible. Instead, he points out that the creed was largely developed by an Italian opportunist, Benito Mussolini. It was the hefty Italian who figured out the main parts—including the glorious theatrical elements. The Germans merely added their own corruptions and attached a peculiarly vicious policy of persecuting, and later exterminating, Jews.

But it is Flynn's description of the economic circumstances in Italy in the late nineteenth and early twentieth centuries—the fertile soil in which fascism took root and flourished—that caught our attention. Italy went to war against Turkey in September 1911. The war was over 12 months later and soon forgotten by everyone. But the impulse that drove the Italians to war in the first place was the focus of Flynn's attention:

> The vengeance of the Italian spirit on Fate was not appeased. Instead, it whetted the appetite for glory. And once more glory did its work on the budget. But once more, peace—dreadful and realistic peace, the bill collector, heavy with her old problems—was back in Rome. The deficits were larger. The debt was greater, and the various economic planners were more relentless than ever in their determination to subject the capitalist system to control.[2]

Perhaps they should have lowered interest rates. Or pressured China to raise its currency. Any policy initiative, no matter how pathetic, could be considered. As Flynn puts it: "Out of Italy [as out of America currently] had gone definitely any important party committed to the theory that the economic system should be free."[3]

Italy had dug herself into a deep hole of debt. Between 1859—when the centralized Italian state came into being—and 1925, the government ran deficits more than twice as often as it ran surpluses. Politicians, who depended on giving away other people's money, found themselves with little left to give away.

"All the old evils were growing in malignance," writes Flynn. "The national debt was rising ominously. The army, navy, and social services were absorbing half the revenues of the nation. Italy was the most heavily taxed nation in proportion to her wealth in Europe."[4]

Of course, there followed many episodes of financial *risorgimento* and many pledges to put the books in order. None of them stuck for long. Italian politicians were soon making promises again.

When grand promises must be fulfilled, debt creeps higher and so does the resistance of taxpayers and lenders, especially from conservative groups. "Hence it becomes increasingly difficult to go on spending in the presence of persisting deficits and rising debt," writes Flynn. "Some form of spending must be found that will command the support of conservative groups. Political leaders, embarrassed by their subsidies to the poor, soon learned that one of the easiest ways to spend money is on military establishments and armaments, because it commands the support of the groups most opposed to spending."[5]

Military spending gives an economy the false impression of growth and prosperity. People are put to work building expensive military hardware.

Assembly lines roll and smokestacks smoke. Plus, the spending goes into the domestic economy. Americans, for example, may buy their gewgaws from China, but their tanks are homemade.

Military adventures not only seem to stimulate the domestic economy; they also goose up popular support for government. Soon, "it was a time for greatness . . ." as Flynn describes the approach of war. War, Giovanni Papini raved, was "the great anvil of fire and blood on which strong peoples are hammered."[6]

There was a time when kings, princes, and emperors ruled the world. Back then, the people knew their place. But in this new, modern world, it became necessary for rulers to appease the masses with various programs designed to fool them into obedience. Armed with ballots, everything seemed possible.

Jose Ortega y Gasset describes the scene:

> Whereas in past time life for the average man meant finding all around him difficulties, dangers, want, limitations of his destiny, dependence, the new world appears as a sphere of practically limitless possibilities, safe and independent of anyone . . . and if the traditional sentiment whispered: "To live is to feel oneself limited, and therefore to have to count with that which limits us," the newest voice shouts: "To live is to meet with no limitation whatever and, consequently, nothing is impossible, nothing is dangerous. . . ."[7]

He might have been describing the mind-set of the contemporary American investor, who sees no limit to stock prices and no risk anywhere. And so he was—70 years ahead of his time.

Voting cannot really increase the masses' well-being. It brings no more hogs to market, builds no more gadgets, improves no meals, nor does it increase the efficiency of the internal combustion engine. But the masses will believe anything; and after Bismarck and Garibaldi came to believe that this new world of assemblies, parliaments, and election fraud offered a better world, it then became the job of politicians to find a way to appeal to these fantasies. This they did, in nineteenth-century Italy as in twenty-first century America, by borrowing money—thus creating the illusion of spending power out of thin air.

From 1859 to 1925, the Italian government ran deficits over 46 years. In only 20 years was the budget balanced. The lire was not a reserve currency; Italian politicos had to do the best they could. But the debts continued and led to war. Not because anyone in particular wanted war or debt for that matter. It was just that one was an evolutionary consequence of the other and both were consequences of the natural urges of democratic society.

> Out of the condition of Italian society sprang certain streams of opinion and of desire that governments acted on and people accepted or at least surrendered to with little resistance, even though they may have not approved or even understood them. Bewildered statesmen turned to government debt as a device for creating purchasing power. No one approved it in principle. But there was no effective resistance because people demanded the fruits it brought. Another was the ever-growing reliance of social-welfare measures to mitigate the privations of the indigent, the unemployed, the sick, the aged. The instruments of debt and spending became standard equipment of politicians. And this need for spending opened the door to an easy surrender to the elements most interested in militarism and its handmaiden, imperialism.[8]

Whenever the debts threatened to overwhelm the nation, inventive politicians found new enemies to distract the people and quiet opponents. "If the country had no natural enemy to be cultivated, then an enemy had to be invented,"[9] wrote Flynn.

Following the war with Turkey, World War I provided fresh diversions. But after the war, the debts mounted even higher. The prewar debt was 15 billion lire. When the war ended it was four times as much. But after the war came new promises: an old-age pension system, unemployment insurance, a national heath care plan. The deficit reached 11 billion lire in 1919, then rose to 17 billion in 1921. How could the debts possibly be paid? Was there any way out, people wondered?

It was at this point that a scoundrel worthy of the crisis arrived on the scene and proceeded to make things worse. Benito Mussolini was the man for the job—energetic, opportunistic—with no scruples or fixed positions to hamper his movements. Mussolini, like Roosevelt, Bush, and practically every politician elected to any office in the entire twentieth century, denounced the loose spending policies of his predecessors and then spent even more. He decried the unbalanced budgets that had brought Italy to the brink of ruin and then piled new debt on the heavy end of the scale. Taking office in 1921, he found himself with a debt of 93 billion lire. By 1923, the *New York Times* estimated that his debt had risen to 405 billion lire, with a deficit for the year of 83 billion lire.

"Spending had become a settled part of the policy of fascism to create national income," concluded Flynn, "except that the fascist state spent on a scale unimaginable to the old premiers."[10]

"We were able to give a new turn to financial policy," explained an Italian pamphlet from the period, "which aimed at improving the public services and at the same time securing a more effective action on the part of the state in promoting and facilitating national progress."[11]

The policy ended in disaster. Spending on domestic programs shifted to spending on military ones. Soon, Italy was at war again. In blood, steel, shame, disgrace, and financial ruin, it settled its accounts.

The romantic lure of empire—the political pull of military spending, the economic delusion, the polished brass and boots—it was all too much to resist. Despite a disastrous experience in World War I, even the fun-loving Italians were soon marching around in jackboots and getting out maps of Abyssinia under Mussolini's new leadership.

Mussolini was the perfect fascist. Like America's leading neoconservatives, he was really a leftist, who saw an opportunity. And also like America's neoconservatives, he was an admirer of Machiavelli, who believed that the ruler "must suppose all men bad and exploit the evil qualities in their nature whenever suitable occasion offers."

Even Americans were impressed. "He is something new and vital in the sluggish old veins of European politics," said Sol Bloom, then chairman of the House Foreign Relations Committee in 1926. "It will be a great thing not only for Italy but for all of us if he succeeds."[12]

In investments, as in war, an early defeat is often more rewarding than a later one. Fortunately for the Italians, the African campaign was a fiasco. In a few years, Mussolini was hanging from a meat hook and Italians went back to making shoes, handbags, and pasta.

MILITARY ADVENTURISM

A characteristic of all empires is an elevation of the military caste. The essential business of empire builders is providing security for parts of the world beyond their own homeland—whether the subject nations want it or not. That is a military exercise. Over time, other forms of business and commerce are neglected. But military might rests on economic might.

People are generally blockheads when it comes to military adventures. Built into their genes is not only the desire to lord it over their neighbors, but also a deep distrust of anyone who fails to do his duty when the nation is at war. That is one of the things that make empires so attractive. Once underway, they meet with little domestic resistance. As time goes by, not only do other forms of business drop by the wayside, so do other domestic concerns. Everything gets sacrificed to the war gods—even the liberties for which they are meant to be fighting.

All that is needed is a war. For that, American imperialists have been blessed twice. First, in 1950, began the war against the Evil Empire. It was a nearly perfect military engagement; it threatened every life in America in a tangible, but not immediate, way. Billions of dollars would have to be spent to protect the nation. Everybody and everything must be available for confiscation, should the need arise. Even money that did not exist— the wealth that future generations had not yet earned—seemed a small price to pay to meet the danger right in front of them.

The *New York Times* of October 31, 1951, noticed the change:

> . . . the Korean War has brought a great and probably long-lasting change in our history and our way of life . . . forcing us to adopt measures which are changing the whole American scene and our relations with the rest of the world. . . . We have embarked on a partial mobilization for which about a hundred billion dollars have been already made available. We have been compelled to activate and expand our alliances at an ultimate cost of some twenty-five billion dollars, to press for rearmament of our former enemies and to scatter our own forces at military bases throughout the world. Finally, we have been forced not only to retain but to expand the draft and to press for a system of universal military training which will affect the lives of a whole generation. The productive effort and the tax burden resulting from these measures are changing the economic pattern of the land.
>
> What is not so clearly understood, here or abroad, is that these are no temporary measures for a temporary emergency but rather the beginning of a wholly new military status for the United States, which seems certain to be with us for a long time to come.[13]

As long as the empire lasts.

On the other side of this vast mobilization was another imperial power doing its own mobilizing—and for similar reasons. Both were in the protection racket. Both benefited—in an imperial sense—from the rivalry. But the Soviet Union's economy had been so wrecked by its economists and central planners, it couldn't keep up. By the 1980s, it was no longer a worthy adversary. By 1989, it came to its senses and got out of the empire business. Dropped tax rates came to an across-the-board 41 percent.[14] And then, went on its way.

During the period of the Cold War—from 1950 to 1989, including the hot periods in Korea and Vietnam—the United States spent a total of $5 trillion protecting the free world from the Evil Empire. If it had not spent a dime, the outcome might have been exactly the same—but we cannot know that.

What we know is that after the collapse of the Soviet empire, only one was still standing. But it left this American empire in an awkward position. It was in the business of providing protection, but from whom? How could it justify high rates of taxation? How could it continue to employ its military men? For a few years—during the Clinton administration—the nation hesitated. But by 2004, the Pentagon budget was nearly 20 percent greater than it was in 1989.

Fortunately for the imperialists, on September 11, 2001, a small group of Muslim terrorists managed one of the most daring and successful attacks in history. With resources no greater than a chemical trace of those of their enemies in the United States, terrorists hijacked commercial airliners and flew them into landmark buildings in New York. The event was seen on television around the world. Within hours, George W. Bush announced a new war—against terrorism. This was an absurd stretch, too. Never before had a war been declared against a tactic. It was as if he had gone to war against naval blockades or fighting on Sunday. Every other empire made war on its enemies or its friends. The Bush administration was making war on no one in particular, and everyone in general. Every fighting force uses terror at one time or another. Besides, *terror* could be defined almost any way you wanted, and is only unacceptable so long as it remains unsuccessful. A terrorist who succeeds gets to have tea with the Queen of England, as did Menachim Begin.

But none of these issues seemed to matter. In the homeland, scarcely anyone complained.

"We are no longer able to choose between peace and war. We have embraced perpetual war. We are no longer able to choose the time, the circumstance or the battlefield."[15] You may think that this is a quotation from a journalist after September 11, 2001. Actually, it is a quote from Garet Garrett, writing about the Cold War in 1952. The comment works for the entire period, just as it would have worked for the Romans almost anytime during their 900-year empire. Or for the Mongols or even the British.

Garrett leaves us another interesting quote from the period:

"Talk of imminent threat to our national security through the application of external force is pure nonsense," said General Douglas MacArthur. "Indeed it is a part of the general pattern of misguided policy that our country is now geared to an arms economy which was bred in an artificially induced psychosis of war hysteria and nurtured upon an incessant propaganda of fear. While such an economy may produce a sense of seeming prosperity for the moment, it rests on an illusionary foundation of complete unreliability and renders among our political leaders almost a greater fear of peace than is their fear of war."[16]

Was he speaking in 1952 or 2002?

Senator Flanders elaborated in 1951:

Fear is felt and spread by the Department of Defense in the Pentagon. In part, the spreading of it is purposeful. Faced with what seem to be enormous armed forces aimed against us, we can scarcely expect the Department of Defense to do other than keep the people in a state of fear so that they will be prepared without limit to furnish men and munitions. . . . Another center from which feat is spread is the State Department. Our diplomacy has gone on the defensive. The real dependences of the State Department is in arms, armies and allies. There is no confidence left in anything except force. The fearfulness of the Pentagon and that of the State Department complement and reinforce each other.[17]

"Senator Flanders missed the point," says Garrett. "Empire must put its faith in arms. Fear at last assumes the phase of a patriotic obsession. It is stronger than any political party."[18]

Neither Flanders nor MacArthur recognized what business America had gotten itself into.

As the imperium moves toward a military footing, civil institutions sink. Senators still debate the merits of particular items of legislation and still sneak pork-barrel projects into military authorizations, but more and more, they become idle windbags rather than real legislators. Even when they see clearly the drift of the continent, they are powerless to stop it. Garet Garrett mentioned the case of Senator Taft discussing the expenses of the Korean War in March 1950.

"I do not know how long this program is going to continue. . . . We simple cannot keep the country in readiness to fight an all-out war unless we are willing to turn our country into a garrison state and abandon all the ideals of freedom upon which this nation has been erected."[19]

Still, Senator Taft was not going to stand in the way of empire. He voted for the appropriations bill.

Fifty-five years later, the people's representatives don't even want to take up the most important issues. Maybe they are too hot to handle. Or maybe, somehow, they know that the important issues are beyond them. It is as if some instinct directs people to doing Nature's own work. Nature will not tolerate an imperial monopoly forever. The empire must find a way to exterminate itself. No one wants to stand in its way. The two most important public issues of the early twenty-first century were the growth of debt in the United States, both public and private, and the stretch of American military resources around the world. Each of these matters had the potential to ruin the imperium itself and gave rise to vital questions. Why are we meddling all over the world? And, how are we going to pay for all the promises we've made? Every publicly elected official should have posed these questions. But almost none did.

Even in 2001, on the matter of war, the United States Constitution was the same as it had been since 1789. "The Congress shall have the power to declare war," it still says. It does not say the president has the power. Nor the Secretary of the Treasury or the Postmaster General. It says Congress. We cannot imagine a graver, more serious act than a declaration of war. We assume that it is just that sort of weight on his shoulders and his conscience that a member of Congress is paid to carry. But when the time came to consider a declaration of war against the lawful government of Afghanistan and then Iraq, out of 98 members of the Senate, not a single one voted against the use of military force in Iraq, and none asked for a declaration of war.

Similarly in matters of domestic policy, Congress becomes more and more marginalized as the work of empire goes forward. Not that it particularly matters. There is nothing necessarily better about a decision made by an elected group of hacks than one made by a dictator, an appointee, or a monarch. We only point out that as empires develop, power develops at the center, around the executive, and radiates outward. The preempire forms are still there. But they become meaningless. The executive can do what he likes, for he controls the business end of the state: the military.

To the extent that it promoted economic progress and prosperity, the Roman Empire did so by establishing public order and otherwise letting people get on with their business. Tax rates probably averaged only about 5 percent of GDP, even lower than the tribute demanded by the Mongols. But as the imperial bureaucracy develops, it has a tendency to clog up the plumbing of commerce with increasingly detailed controls. One measure causes a backup, which in turn provokes remediation by functionaries. Another measure is laid on, which causes even a worse backup. Eventually, people are up to their knees.

This is what happened in Rome. After clipping the coins in the period from Nero to Diocletian, inflation seemed out of control. There were more and more coins. It took more of them to buy the same things every year. Finally, Emperor Diocletian announced his Edict of Prices to stop inflation. Prices for everything—including wages—were controlled. The result, as can be imagined, was even worse disaster.

By the time of the Nixon administration, the water was rising in America, too. We mention it here not to explore the plumbing of commerce but the constitutional system. There is nothing in the United States Constitution allowing a president to fix prices as though he were a Roman emperor. But that is exactly what Richard Nixon did. The measure was desperate, illegal, and so ill-advised as to be financially suicidal. But who opposed it? A few old fuddy-duddies in his own party put up a fight, but most members of Congress seemed not to care.

II

WOODROW CROSSES THE RUBICON

The road to Hell is paved with good intentions.

—Anonymous

5

The Road to Hell

We are dogged by dead men. Down the street from our old office in Paris was the site of the world's first central bank, put up by John Law, before he was forced to hightail it out of town. Around the corner from our new office is the Crillon Hotel, where Theodore Roosevelt, then an assistant secretary of the U.S. Navy, dined in high style while pretending to get the lowdown on the doughboys in the trenches. In the next war, Ernest Hemingway claimed to have liberated the bar at the Crillon from the Nazis as they left for the Rhine.

But it is back in Baltimore, Maryland, where the ghosts haunt us most. In our very own office, according to the local history buffs, Woodrow Wilson got together with the U.S. ambassador to Belgium, Theodore Marburg, and ginned up one of the grandest wish lists of all time—the League of Nations.

An honest, upright man has no place in national politics. A man with his wits about him is too modest for the role. He suffers greatness as a sort of hypocrisy. He has no better idea of how the nation should be led than anyone else—and he knows it.

Dissembling wears him down until he is shouldered out of the way by bolder liars and abject stoneheads. The former will say whatever the voters want to hear—and then go on with disastrous projects. The latter have no plans or fixed ideas of any sort; they merely shake hands and blabber whatever cockamamy nonsense comes into their heads. The former never make good presidents. The latter often do.

93

THE BEST PRESIDENTS

Many of the best American presidents—such as Garfield, Harding, and Arthur—are rarely even mentioned. Lincoln, Wilson, and Theodore Roosevelt, on the other hand, are routinely described as national heroes. Nobody really knows which president was good for the nation and which was bad. We would have to know what would have happened if the man in the Oval Office had done something different. Would the nation be better off if Lincoln had not slaughtered so many Southerners? Would world history have been worse if Wilson had not meddled in World War I? We can't know the answers; we can only guess. But the historians who guess about such matters have a disturbing tilt—not toward mediocrity, but toward imbecility. Like crooked butchers, they advertise our biggest mutton-brains as prime beef—and push their thumbs down on the scales of history to give them extra weight. Those they select as great are merely those who have given them the most meat—those who have made the biggest public spectacles of themselves.

Most historians rate Lincoln, Wilson, and Franklin Roosevelt as our greatest presidents. But all of them might just as well have been charged with dereliction, gross incompetence, and treason. For at one time or another, each of them betrayed the Constitution, got the country into a war that probably could have been avoided, and practically bankrupted the nation.

The presumption that underlies the popular opinion is that a president faces challenges. He is rated on how well he faces up to them. But the biggest challenge a president will face is no different from that faced by a Louis or a Charles—merely staying out of the way. People have their own challenges, their own plans, and their own private lives to lead. The last thing they need is a president who wants to improve the world. Every supposed improvement costs citizens dearly. If it is a bridge, it is they who must pay for it, whether it is needed or not. If it is a law forbidding this or regulating that, it is their activities that are interdicted. If it is a war, it is they who must die. Every step toward phony public do-goodism comes at the expense of genuine private improvements.

That is why a president who does nothing is a treasure. William Henry Harrison was a model national leader. Rare in a president, he did what he promised to do. He told voters that he would "under no circumstances" serve more than a single term. He made good on his promise in the most conclusive way. The poor man caught pneumonia giving his inaugural address. He was dead within 31 days of taking the oath of office.

James A. Garfield was another great leader. He took office in March 1881. The man was a marvel who could write Latin with one hand and Greek with the other—at the same time. He was shot in July and died three months later. "He didn't have time to accomplish his plans," say the standard histories. Thank God.

Millard Fillmore was one of America's greatest presidents. He did little—other than try to preserve peace in the period leading up to the War between the States. Preserving peace was an achievement, but instead of giving the man credit, historians hold up the humbug, Abraham Lincoln, for praise. The United States has never suffered more harm than on Lincoln's watch. Still, it is the Lincoln Memorial to which crowds of agitators and malcontents repair, not the Fillmore Memorial. As far as we know, no monument exists to Fillmore, who not only kept the peace, but also installed the first system of running water in the White House—giving the place its first bathtub. Fillmore was a modest man. Oxford University offered him an honorary degree. But Fillmore couldn't read Latin. He refused the diploma, saying he didn't want a degree he couldn't read.

If Fillmore couldn't read Latin, Andrew Johnson was lucky to be able to read at all. He never went to any kind of school; his wife taught him to read. He is often held up as an example of a failed presidency. Instead, he seems to have made one of the best deals for the American people ever—buying Alaska from Russia for $7.2 million. Who has added so much since? Who has actually made the nation richer, rather than poorer? Johnson did the nation a great service. Still, he gets little respect and practically no thanks.

But our favorite president is Warren Gamaliel Harding.

In his hit book, *Blink,*[1] Malcolm Gladwell tells how Harry Daugherty (a leader of the Republican Party in Ohio) met Warren Harding in 1899 in the back garden of the Globe Hotel in Richwood, Ohio, where both were having their shoes shined.

Daugherty blinked and thought he saw a man who could be president. Journalist Mark Sullivan described the moment:

Harding was worth looking at. He was at the time about 35 years old. His head, features, shoulders and torso had a size that attracted attention, their proportions to each other made an effect, which in any male at any place would justify more than the term handsome. In later years, when he came to be known beyond his local world, the word "Roman" was occasionally used in descriptions of him. As he stepped down from the stand, his legs bore out the striking and agreeable proportions of his body; and his lightness on his feet, his erectness, his easy bearing, added to the impression of physical grace and virility. His suppleness, combined with his bigness of frame, and his large, wide-set rather glowing eyes, his very black hair, and bronze complexion gave him some of the handsomeness of an Indian. His courtesy as he surrendered his seat to the other customer suggested genuine friendliness toward all mankind. His voice was noticeably resonant, masculine, and warm. His pleasure in the attentions of the bootblack's whisk reflected a consciousness about clothes unusual in a small-town man. His manner as he bestowed a tip suggested generous good-nature, a wish to give pleasure, based on physical well-being and sincere kindliness of heart.[2]

Not only did Harding have the looks and the presence, he also had the bad-boy image. Gladwell writes, "Not especially intelligent. Liked to play poker and to drink . . . and most of all, chase women; his sexual appetites were the stuff of legend."[3]

As he rose from one office to the next, he "never distinguished himself." His speeches were vacuous. He had few ideas, and those that he had were probably bad ones. Still, when Daugherty arranged for Harding to speak to the 1916 Republican National Convention, he guessed what might happen.

"There is a man who looks like he should be president," the onlookers would say. Later that day, in the smoke-filled rooms of the Blackstone Hotel in Chicago, the power brokers realized they had a problem. Whom could they find that none of them would object to? Well, there was Harding!

"Harding became President Harding [in 1921]," writes Gladwell. "He served two years before dying unexpectedly of a stroke. He was, most historians agree, one of the worst presidents in American history."[4]

On the surface, he sounds like one of the best. We have never heard of anyone being arrested and charged under the "Harding Act." We have never seen a building in Washington, or anywhere else, named the *Harding Building*. We know of no wars the man caused. We recall no government programs he set in motion.

As far as we know, the nation and everyone in it were no better off the day Warren Harding stepped into office than they were the day he was carried out of it.

Harding was a decent man of reasonable talents. He held poker games in the White House twice a week. And whenever he got a chance, he sneaked away to a burlesque show. These pastimes seemed enough for the man; they helped him bear up in his eminent role and kept him from wanting to do anything. Another saving grace was that the president neither thought nor spoke clearly enough for anyone to figure out what he was talking about. He couldn't rally the troops and get them behind his ideas; he had none. And even if he tried, they wouldn't understand him.

H. L. Mencken preserved a bit of what he called *Gamalielese,* just to hold it up to ridicule:

> I would like government to do all it can to mitigate, then, in understanding in mutuality of interest, in concern for the common good, our tasks will be solved.[5]

The sentence is so idiotic and meaningless, it could have come from the mouth of our current president. But the crowds seemed to like the way he delivered it. He said it with such solid conviction, it "was like a blacksmith bringing down a hammer on an egg,"[6] says Mencken.

Harding was so full of such thunderous twaddle that he stormed into office . . . and then drizzled away until he died. Bravo! Well done.

WILSON CROSSES THE RUBICON

Harding, Arthur, Fillmore—unlike the clumsy giants who left their deep footprints in the earth along Pennsylvania Avenue and trod on practically everyone who got in their way—these midgets managed to make their way through the nation's highest office leaving hardly a trace. That is, they left the country alone.

You will find their pictures on no "dead presidents," that is, on none of the nation's currency. Nor will you find their profiles chiseled on the towering rocks of the Dakota hills. Instead, there you find blowhards such as Theodore Roosevelt and saintly frauds such as Abraham Lincoln. But in the crowded field of contestants for America's worst president, one man stands out. As a world improver, his stature is world class. He was humorless, immodest, and self-righteous.

Woodrow Wilson was the worst kind of politician—he wouldn't lie and couldn't be bought. He was so full of good intentions he could practically pave the road to Hell by himself.

Between the beginning of the twentieth century and the end of World War II, the United States became the world's richest, most advanced, and most powerful nation in history. More people owed more money to America than had ever owed money to any nation anywhere. More people viewed America favorably than ever had viewed any country before. Americans stood astride the globe, a well-meaning and able colossus.

But there never was a silver lining without a cloud wrapped around it. America was too fortunate for her own good. Now, just six decades later, the country is the world's biggest debtor. It is the world's biggest consumer—the "world's mouth." It is the world's most aggressive and meddling military power. No country on earth is so godforsaken as to escape America's notice nor too poor to lend it money. The United States had been the freest country on earth. Now, it has more people locked up in jail than any other country (some of whom it tortures) and employs a huge army of busybodies and snitches all determined that no commercial act between consenting adults will take place without the explicit approval of a half dozen major bureaucracies.

We pause a moment and wonder how we got where we are. Surely, some terrible crime has been committed. We go to the scene to look for evidence. There, we find a few samples and take them over to the lab. And what do we find? The DNA samples are those of Thomas Woodrow Wilson.

We do not blame the man. Or hold him uniquely responsible. His protégé at the Navy Department, Franklin Roosevelt, was an eager accomplice. Lyndon Johnson drove the getaway car. Ronald Reagan, Alan Greenspan, and George W. Bush joined the gang later. But Wilson was the mastermind. It was he who decided to "improve" the U.S. system of government. It was he who also decided to improve much of the world. It was as if he thought all the generations of Americans that preceded him—and all the peoples of the world outside U.S. borders—were a bunch of nincompoops. He, and apparently, he alone was blessed with the ability to see just what the entire world needed. And thus he undertook to change the U.S. Constitution in the most fundamental ways and to reorder the system of international relations that had evolved over thousands of years.

"The spirit of liberty is the spirit which is not too sure that it is right," said Judge Learned Hand in 1944.[7] Such modesty never bothered America's twenty-eighth president.

"A mentally ill, pitiless, mythomaniac, . . . who believed himself in direct communication with God, guided by an intelligent power outside of himself. . . ."[8] Thus did the father of modern psychoanalysis describe Woodrow Wilson. But Freud's judgment of the man was too generous. Wilson was a self-satisfied, sanctimonious delusional bungler who practically single-handedly transformed the country into a mocking shell of what it was supposed to be.

We begin our inspection with a quotation attributed to Wilson after his presidential election victory: "Remember that God ordained that I should be the next president of the United States. Neither you nor any other mortal or mortals could have prevented this."

Is there any doubt that Wilson was mad? He claimed to be a Democrat. Later, he claimed to want to make the world "safe for democracy." But right here, we see he believed in divine providence to decide leadership issues. He had not been elected by the people; he had been chosen by God. Why then, bother to have elections at all?

We also pause to wonder how the former college professor could have known God's mind. We have tried ourselves, many times. Does God intend stock prices to rise, we ask ourselves? Will God let this plane land safely, we wondered recently? Where the hell did God let us leave the car keys? But though we have given the matter a good-faith try, we have never mastered it.

Surely, Woodrow must have supped with the gods. Perhaps he had God's ear or even his throat. For the man could look into the future as easily as we can look into an empty beer stein. He knew not only that he was destined to become president, but that he could build a world even better than the one God had given him—by looking into the future and improving it before it happened and by replacing the private goals and hopes of millions of people with those of his own.

How did he know that the world would be a better place if a Federal Reserve System were set up to control the nation's money? How did he know that Mexico would be a worse country and a worse friend to the

United States—if it had General Huerta at its head, instead of Wilson's man, Carranza? What made him think that his own judgment about what sort of government Mexicans should have was better than that of the Mexicans themselves? What made him think that a democracy was superior to a constitutional monarchy or that World War I would end better if Americans got involved in it?

In his April 2, 1917, speech, in which he urged the nation to war, Wilson noted that the Russians had always been "democratic at heart." "[W]onderful, and heartening things . . . have been happening with the last few weeks in Russia,"[9] he continued. What had been happening was the beginning of the uprising that would later become the Bolshevik Revolution. First, the moderates took over from the Tsar. But the Kerensky government kept Russia in the war. Germany, meanwhile, feared America's entry in the war on the enemy's side. She desperately needed to stabilize the Eastern Front so she could turn her attention to the renewed threat in the West. Her technique was as clever as it was disastrous. She found a windy revolutionary named Lenin who had been exiled from Russia many years before. He was bankrolled, put on a train, and sent back into Russia with the express purpose of making trouble. The trouble he made was the Bolshevik Revolution, which knocked Russia out of the war, just as the Germans had hoped.

Wilson had no clue. He had no way of knowing what would happen anywhere. He was guessing, just like everyone else, and almost always guessing wrong. Many readers will rush to judgment. "He made a mistake," they will say. Or, "How could anyone know that the Russian Revolution would be followed by one of the most cruel and absurd episodes of bad government in the entire sordid, history of the planet?" Since it is impossible to know, they will add, "You just have to do your best. . . . Besides, you have to take action!"

The prejudice for action in public affairs is a constant. And a constant disappointment.

Of course, Wilson could not know what would happen. It was vain to think otherwise. But Wilson did think otherwise and was determined to edit history before it was written—in Haiti, in Mexico, in Nicaragua and then, when the stakes were bigger, in Europe. He even sent troops to Russia to try to beat back the Bolsheviks. But this was typical of Wilson. He seemed to want to intervene everywhere.

THE HALLS OF MONTEZUMA

Americans were perfectly happy with the government of Porfirio D'az in Mexico. But then, the malcontents in Mexico began causing trouble because the most important industries in the country were owned by non-Mexicans. In economic terms it barely matters what passports capitalists carry, but politicians prefer to have locals own local industries, so that they will be closer to hand to lean on. Beyond that, the Mexicans found foreign ownership a useful spoon with which to stir up the mobs. A new president, Francisco Madero, came in after Porfirio was overthrown in 1910. He immediately went to work trying to dispossess the foreigners—many of whom were Americans.

"Give us a dictator we can trust," the dispossessed said to then-president Taft. In February 1913, Madero was overthrown and murdered by General Victoriano Huerta. The new American president, Wilson, did not like the latest regime in Mexico and refused to recognize it. Instead, he backed the opposition movement, led by Venustiano Carranza and his Constitutionalist party. Wilson said he was following a policy of "watchful waiting," but he must have gotten tired of watching after a while. On April 21, 1914, he decided to act. He ordered the bombardment of Vera Cruz. Blowing up another country's city is not an ambiguous act. It is a decisive act of war. The United States Constitution specifically says that Congress, and only Congress, has the power to declare war. But Wilson couldn't wait.

The Mexican "crisis" pot had been on a low boil for months. Foreign ships lay off the coast of several Mexican ports awaiting trouble. An incident in Tampico, where a group of American sailors were detained by Mexican troops, turned up the heat. The sailors were released shortly, with apologies. But Wilson rarely let an opportunity for mishap pass unmolested. He demanded that the Huerta government hoist the American flag over Tampico and give a 21-gun salute to atone for the insult. Huerta would have rather jumped naked into an alligator pond. He refused.

Wilson brought up his marines. But Tampico had no decent place to land them; Vera Cruz was substituted.

The proximate reason for Wilson's attack on Vera Cruz was the approach of a German ship, said to have arms aboard for the Mexican government. Mexico was not at war with the United States. The United States was not at war with Germany. No one was at war with anyone.

Mexico could buy its arms from whatever country it wanted. Wilson's intervention was fantastic, almost unbelievable.

In the battle of Vera Cruz, 90 Americans died and more than 300 Mexicans. What they died for, no one knew. Wilson's military meddling quickly produced the exact opposite result than the one he had expected. His man, Carranza, was so appalled he joined forces with his adversary, uniting the entire country against the United States and demanding the removal of American troops. The Mexican government severed diplomatic relations with the United States and prepared to seize assets of U.S. nationals. Now, the two nations were on the verge of real war. And for what? Mr. Wilson had never met either General Huerta or Mr. Carranza, nor as far as we know, had he ever set foot in Mexico, eaten a single taco, or swallowed a single shot of tequila. Yet, the American president thought he knew best who should be head of state south of the Rio Grande.

The whole affair ended as preposterously and pathetically as it began. The war in Europe began and Wilson's wife died. The president no longer had the time or energy to build a better world in Mexico. After a bit of negotiation, Wilson typed up a press release:

> Both General Carranza and the Convention at Aguascalientes having given the assurances and guarantees we requested, it is the purpose of the Administration to withdraw the troops of the United States from Vera Cruz on Monday, the twenty-third of November. All the persons there for whose personal safety this Government had made itself responsible have now left the city. The priests and nuns who had taken refuge there and for whose safety fears were entertained are on their way to this country.[10]

But the Wilsonian intervention was not over. After the settlement of the Vera Cruz incident, Wilson backed a rival to Carranza—a colorful character named Francisco "Pancho" Villa, who once owned a chain of butcher shops. Villa must have been an early role model for Che Guevara. He loved publicity and was accused of staging battles only to get his name in the paper. Hollywood adored him. If there had been a T-shirt industry in 1916, his picture would have been on millions of them. But Villa was not only comic, he was lethal. On January 10, 1916, his men attacked a group of American mining engineers who had been invited to the area to revive abandoned mines at Santa Ysabel. Villa murdered 18 of them. Then on March 9, he grew more provocative. His men crossed the border to attack a small garrison in Columbus, New Mexico. The town was burned and 17 Americans were killed in the raid. Before you could say *ay Chihuahua,* people all over the United States were foaming at the mouth, eager for war. Once again, Wilson gave up watchful waiting and appointed General John J. ("Black Jack") Pershing to bring him the head of Pancho Villa—dead or alive. This, too, was a failure. Despite the call-up of a punitive force of 12,000 soldiers, Pancho always seemed to get away. "Villa is everywhere, but Villa is nowhere," Pershing told Wilson.

Pershing chased Villa for nine months. He was called home by Wilson two months before the president announced his plans for a new intervention, this time a major league operation. But Villa did not get away for long. He was ambushed several years later and killed.

From humbug, to farce, to disaster, Wilson had written the script for nearly all America's imperial military adventures. The effect of Wilson's interventions in Latin America (he had troops in Nicaragua, Haiti, and the Dominican Republic as well as Mexico) was the opposite of what he had hoped for. Instead of increasing friends of the United States in the region, the number of her sworn enemies multiplied. For the next two generations, the expression, "Yanqui go home" was as familiar as frijoles in many Latin American countries.

THE GREAT WAR

He had a "self-regarding arrogance and smugness, masquerading as righteousness," says historian Paul Johnson of Woodrow Wilson, "which was always there and which grew with the exercise of power." Like all the great empire builders, Wilson was so sure he was making things better he had no need for the polite constraints of bourgeois society, simple truth, or constitutional government. Wilson had "a passion for interpreting great events to the world," he told his first wife. He wanted to "inspire a great movement of opinion."[11] It was not enough to boss around the hidalgos of Latin America; Wilson had an even greater ambition, to lord it over the Europeans, too. Economically, the nation was already on top of the world—U.S. gross domestic product surpassed England's in 1910. Just as every young buck wants to challenge the old bulls, here was America's turn to assert itself militarily among the world's major powers. In answer to the question, why did the United States begin meddling in foreign affairs in the twentieth century, and not before, comes the easy answer: because it could.

On April 2, 1917, Thomas Woodrow Wilson stood before a joint session of Congress and dazzled the assembly with a torrent of rhetorical air. He had hardly to say a word. The animals were already snorting and pawing the ground. The European powers had locked horns. Now, it was America's chance to join the battle and Wilson's chance to become alpha male of the entire world.

"We must put excited feeling away," said the president, and then launched into one of the greatest mob-inciting declarations ever delivered. Wilson was urging Congress to declare war against Germany. The Huns, he said, were governed by a "selfish and autocratic power."[12] What they had done to justify trying to kill them was a matter of great dispute. Robert "Fighting Bob" La Follette, senator from Wisconsin, thought they hadn't done much of anything. They were accused of bayoneting babies and cutting off the arms of boys in Belgium. But when a group of American journalists went on a fact-finding mission to get to the truth of the matter, they could find no evidence of it. Clarence Darrow, the lawyer who later made a monkey out of William Jennings Bryan in the Scopes Trial, said he would offer a $1,000 reward to anyone who came forward whose arm had been cut off by the Germans. A thousand dollars was a lot of money back then (this was when the Fed had barely settled down to work), equal to about $20,000 today. Still, no one claimed the money.

The Germans had also sunk a few ships. But there was a war going on in Europe. Germany tried to impose a blockade of English ports with the only weapon it had, submarines. You took a risk trying to sail into England, especially if your ship was carrying ammunition; everyone knew it. The English were blockading German ports, too. The difference was that the English had a bigger navy and were better at it. There was nothing new about naval blockades. Lincoln had blockaded the South during the War between the States.

It was a long and complicated story. In retrospect, the United States would almost certainly have been better off by staying out of it. Senator Robert La Follette thought so at the time. He told anyone who would listen that the struggle in Europe was best understood as a political and commercial rivalry. The Germans were challenging the English everywhere.

The German economy was growing faster. While Germany industrialized much later than England, she went about it with typical German thoroughness and energy. Output increased over 600 percent from 1855 to 1913. Whereas Britain's empire seemed to be peaking out, the Germans were building new factories and developing new markets. As late as 1870, Britain was responsible for a third of the entire world's manufacturing. By 1910, her percentage had fallen in half; Germany and America both produced more. In Africa, German colonialists were menacing English territories; twice in the years running up to World War I, a crisis in Africa brought the major powers close to war. In Europe, German manufacturers were taking market share from their English competitors. On the high seas, the German Navy was becoming a bigger and bigger threat to the Royal Navy. And so, the English and the Germans were finally having it out. Leave them to it, said Fighting Bob La Follette.

But Woodrow Wilson had his own ideas. "Civilization itself" seemed in the balance, he told the politicians. "We shall fight for the things we have always carried in our hearts—for democracy, for the right of those who submit to authority to have a voice in their own governments, for the rights and liberties of small nations [he did not mention Mexico, Haiti, or Nicaragua], for a universal dominion of right by such a concert of free peoples as shall bring peace and safety to all nations and make the world itself at last free."[13]

When he finished his speech, most of the members of Congress rose to their feet and cheered. Tears streamed down many faces. At last, the United States was going to war! Two million people had already died in the war. For what reason, no one quite knew. Wilson had to resort to bombast and balderdash to try to explain it. It had been just another foolish European war until then—the very sort of war the Founding Fathers had urged their descendants to avoid. Don't go forth looking for "monsters to slay," said Adams. But now the happy moment had come. Now, the United States was ready. Wilson had found a monster. Hallelujah!

Until this date, the war in Europe was just another war in Europe. Not the first, and not the last. As recently as 1870, France and Germany had gone at it. France had attacked. Germany counterattacked so brilliantly, she was able to encircle Paris and lay siege to the city.

The United States felt no desire to enter the Franco-Prussian War. She was still hobbling around on crutches from her own War between the States. And when the war of 1870 was over, the French were forced to pay reparations. But the money paid over to the Germans was quickly recycled back to the French, from whom the Germans bought goods and services. Losing the war turned out to be as good as winning it; France boomed and Germany, too. Apart from that conflict, Europe had enjoyed an entire century of peace and prosperity. The upper brain might have thought— well done, we will hold a steady course. But down in the limbic system, primitive urges were swelling. After such a long period of peace, war might be refreshing. After such a long period of prosperity, they heard the wild call of debt, destruction, and insolvency.

On June 28, 1914, the archduke Franz Ferdinand, of the Austro-Hungarian Empire, and his wife were shot and killed by a malcontent named Gavrilo Princip. No one in America particularly cared. For all it mattered out on the prairie, they would have had the duke stuffed and used as a parlor ornament. Few people had any idea why the Europeans were at war. They had been warned by the Founding Fathers to mind their own business. America had the most dynamic economy in the world; Americans had plenty of business to mind. To sensible people in the United States, minding your own business still seemed like the best foreign policy.

But the editorial pages fulminated with reasons to get into the fight. Nationalism, economic competition, militarism, secret treaties, lofty ideals, low-down secret deals, treachery, rivalry—the answers flew out of the frontal lobe like plastic bags out of a welfare high-rise. Pretty soon, they were hanging from every tree and electric pole.

Even today, you could go from one end of the country to the other asking historians why the United States decided to enter the war or why it entered on the side of England and France instead of on the side of Germany and Austria. You would get plenty of answers, but not a single reason that comes close to justifying the deaths of nearly half a million Americans. You would not, because they don't exist.

Princip was like a character from a Chekov play says historian A. J. P. Taylor. Except that he didn't miss. Did it make sense to sacrifice half a million Americans because Princip hit his mark? Had he been a worse shot, would the war ever have begun? Is that the real reason the war began?[14] Princip's marksmanship did not so much trigger the war as allow it to commence. None of the major powers really wanted war—not in the sense that they expected any benefit from it. None was prepared for it. And yet, none was very good at stopping it. All of a sudden, troops were being mobilized throughout the Balkans. German Kaiser Wilhelm II was alarmed and tried to stop it. On July 30, at 2:55 AM, he sent an urgent telegram to the German ambassador in Vienna: Try mediation, he told the diplomats.

Then, as now, nobody really knew anything. Britain, France, Austria-Hungary, Russia, Germany—all repeatedly misread each others' intentions, miscalculated the effect of their own actions, and completely misunderstood what they were getting themselves into. Many people in Europe at the time had been influenced by the writings of Norman Angell, who believed that war was practically impossible. Angell made a good argument. Modern economies are based on trade, commerce, and manufacture. Wealth no longer rested on land—which could be seized—but on factories, railroads, capital, and business relationships. War destroys capital and stifles economic activity. Therefore, men would not make war; it would be too costly, illogical, and unreasonable.

Norman Angell's book, *The Great Illusion,* was translated into several languages and received high praise from many quarters. One of its most visible admirers was Viscount Esher, chairman of the War Committee in England. Lord Esher gave lectures on the new idea at Cambridge and the Sorbonne. He told listeners that "new economic factors clearly prove the inanity of aggressive wars." No one would make war, said he, because it would cause such "commercial disaster, financial ruin and individual suffering" that people would naturally turn away from it. The whole idea of modern warfare, he explained, was "so pregnant with restraining influences" that war must soon be a thing of the past.[15]

There was also the argument that technology inhibits war. At the beginning of the twentieth century, Winston Churchill said, "Humanity was informed that it could make machines that would fly through the air . . .

"The whole prospect and outlook of mankind grew immeasurably larger, and the multiplication of ideas also proceeded at an incredible rate . . .

"While he nursed the illusion of growing mastery and exulted in his new trappings, he became the sport and presently the victim of tides and currents, of whirlpools and tornadoes amid which he was far more helpless than he had been for a long time."[16]

Not long after the turn of the new century, Orville and Wilbur Wright demonstrated that the promise of air transportation was real. On the windswept banks of North Carolina, for the first time in history, an airplane got off the ground and completed a controlled flight.

The promise was fulfilled. Airplanes worked. Three decades after the birth of airplanes, they were over Churchill's wartime bunker in London, dropping explosives on the city.

"We took it almost for granted that science would confer continual boons and blessings upon us," Churchill explained. But it "was not accompanied by any noticeable advance in the stature of man, either in his mental faculties or his moral character. His brain got no better, but it buzzed the more . . ."[17]

Others expected advances in civilization had made war passé. Freud explained this sentiment in the spring of 1915:

> We were prepared to find that wars between the primitive and civilized peoples, between the races who are divided by the color of their skin— wars, even, against and among the nationalities of Europe whose civilization is little developed or has been lost—would occupy mankind for some time to come. But we permitted ourselves other hopes. We had expected the great world-dominating nations of the white race upon whom the leadership of the human species has fallen, who were known to have world-wide interests as their concern, to whose creative powers were due not only our technical advances toward the control of nature but the artistic and scientific standards of civilization—we had expected these peoples to succeed in discovering another way of settling misunderstandings and conflicts of interest . . .[18]

Only two of the major combatants in World War I, the United States and France, were democracies, more or less officially. But all of them were headed in that direction. In every country, there were parliaments and popular assemblies. Votes were taken. Public opinions were registered. Newspapers shouted out the current prejudices and delivered the latest misinformation. Heads of state hesitated. Autocrats consulted their ministers and advisors. Nowhere in Europe were there any real absolute monarchs. The press, the church, the assemblies, the trade unions, the aristocrats, the bourgeoisie, the industrialists, the bankers, and moneylenders—all had a hearing.

After Wilson declared it a "war to make the world safe for democracy," people began to wonder if democracy itself might have prevented the war. Wilson said as much. "Self-governing nations do not fill their neighbor states with spies," said the chief executive, not quite anticipating the CIA. Nor do they begin "cunningly contrived plans of deception or aggression . . ." he added.[19]

Kerensky, the moderate revolutionary in Russia, declared that democracies never made war on one another. The idea was widely believed at the time, even in America, where two democracies—the North and South—had battered themselves for four years in North America's bloodiest war ever: the War between the States. Nor did anyone bother to wonder why it was that, before their very noses, the worst war in history was taking place between nations that may not have been complete democracies, but were nevertheless more democratic than any in history.

Even today, people still believe that democracies are more peaceful than other forms of government. The United States of America maintains that her form of democracy is so important to the peace and prosperity of the world, she not only invites other nations to join her, she insists. And yet the point has hardly ever been seriously addressed and never proven.

What we do know is that since democracy has become widespread, there has been little letup in the incidence of war and probably an increase in its violence. Unlike the subjects of a tyrant or a monarch, the citizens of a democratic regime are more fully and readily engaged in wartime. When people feel threatened, or feel that they have a stake in the conflict, they are more inclined to devote their energy and resources to victory. Popular newspapers and television work them up to violence easily. Give them the right line of guff and they are prepared to hand over their wallets as well as their lives. France was able to finance 83.5 percent of its wartime expenditures by borrowing. Offering national defense bonds in small denominations, France succeeded, says Hew Strachan, in "mobilizing the wealth of the public."[20]

George Orwell wondered how England could ever triumph over Germany in World War II since socialism was so much better at marshaling the resources of a people in wartime. What he didn't realize was that in wartime, England and America quickly took on many of the attributes of a socialist society such as rationing, censorship, economic planning, and price controls. He also didn't realize that it is not merely the percentage of a society's output that the state is able to grab that counts; what also matters is the total gross amount to grab from. Both of these points were to become critical to the development of global politics in the twentieth century.

Approaching the subject from another angle, we ask ourselves: If democracy was such a good idea, why did people put up with other forms of government for so many hundreds of years? We turn to the dead and ask the question. The answer we get is that most never considered it. Those who did thought democracy a bad system of government.

The Greeks invented it. But their democracy was nothing like our definition of the word. Even America's founders had a deep mistrust of popular democracy. "Democracies," wrote James Madison, "have ever been found incompatible with personal security or the rights of property; and have been as short in their lives as they have been violent in their deaths." Thomas Jefferson believed that "the majority, oppressing an individual, is guilty of a crime, abuses its strength . . . and breaks up the foundations of society." After the Revolutionary War was over, the crafter of the Declaration of Independence also argued that "an elective despotism was not the government we fought for." In the republic they designed and anticipated, few people voted. And then, only for one chamber of the national government: the House of Representatives. The Senate was chosen by the states.

If it was so apparent that American-style democracy was the best system of government ever invented, why didn't the Chinese pick it up? Why did the Chinese never try it in over 4,000 years of civilized community? Surely someone must have thought of it. And how can we be so sure that it really is the best form of government? Isn't it an insult to our ancestors? To the hundreds of generations who never thought of it, or never tried it? And what about all the smart people in all the other countries of the world from the moment man first stood up on two legs to the day before yesterday—why did they so rarely experiment with such a gloriously successful form of government, which as we all know, not only promotes peace and prosperity, but also lifts man up and ennobles him into the most perfect being who ever walked the earth?

We have an answer to propose. Democracy is not really God's choice. It is not really a universal constant; it is not perfect for all people at all times. It is merely an evolutionary development—like a business suit or rap music—sometimes suitable for some people. What has made democracy triumph in the modern world is probably that it is better than monarchy or dictatorship at taking resources from citizens, but rarely takes too much. Totalitarian regimes, such as the Soviet Union, could take nearly all the resources their citizens produced, but it was still not enough to compete with the smaller percentages taken from more democratic regimes. It is also worth noting that democracy has evolved spectacularly over the past 200 years, and especially since Woodrow Wilson redefined it. The American system of the twenty-first century has no more in common with the system set up by the Founding Fathers than, say, a new Mercedes Maybach has with a Tin Lizzie.

In the Great War, almost all the innovations and advances that were thought to prevent war actually made it longer and more brutal—including democracy.

Interlocking treaties were said to prevent any one nation from going to war; instead the system brought in more combatants. Modern methods of production were supposed to make war too economically destructive; instead they brought more weapons with greater killing power to the battlefield. Booming economies had the wealth to spend far more on war than ever before, and to sustain the spending for a longer period of time. Medieval armies could only take the field for a few months. After that, they were exhausted. It was also rare for them to make war in bad weather; they simply didn't have the means to stay at it. Even in modern wars, intensely bad weather puts an end to the fighting, as it did every winter in the Wehrmacht's campaigns in Russia. Modern technology, modern transportation, and modern methods of production all helped put more resources at the warriors' disposal. So did modern democracy. The awakened and awakening democracies in all the major war makers in World War I brought far more popular participation to the war effort— more money, more resources, more soldiers. And all these factors contributed toward keeping nations at war for a much longer period.

But even with all these things, the ability of Germany, Austria-Hungary, Russia, England, and France to sustain a war was still far more limited than one might have thought. Especially in the matter of finance.

Spending in the war exceeded everyone's expectations. After Germany defeated France in 1871, it used the money it received from France in settlement to create a war chest of 120 million marks held in the Julius Tower at Spandau. On the eve of World War I, the amount was doubled to 240 million gold marks, along with an additional 120 million in silver. It seemed like a lot of money. Yet, in 1913, the Reichsbank figured that mobilization alone (to say nothing of wartime losses) would cost 1,800 million marks. Actual expenditure August 1914 was 2,047 million marks. And the war had hardly begun. During the war, Germany's annual expenditure averaged 45,700 million marks, a sum two hundred times greater than the entire contents of the war chest. And the war continued four years. The situation on the Entente side was little different. The war cost far more than expected and needed not only the support of the citizenry, but also of the world's largest democracy—the United States.

No one can know for sure what might have happened. But it seems very likely that without U.S. financial and material support, the Great War would have ended much sooner.

The democratization of the war extended it in another way, as well. The rulers of Britain, Germany, and Russia were all related. Wilhelm II of Germany and George V of England were both grandsons of Queen Victoria. Tsar Nicholas II of Russia was married to their cousin. Nicholas was the cousin of George V through his mother, the Dowager Empress Marie. Before the war, Wilhelm tried to bring Russia into common cause with Germany, sending him a series of letters addressed to "Nicky," from "Willy." Both Willy and Nicky, we soon find, were prepared to make war on each other if need be. But neither they, nor their cousin George V, would do so to such an extent as to endanger their empires, their positions, or destroy the royal houses of Europe. It was precisely because their powers had been weakened that the war continued and expanded to such an extent that two out of three of them not only lost their thrones; their royal houses were extinguished completely. We can't know, but we can imagine that if democracy and Woodrow Wilson had not transformed the war into a bigger event, Willy might have written to Nicky and Georgy and called the whole thing off. But it was too late for that. This was a war between peoples, not royal houses. It was already a largely democratic war, in other words, even before Wilson stuck his nose in it.

The progressive left steadfastly maintained that growing socialism would also make war impossible. Pacifism had always been a major headline in the socialist agenda. They saw war as a by-product of capitalist competition and bourgeois nationalism. Both would be eliminated, "come the revolution." But when push came to shove, socialists in all countries started swinging. The Kerensky government in Russia, after the Tsar's arrest, decided to stay in the war. It called on citizens to fight: "Peasants and workers, all who desire the happiness and welfare of Russia, . . . harden your spirits, collect all forces, and when you have defended the country, liberate it."

Later, in World War II, after Russia had been completely liberated, Stalin found that he, too, had to call on atavistic national sentiments to rally the country behind him. After years of purges, starvation, gulags, and Communist claptrap, the Russians were no longer willing to fight for socialist ideology. But they would still fight for the Motherland.

Both Russia and Germany (and Italy, too) took soft, well-intentioned intellectuals of socialism and put them in uniform. The transformation was a huge success. As an evolutionary strain, National Socialism was much more robust and aggressive than the dreamy, internationalist idealism of the Second International. Here again, the results were just the opposite of what had been expected. Instead of promoting peace, socialism became the most militaristic, warmongering creed on the planet.

Twenty years after World War I, the U.S. government was still scratching its head—wondering how it ever got involved in such a pointless and costly exercise. A committee was set up in Congress to look into the matter. Two years later, the Nye Committee reported that between 1915 and April 1917, the United States loaned Germany 27 million dollars ($470,000,000 adjusted for inflation in 2005 dollars). During that same period, U.S. loans to Britain and its allies totaled 2.3 billion dollars ($40,000,000,000 adjusted for inflation in 2005 dollars). The committee concluded that Americans had entered the war for commercial reasons and on the side of the Allies because it had 85 times as much money at stake.

At least the numbers made sense, from the Americans' point of view. What never quite made sense was why the Europeans went to war in the first place. Many unsatisfying books have been written on the subject. The problem is not that they are incorrect or are not useful explanations; they are reasons as good as any. It is just that they are not sufficient. Looking back nearly 100 years later, we can't see what people got so worked up about. It might just as well have been a religious war, a War of the Roses, or the crusade against the Albigensians.

War is rarely taken up with a cool head. And looking in the head for reasons is as futile as looking for dignity on television. A better place to look is in the heart. Once the mob's sentiment is roused for war, there is practically no stopping it. Mass emotions—whether in the stock market or in war—are infectious. In practically no time, the whole population clamors for uniforms and murder.

"My darling One and beautiful . . ." Winston Churchill began a letter to his wife on July 28, 1914, "Everything tends toward catastrophe, and collapse. I am interested, geared-up and happy."[21] What a rush of excitement swept through Europe in the summer of 1914. Something new. Something big. Something magnificent was underway.

"Strangers spoke to one another in the streets," wrote Stefan Zweig. The Austrian author was a Jew. Later, he would flee another mass movement, but this one, in 1914, he found to his tastes: "People who had avoided each other for years shook hands, everywhere one saw excited faces. Each individual experienced an exaltation of his ego, he was no longer the isolated person of former times, he had been incorporated in too the mass, he was part of the people, and his person, his hitherto unnoticed person, had been given meaning."[22]

There's nothing like a good war to give meaning to empty lives.

"War is the health of the state," Bismarck had said.[23] The European states never felt better than at the beginning of World War I. The words of politicians were reported in all the papers. People who would otherwise never been noticed by the masses were treated as though they were rock stars or sports heroes. Young men lined up to volunteer in the state's armies. Young women joined nursing associations, whose goals were not to take care of people, but to fix up the injured warriors so they could return to battle as quickly as possible. Mothers were honored for their willingness to sacrifice sons to the war effort. Even factory workers were encouraged to think of their work as noble, even glorious—for they were supplying the materiel that made the war possible. Suddenly, everyone had a job to do, an important job.

There was a sense that a war would be good for the spirit and maybe the soul. Poets longed for war to end the "opulence of peace." They saw themselves as suffering from bourgeois prosperity—growing pale, rotting at desks, growing effete over polite dinner conversation. "Today's man," wrote Dezso Kosztolanyi just after the war broke out, ". . . grown up in a hothouse, pale and sipping tea—greets this healthy brutality enthusiastically. Let the storm come and sweep out our salons." Philosopher Max Scheler welcomed the war as "an almost metaphysical awakening from the empty existence of a leaden sleep." Wyndham Lewis wrote that "killing somebody must be the greatest pleasure in existence: either like killing yourself without being interested by the instinct of self-preservation—or exterminating the instinct of self-preservation itself."

While the intellectuals saw the war as "deadly enlivening" to use Rainer Rilke's phrase, the common men and women were titillated, too. Butchers and clerks went home in crisp new uniforms and wives fell in love with them all over again. Freud remarked that his libido had been mobilized for war.

The leaders had their own private joys and sorrows . . . and their own empty lives to fill. Wilson's first wife died in early 1914. German Chancellor, Theobald von Bethmann-Hollweg's wife had died in May 1914. Would he have been so eager for war in July if she had still been alive in June? General Count Franz Conrad von Hotzendorf longed to be a war hero, it was said, so he could win the heart of his beloved Gina von Reininghaus, inconveniently married to someone else. And poor Kaiser Wilhelm, would he have been better at avoiding war if his mother had not rejected him? (The Kaiser had a withered arm, said to be the cause of his mother's coldness toward him.) Wilhelm was "not quite sane," in the judgment of more than one observer at the time. "The Kaiser is like a balloon," Bismarck had said of him. "If you don't hold onto the string you never know quite where he will be off to."[24]

Why look for the causes of such a preposterous war deep in the *isms* that fill history books? The real causes are closer at hand—in the pompous twit of a pedant like Wilson or the bluster of Theodore Roosevelt or in Wilhelm's insecure strut and Bethmann-Hollweg's broken heart. They, and millions more, found the prospect of a short, sanitary war charmingly distracting.

WILSON'S WAR

America had no dog in the European fight. During his reelection battle of 1916, Woodrow Wilson correctly read the public mind. "He kept us out of war," was his campaign slogan.

But there was no glory in sitting on the sidelines. Wilson longed to get into it and imagined that he could transform the war—and the world that came out of it—in his own image. First, it would be a world war, not one confined to the Europeans. And, second, it would have a high-minded purpose: to free the world from tyranny. Never before had such a bloody enterprise been undertaken for what appeared to be such a high-minded reason.

The reasons were just fluff. The real reasons were the same sordid, complex instincts that always lure people to war and ruin. Even the dumbest species have their alphas and omegas—their lead dogs and their drones and mules.

"If it a fearful thing to lead this great peaceful people into war, into the most terrible and disastrous of all wars, civilization itself seeming to be in the balance. But the right is more precious than peace, and we shall fight for the things we have always carried in our hearts," said Wilson.

"To such a task we can dedicate our lives and our fortunes, everything that we are and everything that we have, with the pride of those who know that America is privileged to spend her blood and her might for the principles that gave her birth and happiness and the peace which she has treasured. God helping her, she can do no other."[25]

With this last whoosh of inflated language, the empty bubbles of Mr. Wilson's rhetoric practically exploded. Since the Gettysburg Address, no one in American history had said such a preposterous thing in public that wasn't followed by contemptuous laughter. But it was hardly the last time Americans were to hear such things. In 1961, President Kennedy offered another blank check to the forces of improvement: "We will pay any price, bear any burden, meet any hardship, support any friend, oppose any foe, in order to assure the survival and the success of liberty."[26]

(Science may be cumulative, but war, finance, and love operate in cycles. After 14 years of paying for the Vietnam War, Americans figured it was time to retrench. Richard Nixon addressed the sentiment of the time at his inauguration in 1973: "The time has passed when America will make every other nation's conflict our own, or make every other nation's future our responsibility, or presume to tell the people of other nations how to manage their own affairs."[27] Nixon was wrong. The time had not passed—it was hardly beginning.)

A cynic might dismiss Wilson's high-mindedness as pure claptrap. But it was more than that. The professor of government had managed to take an idea and turn it inside out. He now proposed to waste America's blood on what was practically the exact opposite of the "principles that gave America birth" and squander the happiness and peace she treasured in the process. The Founding Fathers couldn't have cared less about whether Germany or England won the war, to say nothing of the government structure in those countries. They almost certainly would have despised Wilson's busybodying. If they had been subject to the Espionage and Sedition Acts that Wilson put in place to stifle criticism, they probably would have revolted all over again.

Then, as now, critics hacked away at the limbs and branches of Wilson's war fever. What else could they do? They challenged the leafy reasons. None could get at the noxious roots.

After Wilson's speech, practically every member of Congress was on his feet. Amid yelps and war whoops, the world's greatest deliberative body convulsed with excitement. Finally, the war was on.

But there was one important exception: Senator Robert La Follette. A founder of the Progressive Party, La Follette was one of the reasons Woodrow Wilson was elected in the first place. The progressives split the Republican Party vote in two, leaving Wilson—the Democrat—with a 42 percent majority, and so he won on a fluke. La Follette represented Wisconsin, with a large German-American population. But his resistance to war fever seemed to come from his own resources; he held to it longer than politically necessary. He argued against it so strongly that his colleagues thought he was committing political suicide. Many couldn't help but wonder: Is La Follette mad? According to some papers, he was a "Benedict Arnold." He was a "Judas Iscariot," said others. Students at the Massachusetts Institute of Technology (MIT) burned him in effigy, and when La Follette left the Capitol after giving his spirited challenge to the war, another colleague handed him a rope.

But Fighting Bob was not easily bullied, not even after Senator Ollie James of Kentucky rushed at him with a gun in hand. Fortunately for the Wisconsin delegation, Senator Harry Lane of Oregon attacked James with a file and several other senators tackled him.

People were in no mood for question marks. The questions typically come later. In a bubble, or an empire, things that would seem preposterous and absurd under other circumstances—stocks at 200 times earnings, getting yourself killed for no apparent reason—become commonplace. Doubt and skepticism give way to fever.

"It is no time for criticism of the president, of the cabinet, of Congress. . . . It is time for one hundred percent Americanism," said the sage Senator William Squire Kenyon of Iowa. He might have said that it was time to get drunk and dance naked around a fire. The leading politicians were ready for anything as long as it was hysterical. By this time, the superpatriots were out in force and cranked up to 150 percent Americanism. There were rumors that the Huns were stirring up an invasion from Mexico—with an army made up of Mexicans and "armed Negroes." In an exhibition game, baseball legend Ty Cobb beat up another player, Buck Herzog, yelling "German!" People who opposed the war were being accused of cowardice.

In Tulsa, Oklahoma, a crowd hauled a Bulgarian immigrant out of a bar and lynched him. They mistook him for a German. All over the country, people declared they hated Germans, though none knew why. People changed their names to avoid sounding too Teutonic. The *New York Tribune* carried a phony story about a German factory that had been converted to turn corpses into soap. Nothing was too absurd.

(Even after the war, the momentum of hatred took years to halt.) The British continued their blockade of German ports and tightened it after the Armistice was declared. Thousands of Germans—especially children—starved to death. One British journalist visited a maternity hospital in Cologne. He found "rows of babies feverish from want of food, exhausted by privation to the point where their little limbs were like slender wands, their expressions hopeless, and their faces full of pain." But so what, said Clemenceau. There were 20 million too many Germans anyway, reasoned the French premier.

Finally, at 4 PM on April 4, two days after the president's appeal for war, Senator La Follette took the floor of the Senate. Why should Congress get behind the president, he wanted to know? Wilson had been wrong about other things, mightn't he be wrong again?

What about the charge that Germany was sinking ships? Isn't that what nations at war are supposed to do? England had put on a blockade of Germany. Germany had retaliated with its own blockade. American ships could respect the blockades or not. But they shouldn't meekly consent to the English blockade of German ports while being indignant about Germany's blockade of England.

La Follette spoke for two hours and 45 minutes. He ended with tears streaming down his face, for he knew that his words were not enough. He might have been explaining to a pack of hounds why they should let the rabbit go. According to Gilson Gardner, it was "the best speech we will . . . ever hear." But blood was up all over America already. It didn't matter what La Follette said. He was wasting his breath.

Much of what he said concerned who was at fault for the war. Wilson and the warmongers maintained it was Germany's fault. Germany had invaded poor little Belgium, whose neutrality was guaranteed by all the major combatants—including Germany. Yet, Belgium was not really neutral at all; she had signed a secret agreement with Britain.

Germany had started the war, said the Wilsonians. But on the evidence, the Huns no more wanted war than anyone else. The Kaiser himself had tried to stop it. The war began amid a flurry of troop mobilizations, ultimatums, and declarations of war on all sides. Who was really guilty of having begun the war? Who was the aggressor?

Albert Einstein signed a declaration asserting that Germany was innocent. It had not broken international law by invading Belgium, said the text. Nor had Germany committed atrocities against the civilian populations of France and Belgium. In fact, the declaration went on to say that the future of European civilization depended on a German victory. And practically every professor at every German university agreed.

Even old enemies admitted, after the fact, that Germany was no more to blame than anyone else. Lloyd George, Britain's former prime minister, began his memoirs in 1933 by stating that nobody wanted the Great War and nobody expected it. Instead, the nations of Europe merely "slithered over the brink."[28]

Now, America was preparing to slither over the brink, too. Only La Follette and a handful of skeptics stood in her way.

The president claimed that Germany's submarine blockade of England constituted a "war against all nations." Why then, La Follette, wanted to know, was the United States the only one that objected to it? All of Scandinavia, Latin America, Spain—all the world's nations were affected in exactly the same way. But not a single one of them even protested Germany's decision. Certainly, none of them saw the action as a declaration of war.

And then, there was the claim that Germany was under the heel of a "Prussian autocracy." So what, La Follette might have said. What business is it of ours how Germany governs herself? The Wisconsin senator guessed that the average German was more likely to back his government's war effort than Americans were to back Wilson's intervention in Germany's war. And if Wilson was sure of the contrary, let him prove it. Put the matter to a referendum.

But America's entry into what became World War I was never subjected to a popular vote. Democracy is all very well, as long as it takes you where you want to go. Besides, who would really trust the bumpkins to vote on something so important? Wilson knew what was best for everyone—American voters as well as Germans. With little more debate, the U.S. Congress voted to back the president. Only one member, apart perhaps from La Follette, seems to have had any idea what was at stake. William J. Stone, of Missouri, told his colleagues: "I won't vote for this war because if we go into it, we will never again have this same old Republic."[29] The newspapers practically accused him of treason.

Stone was right; but that was the point of the war, to make the United States into an empire. Wilson was proposing to cross the Atlantic as Alexander had crossed the Hellespont and Caesar had crossed the Rubicon.

Every great public movement—and almost every empire—begins in deceit, develops into farce, and ends in disaster. Wilson's war was no different. The idea of making the world safe for democracy was pure humbug. The Europeans had been fighting for two years. If it was a fight for democracy, it came as news to them. After the fighting was over, the French and English laughed at Wilson and ignored his Fourteen Points whenever they conflicted with their own interests. "Mr. Wilson bores me with his Fourteen Points," said Clemenceau, puncturing the American's bubble, "Why God Almighty only has ten."[30]

The American president was appalled and humiliated; he suffered a stroke and never recovered.

Was the world any safer for democracy at the end? Not on the evidence. Just the opposite; in the aftermath of the war, and Wilson's inept settlement, arose democracy's most aggressive and ruthless opponents—men who had ambitions to empire themselves and few scruples about how to achieve it.

ARMISTICE DAY

Finally, 18 months after the United States entered the war, it was over. In much of Europe, the end is still recalled. At 11 AM on the 11th day of the 11th month, bells toll in France. In Britain, everything goes silent. The remembrance is for all the millions of young men who began putting on uniforms in August 1914. These wet, furry balls were plucked from towns all over Europe, put on trains, and sent toward the fighting. Back home, mothers, fathers, and bar owners unrolled maps so they could follow the progress of the men and boys they loved and trace, with their fingers, the glory and gravity of war.

It was a war unlike any other the world had seen. Aging generals looked to the lessons of the American War between the States or the Franco-Prussian War of 1870 for clues as to how the war might proceed. But there were no precedents for what was to happen. It was a new era in warfare.

People were already familiar with the promise of the machine age. They had seen it coming, developing, building for a long time. They had even changed the language they used to reflect this new understanding of how things worked. In his book, *Devil Take the Hindmost,* Edward Chancellor recalls how the railway investment mania had caused people to talk about "getting up steam" or "heading down the track" or "being on the right track."[31] All these new metaphors would have been mysteriously nonsensical prior to the Industrial Age. The new technology had changed the way people thought and the way they spoke.

World War I showed the world that the new paradigm had a deadly power beyond what anyone expected.

At the outbreak of the war, German forces followed Alfred von Schlieffen's plan. They wheeled from the north and drove the French Army before them. Soon the French were retreating down the Marne Valley near Paris. And it looked as though the Germans would soon be victorious.

The German generals believed the French were broken. Encouraged, General von Kluck departed from the plan; instead of taking Paris, he decided to chase the French Army, retreating adjacent to the city, in hopes of destroying it completely. But there was something odd; there were relatively few prisoners. An army that is breaking up usually throws off lots of prisoners.

As it turned out, the French Army had not been beaten. It was retreating in good order. And when Galieni, the old French general, saw what was happening—German troops moving down the Marne only a few miles from Paris—he uttered the famous remark, "Gentlemen, they offer us their flank."

Galieni attacked, driving soldiers to the front line in Paris taxicabs. The Germans were beaten back and the war became a trench-war nightmare of machine guns, mustard gas, barbed wire, and artillery.

By the time the United States entered the war, the poet Rupert Brooke was already dead, and the life expectancy for a soldier on the front lines was just 21 days.

One by one, the people back at home got the telegrams, the letters. The church bells rang. The black cloth came out. And, one by one, the maps were rolled up. Fingers forgot the maps and clutched nervously at crosses and cigarettes. There was no glory left, just tears.

Another poet's mother got the sad news on Armistice Day. A telegram arrived informing the family that Wilfred Owen had been killed. Coming as it did on the day the war ended, the news must have brought more than just grief. "What was the point?" they must have wondered.

Wilfred Owen had wondered, too. His poetry mocked the glory of war. He described soldiers who had been gassed as "gargling" their way to death from "froth-corrupted lungs." Owen saw many men die; it was neither sweet nor glorious, he observed, but ghastly.

It doesn't seem quite right that so many people should have died for nothing. People can't stand the idea. It leaves a hole, a huge gap that the brain labors to fill. Otherwise, the deaths have no meaning. It is not enough to appreciate bravery and self-sacrifice for its own sake. It must make sense. So, bring out the humbug! We found ourselves in Canada's maritime provinces in November 2004, reading the paper. "Don't forget to spend a moment on Remembrance Day," the Canadian Broadcasting Company reminded readers, "to recall those many Canadians who died protecting our liberty and our country."

Not even the maddest of the Wilsonians would have suggested that North Americans' liberty was at stake. The Huns were not going to cross the Atlantic to attack New Brunswick or New York. What did the Yanks and Canucks have at stake? Nothing at all. But people find it easier to die than to think; and for most people, it is probably preferable.

The paper reported that one of the last Canadian World War I veterans had just died at 106 years old. There were only 10 left. (In France, there were 36 still with a pulse as of November 2004.) The old soldiers are dying fast.

Canadian soldiers were among the best colonial troops, said the press report, and the most likely to be killed. If dying in war is sweet, the Newfoundlanders got the most cavities. One out of 4 of the 6,000 men of the Newfoundland Regiment never returned home. But "nothing matched the toll of the massacre at Beaumont-Hamel on the western front on July 1, 1916," reports the *Toronto Globe and Mail*. "About 800 Newfoundlanders charged out of their trenches into the teeth of German machine-gunfire. They had been told that the Germans would be weakened by intense bombardment, that the lethal strings of thick barbed wire strewn across no man's land would be gone and that another regiment would join them. None of it was true. The next morning, only 68 members of the regiment answered the roll call.

"One eyewitness said the Newfoundlanders advanced into the hail of bullets with their chins tucked into their necks, as they might weather an ocean storm."[32]

Then, the old lie swallowed them up, like a tempest.

In the small villages of France hardly a family was spared. Every small town has its monument in a central location to *Nos Heros . . . Mort Pour La France*. Often, the list of names seems longer than the present population. And still people wonder, what happened? We can turn to Wilson's bogus explanation . . . or any one of hundreds. The capitalists are to blame! It's the Germans fault! If only European nations had been democracies! If only Princip had missed his mark!

But there is another way to understand the Great War: A bull market in death began in August 1914; it probably would have ended in 1916 or 1917 but for the fresh new resources of the United States. Wilson longed to give the war meaning by using it to turn America into a world-improving, hegemonic power. All he had to do, he thought, was to prevent an early settlement of the war giving him time to help the French and English win a total victory rather than a negotiated peace. Then, he believed, he would be the true victor. He could come to Europe like an archangel at a Catholic-school picnic. He would walk across the Atlantic and impose his Fourteen Points on the world as if they were written on clay tablets and had been handed to him by God.

MAKING THE WORLD SAFE FOR DEMOCRACY

When Woodrow Wilson stood before Congress and asked for a declaration of war against Germany, the words came out of the advanced part of the brain. They were the nice, multisyllabic, Latinate words you would expect from a former professor of government. They were not simple, honest words, but greasy and meaningless ones, also just what you would expect. It was the kind of bosh you find on a typical high-minded editorial page. It was as if the president opened his mouth and brightly colored bubbles popped out. Airily . . . lightly . . . they floated above the crowds, who craned their necks upward in admiration and awe. They didn't seem to mind that the words were empty. They were gaudy; that was all that seemed to matter.

Wilson's talk of making the world safe for democracy was nothing more than gas. He was proposing to go into the war on the side of the English, who were at that very moment suppressing democracy all over the globe. The Irish, the Indians, the Egyptians—the American president didn't even mention them. Had the upper brain been allowed to do its work, surely it would have told him that if he wanted to make the world safe for democracy, he ought to ask some questions of the nation that held it in check. As a matter of logic he might just as well have entered the war on the side of Germany against England.

But buried deep in the president's sly brain were idealized pictures of the Magna Carta, the robes and wigs of English judges, High Tea at the Savoy, Dickens and Thackeray—all the trappings of the English upper classes as they were imagined by a naïve and admiring college professor from Princeton, New Jersey. The president, his advisors, his cabinet, and his leading allies had such bad cases of anglophilia, they practically stuttered and drooled. And when they stirred the mob with big words, the gaudy balloons they sent aloft meant nothing more than a signal that the fight had begun. The poor schmucks' blood was up already. All it took was a reason and they were ready to die.

A moment of real thought by firing a few synapses in the upper lateral prefrontal cortex would have shown what a losing proposition the European war would likely be. But whatever thinking was taking place was deeper down in the limbic system, not in the lateral prefrontal cortex.

Wilson had already made his decision. And the public, too, was soon engaged. The cannons were drawn up. Medals were polished. In no time at all, people were on their knees pledging all they had to the war effort, giving up their purses, their sons, and their integrity. Around the country, superpatriots were drilling holes through their walls so they could spy on neighbors with names like Bauer and Feldgenhauer. In Baltimore, a former mayor blew his brains out after being charged with being a German sympathizer. Anyone who dared to laugh or cry was soon doing penance or doing time.

War appeals to the limbic system like a new pair of shoes. The yahoos grow taller when war is announced. And when people walk, they take on a proud martial air. Looking around them, they see the bright shine of polished brass and of bombs exploding in air and they are drawn to them like sinners to the sparkling gates of Hell. Politicians feel the need to explain it, to justify it, to dress it up in respectable clothes to hide the jackboots and to slosh on perfume to cover the stench of death. But the words mean nothing. When the sentiments in the limbic system are ready for it, the common man is as eager for war as he is for an extension of his line of credit.

World War I turned out to be a catastrophe as meaningless and senseless as Wilson's words. We look at it here, because it marks the beginning of the U.S. imperium. It helps explain today's world. Now, as then, the yahoos cheer a new group of "Wilsonian" officials. Once again, they think they are making the world safe for democracy. Once again, they believe that almost no price is too heavy for the benefits of the better world they imagine. And once again, they soften up the nation's heads and its money to pay for it.

But it is not the same world that we had in 1917. It is Wilson's world now, the world he helped to make. America is no longer the rising power; China is rising now. America is in Britain's World War I position, trying to hold on to its commercial edge against newer, more aggressive rivals. Americans are no longer lean and hungry for work and profit; now they are the fattest people on the planet and have grown used to living off the hard work of others. "Virtue is what used to pay," said Gordon Tullock. But what used to pay for Americans were the virtues of hard work, thrift, self-discipline, and minding their own business. Americans were virtuous until Wilson took over. Since then, they have given up on what used to pay in favor of what seems to pay right away—meddling, borrowing, and spending—overseas as well as at home.

In the private sphere, a delusional man is soon impoverished, friendless, powerless, and hopeless. All he can do at that point is run for public office: Because in public life, foolish arguments have fewer and less immediate consequences. It is in public life, that people get carried away with theories. "History is an argument without end," said Pieter Geyl. One nation argues that it must dominate its neighbors because it needs "living room." Another says it has a manifest destiny to do so. One public leader says he must create a "co-prosperity sphere." Another says he will make the world safe for democracy. None of these flourishes are rooted in logic or reason, but in the rich, fetid loam of the heart.

Within every world improver and empire builder lurks a vain bird—displaying its tail feathers. And within every democratic assembly is a bunch of stags in rut, waiting for an opportunity to butt heads and make a public spectacle of themselves. For it is neither love nor money that makes the world go 'round—but vanity. Wilson had no particular love and not much money. King George V drew his measure as accurately as Freud, calling him "an entirely cold academic professor—an odious man." But vanity he had in abundance.

PAYING FOR WAR

Nothing softens money up as fast as war. The shells pound it. The bullets puncture it. Armies march on it. And politicians and central bankers stretch it out to the point that it inevitably breaks.

In July 1914, all the major belligerents were on the gold standard— along with 44 other countries. The system was simple and effective. It had fostered an international financial climate so conducive to the growth of capital and trade that most of the West had never been more prosperous. Central banks of the various nations held gold in their coffers. The gold was used to back up the paper currencies. If a nation spent too much on external products, its currency flowed to foreign countries. It came back in payment for either goods or services supplied by the home country. In the event of an imbalance, that is to say when a foreign nation found itself with more of the nation's currency than it could spend on goods and services from that nation, the resulting surplus currency was presented to the central bank to be replaced by gold. Every nation's imbalances were settled in the one thing that none of them could print or counterfeit: gold. If a nation ran a persistent trade deficit, it would find its gold pulled away. This would encourage the central bank to do something to protect it. Usually, interest rates rose, which had the effect of rewarding savings and discouraging the outflow of funds.

The system was neat. It was honest. Which made it ill-suited to the needs of war and empire-builders. War, particularly, was distressingly expensive. Politicians noticed—as monarchs had long ago—that people might be enthralled by the cannon fire, but they hated to pay for it. Typically, according to R. S. Hamilton-Grace, who studied English war financing, about a third of the cost of war had to be covered by borrowing.

Gold was famously uncooperative. It yielded neither to flattery nor to technology. You couldn't pretend it was worth more than it was. And you couldn't create more "out of thin air." Each ounce needed to be dug up out of the earth—at considerable expense. Increasing the money supply— no matter how glorious or worthwhile the cause—was a difficult thing to do. Central banks had only so much gold. If they wanted more, it had to come from somewhere. It had to be saved, put away, stored. The old expression, "you can't get something for nothing," seemed to have been coined to describe the yellow metal. Every ounce of it represented an ounce of thrift, a pound of self-discipline, and a ton of forbearance. It represented money that had not been spent on new clothes, or guns, or food, or entertainment, lodging, tools, roads, or a million other potential uses. Gold was so hard to get that central banks were reluctant to let it go. Kings used to castrate the keepers of their royal mints if they let the gold slip away, either through chicanery or lack of attention. Central bankers were naturally careful with the stuff; caution was in their blood. They knew that if they issued too much paper—that is, if they allowed too many claims against their horde of gold—they risked having it taken from them.

On the other hand, war also was a serious matter. And central banks were asked to help finance the war. This difficult position was made even worse in 1914 when the threat of war caused a drop in stock prices—wiping out much of the liquidity that might be sopped up for wartime finance. The European nations needed to borrow vast amounts to cover the war expenses. But each additional unit of currency further reduced the gold cover, or the ability of the borrowing nation to pay its debts with real money.

Readers will be quick to notice the parallels to the global financial system of 2005. The Europeans wanted to increase the consumption of war materiel. Now, Americans consume other things as if they were fighting for their lives. Cannons and bullets were not much different from big-screen TVs and automobiles; they were quickly used up with no economic progress to show for it. From 1914 to 1918, France and Britain needed U.S. financing to conduct war beyond their means. Now, America turns to its principal suppliers in Asia and asks for credit. Without it, the United States cannot continue consuming at its present rate. In 1914, the world's most important supplier was the United States. France, Britain, and Russia (and to a much lesser extent, Germany, early in the war) had to turn to the United States for supplies. But since they consumed more than they earned, they put their gold reserves at risk. France dealt with this problem early on by simply going off the gold standard. Britain remained on the gold standard throughout the war. But barely, only by the grace of U.S. creditors.

Fortunately for Britain, the United States did not force the issue. (Fortunately for America 90 years later, its major creditors in Asia do not seem to want to force the issue either—at least, not yet. Even without a gold standard, China and Japan could wreak havoc with the dollar any time they chose. For the moment, like America in 1914 to 1916, they are happy to take the orders and increase market share, knowing that their major customer cannot really afford to pay for all that they send her.)

As the war grew more and more grim, not only was the honest money of the gold standard abandoned by most belligerents, the export of gold to settle accounts was expressly forbidden (under cover of fear that the gold would fall into enemy hands). Each nation began increasing its supply of money, issuing more paper currency, borrowing more and more money from foreign (mostly American) and domestic sources, and spending far beyond its means.

France was already heavily in debt when the war began, with a consolidated debt in July 1914 of 27,000 million francs, in arrears already by 967 million. Normally, the French assembly resisted—however weakly—plans to spend more money. But with war cries in their ears and the Huns at the Somme, the peoples' representatives got in the habit of merely rubber-stamping any request that came their way. They voted for credits of 22,804.5 million francs in 1915—an amount that rose every year, reaching 54,537.1 million in 1918. In practice, the government spent far more than the credits that had been voted, using special accounts that we might call "off budget" accounts similar to those used by the Bush administration to pay for the war in Iraq. In 1920, 30,000 million francs—an amount nearly equal to the nation's entire prewar debt—passed through the special accounts (see Figure 5.1).

When America entered the war, its expenditures outdid the other combatants, averaging $42.8 million per day from July 1917 until June 1919. Total federal expenditure rose 2,454 percent in the three years 1916 to 1919. The Federal Reserve issued more and more paper notes; the supply rose by 754 percent between March 1917 and December 1919. The overall money supply increased 60 percent between 1913 and 1918, while GDP increased only 13 percent. The government raised money partly by taxing people much more heavily and partly by borrowing from them. Four "Liberty Loans" were floated during the war years. At the war's end, a "Victory Loan" was offered.

All of this borrowing, spending, and taxing left the world's major economies—especially those in Europe—very fragile. After the war was over, they all attempted to return to the prewar, gold standard that had

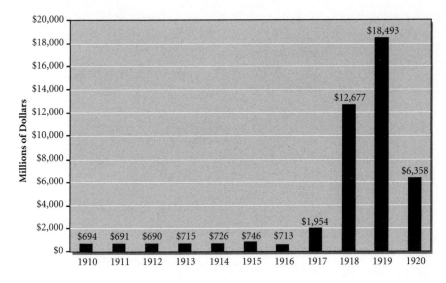

Figure 5.1   **U.S. Federal Outlays, 1910–1920**

Woodrow Wilson is best remembered for his desire to "make the world safe for democracy." However, his involvement in World War I was costly. The one and only respect in which the war paid off was that it turned America into an empire.

Source: "Historical Table," Budget of the United States Government.

worked so well for so long. But they were like the farmers going out to plow their fields in northeastern France; they kept hitting unexploded bombs and blowing themselves up.

Wilson's meddling was disastrous from practically every point of view—except one. The war continued for another 18 months. Not a single major government in Europe survived in its prewar form. "In 1914, Europe was a single civilized community . . ." wrote A. J. P. Taylor, "A man could travel across the length and breadth of the Continent without a passport until he reached . . . Russia and the Ottoman empire. He could settle in a foreign country for work or leisure without legal formalities. . . . Every currency was as good as gold."[33] In 1919, European civilization was a wreck, out of which tough new menaces would be hammered—first in Russia, then in Italy and Germany. Nor did any currency buy as much at the end of the war as it did at the beginning. All the principal belligerents, with the exception of the United States, were forced off the gold standard. The one and only respect in which the war paid off was that it turned America into an empire.

And here we pick up the trail and follow the money that leads to America's empire of debt.

6

The Revolution of 1913 and the Great Depression

eaders of this book will scarcely have given any thought to the
fact that they have never lived in the system of government
argued for by Madison, Jay, and Hamilton in the Federalist
Papers. "It may come as a shock . . ." wrote John Flynn, "to be told that
[you] have never experienced that kind of society which [our] ancestors
knew as the American Republic . . ." Flynn, the editor of the popular
weekly the Saturday Evening Post, had already come to this conclusion in
1955. In his book *The Decline of the American Republic,* Flynn observed
that Americans needlessly "live in the war-torn, debt-ridden, tax-harried
wreckage of a once imposing edifice of the free society which arose out of
the American Revolution on the foundation of the U.S. Constitution."[1]

An empire needs a source of income sufficient to fund its military
campaigns, regulatory regimes, and domestic schemes. It also needs a
strong central authority to direct its ambitious new programs. In one short
12-month span, a year the writer Frank Chodorov calls the "Revolution
of 1913," the empire got the tools it needed. That year—the same year
European countries abandoned the gold standard in preparation for World
War I—the old Republic ceased to exist.

WHERE THE MONEY COMES FROM

America's current system of income tax is a twentieth-century invention.
Previous attempts at creating a national tax had failed or had been thrown

out because they violated tenets of the Constitution deemed essential by the founders. In its first 100 years, the United States supported its federal government with a series of what we would call "sin taxes" today, on whiskey, tobacco, and sugar. By 1817, all internal taxes were abolished by Congress, leaving only tariffs on imported goods as a means for supporting the government.

The first income tax that citizens of the young Republic were forced to endure came about because Congress had been asked to fund the War between the States. In 1862, a tax on incomes between $600 and $10,000 was assessed at the rate of 3 percent, and the Internal Revenue Service (IRS) was created. The war was costing $1.75 million per day.[2] The government sold off land, borrowed heavily, enacted various fees, and increased excise taxes, but it simply wasn't enough. The income tax seemed like the only way to finance the war and service the country's then-staggering $505 million debt. That tax was promoted as a temporary wartime measure. Temporary it was. In 1872, after servicing the Reconstruction, Congress yanked the "temporary" tax.

But that was not the end of it. The income tax appealed to empire builders because it alone offered enough cash to finance the enterprise. But it had another appeal—to the larceny and envy in the hearts of ordinary citizens. Following a banking panic in 1893, Senator William Peffer of Kansas, supported the progressive income tax in this way:

> Wealth is accumulated in New York, and not because those men are more industrious than we are, not because they are wiser and better, but because they trade, because they buy and sell, because they deal in usury, because they reap in what they have never earned, because they take in and live off what other men earn. . . . The West and the South have made you people rich.[3]

That sentiment was puffed up by Nebraska's bellicose world-improver William Jennings Bryan, who argued against the "equal taxation" requirement in the Constitution, in favor of the current progressive one:

> If New York and Massachusetts pay more tax under this law than other states, it will be because they have more taxable incomes within their borders. And why should not those sections pay most which enjoy most?[4]

This logic is simple. People who are more productive should be forced to pay a bigger share of their common expenses. But this kind of logic had no place in a free republic where all men were supposedly created equal; if they were equal they could each carry their own share of the burden of central government. Under this new regime, men were no longer equal, but given differing loads to carry based on the whims of elected hacks.

With considerable foresight, one member of the House of Representatives predicted:

> The imposition of the [income] tax will corrupt the people. It will bring in its train the spy and the informer. It will necessitate a swarm of officials with inquisitorial powers. It will be a step toward centralization. . . . It breaks another canon of taxation in that it is expensive in its collection and cannot be fairly imposed . . . and, finally, it is contrary to the traditions and principles of republican government.[5]

When the tax was again introduced in 1894, a challenge went to the U.S. Supreme Court. In 1895, even among the cacophony of appeals in Congress to "soak the rich," the Supreme Court declared the bill unconstitutional in a 5-to-4 ruling. In writing the majority opinion, Justice Stephen J. Field quoted another case to support his conclusion:

> As stated by counsel: "There is no such thing in the theory of our national government as unlimited power of taxation in congress. There are limitations, as he justly observes, of its powers arising out of the essential nature of all free governments; there are reservations of individual rights, without which society could not exist, and which are respected by every government. The right of taxation is subject to these limitations."[6]

But when the winds of empire blew, the old yellowed paper of the U.S. Constitution went flying. Following The Panic of 1907, President Theodore Roosevelt sided with a faction in the Democratic Party that wanted to amend the Constitution to allow a national income tax. In 1909, President Taft stated that he had "become convinced that a great majority of the people of this country are in favor of vesting the National Government with power to levy an income tax."[7]

Of course, politicians are always able and willing to argue that "the people" want a government to have more power. If the voters see a free lunch in the deal, they're for it. By 1913, just in time for Wilson's emergence on the world stage, the Sixteenth Amendment had been ratified by enough states to put the income tax into law. The Amendment states:

> The Congress shall have power to lay and collect taxes on incomes, from whatever source derived, without apportionment among the several states, and without regard to any census or enumeration.[8]

It wasn't long before Congress exercised its new powers. Wilson even convened a special session of Congress to rush through the first tax law under the Sixteenth Amendment, in which earnings above $3,000 were subject to a 1 percent tax, gradually moving up to 7 percent on higher income levels.

With its rather modest rates, the original income tax was viewed as a benign inconvenience. As early as 1916, however, the top rate was more than doubled from 7 percent up to 15 percent. Then as cash was needed to send Pershing to France, the rate was hiked to a staggering 67 percent in 1917 and 77 percent by 1918. Even the low rates were raised. From their microscopic origin of only 1 percent, the rate settled into a "modest" 23 percent by the end of World War II. But by that time, the people of the old republic had grown to accept an income tax as a necessary evil. Now that the nation was an empire, it needed the money.

In our present era, the complexity of the Internal Revenue Code (IRC) has created an army of specialized lawyers and accountants. Even attempts at reform are out of control. A "technical corrections" bill exceeds 900 pages of adjustments. In fact, by the beginning of the twenty-first century, the tax codes exceeded 7 million words, about nine times longer than the Bible; and the IRS was sending out about 8 billion pages of forms and instructions every year—at the cost of about 300,000 trees! All this effort translates to about 5.4 billion hours spent every year by Americans just complying with the tax rules.

From 1913 to 2005, the income tax has enabled, entitled, empowered, and engorged the federal government, states, and local governments, private enterprises, and millions of private citizens. Spending has grown by more than 13,592 percent.

The income tax gives the federal government a blank check to spend money, even money it does not yet have. The federal government lays a claim on all future economic activity of its citizens; its massive debts are a lien on the earnings of people who have not yet even drawn their first breaths. What's more, the income tax could be used as both an economic tool and as a political weapon. Tax rates could be manipulated, for example, to punish or reward favored political groups.

When the Constitution was ratified in 1789, the colonists in the New World believed they had won for themselves a measure of freedom and independence. "A republic, if you can keep it," Benjamin Franklin warned. But by the end of 1913, a scant 124 years later, Americans were happy to lose their republic; an empire was what they wanted.

AMERICAN CAESARS

But the income tax was only the beginning. If one of the defining features of empire is an open-ended source of funding, another is the shift of power away from the legislature in favor of the central executive. In 1913, a second amendment tipped the scales of authority toward Washington in a way hardly conceived of in the debates of the late eighteenth century. When the Founding Fathers set down the rules for how senators were to be elected, they anticipated a balance between states' rights and the central government. In its original form, the Constitution reads:

> The Senate of the United States shall be composed of two Senators from each state, elected by the people thereof, for six years; and each Senator shall have one vote. The electors in each state shall have the qualifications requisite for electors of the most numerous branch of the state legislatures.

> When vacancies happen in the representation of any state in the Senate, the executive authority of such state shall issue writs of election to fill such vacancies. . . .

The founding fathers saw the indirect election of senators as a means for keeping a balance of power, enabling the states to exert control over the federal legislative branch. The Senate was perceived originally as serving two roles:

> Keeping one eye on states' rights and interests, and the other wary eye on the executive branch, the federal courts, and the House of Representatives. It was contemplated that members of this body would be

older, wiser, more experienced, and better qualified than members of the House and members of state legislatures. Appointed Senators were expected to be somewhat isolated from knee-jerk reactions to current public debates. They would answer for their political acts to state legislatures, and only indirectly to public mobs and voters.[9]

"The preservation of the states in a certain degree of agency is indispensable," stated John Dickinson, the Delaware delegate at the 1787 Constitutional Convention, "It will produce the collision between the different authorities that should be wished for in order to check each other."[10]

James Madison, primary architect of the U.S. Constitution, noted that indirect elections would serve as "a defense to the people against their own temporary errors and delusions [and would] blend stability with liberty."[11]

Each state—acting through its own legislature—should have the right to direct its senators how to vote on issues and how to best represent the state's interests. But along came the great humbug, William Jennings Bryan (again). He maintained the Senate was controlled by corrupt state legislatures. Bryan, who tried to win the presidency three times (in 1896, 1900, and 1908), was described by C. H. Hoebeke, Fellow in Constitutional History at the Center for Constitutional Studies:

> Secretary Bryan put his seal upon the reform that, in the expectations of those who had labored for it, would end the dominance of party "bosses" and the state "machines," stamp out the undue influence of special interests in the Senate, make it more responsive to the will of the people, and of course, eliminate, or greatly reduce, the execrable practice of spending large sums of money to get elected.[12]

The Seventeenth Amendment "improved" the original way that senators were picked by making the election system more democratic. Senators would now be elected by a direct vote of the people of each state. The ills of indirect democracy would thereby be cured . . . by more direct democracy.

As so often happens in the annals of world improvement, the cure was worse than the malady. Corruption and undue influence were not undone by the amendment; they were simply shifted to Washington. The states were reduced to vestiges of their former selves.

Taken together, the Sixteenth and Seventeenth Amendments greatly increased the power of the central government. The original constitutional system involved taxing power at the state level, with revenues submitted to the federal government for the funding of common needs (raising an army, protecting the coast, printing money). Since 1913, the process has been completely reversed. The federal government now collects most of the money from the income tax, and then doles out the revenue to the individual states, usually with many provisos, dictates, and commands attached. This allows the central government to exert great influence over state funding and in many areas not mentioned in the Constitution: highway speed limits, education, health care, medical matters, ownership of weapons, food and drug oversight, police and law enforcement, libraries, the environment, business practices—the list is long and dreary. And now with Homeland Security and the Patriot Act, the list is getting longer.

NEW MONEY

A central bank, as the name implies, is intended as a national center for the control of currency in circulation. It referees the exchange of funds between states and their own banks, and manages debt, both domestically between banks, and internationally between the host country and other governments. The republic, in the years leading up to 1913, had an uneasy relationship, at best, with the notion of a central bank.

Alexander Hamilton, first treasury secretary of the new nation, struggled with high debts from the Revolutionary War. He proposed a central bank to manage the war debt and to create a single currency. In 1791, Congress drafted a charter for the First Bank of the United States. But by 1811, the national emergency had subsided; Congress decided the bank no longer served any purpose, so it was closed.

As a consequence of closing the central bank, state banks flourished. They issued bank notes and the widespread debt-based exchange system went far beyond banking itself. The system grew like zucchini. Every location large enough to have "a church, a tavern, or a blacksmith shop was deemed a suitable place for setting up a bank," said John Kenneth Galbraith.[13] These banks issued notes, and even barbers and bartenders competed with banks in this respect.

But the delightful free-for-all banking situation couldn't last forever. Predictably, the War of 1812 ended with a large war debt and inflation rose to about 14 percent per year. President James Madison signed a new bill in 1816 creating the Second Bank of the United States—with the purpose of again managing debt caused by war.

By the end of the 1820s, a conflict had grown between the bank and President Andrew Jackson, who saw the system as a threat to the virtues of the republic. Jackson argued that the bank should be disbanded. Jackson prevailed, and the bank's charter was vetoed in 1832, with the Second Bank of the United States closing in 1836. The period that followed—1837 through 1862—is known as the era of "wildcat" banks; only state-chartered banks operated, limited to activities mandated by each state's laws.

The legal footing for the creation of currency is limited in the Constitution. Article 1, Section 8 permits Congress to coin money and regulate its value, and Section 10 denies the states the same right. But because any agreed-on medium serves the purpose that we associate with money (an exchange of value) there is no absolute ban on state banks issuing notes. Nor is there any reason a private individual cannot issue his own IOUs, for that matter.

At the beginning of the wildcat bank era, the Supreme Court ruled that state banks had the right to issue notes as media of exchange. When Michigan became a state in 1837, it allowed a bank to gain a charter if it met specific criteria, without also requiring permission from the state legislature. Banks came and went like nail salons. A study of 709 banks in four states found that between 1838 and 1863, half of the banks failed, and a third were not able to honor redemption of notes for gold or silver specie. Overall in the period, banks remained open only five years on average. Widely circulated bank notes—often not backed by reserves—replaced the national currency. States struggled with widespread counterfeiting, inflated note valuation, and the natural instability of the free market.

But the War between the States brought the wildcat banking era to a crashing halt. The first National Banking Act of 1863 brought control over banking to the federal government once again. In addition to creating a uniform national banking system and a single national currency, the new law also provided a secondary market to the U.S. Treasury to finance the growing debts of the Civil War. The change was gradual. By 1870, there were 1,638 national banks versus only 325 state banks. However, state banks continued to operate, having replaced the bank note system with a new concept: the checking account. By 1890, only about 10 percent of the U.S. money supply was represented by currency. The rest was transacted primarily through the bank drafts customers used through their checking accounts.

Then, the same financial crises that induced national support for the income tax, tipped the scales in favor of a permanent national banking system. The Wall Street Panic of 1907 was blamed for the worst depression in U.S. history up to that time. Unemployment climbed to 20 percent. Dozens of banks failed. J. P. Morgan saved several New York banks by granting personal loans.

By 1910, Wall Street executives and Washington politicians saw an opportunity. They met at Jekyll Island off the coast of Georgia, in seclusion and secrecy, to discuss formation of a centralized monetary agency. Senator Nelson Aldrich met with executives of what is today known as Citibank; Morgan Bank; and Kuhn, Loeb Investment House. The so-called Aldrich Plan recommended the formation of 15 regional banks controlled by a national board. The banks would be allowed to make emergency loans to members and create a flexible currency, serving as the monetary arm of the federal government. Although the original plan was defeated in the House, the formula modeled what is now known as the Federal Reserve System.

The legislation, variously called the Currency Bill and the Owen-Glass Act, emerged as the Federal Reserve Act of 1913. It created a dozen regional Reserve Banks to be coordinated by a chairman who would be appointed by the president. While the Constitution grants Congress the right to print money, under the Federal Reserve Act of 1913, Congress approved a plan to delegate this right to the Fed, which is not part of Congress. The U.S. dollar is not issued by the U.S. Treasury but by a privately owned organization, which also influences bank interest rates, the amount of currency in circulation, and even the levels of inflation in the United States. After months of testimony, debate, and over 3,000 pages of documentation of the hearings, the bill was passed and, on December 23, 1913, ratified and signed. For the first time, privately issued debt instruments (currency) would be issued by a private institution but guaranteed by the full faith and credit of the United States.

This last innovation—the establishment of the Federal Reserve System—plays a special role in shaping America's unique system of imperial finance, as we will see later.

A SAFETY NET

If 1913 was the year that set the stage for the empire, the 1930s were years of heavy plot development. Franklin Roosevelt's New Deal had many components but, more than anything else, it was organizing the government for its imperial tasks. In the Old Republic, government was a referee between individuals and between states. Laws were rules of order that were intended to be relatively neutral. Relatively few laws were passed because most of what happened was thought to be out of the range of the rule makers.

But this idea of government changed radically in the 1930s. The government would no longer be accurately described as functioning solely as a law-making and law-enforcing body. This new government would make things better!

It is rarely talked about these days, but at the time the New Deal programs were being passed into law, most people believed they were intended to be temporary measures. At the very least, these programs were never thought to be the cornerstones of a long-term change in the homeland.

In 1935, when the Social Security Act was passed, the promise was that every American would have a secure, if minimal, retirement (if he or she beat the averages and outlived the retirement age of 65). The government, once and for all, would eliminate the common ailments related to old age—sickness, homelessness, disability, and poverty. This was a radical departure from American tradition. The New Deal created a permanent, paternal central government that has only grown more paternal and more centralized in the years since.

Franklin Roosevelt's plan for Social Security was a massive rethinking of the *state,* in the sense that the new system was much more than a simple safety net. It bound ordinary citizens to the federal govern-ment in a way that had not been imagined by the Founding Fathers. People came to rely on the state for their daily bread, and to take a much keener interest in the state itself. Traditional virtues—thrift, independence, self-reliance—were replaced with new virtues: political activism and gaming the system. In the second Roosevelt era, people came to expect the state to take care of things at home; later, they would come to expect the American government to build a better world outside the homeland, too.

While campaigning for presidency, Roosevelt had denounced Hoover as a spendthrift. The democratic platform during the campaign of 1932 called for, among other things, a drastic reduction of government spending by at least 25 percent, abolishing useless commissions and offices, a budget balanced annually, and a sound currency to be preserved at all hazards. But the country was in the throes of the Great Depression.

The causes of the depression have been hotly debated. They go beyond the scope of this book. But the consequences of the economic setback were to spur the nation toward its imperial mission. After the crash of the stock market in 1929, and after the country had entered a deflationary depression in the 1930s, there was little that a man sitting in a chair at 16 Pennsylvania Avenue could do to avert the aftermath of the debt bubble. "Every body tells me what is the matter, but nobody tells me what to do," Roosevelt complained to his cabinet at one point early in his presidency. Soon Washington was flooded with do-gooders chomping at the bit to tell the president what to do. New books published as early as 1932 led the way. George Soule of *The New Republic* penned the influential tract "A Planned Society." Stuart Chase penned another called "A New Deal." Before long, Roosevelt was awash in new ideas. With the new tools from 1913 in his hands, Roosevelt had the ability to turn screws and tighten values throughout the economy. How could he resist?

Among the ideas adopted was one pushed forward by a California physician named Francis Townsend in 1933. The Townsend Plan was designed to extinguish poverty forever. When it first hit the presses, Roosevelt was opposed. But its popularity caught on; two years later under pressure from the voters, Roosevelt introduced the Social Security Act. The organizers of the Townsend Plan became major critics of the government program, complaining that it did not provide enough assistance.

Following the establishment of the act's primary benefit, the old age insurance provision, Congress amended the law four years later to add survivors' insurance. Medicare benefits were added in 1965. By 2005, Social Security and Medicare took up 27 percent of the federal budget. While the program was relatively young, it was a novel idea and controversy surrounded the question of whether the program paid out enough based on the required payroll deductions people paid in. Little concern was given to whether it could remain solvent in the long term.

Other programs introduced as part of the original act included the Federal Unemployment Insurance Act (FUTA), funded by a tax on employers' side of payroll; and Aid to Dependent Children (ADC), now called Aid to Families with Dependent Children (AFDC). Social Security and its related legislation have expanded broadly beyond the biggest pieces, old age insurance and Medicare. The Act began institutionalization of a dual-track system, providing both old age insurance and related benefits, and the other designed to work with the states in a dollar-matching

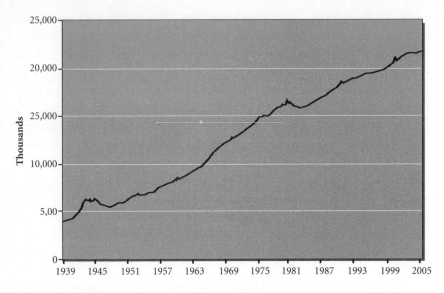

Figure 6.1   **Government Employment, 1939–2005**

The government programs created in the 1930s have required an ever-increasing bureaucracy. All of these programs—outgrowths of Social Security—have expanded today to represent a large, complex, and expensive system of what the Romans called *panem et circenses*—bread and circuses.

Source: Bureau of Labor Statistics.

program for a vast network. Today, the overall program includes national minimum wage and child labor laws; federal disability insurance; Medicaid; public housing and rent entitlements; food stamps; and means-tested income assistance for the elderly and disabled. All these programs—outgrowths of Social Security—have expanded today to represent a large, complex, and expensive system of what the Romans called *panem et circenses*—bread and circuses (see Figure 6.1).

PANEM ET CIRCENSES

That the government should take responsibility for the needy, poor, and disabled is not a new idea at all. The Elizabethan Poor Laws were enacted in England in 1597. The individual duty to provide the "seven corporal works of mercy" predates the modern era. These seven were to feed the hungry, give drink to the thirsty, welcome the stranger, clothe the naked, visit the sick, visit the prisoner, and bury the dead. What is new is the idea that the state should serve as the primary caregiver.

The Elizabethan Poor Laws were based on the premise that the family was primarily responsible for providing help to anyone in need, especially within their own families. Elderly parents were to be cared for by younger family members. Beyond that, the churches were responsible for providing relief. In fact, the community parish was the basic unit of responsibility under the Elizabethan Poor Law system. By 1601, inconsistencies in the administration of relief, the growing problem of burglars and robbers—the "sturdy beggars" of the times—and the difficulty of dealing with those who took advantage of the system led to a consolidation of these poor laws.

The Tenth Amendment to the U.S. Constitution declared, "The powers not delegated to the United States by the Constitution, nor prohibited by it to the states, are reserved to the states respectively, or to the people."[14] While broad, the intent of this amendment is clear: The federal government of the old republic had never been intended to watch over the welfare of its citizens. Yet, the feds now administer more welfare programs than we can imagine. Remembering their names is like learning the logarithmic tables by heart—just as difficult and even more pointless. State programs, while they exist, are often only supplementary. In many instances, funding of state programs is derived from handouts determined and administered by the federal government, invariably with strings attached.

The robust mob of organizations, designed to provide jobs, training, and more, is mind-boggling. These groups included the Civil Works Administration, the Civilian Conservation Corps, the National Youth Administration, and the Works Progress Administration—all agencies of the federal government, all intended to provide services that "are reserved to the states respectively" as identified in the Tenth Amendment.

The largest volume of legislation, however, was passed during the first congressional session, known as the "Hundred Days" (from March 9 to June 16, 1933):

March 9   Emergency Banking Act (expanding federal banking oversight)

March 20   Economy Act (reorganization of federal salary levels and veterans' benefits)

March 22   Beer-Wine Revenue Act (created taxes on alcoholic beverages)

March 31   Civilian Conservation Corps Act (created work camps to train 250,000 men between ages of 18 and 25, and created the CCC).

May 12   Federal Emergency Relief Act (set up system to distribute $500 million to state and local agencies)

May 12   Agricultural Adjustment Act (created farm subsidies)

May 18   Tennessee Valley Authority Act (created authority to the federal government to build dams and power plants and to create the TVA)

May 27   Federal Securities Act (created new regulations in the securities industry and removed the United States from the gold standard)

June 6   National Employment System Act (created the U.S. Employment Service)

June 13   Home Owners Refinancing Act (created the Home Owners Loan Corporation to refinance nonagricultural home loans)

June 16   Glass-Steagall Banking Act (created banking reforms and established the Federal Bank Deposit Insurance Corporation, or FDIC)

June 16   Farm Credit Act (set up provisions to grant refinancing of existing farm loans)

June 16   Emergency Railroad Transportation Act (expanded federal regulation over railroads and transportation companies)

June 16   National Industrial Recovery Act (created the National Recovery Administration and the Public Works Administration)

STUFFING THE COURT

By the time the New Deal legislation had passed into law, a rift developed between President Roosevelt and the Supreme Court. In 1935, the justices—a majority of whom had been appointed by stodgy old Republican presidents—declared much of the New Deal agenda unconstitutional. That year, the Court threw out the Railroad Retirement Act of 1934, a law that had set up pension plans for railway workers. It also threw out one of the most significant pieces of the New Deal, the National Industrial Recovery Act of 1933. In 1936, the trend continued when the Court declared the Agricultural Adjustment Act of 1933 unconstitutional.

The Supreme Court was intended to have the last word for the judiciary branch. It was expected to be made up of wise old men, like a council of elders in more primitive societies. At the time, six of the nine judges were over 70. They were not dead, but they were old enough to know better than to go along with the president's ambitious new programs. Early in 1937, Roosevelt spoke with his advisors about a new draft bill that called for Supreme Court justices to retire at the age of 70. Under the proposed new rule, if they did not retire, the president would be able to appoint a new judge, increasing the number of justices on the Court to 15.

Roosevelt appealed directly to the masses during a Fireside Chat in March 1937. He explained his proposed new legislation and defined both the new imperial executive and its contempt for the wisdom of old age:

> The American people have learned from the depression. For in the last three national elections an overwhelming majority of them have voted a mandate that the Congress and the president begin the task of providing . . . protection [aka. Something for nothing]—not after long years of debate, but now. The courts, however, have cast doubts on the ability of the elected Congress to protect us against catastrophe by meeting squarely our modern social and economic conditions. . . . [S]ince the rise of the modern movement for social and economic progress through legislation, the court has more and more often and more and more boldly asserted a power to veto laws passed by the Congress and by state legislatures. . . . The court in addition to the proper use of its judicial functions has improperly set itself up as a third house of the Congress—a super-legislature, as one of the justices has called it—reading into the Constitution words and implications which are not there, and which were never intended to be there.

> What is my proposal? It is simply this: Whenever a judge or justice of any federal court has reached the age of 70 and does not avail himself of the opportunity to retire on a pension, a new member shall be appointed by the president then in office, with the approval, as required by the Constitution, of the Senate of the United States.[15]

While retirement would not be mandatory as soon as a judge turned 70, the outcome of this proposal is apparent. As soon as a judge did reach that age, the president would certainly appoint a new member. The United States would have ended up with a younger, more obliging Court with a permanent membership of 15. Those bringing appeals forward to the Court would time their filings based on current age, time to age 70, and the president then in office. Even Roosevelt admitted this in a veiled threat to the Court, in the same address. He said "The number of judges to be appointed would depend wholly on the decision of present judges now over 70, or those who would subsequently reach the age of 70."[16]

Congress balked. After months of hearings on the bill, the Senate killed FDR's plan with a 70 to 20 vote. The proposal was sent back to committee and nothing came of it.

But the winds of empire continued to blow hard. Economists, philosophers, radicals, and other malcontents rolled into Washington like tumbleweeds, with plans for centralized control of the economy.

When Roosevelt entered office, having chided the Republicans before him for spending too much money, the federal debt, after 143 years, had grown to $19 billion. Roosevelt—in just four years—borrowed almost as much money as all the dead presidents who came before him. He and members of Congress at the time were disturbed about it, but ideas arise as they are needed. The big spenders needed an idea that would permit huge new levels of government debt. They soon found it: *A government, unlike an individual, can borrow and spend indefinitely without fear of bankruptcy.* A government borrows money from its citizens. Therefore, it owes that debt to its citizens. The debt is therefore owed by the people to themselves. And no matter how large the debt gets, the financial impact on the citizens and the government is negligible. On the subject of what would happen if that debt were owed to foreign bond holders, the Roosevelt era empire builders were less clear.

"The apostle of this sly philosophy was Dr. Alvin Hansen of Harvard," writes John T. Flynn, "When this small book, written by Dr. Hansen's disciples, appeared, the doctor was promptly brought to Washington and installed in the Federal Reserve Board as the economic philosopher of this new dispensation. . . . Now Roosevelt had a luminous guide through the chaos," observed Flynn, "The American economic system planned and directed from Washington and an endless flow of funds to spend, supplied by endless borrowing."[17]

TEN THOUSAND COMMANDMENTS

The Social Security system was considered to be a great improvement of the Roosevelt era. It was supposed to provide a cushion of cash for retired people—so they wouldn't have to eat dog food in their old age. But never was a shiny bell cast by world improvers without a big crack in it somewhere. Economist Martin Feldstein pointed out that if you could count on receiving payments from Social Security, you had less need to save. Fewer savings meant less money for the economy to invest in new industries. Less money invested meant lower productivity and wages. If the government had funded its Social Security system honestly, the missing private savings would have been replaced by public savings in the "Social Security Trust Fund." Instead, the system was unfunded. There were never any savings in the fund—just liabilities from other parts of the federal government. Social Security reduced the availability of capital and indirectly reduced capital investment. Like other taxes, Social Security made people poorer—by reducing the rate of economic growth.

There was also unemployment compensation to blame. When people could expect money even if they didn't work, many would choose to be unemployed, creating an obvious drag on the productive economy. All the hundreds of thousands of pettifogging rules, laws, and regulations acted on the economy like Velcro on a fuzz ball.

By the early twenty-first century the total cost of federal regulation of the economy was all but impossible to calculate. In an annual report called "Ten Thousand Commandments" published by both the Cato Institute and the Competitive Enterprise Institute, the author, Clyde Wayne Crews Jr., makes some astounding guesses: "The exact cost of federal regulations can never be known. Federal environmental, safety, health and economic regulations cost hundreds of billions of dollars every year—on top of official federal outlays." The report continued:

- The 2004 *Federal Register* contained 75,676 pages, a 6.2 percent increase from 2003's 71,269 pages. This is an all-time record.

- In 2004, 4,101 final rules were issued by agencies. This is a slight 1 percent decline from 2003.

- Whereas regulatory agencies issued 4,101 final rules, Congress passed and the President signed into law a comparatively low 299 bills in 2004.

- In the 2004 *Unified Agenda,* agencies reported on 4,083 regulations that were at various stages of implementation throughout the 50-plus federal departments, agencies, and commissions, a 4 percent drop from the previous year's 4,266.
- Of the 4,266 regulations now in the regulatory pipeline, 135 are "economically significant" rules that will have at least $100 million in economic impact. Those rules will impose at least $13.5 billion yearly in future off-budget costs.

Bossing people around like this costs a lot of money. How much?

- Based on a broadly constructed compilation of annual regulatory costs by economists Thomas Hopkins and Mark Crain, regulatory costs hit an estimated $877 billion in 2004, an amount equivalent to 38 percent of all FY 2004 outlays.
- Regulatory costs are more than twice the $412 billion budget deficit.
- Regulatory costs of $877 billion are equivalent to 7.6 percent of U.S. gross domestic product, estimated at $10,980 billion for 2003.
- Federal regulatory costs of $877 billion combined with outlays of $2,292 billion bring the federal government's share of the economy to some 27 percent.
- Regulatory costs also exceed all corporate pretax profits, which were $745 billion in 2002.
- Regulatory costs exceed estimated 2004 individual income taxes of $765 billion, and are far greater than corporate income taxes of $169 billion.

Between them, the Revolution of 1913 and the New Deal prepared the nation for her new role as an empire of debt.

7

MacNamara's War

A joke made its way around the Internet following the train bombings in Madrid in March 2004: "In response to the terrorism events in Madrid, the French government announced a change in its alert status . . . from 'run' to 'hide.' If the threat worsens, the French may be forced to increase their level of security, declaring a move to 'surrender' or 'collaboration' status as events develop."

One of the many conceits Americans permitted themselves in their imperial position was that they bravely faced up to the world's terrorist menace, whereas others—most notably, the French—cowered in fear. But they mistook vanity for courage. The Americans believed their view of how other people should live was so superior that they were prepared to force it on them, even at risk of their own lives.

At about the same time, the editor of the *International Herald Tribune* received a letter in which the writer referred to a big problem in the presidential campaign of Democratic hopeful John Kerry. The poor man was worried about looking "too French," which would be a sign of "weakness" in the eyes of the lumpen voters.

We stopped still in our tracks. We held our breath. Anyone who had ever been in the same room with a history book couldn't help but know that French history is drenched in blood. When it came to butchering each other, what the French didn't know about it probably wasn't worth knowing. There were the wars with the Romans and with the English, and religious wars, wars between princes and between kingdoms, wars for no apparent reason whatsoever. Weakness? Cowardice? A group of

Norman French fighters no bigger than a small-town police force invaded and captured all of England. Bonaparte took on all of Europe and almost beat them.

General Marbot records an incident in Napoleon's campaign against Russia in which a group of French soldiers was cut off from the main force, but was visible from the Emperor's command post. Realizing that they could not expect reinforcements, the brigade sent a message to Bonaparte: "We, who are about to die, salute you." They fought to the last man.

Then, there was the Battle of Camerone. Napoleon's nephew sent troops to Mexico in the 1860s. In the action surrounding the siege of Puebla, a group of 60 French foreign legionnaires was cut off and confronted by an army of 2,000 Mexicans. The Mexican commander asked for surrender. Instead, the French vowed to fight to the death. Trapped in an inn, the soldiers had nothing to eat or drink. Then, the Mexicans set the place on fire.

"In spite of the heat and smoke," explains a report on the Internet, "the legionnaires resisted, but many of them were killed or injured. By five PM on April 30, 1863, only 12 men could still fight with 2nd Lieutenant Maudet. At this time, the Mexican colonel gathered his soldiers and told them what a disgrace it would be if they were unable to defeat such a small number of men. The Mexicans were about to give the general assault through the holes opened in the walls of the courtyard . . . [they] once again asked Lieutenant Maudet to surrender. Once again, Maudet scornfully refused."

The final charge was given. Soon, only five men were left around Maudet; Corporal Maine, legionnaires Catteau, Wensel, Constantin, and Leonard. Each had only one bullet left. In a corner of the courtyard, their backs against the wall, still facing the enemy, they fixed bayonets. When the signal was given, they opened fire and fought with their bayonets. Lieutenant Maudet and two legionnaires fell, mortally wounded. Maine, along with his two remaining companions, were about to be slaughtered when a Mexican officer saved them. He shouted:

"Surrender!"

"We will, only if you promise to allow us to carry and care for our injured men and if you leave us our guns."

"Nothing can be refused to men like you," answered the officer.[1]

More recently, there was the Battle of Dien Bien Phu (May 7, 1954). Writer Graham Greene visited the French just before the shooting started. He found them well supplied—with 48,000 bottles of wine.

The French had a number of advantages similar to the advantages Americans would bring to bear in Vietnam 10 years later. They controlled the air. Using airpower, they brought in 15,000 soldiers and provisions to a remote airfield west of Hanoi. The idea was to install themselves there, disrupt General Giap's supplies, block his move into Laos, and bring him to a pitched battle in which superior French firepower would be decisive.

"A defeat can be borne from a victory," began the *Figaro's* 50-year look back on May 7, 2004. "In order to understand Dien Bien Phu, you have to remember Na-San. This battle, won by the French Army, explains the other . . . and brought the whole thing to disaster. Eighteen months separated them. General Giap, commander of the Vietminh forces, used these 18 months to learn from his defeat. The French high commander, on the other hand, became more sure of himself than ever."[2]

At Na-San, the French established a base on a plateau. Giap attacked. The French were able to hold their ground while the Vietminh staggered away. In a single night, Giap lost 3,000 men. If the French were going to destroy themselves in Southeast Asia, they had to find a better way. They found it at Dien Bien Phu. The broad outlines of the battle were as follows: French parachutists took control of the airfield followed by 15,000 troops under Colonel Christian de Castries. The French dug trenches and set up bases, to which they gave women's names. Dien Bien Phu was not on a plateau, but in a depression, surrounded by hills covered in jungle.

If the Vietminh brought up heavy artillery, the French goose would be cooked. But neither de Castries nor the French high command thought Giap could do it. The surprise began on March 13, 1954. Giap's artillery threw off its camouflage and opened fire in the afternoon. A shell hit the French every six seconds, off and on, for the next 56 days. Then, Giap sent in waves of infantry. Camp "Gabrielle" was taken by the Vietminh and then retaken by the Legionnaires, before being abandoned to the enemy. "Beatrice" was lost after its commander was killed. "Anne-Marie" went down next.

The French held. But the Vietminh noose was getting tighter. On March 26, a plane managed to get off the ground with a cargo of wounded men. It was the last one. After that, the French lost control of the airfields. The only way to get supplies was to drop them from the sky; often they fell into the hands of the enemy. The French were cut off and doomed. Still, they held out hoping a diplomatic solution could be found. It did not come.

The weather turned against the French, says the *Figaro*. They fought in a blast furnace. Then came the rains and they were up to their knees in mud. Doctors operated standing up in it. On May 6, Giap ordered a general assault. "Dominique" and "Eliane" were quickly overrun. On May 7, the order was given to blow up the munitions. Colonel Piroth committed suicide. By 5:30 PM, a cease-fire was sounded, though "Isabelle" held out until 1:00 AM the following day.

After the 56-day siege, French General de Castries radioed his superior in Hanoi, sounding Napoleonic: "I'm blowing up the installations. The ammunition dumps are already exploding. Au revoir."

"Well then," came the reply, "au revoir, mon vieux."[3]

Thousands of French were captured. From the evidence, the Vietminh were not particularly mean to them, but indifferent. The victors had little to eat themselves, and hardly any medicine. The French, many of them wounded, died quickly. They were forced to march 500 to 600 kilometers; many didn't make it. Only about 3,900 of them ever returned to France. Still, the French should cheer. It was a small price to pay to "put an end to illusions," as the *Figaro* described it a half-century later.[4]

General Giap should have been so lucky. Like many colonies, Vietnam had flourished under French administration. There were bars, brothels, and sidewalk cafés in Hanoi. There were elegant hotels and well-dressed women, dignified beach houses near the ocean, and splendid plantation homes in the hills. People could do pretty much as they pleased. France was bringing civilization to the indigenous peoples of Indochina. A fat lot of thanks they got for it. Ho Chi Minh learned French and went to Paris. Scarcely a year or two had passed, and he was printing up leaflets urging his countrymen to kick the French out.

Nguyen Sinh Cung, who would later change his name to Ho Chi Minh, was born on May 19, 1890. He was good at his studies, but he seemed to have an itch for world improvement from the get-go. The urge grew stronger, according to biographer William J. Duiker, when young Ho went to school. He had won a scholarship to the French-run National Academy in Hue. Coming in from the country, he was teased by other students, who thought he was a bumpkin. On one occasion when he lost his temper and slugged a fellow student, a teacher advised him to "channel his energy to more useful purposes such as the study of world affairs."[5]

Ooh la la! If only the teacher had suggested an anger management program instead, maybe the French would still be running the place. The Vietnamese never had it so good, before or after. Ho should have left well enough alone. But Vietnam's history in the twentieth century is a history of people who should have left well enough alone. Old Ho couldn't keep his hands to himself. Then, after Ho took over at the end of World War II, the French should have left well enough alone. And when they washed up, the Americans should have left well enough alone. Time after time, the history of world improvement yields the same lesson: *Leave well enough alone*. And time after time, the world improvers ignore it; they always know better.

But we are getting ahead of our story. When Ho came of age, the gabby talk of independence was running through Europe's colonial possessions like an epidemic of Bird Flu. Locals who had been exposed to a little education were quickly infected and often succumbed. Ho Chi Minh was one of many thousands who got the bug. He had gone to Europe, where he heard Woodrow Wilson's airy song of freedom. It was just after World War I had ended. Paris had a habit of turning a young man's head. Ho's head swiveled around just like everyone else's. Soon, he had joined not only the Annamite Patriots league, but also the communist party. Of all the world improvers of the time, the Bolsheviks had the biggest improvements in mind. Near the close of the war, against all odds, they took over the world's biggest country and were improving it mercilessly. The rest of the improvers looked on in admiration, and turned to Moscow for guidance and money. Ho was no exception.

Ho Chi Minh traveled widely, partly to see how the rest of the world worked, and partly to make contacts that would be useful in his campaign to liberate Indochina from the French. One trip took him to New York and Boston, where he claimed he worked as a cook's helper in the Parker House Hotel in Boston. He also said he once took a trip to the South, where he witnessed the lynching of blacks by the Ku Klux Klan. (Sounds improbable; the Klan did not exactly lynch someone everyday. It is also hard to imagine a young man fresh off the boat from Vietnam standing around to watch the Klan at work; we imagine Ho would have felt like a lamb attending a wolves' picnic.) Ho spent much of the Great War years in

London, working as a sous-chef under the celebrated culinary master, Auguste Escoffier at the Carlton Hotel. In this passage from Ho Chi Minh's biography, wherein he refers to himself as "Ba," we see how close the world came to having another decent pastry chef instead of another indecent world improver:

> Each of us had to take turns in the clearing up. The waiters, after attending the customer, had to clear all the plates and send them by means of an electric lift to the kitchen. Then our job was to separate china and silver for cleaning. When it came to Ba's turn he was very careful. Instead of throwing out all the bits left over, which were often a quarter of a chicken or a huge piece of steak, and so on, Ba kept them clean and sent them back to the kitchen. Noticing this, Chef Escoffier asked Ba: "Why didn't you throw these remains into the rubbish as the others do? "

> "These things shouldn't be thrown away. You could give them to the poor."

> "My dear young friend, listen to me!" Chef Escoffier seemed to be pleased and said, smiling: "Leave your revolutionary ideas aside for a moment, and I will teach you the art of cooking, which will bring you a lot of money. Do you agree?"

> And Chef Escoffier did not leave Ba at the job of washing dishes but took him to the cake section, where he got higher wages. It was indeed a great event in the kitchen for it was the first time the "kitchen king" had done that sort of thing.[6]

Alas, the smell of good works must have been more alluring then the *pain au chocolat*. The world lost a good pastry chef and gained a bad activist. Instead of bringing pleasure to a few hundred, or maybe a thousand, customers, the Annamite Wilson decided instead to launch himself into politics and begin a campaign that would bring misery and death to millions. In London, he warmed up with street demonstrations in favor of Irish independence and a variety of progressive causes. When he read Marx and other revolutionary *penseurs,* his head was turned so far his neck almost broke. Here were people with a grand theory of how the entire world could be improved. And here were people ready to help a skinny, poor young man take over a country.

Ho Chi Minh returned to Indochina, organized the Vietminh and began the long campaign for independence. The struggle was neither easy nor short. If he was to be the *capo* of Vietnam, he had a number of other *capos* to bury first. First, he had the French to deal with. Then, the Japanese. Then, the Chinese. Then the Vietnamese nationalists. Then the French again. More Vietnamese. And, finally, the Americans. Before he was finished, he would have to bury nearly as many people as Alexander or Pol Pot.

Ho Chi Minh's brief visit to the United States had left him somewhat naïve and puzzled about America. Ho had not kept up with Wilsonian improvements in the land of the free. When he addressed the crowd in Ba Dinh Square following the August Revolution of 1945, he spoke not of America as it was, but perhaps as it should have been. It was the America that existed before Wilson improved it. It was the America that minded its own business and had not yet taken the road to empire.

"All men are created equal," said Ho. "They are endowed by their creator with certain inalienable rights; among these are life, liberty and the pursuit of happiness." This statement appeared in the Declaration of Independence of the United States of America in 1776. In a broader sense, it means: All the peoples on the earth are equal from birth, all the peoples have a right to live and to be happy and free.

The Declaration of the Rights of Man and the citizen, made at the time of the French Revolution, in 1791, also states: "All men are born free and with equal rights, and must always remain free and have equal rights."

In this short speech, Ho extended a hand to two nations. One already had not just one empire, but several of them. It had been home to the Empire of the Franks, and then the Holy Roman Empire. Bonaparte made his own empire and his nephew revived it, briefly. The other nation, the United States of America, had been a modest republic only a few years before, but now had imperial responsibilities all over the globe. Ho didn't know it, but if he wanted to rule Indochina he would have to kick both their derrieres.

The August Revolution had been swift and relatively bloodless. On August 14, the Japanese surrendered. All of a sudden, there was an empty hole where an imperial power used to sit. The Japanese were laying down their guns. In Vietnam, they wanted to surrender, but didn't know to whom. French administrators were still in the prisons where the Japanese had put them. So were other allied troops. Chiang Kai Shek's Nationalist Chinese troops would soon be coming down from the north to oversee the Japanese departure. The French would soon be out of jail. Ho's Vietminh forces had to act fast. On the morning of August 25, 1945, his "defense units" swiftly seized government installations and enterprises all over Vietnam. Within hours, the country was under Vietminh control. Vo Nguyen Giap described the joyful scene in Ba Dinh Square, formerly known as Place Puginier:

> Hanoi was bedecked with red bunting. A world of flags, lanterns and flowers. Fluttering red flags adorned the roofs, the trees and the lakes.
>
> Streamers were hung across streets and roads, bearing slogans in Vietnamese, French, English Chinese and Russian: "Viet Nam for the Vietnamese." "Down with French colonialism," "Independence or death," "Support the provisional government," "Support President Ho Chi Minh," "Welcome to the Allied mission," and so on.
>
> Factories and shops, big and small, were closed down. Markets were deserted . . . the whole city, old and young, men and women, took to the streets. . . . Multicolored streams of people flowed to Ba Dinh Square from all directions.
>
> Workers in white shirts and blue trousers came in ranks, full of strength and confidence. . . . Hundreds of thousands of peasants came from the city suburbs. People's militiamen carried quarter-staffs, swords or scimitars. Some even carried old-style bronze clubs and long-handles [sic] swords taken from the armories of temples. Among the women peasants in their festive dresses, some were clad in old-fashioned robes, yellow turbans and bright-green sashes . . .
>
> Most lively were the children. . . . They marched in step with the whistle blows of their leaders, singing revolutionary songs.[7]

At that very moment, about 15,000 French people living in Hanoi, and five thousand French prisoners still being held in Japanese internment camps, along with any number of Vietnamese nationalists, were all preparing to contest Ho's authority. But naïve Ho called on his people to treat foreigners with tolerance and respect and looked to the United States for support. Surely the country that made wars of independence popular would back him up. Ho wrote several letters to the Truman administration asking for help. One requested food for starving people in the North of the country. In 1945, over a million people in Vietnam starved to death. Another letter praised the United States for its humanitarian ideals and asked for American support of the new government. None of the letters was answered.

Americans had come to see the world in a new way. They were an imperial power; they had to think like one. Winston Churchill, representing a declining empire, stood before a crowd in Fulton, Missouri, and said an "iron curtain" had come down separating one empire from another. There was now a "communist bloc" that threatened the "free world." Communism must be "contained," or it would take over the entire world. A new war had begun—the "Cold War."

Typically, the empire builders see the globe in simple-minded terms. It is the only way they can understand it; the only way they can justify their own vain and preposterous interventions. There was no iron curtain in Vietnam, just the same diaphanous fabric that was draped over the rest of the world. Ho Chi Minh explained it to an American official, Archimedes Patti, on September 30, 1945.

At the close of the conversation, Ho recounted to his visitor some of the key events in his life as a revolutionary. Conceding that many Americans viewed him as a "Moscow puppet," Ho denied that he was a Communist in the American sense. Having repaid his debt to the Soviet Union with 15 years of Party work (Ho had been an agent of the Comintern), he now considered himself a free agent. In recent months, he pointed out, the DRV (the Democratic Republic of Vietnam) had received more support from the United States than from the USSR. Why should it be indebted to Moscow?

As they parted, Ho Chi Minh asked his visitor to carry back a message that the Vietnamese people would always be grateful for the assistance they received from the United States and would long recall it as a friend and ally, and that the American struggle for independence would always serve as an example for Vietnam. A few weeks later, another departing U.S. military officer carried a letter from Ho Chi Minh to President Truman. But the likelihood of any U.S. assistance was rapidly dimming. Patti's activities had strengthened suspicions among U.S. officials in both China and the United States, and when his successor cabled Washington that Hanoi would welcome a U.S. effort to mediate the dispute, both Hanoi's offer and Ho's previous letters were ignored.

Americans were once again in no mood for modest restraint, ambiguity, or question marks. Senator Joseph McCarthy was readying his inquisition. Children were pledging allegiance to the flag and hiding under their desks in preparation for a nuclear attack. The enemy was at the gates. It was time for "100 percent Americanism."

Poor old Ho ought to have given up. In a matter of weeks, the French were on the loose and rebuilding their bases. There was an awkward period—a modus vivendi was worked out with the French. They were tolerated, but agreed not to impose themselves. On October 18, the French ship, *Dumont d'Urville,* sailed into Cam Ranh Bay with Ho aboard, back from a peace conference in Paris. But there was no peace. The French were becoming more and more insistent. They drove around in U.S.-made jeeps and carried U.S.-made arms. Ho began to wonder whose side the Americans were on.

Again, as in World War I, the United States seemed to pick its ally without much real thought. In Indochina, for the next quarter of a century, the world improvers would run into each other. Ho wanted to liberate the Annamites from the yoke of colonial rule. Other Vietnamese—Catholics, Buddhists, capitalists, traditional nationalists—wanted to liberate them from Ho. The French, meanwhile, didn't want to liberate them at all—but force them to be good subjects of France's reconstructed empire in the Far East. And America, what did America want? America didn't know exactly what she wanted. But she definitely wanted to throw her weight around.

Ho was duly elected in January 1946. As president of the country, it was not at all clear that he had to run in a district election, but he chose to do so, and won 98.4 percent of the vote. The French were about to nullify the vote and reimpose colonial rule. A moment's thought would suggest that the Americans would side with Ho, or at least stay out of it.

But if America could back the world's two largest colonial empires in World War I—and do so in the name of democracy—there was no effective limit to the hypocrisy of her foreign policy. Besides, once again, she looked up at those big, gaudy bubbles, those empty, floating words, and she was in a trance. This time they did not say anything about democracy. The mood had changed. This time the bubbles said "red menace."

The first Indochina war began on December 19, 1946, when the Vietminh blew up the municipal power station in Hanoi. It ended 89 months later, in defeat for the French at Dien Bien Phu in May 1954. Next it was the American's turn to meddle.

After the fall of Indochina, the French renounced their "civilizing mission" foreign policy. Now, it is the United States that claims to make the world a better place. But when it comes to blockheaded bellicosity and desperate courage, Americans have nothing to teach the French. In comparison to Napoleon's grand campaigns, America's early wars were pid-dling affairs. Its wars against the Mexicans and Spaniards were more sor-did than glorious. Even its Revolutionary War was merely a minor engagement compared with the Napoleonic Wars, and only won because the French intervened at a crucial moment to pull Americans' chestnuts out of the fire. Here, we quote Charles W. Eliot's history, in which he describes how the patriots had fallen "into a condition of despondency from which nothing but the steadfastness of Washington and the Conti-nental army and the aid from France saved them."[8]

In World War I, the French battered themselves against the Germans for two years—and suffered more casualties than America had in all its wars put together—before Pershing ever set foot in France. Again, in World War II, Americans waited until the combatants had been softened up before entering the war with an extraordinary advantage in fresh sol-diers and almost unlimited supplies.

Americans have no history. Probably just as well. The French, on the other hand, have too much. Practically every street in Paris reminds them of a slaughter somewhere. On the Arc de Triomphe, Les Invalides, and dozens of other piles of stone, the names of towns in Germany, Spain, Italy, Poland, Russia, or North Africa are inscribed. Each one marks the deaths of thousands of French soldiers—gone early to their graves for who-remembers-what important national purpose. Every town in France, even the most remote and forlorn little burg, has at its center a pillar of granite or marble—with the names of the men whose bodies were torn to bits by flying lead or corroded by some battlefield disease. A whole race of orphans grew up after World War I and special seats on the subway were designated for those "mutilated in war" including thousands of *sans gueules*—men who had had their jaws blown away and yet survived, too horrible to look on.

The French have had enough of war—at least for now. Let them enjoy a well-earned cowardice.

MacNAMARA'S WAR

On May 1, 1995, the world—or at least the part of it that happened to be gathered at the LBJ Library in Austin, Texas, witnessed a rare and remark-able thing. Robert S. MacNamara was in tears. He had just explained how what he had done as Secretary of Defense during the years from 1961 to 1968 was "terribly, terribly wrong."

"War Criminal says Sorry, Sobs" was how Alexander Cockburn described it in his column in the *Nation,* February 9, 2004. Heads of state, their ministers, and their generals get people killed often. Rarely do they apologize for it. If they're lucky, the war goes their way and they don't have to. If they are unlucky, they get strung up like Mussolini, or they shoot themselves like Hitler. Mr. MacNamara didn't have to do either. The North Vietnamese never posed any real danger to the United States, so there was never much danger in bombing them—unless China or Russia got spooked and fired nuclear warheads toward North America. There was no way Ho and his men were ever going to seize Washington and put U.S. leaders in the dock for war crimes. Nor did Mr. MacNamara, Mr. Kennedy, Mr. Johnson, or any other of the vast cast of earnest incompetents who had a hand in the Vietnam affair ever volunteer for the front lines. If anyone was going to die, it wasn't going to be them. And it was not their money paying for it either.

Mr. MacNamara was never really cut out to be an empire builder. He was too circumspect. The typical world improver goes to his grave believing he has done people a favor and is often bitter that they don't seem to appreciate it. In 1945 when Berlin was near starvation and being overrun by Soviet troops, the Führer complained about the ingratitude of the German people.

Wilson, too, felt abandoned and betrayed—first because Democrats wanted nothing to do with the brain-damaged president in the election of 1920 and second, because in rejecting his League of Nations, Congress seemed to repudiate him and all he stood for.

"I beseech you in the bowels of Christ to consider that you may be wrong."[9] Oliver Cromwell's warning has no effect on real empire builders; you might as well caution sailors against getting drunk on shore leave. No matter what you say, they'll find a way to get themselves in trouble.

According to his memoirs, MacNamara was always plagued by doubts. He seems a decent man, who had no business at the Department of Defense. He said so much himself. "I'm not qualified," he told President Kennedy when the job was offered to him. But he took the post, and over the next seven years, he proved it.

What is astonishing about MacNamara's mea culpa is not his admission that he made a colossal error—though that is extraordinary in itself and places him in a superior category to most public officials—but his candid record of how life-and-death decisions are made by supposedly intelligent and responsible governments.

When MacNamara took over the most lethal armed forces in the world, what preparation did he have? Did he know anything about war? Strategy? The history of combat? He had been a junior officer in World War II doing statistical analysis. Then, he had gone to work for the Ford Motor Company as an executive. Had he even read Sun Tzu or Clausewitz or Machiavelli, or Caesar or Bonaparte? Had he tried to learn a single thing from the millions of dead soldiers, the thousands of battles, the hundreds of wars? If so, he doesn't mention it.

"I entered the Pentagon with a limited grasp of military affairs and even less grasp of covert operations," he says.[10]

What about Vietnam? He knew nothing, zero, about the place. But then, as he points out, neither did Kennedy or National Security Advisor McGeorge Bundy, or military advisor General Maxwell Taylor. The only people in the Western world who knew anything about Vietnam were the French. And the American team decided to ignore the French; they were losers. By this time, the French were becoming cynical about military affairs. Every war they had been involved in since the time of Napoleon had gone bad, even those they won. By contrast, every war America had fought—at least since the War between the States—had been a reasonable success. Americans were still bright eyed, full of energy, ambition, and "can do" spirit. Robert MacNamara was one of the "brightest and best" of the lot—the kind of American who makes you proud to be one. He was a problem solver, a doer, a take-charge guy, the youngest Secretary of Defense ever, badly in need of some Gallic cynicism. He was surrounded by people who were even bigger blockheads than he was. In their minds, they were stopping the advance of communism in Southeast Asia. Could they do so? Why would they want to do so? What would happen if they didn't? Even if they could do it, how should it be done? Could it be done in some other way that didn't involve killing people or spending a lot of money?

You would think that the brightest and best would have thoroughly chatted-out such basic questions. Apparently not. There was plenty of discussion, but the major question was never really answered: What damned difference did it make? Instead, the whole team merely went from one gaff to the next, improvising as they went along. Many were the reasons given why Vietnam was important to America, but all were generalities or theories. If Vietnam fell, so would all of Southeast Asia, like a "row of dominoes," as Eisenhower had put it.[11] Even if that had been true, why did it matter to the United States of America what kind of governments ruled the region? As far as the American republic was concerned, it was of no interest whatever.

But in the new empire, any change of allegiance set off alarms. Mac-Namara, Kennedy, Johnson—all the guardians of Wilsonian foreign pol-icy—heard the tinkle and rushed to take action. They hardly noticed that none had the blurriest notion of what they were really up to. "I am con-vinced that it would be disastrous for the United States and the Free World to permit Southeast Asia to be overrun by the Communist North," said Dean Rusk. Why? Had anyone gone to talk to Uncle Ho? Did anyone know if his plans were compatible with U.S. interests? It did not seem to matter to them. Nor did it matter that the actions they were taking were contradictory to even their own stated aims.

"Some others are eager to enlarge the conflict," said President John-son in 1964. "They call upon us to supply American boys to do the job that Asian boys should do. . . . Such action would offer no solution at all to the real problem of Vietnam. . . . The South Vietnamese have the basic responsibility for the defense of their own freedom."[12]

Thus, did the president repeat what President Kennedy had said before him, and what every American felt in his heart: If the South Vietnamese wanted independence, they could fight for it just as we had. There was a practical consideration behind the sentiment. If the South Vietnamese could not organize or motivate their own people to protect themselves, it would be impossible for foreigners to do the job for them.

No one likes to admit that he is going to war for reasons of vanity or pride. That kind of ambition is, like a bad facelift, not a pretty sight. Or-dinary citizens usually turn away from it; they don't like the idea of get-ting their sons killed and their wallets stolen to support a brassy campaign of self-aggrandizement. So, real ambitions are usually hidden so well that not even the leaders themselves can see their own vanity in them. In 1965, Presidential Military Advisor, General Maxwell Taylor explained: "The situation in Vietnam is deteriorating and without new U.S. action defeat appears inevitable . . . the stakes in Vietnam are extremely high. . . . The international prestige of the United States, and a substantial part of our in-fluence are directly at risk in Vietnam. . . . Any negotiated withdrawal would mean surrender on the installment plan."[13]

Not just Johnson, MacNamara, and Taylor had their pride on the line, but the whole nation. There may never have been a good reason for fighting in MacNamara's war, but Americans began to feel that if they didn't prevail they'd never be able to hold their heads high again.

Still, as late as 1964, Johnson chose not to admit that he would send half a million American boys to do the fighting that Asian boys wouldn't or couldn't do. America was an empire, but still a reluctant one. Maybe he didn't know himself. Besides, it was probably not a good time to mention it. MacNamara, in testimony before defense subcommittees of Congress, failed to disclose the level of troop commitments the administration knew would be required. MacNamara testified to the Defense Subcommittee of the Senate Appropriations Committee on August 4, 1965, that 175,000 troops would have to be deployed by November, to be followed by another 100,000 the following year. He did *not* bother to say that he already estimated the need for an additional 340,000 men to be added to the tour through the draft and extended tours.

Two years later, MacNamara testified before the Senate Armed Services Committee. Asked whether he could provide a monthly breakdown of the costs of Vietnam, he said, "It is almost impossible to do it on a yearly basis, and it is really impossible to do it on a monthly basis. I can tell you how much we are spending in total for defense per month of course, but splitting that into Vietnam and non-Vietnam is honestly almost impossible."[14]

Wilson's platform slogan when he ran for a second term was "He Kept Us out of War." Franklin Roosevelt ran for office saying he would not send troops to fight in Europe's war. And in the election campaign of 1964, Lyndon Johnson maintained that it was still a Vietnamese war, not an American one. The spirit of empire got the better of all of them. Whether you wanted to get into the Vietnam War, or stay out of it, you could find all the reasons and arguments you could want. But the arguments scarcely mattered; temperatures were already rising; war fever was bubbling up all over.

"Aggression and upheaval, in any part of the world," said Lyndon Johnson on the 1964 campaign trail, sounding Wilsonian, "carry the seeds of destruction to our own freedom and perhaps to civilization itself. . . . Friendly cynics and fierce enemies alike often underestimate or ignore the strong thread of moral purpose which runs through the fabric of American history."[15]

By the early 1960s, there was hardly a half-wit in all North America who didn't think that the country was in danger. This time it wasn't the Huns who threatened Western civilization; it was communists. They'd heard it on television. Even the *New York Times* said so.

In a modern democracy, it is relatively easy to stir the masses to absurdity. People are all tuned into the national television stations and read the papers. Just as Americans in 1917 came to believe that their way of life had been put in jeopardy by the Germans, now they came to believe that the communists were a grave and growing threat. If they weren't stopped in Vietnam, said the papers, soon they'd be landing in California. It was preposterous. But that didn't make it unpopular.

In the mid- and late-1960s, the war in Vietnam seemed like the biggest, most urgent foreign policy challenge the United States faced. The French were gone; now Vietnam could be added to America's slushy empire. There was little question in Americans' minds that they could succeed where the frogs had failed. Curiously, but not unexpectedly, public support for the war grew as the United States got itself in deeper. The big question: "Why are we involved in this war?" disappeared, pushed out by a more urgent and practical question: "How are we going to win it?" In the middle of all this, though, the economic aspects (the cost of the war itself) as well as the required level of "boots on the ground" were purposely understated. It was apparent, even within the Johnson administration, that there would be little support for the war if the real costs were known. Head of the Council of Economic Advisors, Walter Heller (who resigned in 1966 and was succeeded by Gardner Ackley) said in 1965:

> We had no concrete idea how much Vietnam was going to cost. First, I think fundamentally it was being underestimated to begin with. And, second, some of the estimates were somehow or another not getting across the Potomac from the Pentagon to the Executive Office Building, at least not to the Council's part of the Executive Office Building. Anyway, the Council was operating partially in the dark.[16]

After supporting the French, the United States backed the regime of the Diem brothers, a pair of staunchly Catholic conservatives with a talent for corruption and political clumsiness, one of whom was married to a sorceress known as Madame Nhu. As a bulwark against the commies, the Diem regime proved as ineffective as it was quirky. The United States gave the go-ahead to a group of generals to replace the brothers. This decision, like so many others, was not taken after careful consideration of the alternatives by the top policymakers. MacNamara says it was inspired by lower-echelon functionaries who set it in motion while Kennedy, MacNamara, and the leading decision makers were on vacation. Then, it took on a momentum of its own. On November 2, 1963, a group of generals led by General Minh rounded up Ngo Dinh Diem and Madame Nhu. Their hands were bound behind their backs and they were shoved into an armored personnel carrier. When the vehicle arrived at General Headquarters, Diem and Nhu had been shot; Nhu had also been knifed several times. The South Vietnamese said it was a suicide. The two were, no doubt, capable of great mischief. But people who have their hands tied behind their backs do not often shoot and knife themselves. The official version of events serves as a eulogy for the entire Vietnam adventure—improbable at the very least, criminal at worst.

Meanwhile, the war ratcheted up another big notch after an incident in the Tonkin Gulf, involving two attacks on U.S. ships. One of the attacks was never confirmed; many think it never happened. The other may have been a mistake. The North Vietnamese now say they never authorized it. Americans said they believed Hanoi was intentionally widening the war. The United States felt it had to retaliate, not for any particular reason, but merely because it felt it had to do something and didn't know what else to do. Before long, the United States had 200,000 of its own troops in Vietnam and was bombing Hanoi "back to the Stone Age."[17]

Finally, after American troop levels in Vietnam reached half a million, and nearly half a trillion dollars (adjusted to year 2000 dollars) had been spent, and noncombatants were being killed or seriously injured at the rate of 1,000 a week (MacNamara's estimate), Americans came to their senses. The idealists left the State Department and the Defense Department. Realists, led by Henry Kissinger, came in and figured out how to abandon South Vietnamese allies and sneak out of the war in the least disgraceful way they could.

Vietnam then did fall to the communists and America's erstwhile allies were reeducated. But was the world better or worse? No one knew or cared. After Americans left the place, except for a lengthy discussion of MIA and POWs, Vietnam disappeared from the news. What people had worried about so much had happened. Ho Chi Minh had won. But it seemed to make no difference to anybody. Did the rest of Southeast Asia fall "like dominoes?" Not at all. Cambodia lost its head in a mad frenzy of murder. What that had to do with Vietnam is not entirely clear; the world breathed a sigh of relief when Vietnamese communists invaded the place to restore order.

FACING THE ENEMY

A quarter century later, MacNamara and a group of associates confronted a team led by his old adversary, Vo Nguyen Giap, in a series of meetings held in Hanoi, between 1995 and 1998. The exchange was advertised as an attempt to learn something. It is recorded in a book by MacNamara, *Argument without End: In Search of Answers to the Vietnam Tragedy.* Appropriately, there is a photo of that arch world improver, Woodrow Wilson, at the beginning of the book. We do not know what inspiration Robert MacNamara drew from Wilson, but we guess it was the worst sort. Wilson had sent 112,000 Americans to their deaths in World War I in an effort to win a war to end all wars. The result was the opposite of Wilson's stated intention. But instead of reaching the obvious conclusion—that Wilson was a dimwit—MacNamara rushed to do something just as foolish.

At the height of the war in April 1969, American troops in Vietnam numbered 543,000, at a cost of $61 billion per year—far, far more than the administration's estimates of $5 billion per year maximum provided back in 1965 (a figure that seemed to emerge time and again amid the vague generalizations MacNamara and others offered).

MacNamara's book makes amusing reading. It describes a futile effort on the part of the American team to get their Vietnamese counterparts to take a measure of the blame for what they regarded as a "tragedy." The Vietnamese saw no tragedy and accepted no blame. Instead, the way they see it, *their country was attacked by foreigners*—first the French, then the Japanese, then the French again, with support from America, and then by the Americans. They had undertaken a long, costly war to liberate the country—against a vastly superior military force. It was no tragedy; it was a crime.

On the American side, MacNamara and his fellow imperialists were determined to keep morality out of the discussion. They regarded the whole affair as a series of unfortunate errors, miscalculations, misunderstandings, and mistakes. They faced their former enemies not as sinners or criminals, but as incompetents. They seemed practically desperate for the Vietnamese to play along, to admit that they, too, made mistakes that contributed to the misunderstanding that led to the tragedy. But the old Annamites wouldn't cooperate.

Asked, for example, if the North Vietnamese hadn't misread the signal implied in President Johnson's bombing campaign that began March 5, 1965 (called "Rolling Thunder"), the Vietnamese delegates protested. They didn't know it was a signal. They thought the Americans were trying to kill them.

In almost every instance, MacNamara and the rest of the American team tried to keep the discussion on strategic issues, diplomatic initiatives, inputs, outputs, throughputs, and other mumbo jumbo. Even three decades after the fact, despite the public weeping, MacNamara seems almost not to notice that he sent men to kill, who were not always too particular about whom they killed. When a man sticks a knife in his neighbor, it is not easy to disguise what is really happening. The event is right in front of him. But the fog of war, as Clausewitz called it, multiplies by the square of the distance from it. In the Oval Office or the war rooms of the Pentagon, the transactions that took place in Vietnam became "costs" or "losses" or "collateral damage." It was as if they were running an insurance company. The losses were regrettable perhaps, but also excusable and generally, forgettable.

The Vietnam War, 1961 to 1975, was far bloodier than we are accustomed to think. America lost 58,000 troops. The Vietnamese lost an estimated 3.8 million, according to MacNamara. Yet, reading the whiz kid's account of his involvement, it is as if he had never met a single one of them. Every human being in the war was treated as war matériel. They were resources, like bombs and cans of Coke. Treated as assets on the military balance sheet, they are expended as though they were inflated currency.

Robert MacNamara saw the war as a bounded, engineering problem. He expected it to be rational, a system that could be modeled and that would yield to practical planning and logical extrapolation. He expected the war could be won simply by increasing the cost to the Vietcong and

North Vietnamese. At some point, the cost would become unacceptably high.

In this sense, he was not unlike the geniuses who ran Long-Term Capital Management into the ground in the late 1990s. They thought the financial world could be modeled, too—just as if it were science. They reasoned that the odds of an investment going up or down could be calculated just as you could figure the odds of hitting an iceberg in the North Atlantic. Then you could make your bets calmly, scientifically; after all, it was just advanced mathematics.

The economists at Long-Term Capital Management included two winners of the Nobel Prize, but their theories were wrong. Neither investing nor war making is a hard science; they are "human" sciences perhaps, closer to art than science. The difference is obvious. You can heat water to 212 degrees Fahrenheit and it will boil—every time (assuming constant pressure). But put a man under heat or pressure, and the fellow could react in any number of different, unpredictable, irrational, and wholly bizarre ways.

Between 1965 and 1975, the United States stepped up its killing campaign. The Vietnamese suffered hundreds of thousands of casualties as the pressure increased. America was turning up the heat, ready for it to boil over and force the North Vietnamese to the negotiating table. The table was set. But the Americans were astonished when no one showed up. It was as if the North Vietnamese didn't care how hot it got. It was as if they ignored all the resources the United States was bringing to bear and the losses that they were inflicting. It was as if they couldn't count!

It made no sense to MacNamara. So, he asked the question of the Vietnamese delegation sitting opposite him in Hanoi, 30 years later. How come all the misery we inflicted on the Vietnamese did not bring them to ask for a settlement? Tran Quang Co replied:

> I would like to answer Mr. MacNamara's question. . . . I must say that this question of Mr. MacNamara's has allowed us to better understand the issue. During the coffee break, an American colleague asked me if I had learned anything about the U.S. during the discussions of the past few days. And I responded that I have learned quite a lot. However, thanks to this particular question, I believe we have learned still more about the U.S. We understand better now that the U.S. understands very little about Vietnam. Even now—in this conference—the U.S. understand very little about Vietnam.

When the U.S. bombed the North and brought its troops into the South, well, of course, to us there were very negative moves. However, with regard to Vietnam, U.S. aggression did have some positive use. Never before did the people of Vietnam, from top to bottom, unite as they did during the years that the U.S. was bombing us. Never before had Chairman Ho Chi Minh's appeal—that there is nothing more precious than freedom and independence—go straight to the hearts and minds of the Vietnamese people as at the end of 1966.[18]

The Vietnam War was not merely a tragedy; or even a crime. It was a farce. American troops had been sent to kill people they didn't know, in a country they had never been, for reasons none of them could understand, by men as benighted as they were. Ho Chi Minh had expected the United States to come to his aid, not to seek his destruction. Yet, MacNamara and President Johnson sent troops to kill people on the basis of an idea so flimsy that, when the war was over, it disappeared without a trace. Gradually, the war was escalated on the basis of a mistake and run as a series of errors, culminating in a disgraceful rout. At every step of the way, American military and civilian officials misunderstood and underestimated their opponents. General William Westmoreland briefed Congress in July 1967: "The situation is not a stalemate. We are winning slowly but steadily, and the pace can accelerate if we reinforce our successes." All we need is more resources!

He could have saved himself the trouble of making it up and taken the communiqué, word for word, sent by French General Raoul Salan, who in October, 20 years before, reported that the Vietminh were on the run. All that was left were isolated bands susceptible to police operations.

"Not once during the war," wrote General Bruce Palmer in his book, *Twenty-five Year War,* "did the Joint Chiefs of Staff advise the commander-in-chief or the secretary of defense that the strategy being pursued most probably would fail and that the U.S. would be unable to achieve its objectives."[19]

Achieve its objectives? No one really knew what America's objectives were. Or if they were attainable. Or, if they really made any difference to anybody in America. The United States had become an empire with scarcely anyone noticing. Its goals were no longer those of its people but of the empire itself. An empire must routinely and habitually contest control of periphery areas. The imperial people had merely come to believe what they had to believe to go along with the program.

The madness began as an oversimplification back in the Eisenhower administration. In 1954, President Eisenhower provided his now famous "domino" speech, by way of explaining that if South Vietnam were lost to communism all of Indochina would fall. In November 1995, General Vo Nguyen Giap put it to Robert MacNamara generously:

> Dominoes, dominoes, dominoes—this theory was an illusion. Whatever happened in Vietnam had nothing to do with what happened in Laos, nothing to do with Indonesia. . . . I am amazed that even the brightest people—people like yourself—could have believed it.[20]

Believed it? What was there to believe? That a state—an abstract as well as physical thing, of 35 million people (in 1965) of various cultures, languages, religions, ethnic and racial groups, political preferences, modernization, and sexual preferences, living in a land of 127,000 square miles (about the size of New Mexico), including mountains, swamps, beaches, plains, jungle, hamlets, and cities could be understood as a small, three-dimensional object painted in two colors! The idea was not stupid. It was just absurd. Einstein had said that things should be made as simple as possible, but no simpler. America's empire builders of the 1960s had gone too far. It was as if they had simplified the Old Testament as: "Jews kick butts in the Holy Land." They had lost the nuances and details that made it interesting.

Whether Laos or Cambodia would be affected by events in Vietnam, no one could say. But what they could say with complete assurance was that Vietnam was not a domino. If proximity caused nations to change their political systems why hadn't West Germany become like East Germany? Why did Switzerland keep its federal system when it was surrounded by centralized governments? And who ever heard of dominoes that fell only in one direction? If the presence of a communist South Vietnam might cause Thailand to topple toward communism, mightn't the presence of Thailand on its border cause South Vietnam to topple toward constitutional monarchy?

It was not merely mad to kill people on the basis of the domino theory, it was Wilsonian. But once the madness took hold, there was nothing stopping it. Soon, almost every member of the chattering classes had decided that what was literally and obviously untrue was worth (someone else) dying for.

Thirty years after the fact, MacNamara seemed embarrassed to recollect why he and his colleagues once thought the matter was so vitally important. They figured the communists were taking over everywhere. If Vietnam also fell to communists, it would be a disaster. But why? No one seemed to recall.

Yes, there were the dominoes. If Vietnam went communist, so might all of Southeast Asia. We now know that it was nonsense. But what if it had been true? If the people of Southeast Asia wanted to "go communist," who were we to tell them not to? It was only because America presumed to be an empire that the question even came up. Empires are involved in constant warfare—the struggle to control vassal states on the periphery. Typically, they do so to maintain order throughout the empire, as well as to obtain new sources of tribute. But our answer presumes a logic that isn't there. Empires fight for dominoes—not for any particular, logical reason, but merely because they are empires.

MacNamara points out that leading intellectuals, the media, politicians, policymakers, and even street bums viewed the war as a struggle between communism and the Free World.

Could not Vietnam have been independent, but neutral in the Cold War? Why did it matter anyway? Vietnam was still a primitive, mostly agricultural nation. Whichever side gained her allegiance, what did they gain? Nobody ever seemed to ask—either themselves or the other side.

"I am aghast at the shallowness of our thinking on the issue of a neutral solution," writes MacNamara. "Why didn't we ask Hanoi for a full explanation of the process they foresaw? If we had asked, and if they had convinced us, for example, that they foresaw reunification taking years, even decades, my god, we would have or should have jumped at it."[21]

In the discussions and confessions 30 years after the end of the war, the Vietnamese said they had been open to suggestion. In retrospect, it looks as though the whole conflict—or at least the bloodiest part—could have been avoided, simply by sitting down and exploring a few issues. But the lunkheads running U.S. foreign policy at the time did not even bother to ask. It was arrogance, no doubt, on the part of MacNamara and others, that prevented anyone in the administration from seriously considering *conversation* as an alternative to brute force.

Bad ideas, foolish theories, misconceived campaigns, misunderstood signals—the war in Vietnam began in almost total ignorance and went downhill. Nobody knew anything worth knowing. Nobody understood anything worth understanding. And nobody did anything worth doing.

But we return to the critical question: Americans were dead set against letting Vietnam "go communist." Why? If a group of people in Columbus, Ohio, decided to pool their property and to live collectively, there would be no terrible outcry. (Though eventually, the Feds would probably get them on a weapons or tax charge.) The only plausible reason for being against communism is that the communists were almost invariably world-improvers themselves. They were not content to collectivize their own property, but insisted on collectivizing other people's property, too. Then, when they had made a mess of their own country, they turned their sights on the countries next door.

The feature that made communism barbaric was not that people shared the same toothbrush or denied the profit motive. Instead, it was the common mark of all barbarism—the readiness to use brute force to get what you want. What marks a civilized society, on the other hand, is a reluctance to use force, preferring persuasion and cooperation over force and fraud.

There are only two ways to get what you want in life. You can get it honestly, by trade, work, or some other bargain—an economic means of some sort. Or, you can get it dishonestly, by stealing it or taking it away from someone—that is, by political means. There is no other way, save a miracle. This distinction works for "things" such as automobiles and whiskey. It also works for other "wants"—such as sex, ambition, and vanity. We can build our reputations and our own *amour propre* by economic means; say, by working hard we can earn money and feel superior to others. Or we can pick a fight with others to prove we can beat them. Into which category does the effort to "bomb North Vietnam back to the Stone Age" fit? American involvement in Vietnam may have been well-intentioned, but it was missing the point.

Martin Luther King confronted the contradiction in a famous speech. "My opposition to the war," he said:

> . . . grows out of my experience in the ghettoes of the North over the last three years—especially the last three summers. As I have walked among the desperate, rejected and angry young men I have told them that Molotov cocktails and rifles would not solve their problems. I have tried to offer them my deepest compassion while maintaining my con-

viction that social change comes most meaningfully through nonviolent action. But they asked—and rightly so—what about Vietnam? They asked if our own nation wasn't using massive doses of violence to solve its problems, to bring about the changes it wanted. Their questions hit home, and I knew that I could never again raise my voice against the violence of the oppressed in the ghettos without having first spoken clearly to the greatest purveyor of violence in the world today—my own government. For the sake of those boys, for the sake of this government, for the sake of hundreds of thousands trembling under our violence, I cannot be silent.[22]

If Western democracies have a virtue, it is that they are gradual and consensual—that is to say, that they are civilized. If suddenly the majority of Americans were to decide that every citizen with red hair should be guillotined, it would be an uncivilized thing to do—even if they had voted on it fair and square. It is the means that are the end. The fact that people are willing to get along with one another without resort to violence is what makes a civilized society, not the fact that the particular day-to-day whims of the masses are enacted into law by a group of legislative hacks. Defending Western civilization by bombing North Vietnam was a bit like what Clovis, King of the Francs, proposed to do after he had become a Christian and learned of Christ's crucifixion. Legend has it that Clovis remarked: "If only I had been there with my armies, I would have had revenge against those Jews."

In his private life, Lyndon Johnson understood what the Vietnam War really meant for America:

> I don't think it's worth fighting for and I don't think we can get out. It's just the biggest damned mess I ever saw. . . . And we just got to think about—I was looking at this sergeant of mine this morning. Got six little kids . . . and he bringing me my things and bringing me my night reading . . . and I just thought about ordering his kids in there and what in the hell am I ordering him out there for? What the hell is Vietnam worth to me? What is Laos worth to me? What is it worth to this country? No, we've got a treaty, but, hell, everybody's got a treaty out there and they're not doing anything about it.[23]

But America went in anyway. And then the bodies came back in plastic bags.

And even after 30 years, it seems not to have occurred to MacNamara that he did anything wrong. Right and wrong seemed to have no place in his analytical brain. Instead, he wondered how he could have done his job better, how he could have fought the war more efficiently, or why he "missed opportunities" to settle it at lower cost. He saw no moral lessons— only practical ones. He looked for no wisdom from the dead, only hints from the living about how to win. If he had only had more information, says MacNamara, his world improvements would have turned out better.

Tran Quang Co put him on the spot:

> Mr. MacNamara admits his mistakes, which we admire, but he unfortunately attributes most mistakes to misjudgments and miscalculations. But we must also ask: What about values and intentions? As I understand it, the right to self-determination—the independence of a nation—belongs to the general values of the world community. What about U.S. support of the French colonialists after World War II, in defiance of its own democratic traditions? What about the direct U.S. military intervention in Vietnam—I mean sending U.S. soldiers to find and kill Southern Vietnamese? And what about the U.S. policy seeking to divide Vietnam for good and to "bomb North Vietnam back to the Stone Age?" We must ask: are these policies consistent with the moral values?[24]

Principles? Morals? There is no room for constitutional restraints, authentic values, or real virtues when you are building an empire. The heart overpowers the brain. Public chatter overpowers private thoughts. Public slogans drown out private acts of decency and courage. Empty words and big theories replace actual thinking. The public itself is charmed and bamboozled, then robbed, killed, or both.

Americans learned nothing from the French experience. De Gaulle warned Kennedy that Vietnam would be a graveyard for American soldiers. It was a "rotten country," he said, unsuitable for Western ways of war. But in the inflationary boom of the first "Guns and Butter" administration, that of Lyndon B. Johnson, Americans thought they could do what the French couldn't. They spent far more money than the French and lost far more men, but Giap beat them, just as he had the French.

While France and America enjoyed their defeats, Vietnam suffered its own dreary independence like a war wound. The whole country oozed a pathetic poverty for the next quarter century, scabbed over with a squalid ideology.

As of 2005, General Giap was still alive. The old man, 91 when he was interviewed by the *Figaro* in 2004, was asked what he thought of America's situation in Iraq: "When you try to impose your will on a foreign nation you will be defeated. Every nation that struggles for independence will win." Woe to empires.

"What we've done," continued the old man, perhaps drifting into senile dementia, forgetting that his comrades set up a police state following his military victory, "was to fight for the right of each man to live and develop as he chooses . . . and the right of each people to enjoy national sovereignty."

8

Nixon's the One

O n August 15, 1971, the administration of Richard Milhous Nixon did something extraordinary. It slammed the "gold window" shut. Henceforth, foreign governments would not be able to redeem their surplus U.S. dollars for gold.

Mention the late president's name, and the average person recalls the crime with which he is so often associated: B&E (breaking and entering) at the Watergate. But while the public's attention was distracted by Nixon's fumbling sidekicks, another team of Nixon goons was pulling off the biggest heist of all time.

A lumpen investor, a university economist, or a Federal Reserve governor might have read the headlines of the past 30 years without noticing how they tucked together. He might have seen the boom in gold of the 1970s, the bubble in Japan in the 1980s, or the subsequent bubbles throughout the rest of Asia as events as independent of each other as a stolen hubcap in New Orleans and a stolen kiss in Boston.

He might also have looked on the boom and bubble in the United States as unrelated and mistaken the run-up in stock prices as a consequence of the New Era wonder age, the new productivity of information age technology, or the newfound wisdom of the guiding hands at the Federal Reserve. He may even have referred to the productivity miracle as the source of such a wonderful thing. Never, on the other hand, would he have imagined that all the great economic and market events of the past three decades found their inspiration in the same place and time: at the hands of Nixon's henchmen in the early 1970s.

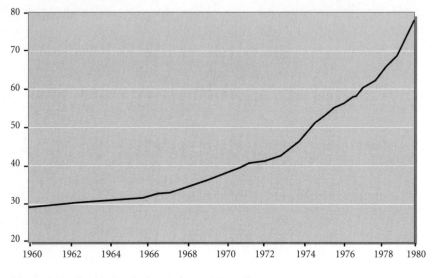

Figure 8.1   **Consumer Price Index, 1960–1980**

Richard Nixon's decision to slam the "gold window" shut has had one demonstrable effect: It set in motion the world-wide credit bubble of the pax dollarium age. As a result, the price Americans have to pay for "goods and services" has risen dramatically—and without a pause—ever since.

Source: Bureau of Labor Statistics.

What was their crime? Breach of contract? Theft? Fraud? Counterfeiting? It was all those things. They breached the solemn promise of five generations of U.S. Treasury officials and set in motion the worldwide credit bubble of the pax dollarium age (see Figure 8.1).

In 1971, the decision to abandon the gold standard was not exactly an improvisation. The decision was part of a series of moves made by the Nixon administration to hold down wages and prices and to check inflation. Consumer prices rose at 4.9 percent in 1970 and inflation looked as though it was going to get worse. Nixon came to believe that he could control the economy, even though this shift in policy contradicted his own political and economy philosophy as stated in the past.

Arthur Burns, chairman of the Federal Reserve during Nixon's administration, had served as an advisor during Nixon's failed 1960 presidential campaign. At that time, Burns warned Nixon that tight money policies would worsen the economy, hurting Nixon and ultimately costing him the election. Burns proved to be right:

Now, a decade later, in May 1970, Burns stood up and declared that he had changed his mind about economic policy. The economy was no longer operating as it used to, owing to the now much more powerful position of corporations and labor unions, which together were driving up both wages and prices. The traditional fiscal and monetary policies were now seen as inadequate. His solution: a wage-price review board, composed of distinguished citizens, who would pass judgment on major wage and price increases. Their power, in Burns's new lexicon, would be limited to persuasion, friendly or otherwise.[1]

Nixon agreed with most of it, except the part about limiting controls to friendly persuasion.

Not since the reign of Diocletian had such a powerful empire attempted such an idiotic thing. As part of the big changes in 1971, Nixon created the Cost of Living Council, organized specifically to administer a 90-day freeze on wage and price hikes. Although this temporary measure was removed, inflation returned. In June 1973, controls were reimposed, shortly before Nixon's resignation. Finally, admitting that these policies did not work as hoped, the wage and price control plan was given up in April 1974 during the Ford administration.

PAYING THE PRICE

Financially, the Vietnam War was a mess. The decision makers had no idea how much the war would cost, or how the bills would be paid. As early as 1965, the MacNamara team had an estimate from Army Chief of Staff General Harold K. Johnson that winning the war would require as many as 500,000 troops and five years of fighting. The policymakers were aghast. They were not prepared to commit to anything like that level of involvement—in terms of the numbers of men as well as the costs involved. The chairman of President Johnson's Council of Economic Advisors (CEA) told the president in 1965, "The current thinking in DOD [Department of Defense], as relayed to me by Bob MacNamara on a super-confidential basis, points to a gradual and moderate build-up of expenditures and manpower."[2]

The debate over the real costs of the war continued throughout the entire period from 1964 through 1968. It wasn't until late 1967, however, that LBJ asked Congress for a 10 percent tax surcharge. That surcharge was approved by mid-1968, but only on condition that Johnson also cut $6 billion from domestic programs—a requirement that hurt him dearly. His beloved Great Society programs, half of the "guns-and-butter" policy defining his presidency, ultimately were curtailed by the escalating costs of the war in Vietnam. But neither the costs of the war nor those of the Great Society were cut enough.

The total spent by the United States on the Vietnam War amounted to more than $500 billion in today's money. That is a lot of money at any time. At first, Johnson assured the nation that the war would not jeopardize his other promises. He had pledged to give away billions of other people's money; the offer was still good, he said. He told Congress in 1966, "I believe that we can continue the Great Society while we fight in Vietnam."[3] As the costs mounted up, government budget officials and his own economic advisors began to worry. The math wasn't working. The president's guns-and-butter policy, a 1960s version of the Romans' bread and circuses was too expensive. They realized they needed more revenue. Rising deficits and rising inflation levels in the United States worried foreign dollar holders, who began calling away America's gold. Only higher tax revenues could cure the problem (see Figure 8.2).

President Johnson stood his ground. He feared that "all hell will break loose," if he were to request a tax increase. Congress would rather cut the butter than raise taxes or give up the guns. The result would be the end of the Great Society.

Lyndon Johnson had no money of his own to fund the Great Society programs he set in place. He could only give money to one voter by taking it away from another one. Peter had to be robbed if Paul was to be paid.

But theft is not murder, and not only will the majority of citizens in a democracy put up with a little thievery, they will welcome it—especially if it is done on their behalf. The most popular American presidents were those who stole most bountifully. The logic of democratic larceny is that there are always more voters receiving tax money than getting it taken from them. That is the real reason Democrats favor doing something "to help the poor"—there are more of them; you can buy their votes cheaply. Wave a $10 bill in front of a rich man and you will get little attention—in a trailer park, you will draw a crowd. Still, in a fluid society like the United States, there are also a lot of people who hope to get rich

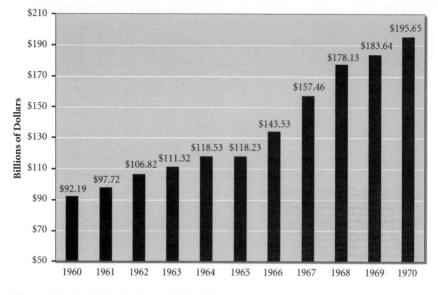

Figure 8.2 **Federal Outlays, 1960–1970**
The total amount spent by the United States on the Vietnam War exceeded $500 billion
in today's money. Lyndon Johnson's guns-and-butter policy, a 1960s' version of the
Romans' bread and circuses, was too expensive. Rising deficits and inflation in the
United States worried foreign dollar holders, who began calling away America's gold.
Source: "Historical Tables" Budget of the U.S. Government.

some day and want to look forward to holding onto their money if it
ever comes their way. So, there is always a certain resistance to higher
taxes, and in 1966 and 1967, Lyndon Johnson was loath to run into it.

But there was resistance to bankrupting the country, too. There were
still a few geezers in Congress who believed in balanced budgets. So, after
the 1966 elections, Johnson's 10 percent tax surcharge was presented.
This, he said, would give the United States "staying power," in its fight
with communism. Robert MacNamara now claims that he knew the war
was hopeless as early as 1964, so staying power was exactly what the
United States didn't need. What it needed was the courage to quit. But it
is this courage that is most lacking in times of war. Men would rather die
than admit that they are doing an asinine and pointless thing.

Johnson's tax hike was opposed in the House by Minority Leader Gerald Ford and Ways and Means Committee Chairman Wilbur Mills. The southern Democrats and northern Republicans wanted spending cuts, not tax hikes. Johnson said:

> They will live to rue the day when they made that decision, because it is a dangerous decision . . . an unwise decision. . . . I know it doesn't add to your polls and your popularity to say we have to have additional taxes to fight this war abroad and fight the problems in our cities at home. But we can do it with the gross national product we have. We should do it. And I think when the American people and the Congress get the full story they will do it.[4]

By 1968, the empire was going broke. Gold reserves were being depleted. Congress had to act, passing the 10 percent tax surcharge along with a budget cut of $18 billion (about a 10 percent cut in appropriations). Johnson had to melt some butter to get more guns.

At the time, Washington still operated on old-fashioned Keynesian economics and a gold standard. Economists believed government could spend more heavily in times of war or times of economic hardship (to "prime the pump"), but it was still widely agreed that what was borrowed must be paid back. Deficits still mattered, partly because they threatened the nation's currency (and its gold backing), and partly because policymakers still thought they would have to make up overspending now by underspending in the future.

Then, as now, taxpayers could be squeezed, but only so hard and only if politically realistic. Otherwise, they would soon start to howl. Redistribution of wealth only works, politically, if someone else's money is being passed around. Taxpayers don't see any advantage in giving up their own money.

Liberal politicians in the 1960s advertised themselves much as George W. Bush does today. They said they were extending freedom at home as well as abroad. "How can anyone say that a nation with an income of more than $800 billion can't afford a $30 billion war?" said Paul Douglas of Illinois.[5]

"Military forces able to defend the cause of freedom in Vietnam and to counter other threats to national security require substantial resources. Yet we cannot permit the defense of freedom abroad to sidetrack the struggle for individual growth and dignity at home," added Johnson.

Vice President Hubert Humphrey joined in, saying that America "can afford to extend freedom at home at the same time that it defends it abroad."[6]

"The United States is not faced—nor could it be faced—with a guns and butter choice. . . . This country has ample resources to prosecute the shooting war and still combat the shortcomings of our own society," continued AFL-CIO president George Meany.[7]

Nor did the people disagree. Americans favored more guns and more butter over a reduction in spending on either front, by a margin of 48 percent to 39 percent, according to a Harris poll.

Until the Vietnam era, after every previous war was over, federal spending dropped. When the Vietnam War ended, however, federal spending continued to go up. The federal budget had been $184 billion in 1969 at the height of the military spending. In 1972, it rose to $231 billion. In 1969, the federal government actually ran a surplus of $3 billion. By 1972, with the war winding down, we expected to see the surpluses continue; but instead the surplus turned into a deficit of $23 billion.

The empire grew, and kept growing. Before launching the attack on the USSR, June 22, 1941, Hitler remarked that the Soviet Union was like a rickety old house. All we have to do, he said, was "kick in the door and the whole thing will fall down." He was 48 years premature. The Soviet Union fell apart in 1989 by itself; America didn't even have to kick in the door. But even after the Cold War was over, the federal budget continued to rise, from $1.14 trillion in 1989 to $1.38 trillion in 1992.

The Great Society was merely the domestic wing of America's new system of imperial finance. Johnson offered more bread and more circuses than any president before him. The five-year cost of administering the Great Society programs was estimated at $305.7 billion (in 2005 inflation-adjusted dollars). This does not include the $250 billion in college loans and grants to 29 million students since 1965 (see Figure 8.3).

The scope of the Great Society was massive, comparable to Franklin Roosevelt's New Deal programs but on a more expensive scale. Even counting only Medicaid and Medicare, the LBJ idea has added trillions to U.S. future obligations:

> During [the Johnson] administration, Congress enacted two major civil-rights acts (1964 and 1965), the Economic Opportunity Act

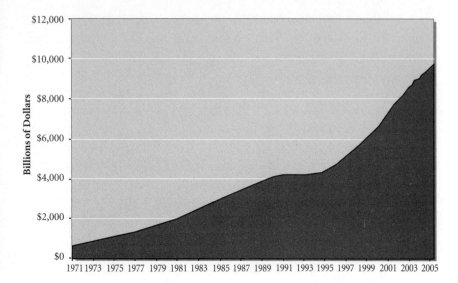

Figure 8.3   **M3 Money Stock**

The great cost of administering the empire requires an ever-expanding supply of the imperial currency. Since U.S. currency has become untethered to gold, the quantity of paper dollars floating around the globe has ballooned significantly, rendering each dollar a little less valuable than the last.

Source: Federal Reserve.

(1964), and two education acts (1965). In addition, legislation was passed that created the Job Corps, Operation Head Start, Volunteers in Service to America (VISTA), Medicaid, and Medicare. Although the Great Society program made significant contributions to the protection of civil rights and the expansion of social programs, critics increasingly complained that the antipoverty programs were ineffective and wasteful.[8]

This expansion had the consequence of creating massive bureaucracies within the federal system. Considering the Medicaid and Medicare costs alone, we have seen exponential growth in current and future obligations, impractical cost-benefit outcomes, widespread waste, and fraud within the medical establishment. The programs were expanded partly to counter growing unrest at home. We should recall that by the end of Johnson's presidency, the country was disturbed. Race riots in the inner cities, massive antiwar protests, and clashes between students and police were commonplace from 1965 onward, and continued into Nixon's reign.

People wanted more bread and circuses. Personal consumption expenditures had expanded significantly since the end of World War II. By 1970, annual expenditures were 4.5 times higher than in 1946. After 1971, when the pax dollarum system began, expenditures grew exponentially. By the year 2000, annual levels were at $6.68 *trillion*—46 times higher than at the end of the Second World War.

But what followed Nixon immediately was an era of financial turmoil that has rarely been equaled in modern history. The U.S. dollar plunged precipitously; U.S. unemployment exceeded 10 percent; oil prices skyrocketed to $39 a barrel; the Dow Jones Industrial Average fell to 570; gold reached $800 an ounce; and U.S. inflation and interest rates climbed to double-digit levels.

Imagine an investor who bought a 30-year U.S. Treasury bond in 1970. Did he not have a right to expect to receive a dollar back for every dollar lent? And shouldn't he have been able to expect that each of those dollars he received—in the year 2000—would be worth about as much as those he had given up?

We can measure the damage by looking at the price of gold. In 1970, each dollar would buy an investor $\frac{1}{34}$ of an ounce of gold. Thirty-five years later, Mr. Market, sitting as judge and jury, tells us that a dollar is worth less than $\frac{1}{425}$ of an ounce of gold.

Investors, taking the U.S. government at its word, have lost trillions. Still, so subtle was the theft that the victims have practically applauded the crime. For the past 20 years they seemed to think it was making them rich!

PAX DOLLARIUM

Globalized commerce, as practiced by the United States since 1971, has a fraudulent side. The hegemonic power uses political means; even when it shops. During the last big boost in the division of labor, in the nineteenth century up until 1913, gold backed the money in which transactions were calibrated. No country—not even an imperial one—could cheat.

If a country consumed more than it produced, other countries found themselves with surpluses of the laggard nation's currency. They then could ask for gold in settlement. Gold was real, ultimate money. No nation could manufacture it. No national assembly could undermine its value or pass a law that increased it. When a nation's gold horde was in danger, it quickly adjusted its policies to correct the imbalance and protect its gold. The dollar, on the other hand, is merely a piece of paper, and since Nixon slammed the gold window shut it is backed by nothing more than the full faith and credit of the United States Treasury. How good a promise is that? No one knows for sure.

The government set up the Federal Reserve in the first place because it wanted a stooge currency. Gold is fine, they said, but it's antisocial. It resists progress and drags its feet on financing new wars and social programs. When we face a war or a great national purpose, we need money that is more patriotic, they said. Gold malingers. Gold hesitates. Gold is reticent. Gold keeps to itself, offering neither advice nor encouragement. Gold has no party affiliation; it doesn't vote. What we need, policymakers said themselves, is a more public-spirited money, a source of public funding, a flexible, expandable national currency, a *political* money that we can work with. We need a dollar that is not linked to gold.

In the many years since the Federal Reserve was set up in 1913, gold has remained as steadfast and immobile as ever. An ounce of it today buys about the same amount of goods and services as an ounce in 1913, and roughly the same amount as it did when Christ was born. But the dollar has gone along with every bit of political gimcrackery that has come along—the war in Europe, the New Deal, World War II, the Cold War, the Vietnam War, the war on poverty, the war on illiteracy, the New Frontier, the Great Society, Social Security, Medicare, Medicaid, the war in Iraq, the war on terror. As a result, guess how much a dollar is worth today in comparison to one in 1913? Five cents.

The Federal Reserve system was set up to provide the nation's empire builders with a convenient, expandable, and compliant money. Whenever they felt they needed more of it, the dollar was right there, ready for duty.

There was a crack in that bell, too. The dollar was ready for service, but its very willingness to serve its masters in Washington made it unreliable to the rest of the world. If the Fed asked the dollar to jump off a cliff, it would do so, no questions asked. This might be a benefit to Washington, but to Tokyo or Peking, it was a risk. At the beginning of 2005, the two nations together held many U.S. Treasury notes that could take a dive at any time.

Since 1971, the United States has added trillions to the world's supply of dollars and credit. During this same time, only about 58,000 metric tons of gold have been brought from the ground. Sooner or later, those extra dollars must be marked to an unforgiving market.

Of course, it hasn't happened yet. Investors are tempted to look out their windows, see the sun shining, and think the good times will last forever. They have no interest in the financial crimes of the Disco Age.

III

EVENING IN AMERICA

The borrower shall be a slave to the lender.

—Proverbs 22:7

9

Reagan's Legacy

It is strange, I mean the way things work out," said a guest at dinner one night. "It seems like a kind of madness wanders around the globe. While, here in Europe, we were trying to batter each others' brains out you, in America, were smart. You were sitting back and taking orders. Now you're the ones who have gone mad."

Our guest had described the world of the nineteenth and twentieth centuries—the days when the idea of an American empire was still repugnant and absurd. While wars, revolutions, and pogroms stormed over Europe—and much of the rest of the world—America kept to itself, reluctant to get involved. Attractive new ideas popped up all over Europe like poisonous mushrooms. But, for the most part, Americans kept their heads. Most went about their business, seeking happiness in their own private ways—trying to get rich. "The business of America is business," Calvin Coolidge explained.

Money isn't everything, we suddenly recalled. Lusting after wealth is not always becoming, not always rewarding, and rarely flattering or dignified. There is something vulgar about the hustle a real business needs . . . like sweat stains on a starched shirt or a cold cup of coffee and stubbed out cigarettes. A man who wants to make a real fortune usually has to grub for it; it's hard to be elegant or refined when you're scratching for cash or market share. But grubbing for money is still better than many other things men do. What follows is a reflection on what the lust for money is better than.

Grubbing for money might be fine for a modest nation working its way up in the world, but is it worthy of a great nation on a roll?

"The trouble with the emphasis in conservatism on the market," William F. Buckley said, "is that it becomes rather boring. You hear it once, you master the idea. The notion of devoting your life to it is horrifying if only because it's so repetitious. It's like sex."

Another old "conservative," Irving Kristol said: "What's the point of being the greatest, most powerful nation in the world, and not having an imperial role?"

"It's too bad," Kristol lamented about money-grubbing, "I think it would be natural for the United States . . . to play a far more dominant role in world affairs . . . to command and to give orders as to what is to be done. People need that."

"When I think of all the crazy things that went on here in France during the last century," continued our dinner guest, "Or maybe I should say in Europe. You know, we invented most of the awful ideas back then. Deconstructionism, Freudianism, Nazism, Conceptualism, Socialism, Syndicalism, Minimalism, Communism, Functionalism . . . come to think of it, almost all the worst ideas came from Europe. And even in America, if I'm not mistaken, almost all the new developments in philosophy, art, and architecture came from immigrants . . . or maybe refugees . . . from Europe. Just about everything. Of course, most of it was harmless. Funny even . . . like Dadaism. But politics wasn't so harmless. But now, the world has turned. Now you do what we did. You come up with the new ideas . . . and you try to force other people to accept them. You have that . . . what do they call it . . . neo–conservatism."

"We sense that we live in a time set apart," said George W. Bush in his State of the Union, 2004, address. What made the time seem so set apart was that the United States had come to resemble a parody of itself; it had come to look like the country leftists had always criticized it for being, but that it had never been: a remarkable combination of self-delusion and self-satisfaction headed for self-destruction. The old conservatives, with their knee-jerk affection for limited government, balanced budgets, and fewer regulations—Republican principles from the Coolidge era—might have saved them, but the old conservatives are gone.

It is a shame about conservatism. Yes, the old sticks-in-the-mud were an impediment to progress. Yes, the old mossbacks were dull and predictable. Yes, their old knees jerked whenever they thought someone might be having fun. Still, we miss those fuddy-duddies. You could count on them to resist the tyranny of the here and now. When something new presented itself, they wouldn't like it. They would resist it, not from any intellectual point of view, but the way a man resists a new pair of shoes or a dog resists a new collar. The new styles might be more fashionable, but that was reason enough to avoid them.

As a creed, conservatism has lost all its adherents, at least in the United States. As a philosophy, it has practically disappeared. As a political movement, it has dropped dead. Everyone likes new things now.

The essential quality of conservatism is not a specific agenda (neither to lower taxes nor to raise the flag), it is merely a way of looking at things—suspiciously; and of reacting to new proposals by dragging one's feet. Conservatives fight against new doctrines like they fight against sushi: Not only is it appalling, it looks as though it might be dangerous, too.

But now the geezers have dyed their hair and had their faces lifted. The codgers refinance their houses, pay with credit cards, and vote for whoever promises them the most of someone else's money. In politics, and in money, the grumps go along with whatever is popular—just like everyone else.

About the only thing you can still count on is vanity—it never seems to go out of style. In the here and now, every generation is the greatest one that ever lived. Every empire is permanent, and everyone who makes trouble for it is an evil subhuman.

In the early part of the twenty-first century, America's neoconservative heirs to the Wilsons—Woodrow Wilson and Ronald Wilson Reagan—became the earth's most dynamic and ambitious empire builders. "These Cold Warriors were mostly liberals of a special, ideologically zealous variety," explained an article in the *American Conservative:*

> Many of them had come from the extreme Left. They had opposed communism because they had universalistic objectives of their own and did not want any competition. These proponents of a single model for all societies were able to form an alliance with putative conservatives, who had come to believe during the Cold War that to be conservative was always to be hawkish and assertive in foreign policy. Used to "standing up for America," these nationalistic and saber-rattling conservatives found in the cause of a better world, a new outlet for their desire to exercise American power.[1]

The neocons preached a rousing sermon of "global democratic revolution," to quote George W. Bush. There is nothing conservative about revolution, but who noticed?

According to former Secretary of the Treasury Paul O'Neill, the leader of the free world had a little trouble following the foreign policy discussions in the White House. But George W. Bush is a shrewd politician who knows a good slogan when someone gives it to him. He saw immediately the advantages of attacking Mesopotamia—it gave him cover to spend more than any president had ever spent, with hardly a peep of protest. Traditional conservatives were struck dumb by this hawkish audacity.

Alas, sometimes it is better to lose a war than to win one. Victory seems to lead to disgrace more often than glory, especially when you are on the road to building an empire. After the West won its Cold War with the Soviet Union, the neocons desperately longed for a new enemy. While they were searching, one found them.

Now, in the opening years of the twenty-first century, the Huns are our friends. And the commies are our new business partners. Now it is the Muslims of the world who must be defeated! The Muslim mind, according to neoconservative scholars, is locked in the past: it mistreats women, it is antidemocratic, antiprogress, nihilistic, and profoundly, irretrievably stuck in a death struggle with the good guys in the enlightened, free, open-minded, fun-loving, capitalist West. Why this should be so has yet to be clarified. Has not the Muslim mind been around for 1,000 years? Did it not evolve according to its own program, just like the Christian mind, the Confucian mind, or the muddled mind of a Democrat? Are there not many millions of Muslims? Are Muslims less smart than Christians or Jews? And yet, the new conservative thinkers could not imagine that the world would be safe unless Muslims were brought into the empire under their heel.

Ronald Reagan had been so successful with his attack on the Soviets' Evil Empire, Republicans hoped for a sequel, never imagining that they might be capable of a little evil themselves. It will be hard, dangerous, and expensive work to transform Islamic civilization, but someone must do it, they say. And only the United States has the military might, the resolve, the courage, the money, and the will to do it. If only the old conservatives' knees still jerked! How they would have harrumphed and gagged.

For here was a new idea—a grand, sweeping new idea—that seemed to call for the most aggressive and activist U.S. foreign policy in American history. Here was a chance for America to entangle itself in foreign military adventures from which it might never get free. Here was an opportunity for the United States to make the Islamic world safe for democracy. Here was a way to improve the world and an almost foolproof way for America to make a public spectacle of itself, go further into debt, and expand its empire!

The old-time conservatives would have been suspicious of such big ideas, especially when they were so flattering. When a man flatters you, it is almost certain that he means to take your business, pick your pocket, or sleep with your wife. When a man flatters himself, he might just as well put a revolver in his mouth and pull the trigger, for he has lost all touch with reality.

We may be the good guys in the here and now, the old-timers would say, but if we want to be the good guys in the future, we have to do good things. They would recall that people who mind business other than their own almost always come to tears. Men are neither good nor bad, the old conservatives would say, but subject to influence.

Traditional American conservatism was not a doctrine of world improvement, but a mood of skepticism toward all "isms" and empire builders.

Political conservatism is undergirded by two important principles. The first principle holds that since most innovations are failures, people should view any proposed change to the traditional order with skepticism. That doesn't mean you can't innovate in a society, but the burden of proof should always be on the world improvers to show that their proposed change will make things better—something they can almost never do.

The second principle of old-time conservatism is the political equivalent of Adam Smith's observation about free markets: "The knowledge required to coordinate and direct a complex, dynamic society is clearly beyond any individual or bureaucratic machine." In short, central planning doesn't work very well, neither in Washington nor in Baghdad. But we add our own little corollary to the knowledge principle—phony knowledge increases the larger the undertaking and the farther you get from it, by the square of the distance and the cube of the scale. That is why the old-time conservatives are suspicious of any grand plan to improve the world—even if it promises to make the world more free.

Old time conservatives don't believe in "freedom." . . . "Just don't tell me what to do," they say.

The world can be improved; we don't deny it. But the only improvements that make the place better are those that remove the eyesores and prevarications of previous improvers. Ronald Reagan's genius was that he was able to see that high taxes and regulation did not make the world a better place, but a worse one. Milton Friedman's three-part formula for better government—cut taxes, cut taxes, cut taxes—seemed like a decent solution.

Reagan had the right instinct. "Get big guv'mint off our backs," was almost his campaign theme song. When he had the chance, he often did the right thing. Faced with a strike by air-traffic controllers—the only union to back his campaign—he fired 10,000 of them. When he saw some "improvement" created by his predecessors, his instinct was generally to get rid of it.

The trouble was that once in Washington, the actor still remembered his lines, but he lost the plot. Almost before he could get his cowboy boots off, he was making improvements of his own.

This was especially notable in what is known as *foreign policy*. Republicans had learned their lesson from the Vietnam War. They still sought to maintain the empire, but by fairly passive means. They merely hoped to "contain" communism—which they saw as a menace. But Reagan fell under the spell of the proto-neoconservatives in Washington. Not content to leave things alone, he decided he could improve the world by actively trying to defeat communism.

This is celebrated as a great and good victory. In her comments on Reagan's death, Britain's Maggie Thatcher said he would be mourned by "millions of men and women who live in freedom today because of the policies he pursued."

Maybe this is true. Maybe it is not. It is impossible to know what might have happened had Reagan left things alone. Most likely, communism would have fallen apart anyway, perhaps sooner. When a man's investments go up, he is a genius. He who failed to invest is seen as a fool. By contrast, when investments go down, it is because of events that could not possibly have been foreseen. Likewise, in politics, the link between action and consequence is forged in a way that always flatters the activists. If something turns out reasonably well, it is because some world improver took action and made it that way. If something turns out badly, it is because someone failed to act when he should have. It is always the activists who get the monuments. Abraham Lincoln is credited with having abolished slavery—at a cost of 618,000 American lives, 2 percent of the entire population. (An equivalent death toll today would wipe out 5 million Americans.) Everywhere else in the world, slavery was abolished—at about the same time—with hardly a single corpse. The Great Emancipator might better be cursed than praised.

Likewise, Woodrow Wilson is given credit for all manner of extravagant improvements. People rarely mention that he almost single-handedly brought about World War II with his meddling in World War I. Instead, when the subject of World War II comes up, Neville Chamberlain's name arises almost immediately. The poor man gets the blame for trying to avoid war—that is, for not taking action when he should have.

Reagan "also helped engineer a huge surge in American patriotism," writes Ross MacKenzie. "The Carter years were a period of American self-doubt about the economy and about American power (with the memory of Vietnam still tormenting most policymakers). Mr. Reagan set about wiping this away. He increased military spending by 25 percent between 1981 and 1985. He talked to the American people, not about malaise (as Mr. Carter had done), but about 'morning in America.' By the end of his second presidency, much of the talk about American decline had gone out of fashion: the country regarded itself once again not only as the world's greatest superpower, but also as the world's most dynamic economy."[2]

Now, we look around and we see no trace of self-doubt. Instead, we see a bubble in confidence. That alone would be no disgrace, but it comes with the most immodest plans for world improvement and the biggest rush of liquidity the water planet has ever seen.

". . . As we begin, let us take inventory," said Ronald Reagan at his inauguration. We find that his head and heart were in the right place; he sought, at least he claimed, not to praise the improvements of the past, but to bury them.

> We are a nation that has a government—not the other way around. And this makes us special among the nations of the Earth. Our Government has no power except that granted it by the people. It is time to check and reverse the growth of government which shows signs of having grown beyond the consent of the governed. It is my intention to curb the size and influence of the Federal establishment and to demand recognition of the distinction between the powers granted to the Federal Government and those reserved to the States or to the people. All

of us need to be reminded that the Federal Government did not create the States; the States created the Federal Government.

Now, so there will be no misunderstanding, it is not my intention to do away with government. It is, rather, to make it work—work with us, not over us; to stand by our side, not ride on our back. Government can and must provide opportunity, not smother it; foster productivity, not stifle it.

If we look to the answer as to why, for so many years, we achieved so much, prospered as no other people on Earth, it was because here, in this land, we unleashed the energy and individual genius of man to a greater extent than has ever been done before. Freedom and the dignity of the individual have been more available and assured here than in any other place on Earth. The price for this freedom at times has been high, but we have never been unwilling to pay that price.

It is no coincidence that our present troubles parallel and are proportionate to the intervention and intrusion in our lives that result from unnecessary and excessive growth of government. It is time for us to realize that we are too great a nation to limit ourselves to small dreams.[3]

Ronald Reagan called himself a conservative. This part of his inaugural address made us think he really was one. But people come to believe what they must believe in order to play their roles—even conservatives. Reagan's real revolution lay in redefining conservatism as an activist, imperial creed. First, the neocons took over foreign policy. Soon, Americans were stirring up trouble everywhere, from Latin America to Afghanistan. Then, they took over domestic policy. In a few cases, the ghastly remnants of previous improvers—such as 70 percent top marginal rates—were knocked over. In more cases, new edifices were built up. But the major failure was that the sharp tax cuts of 1981 were not followed by sharp spending cuts. Instead, spending went up. And not just on defense. Reagan had pledged to abolish the Department of Education. Instead, he increased its budget by 50 percent.

The Reagan Revolution transformed the Republican Party. Rather than continuing to fight a rearguard action against leftist activists, Republicans were emboldened to take the lead, becoming activists themselves. This they did by relying on a monumental fraud.

Murray Rothbard watched Republicans scam themselves. He wrote:

In the spring of 1981, conservative Republicans in the House of Representatives cried. They cried because, in the first flush of the Reagan Revolution that was supposed to bring drastic cuts in taxes and government spending, as well as a balanced budget, they were being asked by the White House and their own leadership to vote for an increase in the statutory limit on the federal public debt, which was then scraping the legal ceiling of one trillion dollars.

They cried because all their lives they had voted against an increase in public debt, and now they were being asked, by their own party and their own movement, to violate their lifelong principles. The White House and its leadership assured them that this breach in principle would be their last: that it was necessary for one last increase in the debt limit to give President Reagan a chance to bring about a balanced budget and to begin to reduce the debt. Many of these Republicans tearfully announced that they were taking this fateful step because they deeply trusted their president, who would not let them down.[4]

"Famous last words," wrote Rothbard.

In a sense, the Reagan handlers were right: there were no more tears, no more complaints, because the principles themselves were quickly forgotten, swept into the dustbin of history. Deficits and the public debt have piled up mountainously since then, and few people care, least of all conservative Republicans. Every few years, the legal limit is raised automatically. By the end of the Reagan reign the federal debt was $2.6 trillion; now it is $3.5 trillion and rising rapidly. As we write, September 2005, it is almost $8 trillion. And this is the rosy side of the picture, because if you add in "off-budget" loan guarantees and contingencies, the grand total federal debt is $20 trillion. That is merely the current debt. As we will see later, when Treasury Secretary Paul O'Neill totaled up the present value of future obligations minus expected tax revenues he came to a figure more than twice that large.

Before the Reagan era, conservatives were clear about how they felt about deficits and the public debt: a balanced budget was good, and deficits and the public debt were bad. In the famous words of the left-Keynesian apostle of "functional finance," Professor Abba Lerner, there is nothing wrong with the public debt because "we owe it to ourselves." In those days, at least, conservatives were astute enough to realize that it made an enormous amount of difference whether—slicing through the obfuscatory collective nouns—one is a member of the "we" (the burdened taxpayer) or of the "ourselves" (those living off the proceeds of taxation).

Since Reagan, however, intellectual-political life has gone topsy-turvy. Conservatives and allegedly "free-market" economists have twisted themselves inside out trying to find new reasons why deficits don't matter.

Today, if you were to pose the question to the small-town Republican, you might still find a faint residue of the Old Religion. But the poor man has been betrayed by his party, by his representatives, by politics itself, by the lure of empire, and by his own vain and fatal urges. He has come to believe what he must.

There were four key elements to Reaganomics. Restrict the money supply to slow inflation (admirably carried out by Paul Volcker at the Fed). Cut taxes (a 25 percent across-the-board tax cut was enacted in 1981). Balance the budget by controlling domestic spending. (A complete failure—deficits grew larger than ever.) And reduce government regulation. (Ditto.)

The first two objectives were more or less achieved. They produced more or less what Milton Friedman expected. But neither was an activist measure. Both merely undid some of the worst damage done by previous officeholders. Lyndon Johnson, Richard Nixon, and Jimmy Carter had made a mess of the economy. Ronald Reagan and Paul Volcker helped clean it up. But even the cleanup lacked the necessary suds and elbow grease. Instead, the dirt and clutter were mostly let alone, while new trash was heaped on.

The big cut in taxes gave people more money to spend. It was equivalent to an increase in demand. Consumers began a buying spree, while government borrowed the money to fund the deficit.

Where did the extra spending power come from? Few people asked. If they had thought about it, they would have realized that, collectively, they were merely going further into debt to upgrade their standards of living. If they had reflected on it deeply, they would have realized that they were running up bills that future generations would have to pay; they were spending money that their children and grandchildren hadn't earned yet. For what was a national debt, but an intergenerational obligation, a burden placed on infants by their parents and grandparents?

Hardly anyone thought about it then—or since.

Reagan's *supply-side economics* was meant to be different from Keynesian economics in that it celebrated the power of the free market to create wealth. If only the restrictions imposed on the economy by previous generations of world improvers could be removed, they said, the economy would boom and people would get rich.

Thus, it came to be that taxes were cut and the economy boomed. But what the new supply-siders had done was nothing more than administer an old-fashioned Keynesian boost. John Maynard Keynes, a British economist of the early twentieth century, had given world improvers a tool. He showed that nations could be winched out of recessions by easy credit and government spending. When private spenders eased off, he noted, government could take up the slack—by running deficits. Where would the money come from? He expected governments to run surpluses in good times so they would have money to spend in bad ones. Had government actually done so, the Keynesian system would have at least been honest. But this was the part the politicians never particularly liked, and the part of his plan they never could quite follow. It was all very well to spend money. Only curmudgeonly conservatives complained about that. Otherwise, spending money made everyone happy. But *not* spending money was another matter. Not spending meant less bread and fewer circuses, and fewer clowns on the public payroll. It meant explaining to voters that they wouldn't get the new road or new medical services that had been promised. It meant lower demand and less new money in circulation, the very opposite of the boom everyone loved so much.

Politicians had no trouble giving the economy the boost that Keynes had suggested. But when it came to saving money to have something to give a boost with, the time never seemed quite right. The moment for underspending never seemed to come. Like fat men at a wedding feast, policymakers told themselves they would eat less after the party was over, to make up for their gluttony now. But in public finance, there is never a good time for fasting.

When the Reagan team arrived in Washington, the nation had been living with Keynesian deficits for many years. Savers and lenders had grown wary. Consumer price inflation hit 13.5 percent in 1980. Lenders feared it would go higher still. They demanded protection. In 1980, 30-year mortgages could be had at 15 percent interest. By the following year, the mortgage rate rose to a peak of 18.9 percent.

But then, Paul Volcker's anti-inflation policies at the Fed began to pay off. Investors did not yet know it, but the bond market had found its bottom. For the next two and a half decades, bonds would go up. Bond yields—a measure of what people must pay to borrow—went down. Thus, were the two cornerstones of the Reagan era in place—lower taxes and lower real cost of credit. Neither was an improvement to America's system of imperial finance. Both were merely corrections to previous meddling. Taxes had been raised so that the government would have money to spend on its imperial programs: bread and circuses at home; wars at the periphery. High bond yields (a high cost of credit) were the result of Keynesian policies. Neither problem was caused by neglect. Instead, both were the inevitable debris of previous improvements, previous innovations in the field of economics, and previous generations of self-aggrandizing empire builders posing as do-gooders.

After Reagan's tax cuts, U.S. gross domestic product (GDP) grew at an average rate of 3.2 percent per year throughout the eight years of Reagan's two terms. This was a bit more than the 2.8 percent average gain in the eight years before and substantially more than the 2.1 percent of the eight years following. Still the growth was slower than it had been in the 1960s, after Kennedy's 30 percent tax cut of 1964 produced 5 percent annual GDP rates. Meanwhile, real median household income rose from $37,868 in 1981 to $42,049 in 1989. This, too, was much better than the rate of growth before or after the Reagan years. But much of it—maybe all of it—came not from real increases in wages, but simply from more people working longer hours, as we illustrated in our previous book.

Real wage increases require three things: First, the society must save money so that it has the capital to invest. Second, it must invest the savings in profitable businesses. Third, these capital investments must result in increased productivity.

Alas, none of these things happened. Instead, these three critical things began trending in the wrong direction. National savings—including public savings—fell from 7.7 percent in the 1970s to only 3 percent by 1990. Business investment fell from 18.6 percent of GDP in the 1970s to 17.4 percent in the 1980s. And productivity? In the 25 years after World War II, output per employee had risen at an average rate of 2.8 percent per year. During the 1980s, this rate fell to less than 1 percent.

There was a bump in productivity after 1995, but this was largely a feature of the Labor Department's new way of calculating it. With falling savings, falling business investment, and (consequently) falling productivity, you could not expect the economy to do very well. It didn't.

While the supply side of supply-side economics was a total flop, the demand side was a stunning success. The Reagan team at least figured out how to pay for an empire: Borrow.

As a percentage of GDP, federal government receipts fell from 20.2 in 1981 to 18.6 in 1992. But spending rose from 22.9 percent in 1981 to 23.5 percent in 1992. Naturally, debts rose.

By the end of 1992, the federal debt was more than $4 trillion. When Reagan took over, it was less than $1 trillion.

No fraud is so lovable as the illusion of getting something for nothing. But something-for-nothing was just what the new conservatives now promised voters—just like the Democrats. The difference was that the Democrats pledged to steal the money from the rich (Republicans). The Republicans promised to create it in a free economy, like Jesus multiplying the loaves and fishes at Beth Saida. "Voodoo economics," was how George Bush described it.

ORIGINS OF SUPPLY SIDE

When supply-side economics first appeared in the American press, real economists were perplexed. They had never heard of it. There were no university departments specializing in it. There were no peer-reviewed papers. There were no scholarly books describing it. There were scarcely any economists claiming to be supply-siders. It was, apparently, a school of thought without a school. Some wondered if it also lacked a thought.

Traditional economists—mostly empire builders and world improvers, but of the Keynesian variety—had gotten themselves stuck on a teeter-totter. On one end sat inflation. On the other was employment. They could press down on one end, but the other would rise up and hit them on the chin. There seemed to be no way out. No free lunch. It seemed that they would have to pay for every something with something else. If they wanted to reduce inflation, it would cost them jobs. If they wanted to increase employment, consumer prices would rise.

Milton Friedman, among others, warned that Keynesianism was just folderol. As soon as people realized what the government was doing, the jig would be up. They would merely raise prices in anticipation of inflation, without increasing production. *Stagflation*—rising prices in a sluggish economy—would result. Other economists pointed out that any attempt to manipulate the business cycle would fail for the same reason. Once the policy were known, people would adjust their behavior to it, nullifying its effectiveness. They would not mistake inflation for greater demand: they would not increase production; they would not hire more workers; they would not spend more money. The only thing the policy-makers could possibly do that would have an effect would be something people did not expect. And that could only be a policy of random manip-ulations—which would cause further confusion and who-knew-what re-sults. Keynesians, even new Keynesians, never had any real answer to this problem. But that didn't stop them. They decided to ignore it. Meddlers and empire builders can't be bothered with theoretical problems; they are too busy creating a better world!

Stagflation came in the 1970s, just as Milton Friedman had said it would. It was not the better world the Keynesian economists had hoped to create. But it was the world they got. (Like everyone else, world im-provers don't get exactly what they expect; they get what they deserve.) Stagflation posed a problem with no easy solution. Prices were rising, but employment was flat. Policymakers wanted to increase employment, but they were loath to add more inflation. They could try to lower inflation, but that would hurt employment even more.

Along came the supply-siders. They had no real solution. But at least they had a way to hide the problem. What both the public and the politi-cians wanted, they noted, was employment without price increases. They wanted a booming economy and no inflation. Voters wanted money from government; they also wanted to lower taxes.

The trouble with traditional conservative economists was that they were always pointing out the true cost of things. "There's no such thing as a free lunch," was practically tattooed on their foreheads. Conserva-tive economists typically argued against government debt, against deficits, and against more spending, against activism in all its forms; they knew there would be a price to be paid for it, eventually. This at-titude made conservative economists deeply unpopular. They were, after all, party poopers. Who would want such a killjoy around? None could ever be elected to high office. The essence of politics was promis-ing things that couldn't be delivered honestly. If a man could get no more from an election than what he actually earned, why would he bother to vote at all?

The supply-siders' proposal seemed to offer something for everyone—at no cost to anyone. Taxes could be cut, said Arthur Laffer; lower taxes would create such a boom that output would go up—eliminating inflation. Government revenues would go up, too—even at lower tax rates. The budget would be balanced. Most importantly, it offered a way to get conservatives elected—by turning them into big spenders.

REAL BOOMS VERSUS THE PHONY VARIETY

Real booms need real money. Typically, people save money when they are wary and spend it when they are flush. The spending is real. The money is real. The boost in sales is real. The profits are real.

But a boom that people build on phony money is itself phony. Every step of the way takes them in the wrong direction. The demand is an illusion. The spending is a mistake. The money is suspect. And the resulting business profits are not merely temporary, they are nothing more than next year's sales disguised as this year's earnings.

A man who borrows money to begin his spending spree contributes nothing to the economy. Every dollar he spends must someday be withdrawn. It must be paid back. Imagine that he borrows $1 million. In a small town, that sum might be enough to set off a boom. He buys a new car. He goes out to the restaurant. He gives money to church and charities. He takes a holiday. He orders a new suit. He builds a new wing on his house. Soon, the money is out of his pocket. But it is not gone. It has found a new home in pockets all over town. And now the butcher, the baker, the builder, the travel agent, and many others are all planning little additions to their own standards of living.

But imagine the disappointment when, the following year, the man who spent so freely no longer comes around. He is not seen at the tailor, or at the travel agent, or at the restaurant, or the car dealer. He is not even seen so frequently at his old haunts. Not only does he not spend as freely as he did the year before, he barely spends at all. For now he must cut his regular spending by enough to pay back the $1 million plus interest. Net spending in the town will actually go down, over a multi-year period, by the amount of interest he pays (assuming that the loan comes from outside the community).

(We invite readers to consider the current U.S. situation—when loans from overseas surpass $600 billion per year.)

The supply-siders' key insight was that government is essentially a parasite. It lives off its host like a leech. And like any bloodsucker, it has to be careful not to suck too much. Otherwise, it will weaken its host and maybe even kill it. Or, if it sucks too little, it fails to fully exploit the opportunity and invites competition.

The supply-siders' concept was hardly a formula for maximizing individual freedom. On the contrary, it was a formula for financing an empire by increasing government revenues. Arthur Laffer's curve merely illustrates a rational bloodsucker's optimization strategy; he will get the most at a level that is neither too high nor too low. A government that imposes tax rates that are too high, weakens the economy and ends up with less resources than it might otherwise have. This was a problem with communism—it asked too much of its citizens. The poor schleps were drained dry. Democratic regimes in the West took a lower percentage of their citizens' output. But their hosts thrived, giving the government more money to spend. The government of the Soviet Union took less from each citizen than the United States did, but it took a much higher percentage of each citizen's output. This was why the West won the Cold War; it had fixed its tax rates lower.

But Reagan's tax cuts were an empty gesture. Without offsetting cuts to federal spending, deficits increased. What really matters to an economy is not the nominal tax rates, but the percentage of the economy's resources taken away by the government. Actual tax rates in the Soviet Union were zero. The communists claimed the right to 100 percent of production, a portion of which was turned over to citizens for personal use. The government's percentage of production, or what might be called its *real tax rate,* while difficult to measure, was very high. That, combined with even more government meddling than in the United States, doomed the Soviet experiment.

Reagan cut nominal tax rates, but government consumed more and more resources. The leech grew. Lower tax rates gave citizens the impression that they had more money to spend. Individually, they did. Collectively, they did not. The program was merely a monumental legerdemain. For every tax-cut dollar that a citizen spent, the federal government had to borrow as much as $1.18 (with interest).

Still, citizens thought they had more to spend. They spent it. It was this extra spending—this Keynesian boost of money borrowed by the federal government to replace the forgone tax revenues—that picked up the economy.

And now, pardon us if we go over to this dead horse and lay on the whip again. Reducing taxes is a conservative, anti-activist, anti-world-improving, anti-political, anti-empire gesture. Taxes are imposed by people who pretend that the world will be a better place if your money is taken from you and redirected to others' pockets. Cutting taxes is a way of removing the improvement residues of the past. It is a way of tipping society away from the political means of doing things back toward civilized, consensual, economic life. The lower the taxes—and here, we speak of real tax rates (the amount of resources consumed by the government)—the more modest the world-improvers' ambitions. Lowering tax rates was the right idea. But lowering only nominal tax rates, while simultaneously increasing the government's resources, was a sham.

Since the tax cut was a sham, so was the resulting boom. It was inspired by consumer demand that didn't exist. But the financial world is a complicated, confusing affair with many promiscuous liaisons. Events are engendered by other events. They are *path dependent,* as economists say. One event fathers another. Life was good in the Reagan years. The supply-siders patted each other on the back. "We did it," they congratulated each other. Someone should have asked for a paternity test.

Whereas tax cuts gave consumer spending a temporary boost, bond yields began a long, solid downtrend. The lower cost of credit was a plus for the economy and for the financial markets—at least as important as tax cuts. Falling interest rates made it cheaper to borrow. From experience, people expected prices to go up—which would lower the cost of their loans still further. Rising prices would also undermine the value of their savings. They did the reasonable thing: They borrowed.

Stocks rose. Things were looking up. It was "morning in America." The questions would have to wait until evening.

FUNNY NUMBERS

Since 1913, the costs of do-gooders, empire-builders, and world-improvers has been adding up. By the 1970s, it had begun to depress productivity rates. Instead of growing at 2.8 percent per year (the rate since World War II), productivity rose only about 1 percent from 1973 to 1984.

Since then, the rates themselves have become fraudulent: In 1995, Department of Labor officials began to crunch the numbers into such odd and awful shapes, even their own mothers would no longer recognize them. The practice known as hedonic price indexing based on "chained dollars" was put into place. Computers came to be valued for their potential to increase productivity rather than their actual cost, dramatically inflating both the importance of the tech sector in the economy, and overstating GDP so as to make the number useless.

Nearly half the items in America's measure of consumer price inflation are "adjusted."

Between 2000 and the end of 2004, for example, spending on computers rose 9.3 percent. Since computers became more powerful, however, the number was enhanced to 113.4 percent. Other numbers in the consumer price inflation calculation were adjusted by the substitution effect. If steak rose in price, the statisticians assumed people switched to mutton, thereby reducing their cost of living.

So did they adjust the price of housing. It cost a lot more to own a house in 2005 than it did in the year 2000, but the boys went to work on the numbers with pliers and a torch. Soon they had twisted the cost of actually owning a house into the cost of renting the same house; "owners' equivalent rent" they called it. Because the imperial central bank has held interest rates below the consumer price index (CPI) rate for the past three years, people who previously would have rented, now buy. This has reduced rents even while it increased house prices. Voilà! The CPI, of which more than a quarter is the cost of housing, was held down. The credit bubble had a similar effect on used cars. Zero financing deals turned heads away from used cars and toward new ones. Used car prices fell—and so did this component of the CPI. Together the two items alone—housing and used cars—were responsible for a 1.7 percent drop in core CPI between November 2001 and December 2003.

While everyone knows it has become much more expensive to make ends meet, these distortions keep the official CPI low and the gross domestic product (GDP) figures high. (Nominal output is reduced by the official CPI number to give the real GDP figure. The lower the CPI, the higher the resulting GDP figure.) The productivity figures are also beaten senseless. Output per hour is distorted by the measure of output itself, which includes both hedonic quality enhancements and inflation adjustments.

FORGETTING TO DUCK

We turn back to the Gipper. When Ronald Wilson Reagan was finally carried off in June 2004, the nation said goodbye with a soft heart and a head that had turned to mush. His obsequies were as full of humbug as a national election. The man deserved better. He should have been carried off by six jolly cowboys and bid farewell by honest drunks.

Instead, Reagan was given a send off worthy of a world-class mountebank. We were told that he was responsible for a huge economic boom in the land of the free. He cut marginal tax rates. He helped get the government off our backs. He defeated communism.

Rod Martin wrote a book praising Ronald Reagan for "saving the world . . . without Reagan," he says, "We might all be speaking Russian!" We have nothing against Russian. But we doubt that, in any reasonably imaginable circumstances, Americans could all have learned to speak Russian in a single generation. They are not that good at languages. But it illustrates how the world-improvers think; if you want to make a better world, you must make others do just as you do. Martin could not imagine a Russian "victory" without imagining that we had to learn to speak the Russian language. He probably thought we would have to learn to like vodka and dance like Cossacks, too.

> [Reagan's] certainty that people everywhere yearned for freedom and that free markets could always outproduce centrally planned slavery drove his strategies where realpolitik could never go. He replaced both containment and détente with his "Reagan Doctrine," proclaiming America would actively roll back its foe by helping freedom fighters behind the Iron Curtain.[5]

What made Reagan so sure that people everywhere yearn for freedom is a mystery; there is no evidence of it. Even Americans, who claim to love freedom as much as anyone, are much more interested in low mortgage rates. They would scrap the entire Bill of Rights in less than 24 hours if it meant guaranteed 10 percent annual real estate gains. And if free markets could always outproduce centrally planned slavery, why was he worried about losing out to the Soviets? It was obvious we could beat them—because we could afford far more and better weapons.

Realpolitik was Kissinger's approach to foreign policy. It began by taking people as he found them, whether they wanted Western-style freedom or not, and making the best of the situation. This meant generally trying to avoid conflict without surrendering strategic interests—even imperial ones.

The neo-Wilsonians advising Reagan came up with a more daring doctrine. They wanted to get Kissinger out of the way and remake the world in their own image. Martin does not mention that among the "freedom fighters" that the United States decided to support was, notably, Osama bin Laden. The present War on Terror was largely an invention of the neoconservatives. They helped create the enemy and then developed a war against him.

Martin continues:

> And free men everywhere, [Reagan] believed, would lay down arms, take up tools and build a new, peaceful, prosperous world for themselves and their posterity, given the chance.[6]

We have never met Rod Martin; we presume he is an honest and decent man. Yet, in this ode to Ronald Reagan and George W. Bush, the man seemed to have taken leave of his senses altogether. Men—free or not—occasionally pick up weapons and begin killing each other. If liberty has anything to do with it, there is no proof for it in the historical record.

Yet, Reagan's anti-communism resonated with the voters. He had spent a good part of his career telling the world how bad the communists were. But what was it that was so bad about them? And what business was it of his?

Why was Ronald Reagan so eager to get rid of Bolshevism? As long as you didn't have to live in a communist country, what would it matter to you? Many smart people thought it was a better way. What made the communists a menace was not that they were intent on improving their own world with the benefits of collectivism, but that they were determined to improve our world, too. What made them obnoxious was not their own goofy creed, but their determination to do precisely what Ronald Reagan wanted to do, remake its adversary into something more like itself. Reagan had branded the Soviet Union "an evil empire." But behind the words was a monstrous conceit that, by some special grace of God, he knew how people everywhere were meant to live and how they were meant to govern themselves. It did not matter that 3,000 generations who had come and gone had had other ideas, nor that a third of the world's people alive in 1981 had other ideas. Reagan thought he knew what was best for everyone.

In a strictly economic sense, communism was America's greatest ally. For many decades, it kept millions of people penniless—unable to compete for the world's oil and other resources. While the United States guzzled cheap oil for half a century, communism retarded the economic development of its competitors. Now, every remaining barrel of oil comes on the market with people bidding for it from all over the planet—Americans, Europeans, Russians—and 3 billion Asians, too!

The Soviets were so discouraged by the Reagan Revolution, we are told, they decided to give up being Soviets; now, they are Russians or Lithuanians or Khazaks. The Chinese were so impressed, they decided to loose the dogs of capitalism; now they are nipping at our heels and stealing our food.

MARX'S REVENGE

For the first time in two-hundred years, the West (including Westernized Japan) faces real competition. The world's largest nations—China, India, and Russia—sat on the sidelines for most of the nineteenth and twentieth centuries. They were too remote and too backward to participate in the great boom that lifted living standards during the reign of the British Empire in the nineteenth century. GDP per capita rose from barely over $1,000 (in 1990 dollars) in the United States at the beginning of the nineteenth century to more than $5,000 by its end. China, on the other hand, had a GDP per capita of about $600 when the nineteenth century began. By its end, the figure had fallen to around $525. Indian numbers were about the same, but in the other direction, with a small gain in the nineteenth century—probably the result of British colonial development. In the twentieth century, Russia, China, and India all became victims of self-inflicted wounds; various forms of socialist claptrap took them out of economic competition.

But now they are back, and it is a whole new ball game, as they say. These countries are either on the periphery of U.S. imperial protection, or beyond the pale altogether. Either way, they benefit from the order created by the U.S. imperium. Foreign workers seem to be able to make anything we can make—but at much lower cost. India is growing at 8 percent a year, China at 9 percent—Russia is booming too. In addition, they are turning out millions of young people who can make things—graduates in the practical arts and sciences—better and cheaper than we do in the United States or Europe. What's more, the foreigners take the old virtues seriously. They save their money—the saving rate in China is as high as 40 percent of the national income, according to official sources. These savings give them huge piles of capital with which to build more modern factories and more convenient infrastructure.

The price of labor in the rich countries is high. The average cost of an hour of someone's time in the United States—including social charges—is $20.73. The average cost of someone's time in China, on the other hand, is somewhere between 13.5 and 65 cents, depending on the source. As long as capital, expertise, and finished products are free to move around, it is likely that the two numbers will grow closer together. The consumer doesn't particularly care who assembled his gadget; he only cares that he can buy it at the lowest possible price. Labor is a big component of the price of most things, so both manufacturers and consumers appreciate lower labor prices. Our old incompetent enemies have learned how to compete.

We were told that America became much richer because of Reagan's improvements, but if that is so, why did real wage rates not rise? A man sweats, humps, busses, totes, and schleps today, on average, for about the same wage he got before the Reagan revolution fired its first shot. But that is not to say that everything is just the same. Far from it. Today, people own less of their own homes—homeowner equity (the portion not mortgaged) has fallen from nearly 70 percent in the late 1970s to less than 55 percent in 2005. Plus, the average person owes more money to more people than ever before. Household debt in the fall of 2005 is 113 percent of annual income on average; prior to 1980, it was 58 percent. Today, fewer people have secure sources of money for their retirement. More than two-thirds of older households—those headed by people 47 to 64—had someone earning a pension in 1983. By 2001, fewer than half did.

The Reagan Era came with a relatively new idea, that people should be responsible for their own pensions. Companies stopped offering fixed-benefit pension plans. But by 2000, old people were feeling the effects. They were not as well off as they had expected to be. When the holdings of typical households were analyzed, today's near-retirees turned out to be a little poorer, in constant dollars, than the previous generation was when it approached retirement in 1983.

Edward Wolff, an economist at New York University, looked at 18 years of household financial data from the Fed. Somehow he retained his sanity long enough to discover that the net worth of the average older household declined by 2.2 percent, or $4,000, during the period [1983–2001] to $199,900.

We look on that fact in shock and awe. How could it be that after the biggest explosion of wealth-creation in the history of man, the average man is not richer, but poorer?

We recall the Carter years: The nation was at peace. Despite inflation, Americans were still getting richer. Wages were rising. The country still enjoyed a positive balance of trade, and the rest of the world still owed it more than it owed to foreigners.

But in 1980, stocks had been going down for 14 years and bonds had been in a bear market that began in 1945. With eyes in the back of their heads, people must have looked out and seen nothing but trouble. The Vietnam War was still in the near background. And Richard Nixon. And Jimmy Carter himself. Americans were discouraged, we are told; they had lost confidence in themselves.

Then, along came Ronald Reagan with a message of hope, optimism, and something-for-nothing. The supply side, the Laffer Curve! Suddenly it seemed possible to spend more . . . and still have more! Government could cut taxes—and get more revenue, said Laffer. Forget the deficit; it will take care of itself. Somehow. The average man figured he could do the same: borrow more, spend more, and he would get rich.

Pensions were out. Free people could look out for themselves. They could set up their own 401(k) plans and make money in common stocks. All you had to do was buy the companies you liked, said Peter Lynch.

And the companies themselves no longer had to worry about their employees. Managers could focus on cooking the books to give the impression of maximizing shareholder value. America soon became "Shareholder Nation"—a whole country of capitalists, all getting rich in the freest, most dynamic economy the world had ever seen.

Now we see that the whole thing was a huge swindle. Supply-side policies never really increased the supply side. Government never actually lightened up to let people live their own lives in their own ways. Employees never quite got around to putting money into their 401(k) plans; they were too busy trying to keep up with the credit card bills. And managers soon realized that maximizing their own incomes with stock options, bonuses, and rich retirement plans was more rewarding than looking out for shareholders.

The shareholders themselves—the millions of lumpen pseudo-investors who owned mutual funds—couldn't tell the difference. They had neither the time, the money, nor the training to be real capitalists; they were merely chumps for Wall Street.

And now, here we are, a quarter-century since Reagan won the White House: We are at war, with the biggest trade deficit, the biggest federal debt, the biggest financing gap, the lowest interest rates in 45 years, and the most consumer debt ever. In real terms, the average man earns less per hour worked than he did in the Carter years. And the typical household approaches retirement poorer than it would have been in 1980.

America was the world's biggest creditor when Ike was president. By Ronald Reagan's second term, about 15 years into the pax dollarium era, the nation slipped to net-debtor status. In the following 15 years, it broke all records—becoming the world's biggest debtor and the greatest debtor of all time.

But Thomas Gale Moore, then a member of President Reagan's Council of Economic Advisors, must have anticipated Ben Bernanke when he noticed the United States crossing the creditor/debtor threshold in the mid-1980s. Not to worry, said he, "We can pay off anybody by running a press."

In 1980, people still held parties when they paid off their mortgages. Paul Volcker said that he would bring down inflation rates, and he meant it. You could buy a stock for six times earnings and lend your money to the U.S. government for a 15 percent yield. Lenders demanded that much because they remembered the inflation of the 1970s. They knew that not every investment story had a happy ending.

Back then, the United States still made things. General Motors was our biggest employer; you could tell what year a car was made by looking at the tail fins, they got better every year. When Eisenhower was in the White House and William McChesney Martin was at the Fed, the United States had most of the world's gold and most of the world's credit. This happy state of affairs persisted until the reign of Ronald Reagan and Alan

Greenspan, when Wal-Mart—a retailer, not a manufacturer—became its biggest employer.

The foreigners own more and more of what used to be American wealth-producing assets. When Ronald Reagan arrived at the White House, foreign-owned U.S. assets were less than 15 percent of GDP. Now, they're over 78 percent. And they are growing rapidly.

SUNRISE, SUNSET

Under Ronald Reagan, Americans thought they had rediscovered their youth. They couldn't remember ever feeling more confident or more optimistic. Then, 12 years later, in George W. Bush, Republicans thought they saw their hero reincarnate, with another 20 years of prosperity ahead.

And why shouldn't it be morning in America again?

We answer the question directly. It is not morning in America because it is evening. There is no bull market because there is a bear market. People are not getting richer because they are getting poorer. It is not 1981 because it is 2005.

Readers who find this an unsatisfying explanation are reminded that it is not your authors who set the planets in motion around the sun and created man—such as he is—out of the dust of the earth. Morning often looks a lot like evening—if you face the wrong way at the right time. But it is the opposite end of the day's cycle.

In 1982, interest rates were high and stock prices were low. In 1982, there were a few people who wanted to buy stocks, and many who didn't. In 1982, America, Inc., looked like a has-been economy. Its currency was widely considered near-trash and its bonds were described as "certificates of guaranteed confiscation."

You could buy nearly the entire Dow for just one ounce of gold. Now it takes 22 ounces. The trend of the time, in 1982, was down. Then, as now, smart people considered it eternal. *BusinessWeek* proclaimed that equities were not just in a cyclical downturn, not just sick, but dead.

As the moon looked down in the summer of 1982, it shone on a wall of worry so high that only a knuckleheaded contrarian would think of climbing it. Every headline seemed to give another reason the bear market would last forever. Every poll showed that consumers expected it. Every price seemed to confirm the everlasting trend; the sun had set forever; the black of night was permanent.

And yet, at that very moment, had an investor turned around, he would have noticed a brightening in the eastern sky. Over the next 18 years, the sun rose higher and higher, until investors were so encouraged by the favorable growing conditions that they scattered their seed like confetti at a parade. Did anyone doubt that it would take root in the hard concrete of lower Manhattan's financial hothouse or the thin soils of the technology sector?

But the year 2005 is everything the year 1982 was not. Today, there are many people who want to buy stocks and few who don't. Interest rates are nearly as low as they have been in half a century and stocks are as high as they have ever been. Consumers—who were relatively reluctant to spend in 1982—pick their own pockets today. The latest figures—from April 2005—show consumer spending increasing at five times the increase in wages and salaries.

And housing is booming. In many parts of California, prices of houses are going up 10 times faster than the rate of core inflation.

Can these sunny trends continue forever? They never have before. And no theory of economics explains how they might. Instead, the typical pattern is for night to follow day. It is also typical for the dumb things people did when they were feeling flush to be corrected by recession and bear markets.

There is one more big difference. In the hot sun of the Reagan recovery, overseas investors, who had previously been cool on America, warmed up. Now, we start from a very different position. Foreigners have been hot for U.S. assets for years—an attitude we have come to count on, because we need $2 billion in capital inflows every day to cover our foreign-trade deficit. What happens as they cool off again?

Of course, they will cool off. Americans cannot expect foreigners to support them indefinitely. Someday, perhaps soon, they will realize that their main customers cannot pay their debts; they will get tired of lending to them.

Then, the long, dark night will begin. It will not last forever. In our previous book, we foresaw a "long, slow, soft slump" coming. But just as every sunny day comes to an end sometime, so does even the darkest night. If Americans keep their wits about them, they can hope to get through it and begin another sunny period bright and refreshed.

A WORLD OF DEBT

Pete Peterson attempted to gauge the difficulty of determining the burden we've now placed on future generations. "Estimates vary," Pete Peterson points out in *Running On Empty,* his vast inquiry into the impending bankruptcy of the U.S. government, "depending on methodology, but the numbers are all vast." Peterson points to studies done on the future obligations of the Social Security and Medicare trust fund alone. In 2003, the American Enterprise Institute projected a $45 trillion shortfall; $47 trillion countered the International Monetary Fund in 2004; the National Center for Policy Analysis and the Brookings Institution came up with $50 trillion and $60 trillion, respectively, in their own research reports published in 2003.

Those are all incomprehensibly large numbers, of course, but the biggest of the projections came in 2004 from Social Security and Medicare trustees themselves. They estimated the unfunded benefit liabilities to have a current value of $74 trillion dollars.

As an empire matures, the imperial citizens believe more and more extravagant things. By the opening of the twenty-first century, Americans were spending more than they earned. Each day brought more new debt than real new wealth. Yet, between 2002 and 2005, every quarter showed growth in GDP. Americans mistook this growth for progress. They knew they had the world's best economy, its best system of government, and its finest culture. They could not imagine that they were growing poorer. But here we turn again to the living and the dead for elucidation. Supply-sider Jude Wanniski admits that real growth has come almost to a halt:

> In the United States, my own work shows that between 1945 and 1971, when the dollar was fixed to gold at $35 oz under the 1944 Bretton Woods arrangement, the real economy in the US grew by 4 percent per year. From 1971 when the dollar was floated to 2004, real growth of the US economy has only managed a pitiful 0.3 percent per year.[7]

The growth, such as it is, in the American economy, has come about by virtue of increased emphasis on the present tense. Americans came to despise the past and neglect the future. The lessons of the dead and the desires of the unborn were both ignored. Instead, all that seemed to matter was consumption in the here and now.

A dead man, F. A. Hayek, explains the consequences:

> The economy in its entirety must continue to decline so long as more is being consumed than produced, and some part of consumption therefore takes place at the expense of the existing capital stock.

Without a theory, Hayek might have said, the facts are as mute. But by the year 2005, both facts and theories had become blabbermouths. The trouble was that the facts had been corrupted so they no longer told the truth. And the old theories that might have been used to interpret the facts had been abandoned in favor of new, more convenient delusions. Americans could now run up as much debt as they wanted, said the new theorists.

The American economy may or may not be "growing" in 2005. But if traditional, time-tested theories about how wealth and poverty are correct, thank God it is not growing more. Every step it takes moves it deeper into debt and closer to bankruptcy.

10

America's Glorious Empire of Debt

L et us take a moment to stand back and gaze at America's great Empire of Debt. It is the largest edifice of debt ever put up. It sustains the most magnificent world economy ever assembled. It supports more people in better style than any system ever before devised.

Not only is it incomparably effective, it is also immeasurably entertaining. For it has its burnished helmets and flying banners; its intellectuals and its gladiators; its Caesars, Antonys, Neros, and Caligulas. It has its temples, its forum, its Capitol, its senators; its praetorian guards; its via Appia; its proconsuls, centurions, and legions all over the world as well as its bread and its circuses in the homeland, and its costly wars in periphery areas.

The Roman Empire rested on a classical model of imperial finance. Beneath a complex and nuanced pyramid of relationships was a foundation of tribute formed with the hard rock of brute force. America's Empire of Debt, on the other hand, stands not as a solid pyramid of trust, authority, and power but as a rickety slum of delusion, fraud, and misapprehension.

"My tax guy has been bugging me. . . . You know, real estate is where it is at." In June 2005, NBC quoted a young woman who had bought a second home at a Colorado resort. According to the report, more than a third of the houses sold in the previous 12 months were not primary residences, but second homes or investments.

Down at the bottom of the pyramid are petty agents spreading deceit and misinformation—such as the aforementioned "tax guy." You would think a young woman could trust her certified tax advisor to give her sound counsel. Instead, he urges her to speculate on the most bubbly property market in American history. Naturally, she went for it, aided no doubt by a whole industry of professional dissemblers. Press reports tell us that appraisers routinely stretch valuations to help close a deal. Mortgage lenders know perfectly well the appraisals are lies, but they wink at them with one eye while winking at the borrower's phony income declaration with the other. Again, according to the press reports, lenders no longer verify income claims. They have gone blind!

In California, house prices have raced so far ahead of incomes that barely one in ten buyers can afford the median house. Yet thanks to "creative finance," more houses are being sold than ever before.

Thus the foundation of the debt pyramid is laid down in a bed of mutual deceit and cupidity, and covered with another level of fabrications. Lenders do not stick around to see how the loans work out. Instead, they pretend the credits are good, and package the mortgages into convenient units so that investors can buy them. The financiers know damned well that many buyers can't really afford to pay for the houses they buy, but they see no point in mentioning it. Nor do the investors want to know. They're in on the scam, too. The smartest of them even have figured out how it works: The Fed holds down short-term rates below the inflation rate so that investors in long-term mortgage financing and buyers of U.S. Treasury obligations can make an easy profit.

Further up the steps of imperial debt are whole legions of analysts, economists, and full-time obfuscators whose role is to make us all believe six impossible things before breakfast and a dozen more before dinner. Economists at the Bureau of Labor Statistics do to numbers what guards at Guantanamo did to prisoners. They rough them up so badly, they are ready to say anything. In June 2005, it was reported that productivity was increasing at a 2.9 percent rate—the fastest pace in nine months. Productivity is supposed to measure output per unit of time. But the yardstick was bent by the government's statistical brownshirts, who said that if a computer this year can process information 10 times as fast as one produced last year, the worker who assembled it has multiplied his output 1,000 percent. This abuse of statistics is what allows Americans to deceive themselves about their own economy. It is healthy, they say. It is growing. It is stable.

Economists, commentators, and policymakers take up these distortions and add their own twists. It is obvious to anyone who bothers to think about it that an economy that spends more than it earns is in decline. But try to find an economist willing to say so! They've all become like rich notables in the time of Trajan, doing the emperor's work whether they are on his payroll or not. They will tell you the economy is expanding, but it is an expansion similar to what happens when a compulsive eater escapes from a fat farm. The longer he is on the loose, the worse off he becomes. It is an expansion of consumption, not wealth-producing, job-creating investment.

On the issue of the trade deficit, they will say what the senators and consuls want to hear, as Levey and Brown did in *Foreign Affairs* magazine: "The United States' current account deficit and foreign debt are not dire threats to its global position, as would-be Cassandras warn. U.S. power is firmly grounded on economic superiority and financial stability that will not end soon."[1] In fact, the story of international trade, circa 2005, is the most preposterous tale economists have ever heard. One nation buys things that it cannot afford and doesn't need with money it doesn't have. Another sells on credit to people who already cannot pay and then builds more factories to increase output.

Every level colludes with every other level to keep the flimflam going. On the banks of the Potomac, people of all classes, rank, and station are pleased to believe that all is well. And there, at the Federal Reserve headquarters, is another caste of loyal liars. Alan Greenspan and his fellow connivers not only urge citizens to mortgage their houses, buy SUVs, and commit other acts of wanton recklessness, they also control the nation's money and make sure that it plays along with the fraud.

From the center to the furthest garrisons on the periphery, from the lowest rank to the highest—everyone, everywhere willingly, happily, and proudly participates in one of the greatest deceits of all time. At the bottom of the empire are wage slaves squandering borrowed money on imported doodads. The plebes gamble on adjustable rate mortgages (ARMs). The patricians gamble on hedge funds that speculate on huge swaths of mortgage debt. Near the top are Fed economists urging them to do it! And at the very pinnacle is a chief executive, modeled after whom

. . . Augustus or Commodus? . . . who cuts taxes while increasing spending on bread, circuses, and peripheral wars.

The spectacle is breathtaking. And endlessly entertaining. We are humbled by the majesty of it. Everywhere we look, we see an exquisite but precarious balance between things that are equally and oppositely absurd.

On the one side of the globe—in the Anglo-Saxon countries in general, but the United States in particular—are the consumers. On the other side—principally in Asia—are the producers. One side makes, the other takes. One saves, the other borrows. One produces, the other consumes.

This is not the way it was meant to be. When America first stooped to Empire, she was a rising, robust, energetic, innovative young economy. And for the first six decades of her imperium—roughly from 1913 until 1977—she profited from her competitive position. Every country to which she was able to extend her pax dollarum became a customer. Her businesses made a profit.

But gradually, her commercial advantage faded and her industries aged. The very process of spreading the soft warmth of her protection over the earth seemed to make it more fertile. Tough, weedy competitors sprouted all over the periphery of the empire—first in Europe, then in Japan, and later, throughout Asia, even areas she had never been able to dominate.

By the early twenty-first century, the costs of maintaining her role as the world's only superpower, and its only imperial power, had risen in excess of 5 percent of her GDP, or $558 billion per year. Not only had she never figured out a good way to charge for providing the world with order, now order was working against her. The periphery economies grew faster. They had newer and better industries. They had higher savings levels and much lower labor rates. They had few of the costs of bread or circuses and none of the costs of policing the empire. They were freer, lighter, faster. Every day, the competitors took more of America's business, assets, and money. If the empire were an operating business, accountants would say it was losing money.

The empire no longer pays because the entire Western world—including Japan—has lost its competitive edge. Globalization of the pax dollarum era served the United States well after World War II. America was the world's leading exporter. But Europe also thrived in the 30 years after the war—*les trente glorieuses,* as the French call them. Then, in the 1980s, the Japanese took over as the leading economy of the advanced world.

And now, the pax wrought by the American empire works against America. Asian factories are newer and more modern. Asian workers are younger and cheaper. Now, every business day that passes, the Asians grab a little more of the U.S. market. And every business day puts Americans $2 billion further beholden to its mostly-Asian creditors.

"GM plans to cut 25,000 jobs in the U.S." The headline appeared on the front page of the *International Herald Tribune* in mid-June 2005. Elsewhere in the paper was a status report explaining that China's Chery Automobiles plans to begin exporting the first of 250,000 Chery Crossovers to the United States in 2007. For every job lost by America's preeminent industrial company, China was planning to export 10 new cars.

It was not just manufacturing that was moving to periphery states. The advent of high-speed, inexpensive communications, along with cheap computing power, has allowed Asians to compete in service sectors as well. Anything that can be digitized can be globalized—architecture, law, accounting, administration, data processing of all sorts, call centers, record keeping, marketing, publishing, finance, and so forth.

What is left for the developed economies? What could they do? Here is where European and Anglo-Saxon economies part company. The Europeans emphasize high value-added products such as luxury goods and precision tools. They cling rigidly to the wisdom of the old economists, refusing to expand consumer credit and refusing to use massive doses of fiscal stimuli to increase overall demand. House prices rise sharply in Paris, Madrid, and Rome. But there have been few signs of speculation. Houses are not refinanced readily. They are not "flipped." There is little creative finance. Nor has there been a big run-up in consumer debt, or a big run-down in savings rates. Credit cards are still comparatively rare. Unemployment is high, for Europe's policy managers have tolerated neither marginal jobs nor marginal credits. Europe is rigid and dull, economically, but relatively solid, with a positive balance of trade.

The Anglo-Saxon countries took a different route. During a time when the Bank of England has regularly moved interest rates up and down to deal with changes in economic conditions, the ECB sat on its hands.

The general consensus was that Europe would have been better off if it had acted a bit more like the Anglo-Saxons, by manipulating interest rates to encourage consumer debt. American economists imagined themselves carefully analyzing the data and coming to a logical conclusion. What they did not realize was that their numbers, conclusions, and views of the world had become nothing more than stones in the immense pyramid of *consuetude fraudium* of the advanced empire.

The numbers were frauds. If you were to look at the percentages fairly, the European economy actually looked no worse than its Anglo-Saxon competitor—with a similar rate of growth, higher unemployment, but better productivity and less debt.

As the Anglo-Saxon economies lost their competitive edge in manufacturing, they tried to make up for it by encouraging consumption. This is the biggest fraud of all. At first, higher consumption feels good. It is like burning the furniture to keep warm; it feels good for a moment. But the sense of well-being is extremely short-lived. When people borrow and spend, they feel as though they are getting richer—especially when their houses are rising in price. The increased consumption even shows up, indirectly, in the GDP figures as growth. But you don't really become wealthier by consuming. You become wealthier by making things you can sell to others—at a profit. The point is obvious but, at this stage of imperial finance, it was inconvenient.

The homeland's losses—measured by a negative balance of trade—began in the mid-1970s. Less than 30 years later, both government and consumers were running up debts at an alarming rate. What else could they do? The only way Americans could continue their imperial role—which meant more to them than ever, since it was now the only source of national pride left to them—was to borrow (see Figures 10.1 and 10.2).

The global economic system in the pax dollarium era was perfectly balanced. For every credit in Asia, there was an equal and opposite debit in the United States. And for every dollar's worth of demand from the United States, there was a dollar's worth of supply already waiting in a container in Hong Kong.

But while the imperial finance system was flawless, its perfections were devastating.

For the moment, in mid-2005, Americans salute their imperial standards. They gratefully paste the flag to their car windows, their jackets, their hats, their beer mugs, their shirts, and even their underwear (never once in Europe have we seen anyone with a national flag anywhere except at a parade or a public building). Americans are proud of their empire—and should be. Without it, they could never have gotten so far in debt. What central banker would fill his vault with Argentine pesos or

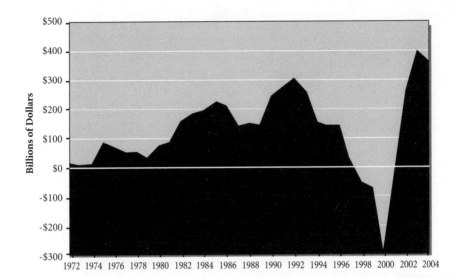

Figure 10.1 New Borrowing by Federal Government
The homeland's losses—measured by a negative balance of trade—began in the mid-1970s. Less than 30 years later, both the government and consumers were running up debts at an alarming rate. The only way American's could continue their imperial role was to borrow.
Source: Federal Reserve.

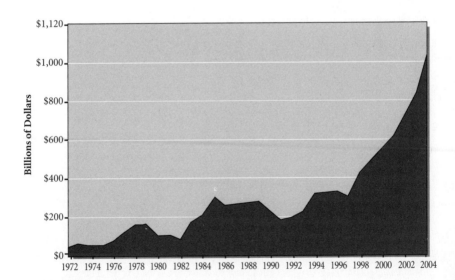

Figure 10.2 New Borrowing by Private Households
Source: Federal Reserve.

Zimbabwe dollars? What drug dealer or arms seller would want Polish zlotys in payment? What insurance company would want to buy Bolivian or Kyrgzstan bonds to cover its long-dated liabilities? The dollar has not been convertible into gold for 34 years. Yet, people still take it as though it were as good as the yellow metal—only better. Ultimately, lending money to a foreign government is a bet that the government will put the squeeze on its own citizens to make sure you get paid. The United States doesn't even have to squeeze. When one foreign loan comes due, other foreigners practically line up to refinance it; it is as if they were drinks to a street bum, just to gawk and wonder when he might pass out.

HOW THE PUBLIC DEBT INCREASED

"Since Prime Minister Sir Robert Walpole's introduction of the funding system in England during the 1720s," writes H. A. Scott Trask for the Mises Institute, "the secret was out that government debt need never be repaid. . . . Walpole's system proved its worth in financing British overseas expansion and imperial wars in the eighteenth and nineteenth centuries. The government could now maintain a huge peacetime naval and military establishment, readily fund new wars, and need not retrench afterward. The British Empire was built on more than the blood of its soldiers and sailors; it was built on debt."[2]

The new system was slow to catch on in America. Jefferson was against it. In 1789, in a letter to James Madison, he wondered whether "one generation of men has a right to bind another." His answer was "no." "The earth belongs in usufruct to the living," he concluded. "No generation can contract debts greater than may be paid during the course of its own existence."[3]

An intergenerational debt is an odd thing. Say a man buys a house. He may leave the house to his children, with a mortgage owing. The children were not party to the mortgage contract, but they take the bequest in good grace.

The house may have a mortgage or it may need a new roof. A gift is a gift, encumbered or not. If it is too heavily burdened with debt, they could simply turn it down; they never made a deal with the mortgage company and are under no obligation to pay it.

Suppose it is credit card debt. Say the man used the money to take a trip around the world. But the trip wore him out; no sooner does he return home than he collapses of a heart attack. Are the children under any obligation to pay the credit card bills? Not at all.

But comes now, "public" debt. What kind of strange beast is this? One generation consumes. It then hands the next generation the bill. The younger generation never agreed to the terms of the indebtedness. They are party to a contract—and on the wrong end of it, we might add—that they never made. Indentured servants only had to work seven years to pay off their indenture. This new generation, on the other hand, will have to work their entire lives.

Such arrangements are often excused as part of the "social contract." But what kind of contract allows one person to take the benefits while sticking the costs to someone else?

But dead men don't talk, and the unborn don't vote. Politicians in America—just as those in Britain, Italy, and Germany—gradually came to see that they could get the benefits of spending money in the present, while passing on the debts to the next administration and the next generation. Then, as now, war provided cover for excess spending. First, there were the debts from the American Revolution, which were paid down quickly. Then came the War of 1812, Mexican War, and the War between the States. Each time, spending was increased, debts were taken on, and then, after the war, the debt was paid down, or paid off completely.

World War I saw federal debt explode from $3 billion to $26 billion. Presidents Harding and Hoover paid it down to $16 billion. But then came the Great Depression, Roosevelt, and World War II. By 1945, federal debt had reached $260 billion. Then came something new. The war did not end. It continued as the Cold War, and instead of the debt being paid down, it was increased.

Under Ronald Reagan, America's debt seemed on course for Mars. Less than $1 trillion in 1980, it soared to $2.7 trillion before Reagan left office. One might have expected some relief after the Cold War was over. But the habit of debt is hard to break. By the time George W. Bush took office, the debt had risen to $5.7 trillion.

Mr. Bush, a conservative, might have seized the opportunity to pay down the debt. The nation was at peace and expected huge budget surpluses. He promised as much when he stood before a joint session of Congress in 2001 and announced his budget.

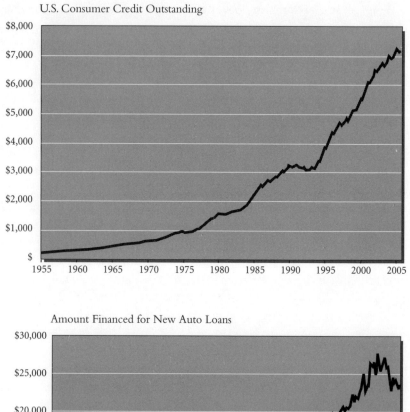

U.S. Consumer Credit Outstanding

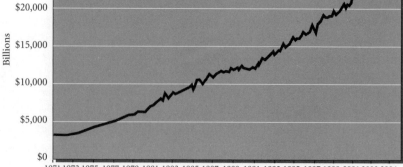

Amount Financed for New Auto Loans

Figure 10.3 **U.S. Consumer Credit Outstanding and Amount Financed for New Auto Loans**
Source: Federal Reserve.

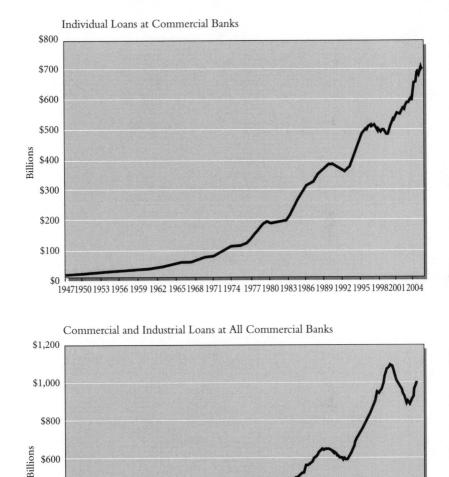

Individual Loans at Commercial Banks

Commercial and Industrial Loans at All Commercial Banks

Figure 10.4 **Individual Loans at Commercial Banks and Commercial and Industrial Loans at All Commercial Banks**

As the empire matured, Americans embraced new ideas and attitudes. People switched their attention from assets to cash flow, from balance sheets to monthly statements, from building long-term wealth, to paycheck to paycheck financing, from saving to spending and from "just in case" to "just in time."
Source: Federal Reserve.

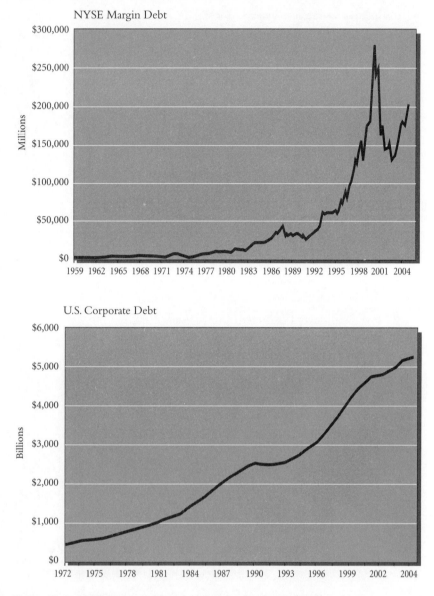

Figure 10.5 **NYSE Margin Debt and U.S. Corporate Debt**
Sources: New York Stock Exchange and Statistics Bureau (Japan).

Home Mortgages Outstanding

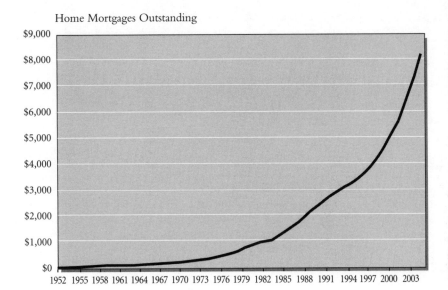

Real Estate Loans at All Commercial Banks

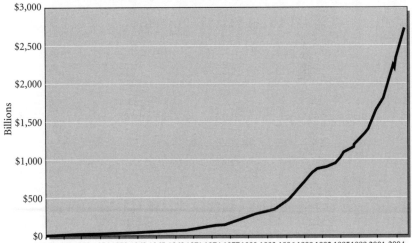

Figure 10.6 **Home Mortgages Outstanding and Real Estate Loans at All Commercial Banks**

Consistent with speculative bubbles throughout history, the great Tech Wreck on Wall Street circa AD 2000—which was itself financed by corporate borrowing—was followed by a dramatic rise in speculation on real estate . . . also, on a borrowed dime.

Source: Federal Reserve.

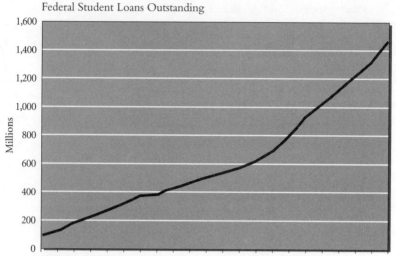

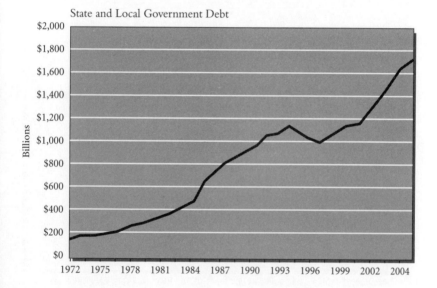

Figure 10.7 **Federal Student Loans Outstanding and State and Local Government Debt**
Sources: New York Stock Exchange and Federal Reserve.

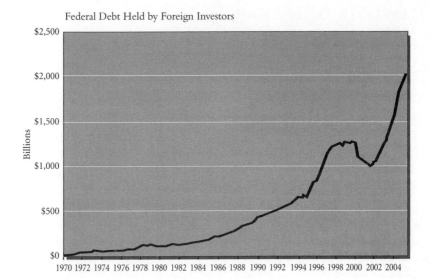

Federal Debt Held by Foreign Investors

Figure 10.8   **Federal Debt Held by Foreigners**
As the gusts of credit, debt, borrowing, and spending blew across the nation, very few of the old attitudes and institutions were left standing. By the early twenty-first century Americans borrowed money for everything they wanted: They borrowed to go to school, to drive in late model SUVs, to finance new football stadiums, and to convert aging industrial districts into shopping meccas. How was all this borrowing made possible? It was made possible by the kindness of strangers.
Source: U.S. Treasury Department.

"That night," Paul O'Neill tells us in the book by Ron Suskind, *The Price of Loyalty,* "Bush stood before the nation and said something that knowledgeable people in the U.S. government knew to be false."[4]

Generations of Republicans had promised balanced budgets. Only war had permitted them to continue running up debt. With no war, the Republicans squirmed. But since 1917, wars had always seemed to come along just when they were needed, and now they included a remarkable event: 9/11. All of a sudden, another strange war was announced against an enemy no one could find on a map—a *War on Terror.* Now, the war, the spending, and the debts could go on forever.

In the following 24 months, the Bush administration added more debt to the nation than had been built up in the first 200 years of its existence.

MAESTRO'S PERFORMANCE

In February 2005, Alan Greenspan gave a speech in honor of the first modern economist—Adam Smith. The Fed chairman journeyed to Fife College, in Kirkcaldy, Fife, Scotland, where Smith was born in 1723. There, he commented on Smith's work: "Most of Smith's free market paradigm remains applicable to this day," said he.[5]

In particular, the world seems to have discovered that independent buyers and sellers are better at delivering the goods than government planners.

This would have come as a shock to George Orwell. Writing at the beginning of World War II, Orwell expressed the belief of millions: "I began this book to the tune of German bombs. . . . What this war has demonstrated is that private capitalism—that is, an economic system in which land, factories, mines and transports are owned privately and operated solely for profit—does not work. It cannot deliver the goods."[6]

Orwell was wrong. Capitalism delivered the goods better than socialism, a fact that even nearsighted journalists and central bankers were eventually able to see. But even after the fall of the Berlin Wall, continued America's most celebrated central banker, there was "no eulogy for central planning."

Adam Smith had proposed a useful metaphor to help explain how a system of private, individual decision making—which must have looked chaotic to a top-down observer—actually functioned to the betterment of all. A rise in the price of pigs, for example, sends a signal to the hog raisers to produce more. Thus, the market is guided by an "invisible hand" to produce exactly as much of a thing as people really want and can really afford.

Quick-witted readers will already be gurgling with indignation. Markets work best without the heavy hand of regulation, Greenspan acknowledged. But he seemed to exempt, conveniently, the credit markets. The maestro's speech hit a false note; rather like President Bush's approach to evangelical democracy, it seemed to miss the point. Instead of letting lenders of credit and demanders of it be guided by an "invisible hand," for years the Fed chief's boney paws have drawn them together. Mr. Greenspan's "Open Market Committee," not the open market, has largely determined the rate at which lenders will lend, short term, and at which borrowers will borrow.

Why is it that what is good for the goose of lumber markets, stock markets, grain markets, laptop computer markets, and almost every other market under Heaven is not good enough for the gander of the credit market? The answer is not one of logic, but of convenience. Most of the time, political leaders prefer easier credit terms than buyers and sellers would determine on their own. In setting its key rate, the Open Market Committee is likely to set a rate that is to the politicians' liking.

New Yorker columnist James Surowiecki's book, *The Wisdom of Crowds,*[7] makes the point that two heads are better than one. Groups of people can be smarter than individuals. A market, theoretically, can do a better job of finding the right price for a thing. A market is supposed to aggregate the private opinions and independent judgments of thousands of individuals. Generally it succeeds. But on occasion, the market slips into crowd-like behavior—whipped to excess by the financial media or the financial industry.

And sometimes, the whole market is deceived by its own central planners. Rather than allow lenders and borrowers to decide for themselves what rates they would accept, the central planners at the U.S. Federal Reserve decided for them. How they can know exactly what lending rate such a large and infinitely complex economy needs has never been explained. But, historically, from the Fed's lowest rate to its highest, there are about 1200 basis points. On those odds alone, they have almost certainly chosen the wrong one. There are times—indeed most of the time—when political leaders prefer easier credit terms than buyers and sellers determine on their own. In setting its key rate, the Open Market Committee tends to set a rate much more to the politicians' liking than the one offered by Mr. Market. A lower rate, that is. But as Schumpeter points out, any stimulus in excess of actual savings is a fraud.

This artificially low rate gives the illusion that there is more money available than there really is. Hardly anyone ever complains. Consumers feel they have more money to spend than they really have. Producers sense a demand that really isn't there. Undeserving politicians get reelected. And conniving central bankers are reappointed.

The "information content" of the Fed's low rate misleads everyone. They proceed happily on the long, slow process of ruining themselves, unaware that they are responding to an imposter. Only much later does the deception become a problem.

Friedrich Hayek explains:

> The continuous injection of additional amounts of money at points of
> the economic system where it creates a temporary demand, which must

cease when the increase of money stops or slows down, together with
the expectation of a continuing rise in prices, draws labor and other resources into employments which can last only so long as the increase of
the quantity of money continues at the same rate—or perhaps even
only so long as it continues to accelerate at a given rate . . . would rapidly lead to a disorganization of all economic activity.[8]

The way it works is simple: An economy is geared to produce for
real demand.

Or it is misled by artificially low interest rates to produce for a level of
demand that doesn't exist. The deceit can go on for a long time. But,
eventually, some form of adjustment must take place—usually a recession
restores order by reducing both production and consumption. Generally,
the correction is equal to the deception that preceded it.

But the Bank of Alan Greenspan thinks it can avoid these periodic
bouts of sanity. Fed Governor Ben Bernanke proposed "global cooperation"
in a November 21, 2002, speech. Then, in May 2003, he went to Japan urging concerted action. The Fed was prepared to sacrifice the solvency of
American consumers, he told the Japanese. Tax cuts and low interest rates
could still induce them to buy things they didn't need with money they
didn't have. But Japan had to help hold down U.S. interest rates—by buying up dollars and dollar-denominated assets, notably U.S. Treasury bonds.

This is what happened next, according to Richard Duncan: "In 2003,
and the first quarter of 2004, Japan carried out a remarkable experiment in
monetary policy—remarkable in the impact it had on the global economy and
equally remarkable in that it went almost entirely unnoticed in the financial
press. Over those 15 months, monetary authorities in Japan created ¥35 trillion. To put that into perspective, ¥35 trillion is approximately 1 percent of
the world's annual economic output. It is roughly the size of Japan's annual
tax revenue base or nearly as large as the loan book of UFJ, one of Japan's four
largest banks. ¥35 trillion amounts to the equivalent of $2,500 for every
person in Japan and, in fact, would amount to $50 per person if distributed
equally among the entire population of the planet. In short, it was money
creation on a scale never before attempted during peacetime."[9]

Why did the Japanese create so much money? Because they needed
to buy from their citizens the dollars they had accumulated by selling
things to Americans. Had they not done so their currency would have
gone up—making their products less competitive on the U.S. market.

Had they not done so, the dollar would have fallen much further against other currencies. Had they not done so, the Japanese would not have had the dollars to buy U.S. Treasury bonds. And had they not bought so many of them, U.S. interest rates would have risen, consumers would have had less money to spend, and probably the whole world would have had an economic crisis.

"Intentionally or otherwise," Duncan continues, "by creating and lending the equivalent of $320 billion to the United States, the Bank of Japan and the Japanese Ministry of Finance counteracted a private sector run on the dollar and, at the same time, financed the U.S. tax cuts that reflated the global economy, all this while holding U.S. long bond yields down near historically low levels.

"In 2004, the global economy grew at the fastest rate in 30 years. Money creation by the Bank of Japan on an unprecedented scale was perhaps the most important factor responsible for that growth. In fact, ¥35 trillion could have made the difference between global reflation and global deflation. How odd that it went unnoticed."[10]

FLIGHT TO HAZARD

As the empire matured, Americans developed new ideas and attitudes to go with it. We have already shown how they took on the beliefs of an imperial race, ready to mind everyone's business but their own. Financially, their beliefs changed, too; people switched their attention from assets to cash flow, from balance sheets to monthly operating statements, from long-term wealth-building to paycheck-to-paycheck financing, from saving to spending, and from "just in case" to "just in time."

It was a flight to hazard that became more hazardous with every takeoff and landing.

It was as if a strange new trade wind had been stirred up in the Pacific and blew across the country. Year after year, it blew stronger, until practically every tree and street sign, all across the country, leaned toward empire. Gradually, all of America's institutions and attitudes were bent by the new wind.

The federal government ran a fairly tight ship until the Johnson and Reagan years, and then the wind caught it. Soon, it was under full sail, flying toward record deficits and unheard-of debts.

The Federal Reserve braced itself under the iron hand of Paul Volcker (1981–1987). Then, it was Alan Greenspan's turn at the helm. Soon, the Fed was not only bent over along with everyone else, but actually flapping away itself—increasing the blow.

Consumers had a hard time keeping their feet on the ground. Every time they ventured outdoors, the strong wind pushed them toward more and more dangerous debt. Where once they considered a heavy mortgage a risky thing, they came to see it as no risk at all. The gush of air picked up their houses and lightened the load. As interest rates dropped, they couldn't wait to refinance and then refinance again, each time "taking out" a little more equity.

The wind bent consumers' attitudes toward debt and twisted the lending industry into such comely new forms: How could they resist?

In the spring of 2005, *Grant's Interest Rate Observer* paused to observe something unusual: Rarer even than a banker with a heart, it had discovered one with a brain.

Mr. Karl B. Hill is a banker from a small town that must be in a gully; the winds of modern debt-financing didn't seem to reach it.

"We feel the U.S. is in trouble, with major weaknesses and unpleasantness ahead," he says. "Whether inflation or deflation lies ahead, or some kind of both, we believe many borrowers will be unable to repay their loans as scheduled." None of the reasons Mr. Hill mentions are original: little savings, little investment in productive industry (much of what is invested goes into short-lived software), and the illusion of wealth that accompanies rising house prices. With little real investment in new factories or new methods of production, few good-paying new jobs are created. In such an economy, a banker without a brain walks lightly and lends heavily. For the president of Monroe County Bank, on the other hand, you get the impression that every step toward a new loan is uphill. He lends almost reluctantly, wondering how borrowers will be able to repay.

While other bankers were moving more and more of their money into real estate loans, Mr. Hill was warily reducing his bank's exposure—especially to residential property. Home mortgages were less than a third of commercial bank loans in 1980. Now they are nearly two-thirds. Other bankers will lend to anyone who can sign his name, provided he is buying a house. Mr. Hill wants to know how the borrower will be able to pay back his loan if—heaven forfend—his house doesn't go up in price by 20 percent this year.

These were not the sort of practices that would make Mr. Hill's establishment the "Bank of the Year" or get his photo on the cover of *Business Week*. Not in the year 2005. His is not the Bank of the Present. It may be the Bank of the Past. That it may also be the Bank of the Future is the guess that keeps us going.

Not only is the Monroe County Bank out of step with most of today's lending institutions, it seems to be marching in the opposite direction—back to the future. We have never met the man or visited his office in Forsyth, Georgia. But were we to enter the bank, we would expect to find a man behind an old-fashioned ledger at an oak desk . . . and a spittoon in the corner. Were we to ask for a loan, we would expect a disapproving look, followed by a polite, but severe inquiry into our personal finances. No, these are not the methods of the typical banker in the eighteenth year of Alan Greenspan's reign at the Federal Reserve System.

Nor is Mr. Hill's approach to the credit industry particularly profitable. He admits he would earn more money by doing what other bankers do. Most bankers borrow short and lend long. As long as long rates are higher than short rates—and he does his math right—he will make money. Mr. Hill's approach, borrowing long and lending short, is a curiosity in the banking industry. It forgoes current profits, in favor of a more solid balance sheet. And when long rates rise, which they will do, sooner or later—both Mr. Hill and your authors are sure of it—Mr. Hill will have the last laugh. Compared with most bankers, it will be far easier for him to collect his credits and pay his liabilities.

Stocks are buoyed up or thrown down as the market's view of the firm's value changes. Profit-making enterprises' value depends on how much profit they make, a figure subject to both change and speculation. But the value of a house changes little over time. Year after year, it is the same roof, the same walls, the same cozy warmth and convenience. The value that an owner-occupied house gives cannot be amended, jiggled, bent, written down, cooked up, or restated. No clever CFO can smooth its earnings. No fast-talking promoter can hype up next year's sales. It is what it appears to be and nothing more: home sweet home.

But with the complicity of the entire credit industry, except for one bank in Forsyth, Georgia, Americans have come to believe that the very same dull and lifeless bricks they know so well—along with the fading paint, the stained carpets, the leaking taps, and cracking driveways—have a near-magical quality; they can make them rich. They believe that the house is an "investment," different from stocks only in that it is safer and more profitable. They know from their own, direct experience that the house is not a profit center, but a cost center. Each month, the place must be maintained. Money must be spent on it. They also know that—other than the aforementioned service the house renders to its occupants—there is no output. There is nothing that comes out the backdoor that can be sold. As a business, it is a losing proposition, and they know it. It produces nothing; no revenues are realized. No profits are earned.

And yet, the homeowner also believes that he can go to friendly lenders from time to time and "take out" cash—as if the place had been accumulating earnings. What he is taking out, he believes, is merely surplus equity. He figures that if last year he had, say, $200,000 worth of house, this year he must have $250,000 worth of house. He can "take out" the $50,000 extra and spend it—just as if the house had earned $50,000 in profit—and still have his $200,000 worth of house.

He does not ask himself where that $50,000 came from. He does not find it at all extraordinary that an item he knows to be a cost center could also produce more in "profits" each year than he earns in income! Nor does he wonder how there could be so much untapped value locked up in his house, when he knows full well that he and his family use every room.

Mr. Karl B. Hill considers this wealth an illusion, as we do. He believes it will lead to big problems among both borrowers and lenders. To avoid the big problems personally, Mr. Hill, like Warren Buffett, lives in the same house he bought nearly 40 years ago.

Mr. Hill requires prospective borrowers to show him their finances without considering the house they live in. Whatever value there is in the lived-in house, he says, is "inactive." It doesn't really earn any money for you; if you were to sell it, you would just have to buy another one. And you can't ship it to China to pay for your flat-screen TVs or to Japan to pay for your SUV.

It is not that Mr. Hill is necessarily opposed to the great empire; he just doesn't seem to care. But a view more typical of the average lender, and average economist, was expressed by a pair of economists, mentioned briefly earlier, writing in the *International Herald Tribune*. Mr. David H. Levey was formerly managing director of Moody's Sovereign Ratings Service. Stuart S. Brown is a professor of economics and international relations at Syracuse University. The two argued that "U.S. Hegemony Has a Strong Foundation." The two are talking big. They are talking macro-economics, with no trace of Mr. Hill's modest insights, or his private knowledge, or his 37 years of experience lending money, or the keen and immediate attention of having his own money at stake.

What Levey and Brown were trying to tell us is that we have nothing to worry about. Yes, it is true that we Americans spend 6 percent more every day than we earn. Yes, $11.5 trillion worth of U.S. assets are in foreign hands and our net international investment position has gone negative at more than 3 trillion. And yes, it is true that we save nearly nothing. But we can still feel good about ourselves, they say.

The numbers obscure "the United States' institutional, technological and demographic advantages," they say. What are those advantages? The two never quite said. But what could they say? Other countries have different institutions. Others have different demographics. Others use different technologies. Who knows which are an advantage and which are a hindrance? You only know—and then, only by inference—after the fact. At the height of its bubble in 1989, it was widely presumed that Japan had all the advantages. Hardly a single issue of the business press failed to mention them. Now, 15 years and a major slump later, Japan seems to have all the disadvantages, while the advantages somehow crossed the Bering Strait into North America.

Today, the mainstream press tells us how dynamic, flexible, and open the U.S. economy is. At the end of their article, Messrs. Levey and Brown told us that the only real threat is that "protectionism and isolationism at home will put an end to the dynamism, openness and flexibility that power the U.S."[11]

We can't help but remember French military policy after the Franco-Prussian War. Led by Colonel Grandmaison, the French allowed words to replace tactics and strategy. *Élan* was the word. It meant "spirit" or "force of will." When World War I began, the French attacked on horseback, swords glittering. What élan! What style! What blockheads. The German machine guns opened up and soon the ground was covered by handsome young soldiers. Élan proved great for poets but bad for France's military.

And now, Americans put on their own gaudy tunics—so proud of their "dynamism," their "flexibility," their "openness." Who cares that they spend more than they can afford? Who worries that we have no savings and now depend on the kindness of strangers to maintain our standards of living? Who realizes that the Chinese or Japanese could bring the U.S. economy to its knees with a single word?

But what about our houses? Aren't we rich? So what if the Chinese and Japanese sell our bonds, we still have our houses!

The two economists note that "when you include capital gains, 401(k) retirement plans, and home values, U.S. domestic saving is around 20 percent of GDP, the same as in most other developed nations."[12]

They should talk to Mr. Hill. They don't seem to realize that home values are "inactive." We have yet to hear of a factory built with increases in house prices. We have yet to see a debt paid from a rising house price—without an equal debt arising somewhere else.

"Much of our meager savings and massive borrowing has gone into housing," says the Monroe County banker. "How convenient it would be now if mansions and subdivisions could be exported, to improve our foreign trade balance. Since they cannot be exported, perhaps the foreigners who own our massive debts can be repaid by coming to live in our Mc-Mansions, with homeowners serving as houseboys and house maids to the visiting Japanese and Chinese owners of our debt."

The United States economy is growing, says Paul Volcker, "on the savings of poor people." Or, as Marshall Auerback puts it, we have become a "Blanche Dubois" economy—we have delusions of grandeur, and yet, we are completely dependent on the kindness of strangers just to keep going. Poor people make things, and then finance the consumption of them by rich people.

Americans deceive themselves with the fanciful notion that people who live in hovels, eat disgusting animals, and earn less than $\frac{1}{20}$ as much per hour will be willing to finance our new houses and new wars forever. Why? Our economy is so "dynamic" . . . so "flexible" . . . so "open"—the poor peasants can't resist!

FRUGAL TO A FAULT

As the gusts of credit, debt, borrowing, and spending blew across the nation, very few of the old attitudes and institutions were left standing. Apart from Karl B. Hill and a few others, lenders stopped worrying about the quality of their borrowers. Savings and loan businesses might as well have dropped the word *savings* from their names. And calling lenders *thrifts* was practically a lie; the whole industry bent to a new task—to load up consumers with as much debt as possible.

There was a time when thrift was a virtue. "A penny saved is a penny earned," dead people whisper. Accountants with sharp pencils even noticed that a penny saved was more than a penny earned, 40 to 50 percent more; it was not subject to state, local, and federal income taxes.

But in America, circa 2005, thrift came to be regarded no longer as a virtue, but as a mental disorder.

Evidence came from a magazine spotted on Long Island, again through the ever-observant *Grant's Interest Rate Observer.* The publication, entitled *Real Simple,* told the story of a poor woman named Morning Naughton, 34 years old in the flesh, hundreds of years old in spirit.

If the phone didn't ring at an expensive jewelry store, it was Ms. Naughton who wasn't calling. If no one was admiring the new SUVs in a North Carolina showroom, it was Ms. Naughton who stayed at home. If you were to check the credit card records for sales of expensive vacations, fancy hotel rooms, extravagant fur coats, or top restaurants, you would not find Ms. Naughton's name.

Alas, said *Real Simple,* the woman had a real problem; she was "frugal to a fault."

"She has never had credit card debt, she pays all her bills on time and she typically saves $500 each month—on a salary of about $30,000," we are told.

"Her husband, Jason Michaels . . . worries about her inability to indulge herself . . . or him." The plot thickens. "And he wonders if her scrimping sends the wrong message to their child." "I realize she can't help herself," says Jason. "But her obsession with saving can drive me nuts."

But never was there a problem under the bright sun of America that didn't have some sort of fraud creeping in the shadows behind it. Reading about Ms. Naughton, economists saw a threat; if other consumers were to do the same, the whole shebang would be in trouble. Psychologists, on the other hand, saw an opportunity; some would prepare 12-step programs to help overcome it. Others would offer drugs and counseling.

Both economists and psychologists can relax. If frugality is a disorder, it is too rare to worry about. The odds of coming down with it are as remote as integrity in public office. Besides, thrift—even if it were a disorder—is one that comes and goes. If people are saving too much, or too little, just wait; it will go away.

Ms. Naughton—through no fault of her own—tumbled into an un-usual situation. One generation creates; the next dissipates. One genera-tion earns; the next burns. One generation composes, the next disposes. Morning Naughton was merely born at the wrong time.

"In the 1970s," began a recent letter from a reader of our daily e-mail, the Daily Reckoning, "I recall seeing many people, children of the Depres-sion, ravaged by inflation. They remembered the 'bad times' and were loath to take on debt—even if it would have been prudent to borrow and pay back in cheaper dollars. In the face of rising prices, they would slam their wallets shut or buy used, rather than new—'I'd never pay that much for a new car!' They held their dollars, steadfastly refusing inflation hedges, and watched, even increased their dollar position, as the inflation storm ravaged their holdings."

"When Morning was 9," continues the *Real Simple* analysis, "her parents divorced, and she moved with her father to Cape Cod. Her dad did some construction work to make money, but he was an artist at heart. . . . She worked at a multitude of odd jobs, including baby sitting, to make money. At age 10, she opened her first savings account. At 13, she started paying all the bills by filling out the information and having her dad sign the checks. . . . 'My childhood left me with this extreme anxiety about parting with money. I always need a safety net.'"

She may be the only American on two legs who still worries about falling. But she can always try therapy. "Were it not for her husband and child, Morning . . . might not be motivated to change," *Real Simple* explains.

"After more than 20 years of belt-tightening, Morning knows she needs to relax. 'I don't want [my son] Spencer to grow up with the same money anxieties I have,' she says. 'Being so frugal has become a burden, and I want to change. But it's hard after a lifetime of being this way.'"

We wish her luck. But we offer advice: Don't change too much. Old habits might turn out to be useful. Who knows? Frugality could make a comeback. It always does.

THE OWNERSHIP SOCIETY

A great empire can be viewed as a vast public spectacle. It begins with a bold crime, develops into a farce, with petty acts of tomfoolery and fraud along the way, and ends in shame, regret, and disaster.

The Medicare Drug Benefit program, enacted during Bush's first term, was meant to cost $400 billion during its first 10 years. Turns out, the official estimates included 2004 and 2005, that is, two years before the program existed. The real 10-year cost of the program floated through the news months later at $720 billion. Americans voted for their representatives in Congress and the White House; the politicians voted for the free drugs. Thus, was the divine right of the majority—the brute power of the many to tell the few what to do—purified by the ballot box. The polite forms of the old republic were respected. But the essential act was a sin and a crime. Why should some Americans get drugs at other Americans' expense? Is it not larceny on the part of one and complicity on the part of the other? And how will those "others" pay for it; are they not already on the hook for $44 trillion in unfunded federal obligations?

But now the scam is the law of the land.

George W. Bush wants to create an "ownership society." But it is a strange form of ownership. Much of what Americans believe they have a right to belongs to someone else. Their retirements and health benefits, for example, must be stolen from other people before they can be handed out. Even things they think they paid for are actually on the balance sheet of other people. More and more houses are really owned by mortgage finance companies. Cars are owned by GMAC and other auto financers. People expect to retire on the equity locked up in their houses. But they own less of their own houses than ever before; now, someone claims to own them, too—the lenders. And Social Security? A forensic accountant could pore over the books for a thousand years and never find a trace of the cash supposedly stashed away for Americans' retirement. It doesn't exist.

Mr. Bush says he wants to change that. He wants Americans to own their own retirement funds—with private accounts invested in stocks. The young have wised up to Social Security. There is no way they can get a decent return on investment in Social Security; they want out. The old are alarmed too; they're afraid that the something for nothing they've grown to expect will turn out to be more nothing than something. And the Bush administration wants votes from both groups. So, it does what you would expect; it deceives and dissembles.

It doesn't matter what we think about it. Empires—like history— have thoughts of their own, and a will toward their own end.

11

Modern Imperial Finance

A new piece of research from Princeton's Center for the study of the brain was reported in the press in April 2005.[1] Poking around, the scientists thought they found something new that would explain Americans' reluctance to save money.

Decisions are made in two parts of the brain, the researchers told us. The first part is the lateral prefrontal cortex. This is where advanced, logical thinking is supposed to happen, such as when a person decides which investment to make or which automobile offers the most value for the money. Deeper down in the gray matter is another decision center, the more primitive limbic system, where he actually decides which car to buy—usually the one that best suits his own prejudice. If he thinks he is a manly man, he buys a big American-made truck, or maybe a Hummer. If he prefers to think of himself as an intellectual, he goes for a foreign make, maybe an Audi or a Volkswagen. Behind the wheel of a German car, he feels at one with Hegel and Schopenhauer. Or, if he is a hip environmentalist, he will want to advertise that, too; in a sleek hybrid he will feel as smug as a teetotaler in a beer hall.

Researchers believe that the limbic system decides our likes and dislikes, and tells us how to react to immediate stimuli. When a dump truck cuts you off in traffic, the limbic system almost automatically wants to cock your right arm and middle finger in the traditional salute, before your lateral prefrontal cortex can warn you against the gesture.

In the upper part of the brain, Americans realize that they need to save for their retirement. But the limbic system insists on buying a new wide-screen TV instead. Though the researchers' report was circulated in the media as though it meant something, it left us only more puzzled than before. When did Americans acquire this limbic system, we wondered? Up until 1980, American savings rates were around 10 percent of incomes. Did some kind of evolutionary mutation occur in the early years of the Reagan administration?

And how come the Chinese don't seem to have the same problem? They are said to save 25 percent of their incomes, while we save less than 1 percent. Someone ought to pry open a Chinese skull and take a peek to verify this, but our guess is that the Chinese have limbic systems, too.

At least the scientists were wise enough to realize that not every thought that passes through the human brain makes any logical sense. The most powerful thoughts—strong enough to put the average American's retirement financing, and even his life, in jeopardy—are not logical at all, but instinctive, atavistic, and primordial.

GLOBALIZATION AND ITS DISCONTENTS

Two thousand years ago, St. Peter urged a crowd to "turn away from this lost generation." W. H. Auden spoke of the "low, dishonest decade," before the Great War. Could our own generation be low, dishonest, and lost? We have come to believe that things will last forever that couldn't possibly be true for even a minute. In the spring of 2005, Fed governor Ben Bernanke told Americans that they were doing the world a great favor by borrowing its surplus savings. The globe suffers from a "glut" of savings, said he. Americans counted on overseas savers to lend them money. The overseas savers, said Bernanke, counted even more on American spend-thrifts to borrow it.

The trouble with this analysis is not that it is flawed; but that it doesn't go quite far enough. The transaction Bernanke described is only half complete. It is like a man who gets dressed in the morning by putting on his shirt, but forgets his pants. He goes out on the street and looks ridiculous. Anyone who looks at Bernanke's half-dressed explanation wants to point and giggle. He has forgotten the essential part—how and when the lenders get repaid. The borrower only does the lender a favor when he is capable of repaying it on the agreed terms. If he cannot, the transaction becomes a big disappointment for the lender. Incomes in the United States are stagnant, or actually falling. We face more and better-organized competition than at any time since the beginning of the industrial revolution. The pool of people in the world willing to work hard for $3,000 a year is enormous. Given such competition, why would U.S. wages go up? And without higher wages, how will Americans ever pay back what they have borrowed?

But the world's financial plumbing has become so curiously put together that the oddest things have been mistaken for commonplace. We turn on the stove and champagne fizzes out. We open the faucet and it runs with Kentucky bourbon; the whole thing is strange, but it doesn't take long to learn to like it. The U.S. economy has been so strong for so long, people all over the world have come to accept its currency as though it were real money; they take it and ask nothing in return. In exchange for a shipment of TV sets, the Japanese take a wad of $100 bills and call it even. And here is another remarkable thing: The bills tend to stay overseas—where they are used to buy another form of U.S. paper, Treasury bonds. The United States can print as many $100 bills as it wants. So can it issue as many bonds and notes as it pleases. As long as people don't try to exchange them for other forms of wealth—all is well.

Rev. Al Sharpton is clean. He is not an economist. He is against outsourcing. That those qualifications did not cinch the 2004 Democratic presidential nomination for the man disappointed many people. That he had not been outsourced himself disappointed many others. For surely a clever fakir could be found in India who would be ready to make a public spectacle of himself at half the price. For that matter, all of Washington could be outsourced to the banks of the Ganges at a fraction of the price, but no one has yet suggested it.

Joined by Dennis Kucinich and Ralph Nader, Sharpton argued that the United States should disavow free trade altogether. As long as we are members of the World Trade Organization, explained Kucinich in a debate, we cannot "protect the jobs . . . this is the reason why we have outsourcing going on right now. We can't tax it. We can't put tariffs on it."[2]

To be nonpartisan about it, all the candidates' positions on outsourcing were preposterous or scurrilous. There were those who wanted to stop it. And those who saw no problem with it. Every opinion was fraudulent, delusional, or dumb. It was widely believed that the Chinese were stealing American jobs. Their factories hummed and belched smoke while U.S. factories went silent and sent up weeds in the parking lot.

The world has been globalized for a long time. An Englishman in 1910 could sit in his parlor off St. James Park at the center of what was then the world's greatest empire and drink tea that came all the way from Ceylon in cups that came all the way from China. Then, putting down his drink, he could pick up a Cuban cigar, put it to his lips . . . and perhaps sprinkle a few ashes on the carpet that he had bought in Egypt or the leather boots he had ordered from a shop down the street that sold Italian goods. He could buy stocks in New York as easily as he could pick up oranges from Spain or the latest French novels to make their way across the channel.

But globalization is not without its discontents. In 1910, England had been the world's number-one super-power and the world's greatest economy for two centuries. But global competition had recently edged the British out of the top spot. American GDP surpassed it at the turn of the century. Germany marched by a few years later. Relatively, England, that "weary Titan," was in decline, and the globalized economy that the British Empire helped create worked against it.

Still, why would the English complain? They lived well—perhaps better than anyone else. Even if they didn't, they thought they did. The rest of the world was content. People liked buying and selling. People in Europe liked globalization, because it brought them oranges in the wintertime. People in the warm latitudes liked it because now they had someone to buy their oranges. Even then, people spoke of the "annihilation of distance" and assumed that more miles would be destroyed in the years to come.

Globalization is nothing more than the extension of the division of labor across international boundaries. One of your authors passes much of his time in France. In his little village are the vestiges of a self-contained community. As recently as the end of World War II, almost everything people needed was produced right there. The farms grew wheat. Farmers raised vegetables, cows, pigs, and chickens. There was a machine shop, a forge, and a woodworking atelier. There still remain the *Versailles boxes,* in which lemon trees were planted. The boxes allowed the trees to be moved into heated space in the winter. Otherwise, they would freeze and die.

But as distance was annihilated, commerce in lemons was born. There was no longer any need to plant lemon trees in transportable wooden boxes when lemons could be shipped, quickly and cheaply, by the millions. One country can produce lemons. Another can produce machine gun cartridges. Individuals, towns, enterprises, regions, can divide up the labor, work more efficiently, and produce more things at lower cost. Everyone involved gets a little richer.

You'll recall our distinction, dear reader: There are only two ways to get what you want in life. You can do so honestly or dishonestly. You can get it by working for it or by stealing it. You can get it by trade and commerce or by force and fraud. You can get it by civilized methods or by barbaric ones. You can get rich by "economic means" or by "political means," as the great German sociologist Franz Oppenheimer put it. Globalization is merely an elaboration of the economic means of getting things. It requires civilized relationships for trade to work; people must get along with each other. They must rely on others—even other people in strange, faraway places—for important, maybe even essential items. They must also be able to count on the medium of exchange for trading goods and services. If they can't trust the imperial money, they will switch to something else.

The end of history has been announced several times. But it never seems to arrive. People always tend to think that what is will remain, that present trends will continue at least indefinitely, and perhaps forever. When the going is good, they tell themselves that the odds of anything going wrong are like the extreme edges of a bell curve—vanishingly small. But people badly "underestimate the persistence of history's traditional side, the rise and fall of empires, the rivalry of regimes, the disastrous or beneficent exploits of great men," wrote French historian Raymond Aron. That is to say, they tend to ignore the political means that shake things up and the rare "fat tail" events that make history interesting. Fat tails are those uncommon things that bunch up way out on the extremities of bell curves. They are things that shouldn't happen very often, but that tend to happen more often than people expect. That is why the tail ends of bell curves have little bulges in them—or *fat tails*.

Such a fat tail happened in 1914. A European war came after nearly 100 years of peace and progress. People thought the war could not happen. And if it did happen, they said, it would be short and sweet. As we have seen, they were wrong on both points. Again, in the 1930s, came another "fat tail" event—a great depression. And once again, globalization entered a shrinking phase.

Some experts think globalization can only flourish under the protection of an imperial armada, such as that of Great Britain in the nineteenth century or the United States in the twentieth. They are plainly wrong. Sometimes trade arrangements are elaborated. Sometimes they are trimmed back. The presence or absence of a sheltering empire is a factor, but certainly not an essential one. Switzerland has always enjoyed healthy trade with its neighbors, despite never being part of an imperial system. And even within an empire (such as within the Soviet Union), trade might be more difficult than trade between independent states.

Still, in the free world until 1989, and now almost everywhere, a pax dollarium might have greatly aided the cause of globalization throughout the second half of the twentieth century. America—and much of the rest of world—enjoyed a great boom after World War II. They were years of high growth, low inflation, and high employment. Tom Wolfe called it a "magic economy." Real incomes doubled from the late 1940s to the early 1970s. So did household income and consumption per capita. People were twice as rich because they produced twice as much as they. had a quarter century before. Productivity, or output per worker, rose 100 percent.

But in 1973—two years after Richard Nixon took the nation off the gold standard—the economy lost its magic. No one knows exactly why. But that didn't stop people from having opinions about it. Conservatives thought economic policy had been too socialistic; there were too many rules, too many taxes, and too many government expenses. Liberals thought there needed to be more controls; economists needed to manage the economy better, like the Japanese did. They also blamed free trade, which they saw as a threat to America's developed industries.

It took many years to achieve, but year after year, all the world's leading industrialized nations added laws, regulations, and taxes designed to make things better. And all these Wilsonian improvements cost money, reduced investment, or merely slowed down the economic machinery.

Taxes took resources out of the productive economy and moved them into government spending—which was essentially current consumption, with little future payoff. Taxes also discouraged investment by reducing real rates of return. This was especially important as inflation rates rose because taxes applied to the entire nominal gain, not the actual, real profit. An investment might double in nominal value. But if the value of the currency fell in half during the same period, the investor had not made a dime. Still, the Internal Revenue Service would tax his nominal profit as if it were real. Also, as the government began supplying more and more "bread" to those who needed it—welfare, social security, health benefits, job protections, entitlements—people saw less need to stock their own cupboards.

In September 2004, the personal savings rate among Americans was just 0.2 percent of disposable personal income. When Ronald Reagan first entered the White House, the rate was over 8 percent. "Gross national savings" (calculated by deducting capital imports from total domestic savings) were nearly 20 percent of GDP in 1980. They fell to 15.6 percent in 1989 and currently are less than 14 percent.

Net national savings are even worse. You get the net figure by subtracting depreciation of the capital stock. As the economy became more and more reliant on communications technology, the rate of depreciation increased. New computer systems and communications software just don't last as long as a new auto plant. Net national saving had been 8 percent of GDP in the 1970s. It averaged only 3.4 percent in the 1980s. By the 1990s, it was down to 3 percent. And in 2004, the number sank to 1.6 percent.

With no savings of its own, the country relied on foreigners to do the savings. But not only did the foreigners have to save, they had to be willing to buy U.S. financial assets—mainly Treasury bonds—denominated in U.S. dollars. If they grew tired of it, or wary of it, the dollar could collapse.

The odd thing about the spurt of globalization in the first five years of the twenty-first century was that it was so lopsided. The United States took, but it didn't give. It borrowed, but it didn't pay back. It bought, but it didn't sell. It imported, but it didn't export. The only reason foreigners put up with it is that they assumed their dollars would be as valuable in the future as they are now. They assumed that the trends of the previous 50 years would continue unchanged. They assumed that no terrorists would knock off an archduke, that they would never want for bread, and no fat tail would plop itself down in the currency markets.

Americans and their politicians preferred to see neither a glass half empty nor a glass half-full, but one that was full to the brim. Of so little interest and importance was the trade deficit that, at the nation's two political conventions, it was hardly mentioned. Everything was almost perfect, said the Republicans—and getting better and better every day. Everything was almost perfect, said the Democrats—but the Republicans were making a mess of it. "Outsourcing" was a problem, all agreed. The trade deficit, on the other hand, didn't matter.

Back when Paul Volcker was at the Fed, the central bank's role was to "take the punch bowl away" before the party got out of hand. Volcker did it at the end of the 1970s—sending Treasury yields above 15 percent. The party animals were so mad, they burnt an effigy of Volcker on the Capitol steps. Still the Fed brought inflation under control and prepared the way for the boom of the 1980s and 1990s. But by 2005, the party had gotten so wild that people were dancing on tables and putting lampshades on their heads. And Ben Bernanke and Alan Greenspan were creeping over to the punch bowl with grins on their faces and bottles of gin in their hands.

TAKE IT AWAY, MAESTRO

In the spring of 2005, the American economy had been in "recovery" for over 37 months. It was an odd recovery. No one was quite sure what it was recovering from. There had been a recession in 2001 and 2002. But it was a curious recession. GDP growth went negative. Yet, consumer spending and credit continued to expand. If recessions were meant to correct the mistakes of the previous expansion, this one was a failure. Consumers should have spent less and increased savings. Then, after the recession was over, they should have had money to spend in the following expansion and a pent-up desire to buy what they had not bought during the recession.

The expansion was doomed from the beginning. Consumers had never stopped spending. So, when the economy turned around, they had saved no money. The only way they could continue spending was by borrowing more. The Fed helpfully dumped more alcohol in the bowl—lowering rates to make it easy for them. But by this time, the whole economy had become so woozy that the extra consumer spending had much less positive effect on the real economy than had been hoped. Americans borrowed and spent. But, in the new globalized economy, much of what they bought came from Asia—particularly China—which could turn out consumer goods at a lower cost than the United States.

What America really needed was not a consumer binge, but a capital spending boom. It needed to invest in new factories, new plants, and new jobs. The jobs would have given consumers real new income, with which to buy more goods and services and sustain the expansion. But gross investment—which had averaged 18.8 percent in the pre-Reagan years—had begun dropping the year Reagan entered the White House. By 2004, it had fallen to 1.6 percent—even dipping below zero periodically. People were spending, but on consumption, not future production. The gewgaws and gadgets bought from China merely put Americans further into debt. Neither jobs nor incomes improved. Typically, at this stage of a recovery (June 2005), 10 million more new jobs should have been created. Likewise, incomes went up $300 billion less than they should have, based on the pattern of previous recoveries.

Many economists—including Alan Greenspan—maintained that the lack of jobs was a sign of something good happening. "Productivity," they said, "accounts for most job losses, not outsourcing."

"Over the long sweep of American generations and waves of economic change," explained the maestro, "we simply have not experienced a net drain of jobs to advancing technology or to other nations."[3] Could something be different this time? Could this be a kind of "new era" in American economic history? The answer we give is "yes" . . . but we will give it later. Here, our burden is more modest, and our proof comes more readily to hand. For here, we argue only that America's leading economic and political policymakers are either rascals or numskulls.

Major tops in the credit cycle seem to correspond with major bottoms in economic thinking. From high offices all over the nation come the explanations, excuses, rationales, and obiter dicta; we don't know whether they are corrupt or merely stupid. But when the guardians of the public financial mores begin urging people to acts of recklessness, we cannot help but notice. Buy more, says one Fed governor. Borrow more, says another. Don't worry about debt, interest rates, or the loss of jobs, says the captain of them all. It is as though the National Council of Bishops had come out with a public statement urging wife swapping. The experience may not be unpleasant, but it is unseemly of them to say so.

"Go out and buy an SUV," urged Fed governor Robert McTeer.[4] Seventeen million people heeded his call each year, from 2001 to 2005.

On February 23, 2004, the Fed chief urged Americans to switch from fixed rate mortgages to ARMs—mortgages with adjustable rates, which left them much more exposed to interest rate increases, at the very moment when the Fed was increasing them.

If anyone could be held directly and immediately responsible for the record level of America's foreign and domestic debts, it was Alan Greenspan. He had brought about a binge of borrowing by lowering interest rates down to Eisenhower-era levels. But spiking the punch was not enough; he was urging consumers to have another drink.

The Fed chairman had an uncanny way of arriving at ideas at a time when they would be of most benefit to his own career and of most danger to everyone else. To Greenspan, the conservative economist, the stock market looked "irrationally exuberant" in the mid-1990s, until a member of Congress pointed out to him that he would be better off keeping his mouth shut. A goldbug in the 1970s, Greenspan has now become the biggest purveyor of paper money the world has ever seen. Similarly, large federal deficits seemed at odds with his creed until it suited him to think otherwise. The new American empire needed easy money and almost unlimited credit: Alan Greenspan made sure they got it.

Markets make opinions, say old-time investors. Mr. Greenspan's opinions neatly corresponded with the market for his services. As the debts and deficits mounted up, Greenspan underwent an intellectual metamorphosis. An article in the *New York Times* explained:

> Many mainstream economists are worried about these trends, but Alan Greenspan, arguably the most powerful and influential economist in the land, is not as concerned:

> In speeches and testimony, Mr. Greenspan, chairman of the Federal Reserve Board, is piecing together a theory about debt that departs from traditional views and even from fears he has himself expressed in the past.

> In the 1990s, Mr. Greenspan implored President Bill Clinton to lower the budget deficit and tacitly condoned tax increases in doing so. Today, with the deficit heading toward a record of $500 billion, he warns more emphatically about the risks of raising taxes than about shortfalls over the next few years.

> Mr. Greenspan's thesis, which is not accepted by all traditional economists, is that increases in personal wealth and the growing sophistication of financial markets have allowed Americans—individually and as a nation—to borrow much more today than might have seemed manageable 20 years ago.

And here the article strikes gold:

> This view is good news for President Bush's re-election prospects. It increases the likelihood that the Federal Reserve will keep short-term interest rates low. And it could defuse Democratic criticism that the White House has added greatly to the nation's record indebtedness.[5]

Out of convenience, rather than ideology, Mr. Greenspan came to see goodness in all manner of credit. Since he became head of the Federal Reserve system, debt levels have risen from $28,892 for the average family in 1987 to $101,386 in 2005. Mortgage foreclosure rates, personal bankruptcies, and credit card delinquencies have risen steadily and are now at record levels. Mortgage debt rose $6.2 trillion during his tenure at the Fed. By January 2005, it had reached $8.5 trillion, or approximately $80,849 per household.[6]

But none of this seemed to bother the chief of America's central bank nor its chief politicians.

WHAT HATH ALAN WROUGHT?

For years, we have been working on Greenspan's obituary. As far as we know, the man is still in excellent health. We do not look forward to the event; we just don't want to be caught off guard. Maybe we could even rush out a quickie biography, explaining to the masses the meaning of Mr. Greenspan's life and work.

We see something in Alan Greenspan's career—his comportment, his betrayal of his old ideas, his pact with the Devil in Washington, and his attempt to hold off nature's revenge at least until he leaves the Fed—that is both entertaining and educational. It smacks of Greek tragedy without the boring monologues or bloody intrigues. Even the language used is Greek to most people. Though the Fed chairman speaks English, his words often need translation and historical annotation. Rarely does the maestro make a statement that is comprehensible to the ordinary mortal. So much the better, we guess. If the average fellow really knew what was being said, he would be alarmed. And we have no illusions. Whoever attempts to explain it to him will get no thanks; he might as well tell his teenage daughter what is in her hotdog.

Alan Greenspan is the most famous bureaucrat since Pontius Pilate. Like Pilate, he hesitated, but ultimately gave the mob what it wanted. Not blood, but bubbles. Greenspan's role in the empire is more than that of a Consul or a Proconsul. He is the Prefect. He is the quartermaster who makes sure the empire has the financial resources it needs to ruin itself.

We don't know how heaven will judge him. According to the central bankers' code, Greenspan has committed neither sin nor crime. He is seen as a paragon of virtue, not vice. Yet, as Talleyrand once remarked to Napoleon, "Sire, worse than a crime, you have committed an error."

When the winds of imperial debt-finance blew, Mr. Volcker planted his feet and stuck out his jaw. His successor, Mr. Greenspan, tumbled over. The Fed chairman's error was to offer more credit on easier terms to people who already had too much. During Greenspan's reign at the Fed, more new money and credit has been created than under all the rest of the Fed chiefs combined. Consumer debt rose to its highest level in history, the ratio of debt to income also rose higher than it has ever been. The effect was to inspire bubbles all over the world and to transform the United States from the world's largest creditor to its biggest debtor.

What the Greenspan Fed had accomplished was to put off a natural, cyclical correction and transmogrify an entire economy into a monstrous *economic* bubble. A bubble in stock prices may do little real economic damage. Eventually, the bubble pops and the phony money people thought they had disappears like a puff of marijuana smoke. There are winners and losers. But in the end, the economy is about where it began—unharmed and unhelped. The households are still there and still spending money as they did before. Only those who leveraged themselves too highly in the bubble years are in any trouble.

But in Greenspan's bubble economy, something awful happened. Householders were lured to take out the equity in their homes. They believed that the bubble in real estate prices created wealth that they could spend. Many did not hesitate. Mortgage debt ballooned in the early years of the twenty-first century—from about $6 trillion in 1999 to nearly $9 trillion at the end of 2004—increasing the average household's debt by $30,000. Americans still lived in more or less the same houses. But they owed far more on them.

We had given up all hope of ever getting an honest word out of the Fed chairman on this subject when, in early February 2005, the maestro slipped up. He gave the aforementioned speech in Scotland entitled "Current Account." Jet-lagged, his defenses down, the poor man seems to have committed truth.

"The growth of home mortgage debt has been the major contributor to the decline in the personal saving rate in the United States from almost six percent in 1993 to its current level of one percent," he admitted. Thus, did he bring up the subject. Then, he began a confession: The rapid growth in home mortgage debt over the past five years has been "driven largely by equity extraction,"[7] said the man most responsible for it. By this time, listeners were beginning to take notes. And pretty soon, even the dullest economist in the room was adding two plus two. Mr. Greenspan lowered lending rates far below where a free market in credit would have put them. With little to be gained by putting money in savings accounts and a lot to be gained by borrowing, households did what you would expect; they ceased saving and began borrowing. What did they borrow against? The rising value of their homes—"extracting equity," to use Mr. Greenspan's jargon. The Fed chairman had misled them into believing that the increases in house prices were the same as new, disposable wealth.

But the world's most famous and most revered economist didn't stop there. He must have had the audience on the edge of its chairs. He confessed not only to having done the thing but also to having his wits about him when he did it. This was no accident. No negligence. This was intentional.

"Approximately half of equity extraction shows up in additional household expenditures, reducing savings commensurately and thereby presumably contributing to the current account deficit. . . . The fall in U.S. interest rates since the early 1980s has supported home price increases," continued America's answer to Adam Smith.[8]

"Lacking in job creation and real wage growth," explained Stephen Roach, "private sector real wage and salary disbursements have increased a mere 4 percent over the first 37 months of this recovery—fully ten percentage points short of the average gains of more than 14 percent that occurred over the five preceding cyclical upturns. Yet consumers didn't flinch in the face of what in the past would have been a major impediment to spending. Spurred on by home equity extraction and Bush administration tax cuts, income-short households pushed the consumption share of U.S. GDP up to a record 71.1 percent in early 2003 (and still 70.7 percent in 4Q04)—an unprecedented breakout from the 67 percent norm that had prevailed over the 1975 to 2000 period . . ."[9]

Since the fall of the Berlin Wall, nearly everyone seems to agree that central planning is bad for an economy. The central planners, as any Economics 101 student can tell you, do a poorer job of delivering the goods than the "invisible hand" of Mr. Market.

Joseph Schumpeter sharpened the point: "Our analysis leads us to believe that recovery is only sound if it does come from itself. For any revival which is merely due to artificial stimulus leaves part of the work of depression undone and adds, to an undigested remnant of maladjustments, new maladjustments of its own."

The U.S. economy faced a major recession in 2001 and had a minor one. The newborn slump was strangled in its crib by one of the most central planners who ever lived. Alan Greenspan cut lending rates. George W. Bush boosted spending. The resultant shock of renewed, ersatz demand not only postponed the recession, it pushed consumers, investors, and businesspeople to make even more egregious errors. Investors bought stock with low earnings yields. Consumers went further into debt. Government liabilities rose. The trade deficit grew larger. On the other side of the globe, foreign businessmen worked overtime to meet the phony new demand; China has enjoyed a capital spending boom as excessive as any the world has ever seen.

Our own Fed chairman, guardian of the nation's money, custodian of its economy, night watchman of its wealth: How could he do such a thing? He turned a financial bubble into an economic bubble. Not only were the prices of financial assets ballooned to excess, so were the prices of houses and the debts of the average household. And the economy itself was transformed. By 2005, the housing bubble was no longer an investment phenomenon, but an economic one affecting almost everybody. In some areas, half of all new jobs were related to housing. People built houses; people financed houses; people remodeled houses; people sold houses to each other; people put in so many granite countertops that whole mountains had been flattened to quarry the stuff.

12

Something Wicked
This Way Comes

The force of a correction is equal and opposite to the deception and delusion that preceded it. Alan Greenspan, George W. Bush, and all the great nabobs of positivism assure us that there is nothing to fear. Our favorite imperial columnist, Thomas L. Friedman of the *New York Times,* explained that "the next big thing almost always comes out of America . . . [because] . . . America allows you to explore your own mind."[1] Friedman believes the world would be a better place if America were more aggressive about "empowering women" and "building democracies." He also thinks that technical innovations give America a permanent advantage. Americans are always innovating, always figuring things out. Heck, we even invented outsourcing, says Friedman:

> This is America's real edge. Sure Bangalore has a lot of engineering schools, but the local government is rife with corruption; half the city has no sidewalks; there are constant electricity blackouts; the rivers are choked with pollution; the public school system is dysfunctional; beggars dart in and out of the traffic . . .[2] and so forth.

Among the things Mr. Friedman seems to lack is a feeling for verb tenses. He goes to Bangalore and notices that it is backward. His conclusion is that it will always be so. "Is" is forever in Friedman's mind. "Will be" has no place. It is as if he looked at the stock market in 1982. "Stocks are cheap," he might have said. "Stocks elsewhere are expensive," he might have added, without it ever occurring to him that they might change places. And yet, why else would anyone outsource work from Baltimore to Bangalore unless Bangalore was relatively, though not necessarily permanently, cheaper? Let us imagine that Bangalore had no electricity blackouts or pollution or beggars. Let us imagine that it was like Beverly Hills or Boca Raton. We might just as well imagine that stocks were expensive in 1982. Of course, if they had been, there never would have been the bull market of 1982 to 2000. It is only because they were cheap in the past that they had the potential to be expensive in the future. And it is only because Bangalore is a Third World hellhole that it is cheap enough to take work away from overpaid Americans 10,000 miles away. Whether it will, neither Friedman nor we can know.

We always try to get our day off on the right foot by reading Friedman's column before breakfast. There is something so gloriously naïve and clumsy in the man's *pensée,* it never fails to brighten our mornings. It refreshes our faith in our fellow men; they are not evil, just mindless. We have never met the man, but we imagine Friedman as a high school teacher, warping young minds with drippy thoughts. But to say his ideas are sophomoric or juvenile merely libels young people, most of whom have far more cleverly nuanced opinions than the columnist. You might criticize the man by saying his work is without merit, but, too, that would be flattery. His work has negative merit. Every column subtracts from the sum of human knowledge in the way a broken pipe drains the town's water tower.

Not that Mr. Friedman's ideas are uniquely bad. Many people have similarly puerile, insipid notions in their heads. But Friedman expresses his hollow thoughts with such heavy-handed earnestness, it often makes us laugh. He seems completely unaware that he is a simpleton. That, of course, is a charm; he is so dense you can laugh at him without hurting his feelings.

Friedman writes regularly and voluminously. But thinking must be painful to him; he shows no evidence of it. Instead, he just writes down whatever humbug appeals to him at the moment, as unquestioningly as a mule goes for water.

One of the things Friedman worries about is that the world will "go dark." As near as we can tell, he means that the many changes wrought after 9/11 are changing the character of the nation, so that "our DNA as a nation . . . has become badly deformed or mutated." In classic Friedman style, he proposes something that any 12-year-old would recognize as preposterous: another national commission! "America urgently needs a national commission to look at all the little changes that were made in response to 9/11,"[3] he writes. If a nation had DNA and if it could be mutated, we still are left with the enormous wonder: What difference would a national commission make? Wouldn't the members have the national DNA? Or should we pack the commission with people from other countries to get an objective opinion—a U.N. panel and a few illiterate tribesmen for cultural diversity?

Friedman's oeuvre is a long series of "we should do this" and "they should do that." Never for a moment does he stop to wonder why people actually do what they do. Nor has the thought crossed his mind that other people might have their own ideas about what they should do and no particular reason to think Mr. Friedman's ideas are any better. There is no trace of modesty in his writing—no skepticism, no cynicism, no irony, no suspicion lurking in the corner of his brain that he might be a jackass. Of course, there is nothing false about him either; he is not capable of either false modesty or falsetto principles. With Friedman, it is all alarmingly real. Nor is there any hesitation or bewilderment in his opinions; that would require circumspection, a quality he completely lacks.

Friedman fears he may not approve of all the post-9/11 changes. But so what? Why would the entire world "go dark" just because America stoops to empire? The idea is nothing more than another silly imperial conceit. America is not the light of the world. Friedman can stop worrying. The sun shone before the United States existed. It will shine long after she exists no more. But, without realizing it, imperial conceits are what Mr. Friedman offers, one after another. He knows what is best for everyone, all the time.

But even at his specialty, Friedman is second-rate. It is not that his proposals are much dumber than anyone else's, but he offers them in a dumber way. He sets them up like a TV newscaster, unaware that they mean anything, not knowing whether to smile or weep. He does not seem to notice that his own DNA has mutated along with the nation's institutions . . . and that he does nothing more than amplify the vanities and prejudices that pass for the evening's news. Is there trouble in Palestine? Well, the Palestinians should have done what we told them. Have peace and democracy come to Iraq? If so, it is thanks to the brave efforts of our own troops. Is the price of oil going up? Well, of course it is; the United States has not yet taken up the comprehensive energy policy he proposed for it. Friedman's world is so neat. So simple. There must be nothing but right angles. And no problem that doesn't have a commission waiting to solve it.

It must be unfathomable to such a man that the world could work in ways that surpass his understanding. In our experience, any man who understands even his own thoughts must have few of them. And those he has must be simpleminded.

But we enjoy Friedman's commentaries. The man is too clumsy to hide or disguise the awkward imbecility of his own line of thinking. The silliness of it is right out in the open, where we can laugh at it. Arabs ought to shape up and start acting more like New Yorkers, he believes. If they don't want to do it on their own, we can give them some help. He says we can send "caring" and "nurturing" troops to "build democracies" in these places and "protect the rights of women." But he doesn't understand how armies, empires, politics, or markets really work. American troops can give help, but it is the kind of help that Scipio gave Carthage or Sherman gave Atlanta. Armies are a blunt instrument, not a precision tool.

Friedman urged the Bush administration to attack Iraq. But the man has a solution for every problem he causes. "So how do we get the Sunni Arab village to delegitimize [we love these big words—every one of them hides a whole dictionary of lies, fibs, prevarications, *malentendus,* misapprehensions, miscalculations, guesswork, hallucination, conceit, and mendacity] suicide bombers?"

Simple. Propaganda! "The Bush team needs to be forcefully demanding that Saudi Arabia and other key Arab allies use their news media, government, and religious systems to denounce and delegitimize the despicable murder of Muslims by Muslims in Iraq."[4]

That ought to do it. What is wrong with the Bush team? Why didn't they think of that? "Forcefully demand" that the Arab states do more propaganda. Yes, problem solved.

By the way, your authors have no position on foreign policy. We only notice that the people who do have them are idiots.

Still we are not going to criticize Friedman. There is no sport in it. The poor fellow is evidently handicapped. He only sees things in two dimensions, like a drawing by a five-year-old with only one eye. He seems to have a one-eyed proposal each week: a "Reform Revolution" (whatever oxymoronic thing that is); "nation building"; "a Manhattan project to develop a hydrogen-based energy economy"; a "National Commission for Doing Things Right"; a "Patriot Tax" of 50 cents a gallon on gasoline; a "Reform India" proposal; and many others too numerous and absurd to mention.

Looking at the issue with two eyes and rounding on it a bit to get a better view, we see that things are not nearly as simple as Friedman must imagine. Things do not respond to commissions and good intentions. People do not always get what they want; sometimes they get what they deserve.

America's roly-poly empire of consumer capitalism, pax dollarium, airborne diplomacy, and debt has established order throughout most of the world. That order was immensely helpful to Americans in the first 60 years of the U.S. imperium. We made things that we could sell throughout the world—at a profit. Today, the world still turns, but maybe not in our direction.

There is a dark side to the human character. After people have enough to eat and a roof over their heads, they care more about their relative wealth than their absolute wealth; they care more about their status than their souls. The present imperial order benefits foreigners more than Americans. Real wages are rising in Asia. In the United States, they are stagnant. In relative terms, Americans are likely to continue to get poorer, even if they eliminate their trade deficit.

The logic of human jealousy—and imperial finance—has now shifted. The United States should not be willing to continue providing a public good—order—for no other return than the opportunity to compete on a level playing field. Industries in the United States are now losing that competition. Americans are beginning to resent it. They are likely to insist that either we retire from the empire business; or we take it up in a way that impedes globalized economic progress.

Looked at this way, the Bush administration's many actions make more sense. Why invade Iraq? Because it creates disorder. Military adventures are risky and destabilizing. And they are a shift from civilized means for getting what you want to using political means, which are not only inherently disorderly but also favor America's military strengths while minimizing her commercial weaknesses. Why pressure China to revalue the yuan? Because it creates disorder. The yuan had been stable for 10 years—pegged to the U.S. imperial dollar at a fixed rate. The United States insisted that the yuan move up and threatened to impose tariffs and trade barriers. Why? Because the trade barriers directly interfere with the orderly give-and-take of commerce and slow our competitors' growth. Why run up huge federal deficits? Why give away money at the cost of consumer price inflation? All these things are deeply disturbing to the world financial system; they breed disorder.

What Friedman has not seemed to notice is that America's advantage is past tense. If the United States really had been creating new products and new jobs, the evidence would be in the figures. America's trade figures would not be preceded by a minus sign, but by a plus, as they had been prior to Ronald Reagan's entering the White House. America's job numbers, too, would have been different. The number of new jobs created in a single month—say, February 2004—would have been more like 200,000 (which would have been "normal" for that stage of the recovery) rather than the measly 21,000 that showed up.

Never before, since the beginning of the industrial revolution 300 years ago, have there been so many people outside the Western world ready, willing, and able to compete with us. Never before have they had so much available capital. While Americans spend all their money—and then some, the average Chinese worker saves more than 20 percent of everything he earns.

There are more engineers in the city of Bangalore, in India, than there are in the state of California. They work well and cheaply, taking home an average annual pay of about $6,000. And they seem to be just as innovative as their American counterparts. The software for DVDs was developed in Bangalore, not in Silicon Valley, says the French newspaper, *Libération*. In the seven short years of its existence in Bangalore, the Philips research center alone has come up with 1,500 new inventions.

Foreign workers have been cutting into American salaries for many years. Assembly line workers in Taiwan, Mexico, and other places have undermined factory wage growth in the United States. Over the past 30 years, real hourly earnings on the shop floor have gone nowhere. No one particularly cared—because America's economy was shifting to service and consumption anyway. Factory workers were out of fashion and out of luck. But now it is the accountants, architects, and paper shufflers whose jobs are threatened. Even lawyers are worried; law firms are outsourcing routine legal work to India.

These trends might not have worried Democrat economists any more than they troubled the Republicans, but 2004 was an election year, so they couldn't pass up an opportunity to get their names in the paper. Pandering to the lumpen masses, the Democrats offered to "do something" to "protect American jobs."

A lot of dopey things are said to voters with the cameras running. But no one is going to look the American worker in the face and tell him that he earns too much money for what he does. A politician might as well pour gasoline over his head and light a match; the media would scorch him in a matter of minutes; his career in politics would be in cinders.

We are not running for anything. And if by some misfortune we were elected to public office, we would immediately confess that we had spent a drug-crazed night with a Russian prostitute and demand a recount. So, we offer this little reflection on outsourcing with nothing at risk but our reputation, which is to say we have little to lose.

For many, many years, Americans have had the high ground in the international labor market. The playing field was tilted in their favor by the skills, capital, infrastructure, institutions, and habits built up over many generations. They will still have an advantage for many years, but Friedman is right about one thing: The playing field gets more level every day.

Huge economies—principally India and China—are on the rise, whether we like it or not. By the middle of this century, estimates a Goldman Sachs study, Russia's living standards will be some 40 percent higher than America's are today, China's will have reached the same level as Japan's today, Brazil's will be about the same as Britain's today. Indians will have about the same incomes as Italians have today.

Here are some of its other conclusions:

- The four largest emerging economies, which the bank calls the BRICs—Brazil, Russia, India, and China—could within 40 years become larger in combination than the "G6"—America, Japan, Germany, Britain, France, and Italy.

- Currently they are less than 15 percent of the size of the G6. In U.S. dollar terms, China could overtake Germany in the next four years, Japan by 2015, and the United States by 2039. India's economy could be larger than all but the United States and China in 30 years.

- Over the next five years, China's GDP per head is expected to grow at an average of 11.2 percent a year, Russia's by 10.3 percent, India's by 7.5 percent, and Brazil's by 6.3 percent. The equivalent projections for today's giants are just 1.7 percent for the United States, 0.9 percent for Japan, 2 percent for Germany, 1.9 percent for Britain, and 1.5 percent for France.

- Living standards in the United States will continue to grow, too. Americans' GDP per head is expected to rise from $38,700 to $83,700, Britain's from $26,000 to $59,000, Germany's from $23,100 to $49,000, and Japan's from $34,300 to $66,800.

Reagan and his disciples may or may not have defeated communism. But once freed, the economies of Russia, India—and in a most curious way, China—posed tougher competition than America had ever seen.

THE GREAT CONCEIT

While foreigners got richer, U.S. passport holders became delusional. They believed that they could get richer without saving or earning more money.

In the United States, household consumption is 71 percent of GDP. People think they are getting richer because they have money to spend—borrowed money. But what makes a man, or a nation, rich is not spending—it is *not* spending. We wouldn't think it necessary to say so except that so many people still seem to believe the opposite. They see the GDP numbers as signs of a "healthy, growing" economy. But what is growing in the United States is the very thing that makes the economy unhealthy—consumption. For every dollar of product that the United States sells abroad, it buys $1.60 worth of imported items, almost all of it consumer goods.

China, as we all know, is on the opposite side of the planet. Over there, people make the things that we buy and don't buy the things we make. American households are rich and buy a lot. Chinese households are poor and buy little. Americans save little; the Chinese save a lot. Only 42 percent of Chinese GDP is domestic consumption. Another 35 percent is devoted to exports. And nearly half of all the money spent in China, according to Stephen Roach, is for fixed investment.

Both economies are preposterously imbalanced. Both will probably fall down and break apart. But when the pieces are picked up, the Chinese will find themselves with the ability to produce wealth—things that people are willing to buy. America will find itself with less money to buy them with and fewer people willing to provide credit.

WHENCE COMETH THE TRADE DEFICIT?

It ariseth when Americans buy more from non-Americans than they sell to them. Each year that passes, Americans buy, net, about $700 billion more in foreign imports than they make in overseas sales. That United States businesses are more profitable than their Asian counterparts makes no difference. That the American economy is the most dynamic, flexible, and delicious confection ever put up on God's green earth is as irrelevant as tree rings. That foreigners want a piece of America is flattering, but it is also as much a non sequitur as hemorrhoids.

Nor does it especially matter why Americans overspend. They have their reasons. But even if they had no reason, the result would be the same.

If the nation were a corporation, the difference between what came in and what went out—in dollar terms—would be the measure of its "loss from current operations." If it were a family, it would be the rate at which it impoverished itself. If it were a business running such an imbalance for so many years, it would have gone bankrupt long ago. Even a lesser nation would have run into trouble years ago. Only an imperial power with the world's reserve currency could have gotten away with it.

Even if it were true, it is not particularly important that the U.S. economy is growing faster than its competitors as Mr. David Malpass claimed (in the *Wall Street Journal*). Nor does it matter that Asians have "no choice" but to buy U.S. dollar assets, as other commentators maintain. Nor is it pertinent that the foreign investments represent a kind of tribute paid to the imperial power.

The grim and unyielding fact is that each day, Americans grow "richer" in SUVs, flat-screen TVs, and other consumer flotsam and jetsam that come mostly from Asia (where the trade deficit is concentrated), while the Asians grow richer in U.S. financial assets, notably Treasury bonds. Since 1990, foreigners have acquired $3.6 trillion worth of U.S. assets as a direct consequence of the trade deficits.

At a micro level, individually, this makes no great difference. We only bring it up to mock others who brought it up before us. A man decides for himself if he'd rather have a big TV or a Treasury bond. It is not for us to say he has made a good choice or a bad one. But Americans are not merely trading a financial asset for a consumer asset. They have few financial assets to trade. People do not dip into capital to spend at Wal-Mart. They dip into debt. With no savings to spend, they cannot trade a financial asset for consumer fluff. So, they must trade a financial liability.

This is just another consumer preference. It is no concern of ours if a man decides he wants a big-screen TV so badly he's willing to go into debt to get it. He would rather have the additional debt than forgo the TV. But we suspect his preference rests on either delusion or fraud. The preference assumes he will give up spending in the future for spending in the present. Most likely, he expects to give up neither.

Every empire begins with a humbug. Later it develops into mass illusion, self-congratulation, hallucination, farce, and finally disaster. Until the disaster comes, you never know quite where you are. Because for every imbecility that comes along, there are dozens of eager intellectuals ready to promote it and at least half the population is ready to believe it.

So it is that almost every day, we see a piece in the *Wall Street Journal* explaining that trade deficits are no trouble. And at a certain level, they are no trouble at all. It does not matter to God who owes what to whom. Or even if it does, he keeps quiet about it.

Some kibitzers point out that the United States ran trade deficits for much of its early history and that fast-growing countries always have current account deficits. After all, they are building something for the future—factories, plants, machines—that takes capital. Then, when the factories are built, they produce earnings and profits, which are used to pay back the debt. In this instance, the debtor comes out ahead.

Oh, the reverie of it! But when did you last see a factory, refinery, or mine under construction in America? The last one we recall was a shiny new brewery outside Baltimore—and that must have been 40 years ago. Since then, it has gone out of business.

Many economists believe we no longer need factories. They think the information revolution has many more good things to give us. We're not aware of any benefits, yet, from the information revolution, but we're prepared to believe there might eventually be some. But information is notoriously light on its feet. More and more U.S. tax forms—which are nothing more than information—are being processed in India. And American companies are actually outsourcing more and more of the "information" component of modern products. They no longer go to Taiwan and ask the locals to "make this." Now, they go to Taiwan to see what the locals are making that they can sell back home. More and more, U.S. companies don't even participate at the design stage.

"What we are seeing," says Paul Craig Roberts, is the "rapid transformation of America into a 3rd world economy."[5] American firms are increasingly left with only brands to market. But even those won't last forever, after customers realize that the real innovation, design, and manufacture genius is overseas. Just as car buyers took up new brands as quality increased in Japan, so will they soon take up new brands in other industries. Soon, Americans will not only want to spend on foreign-made goods, they will have to.

The cycle is typical of empires in their mature stages. Even in decline, people still look to the homeland for fashion cues. Music, education, theater, dress, architecture, and manners are exported from the center to the periphery long after commerce in more practical goods has reversed direction. Even today, Vienna remains a regional cultural center—as do Paris and Rome. Parents from former colonies still dream of sending their children to Cambridge and Oxford.

Meanwhile, the Newman brothers, Dan and Frank, in the *Wall Street Journal* point out that the outflow of dollars is no cause for concern, because the dollars just come back to us. We concede they do or, they will. But they don't come back as the same good-natured working stiffs they were when they left. Instead they come back from abroad in finer clothes, with finer manners, and with a better accent. They come back as rentiers. They went out as a credit and come back as a liability. The next thing you know, they are putting their feet on the furniture and acting as if they own the place. Instead of helping the average man earn a living, they make it harder for him. For now they must be supported, too. Interest must be paid on debt or compounded into more debt. Either way, day by day, the burden just grows heavier.

We know from experience that our moods can change for no apparent reason. One day, we are happier then usual. The next, on exactly the same set of "facts," we are gloomy. One day, we are prepared to start a war. The next, trouble is the last thing we want. One day we think $20 is a fair price to pay for $1 of earnings. The next, even $10 seems too much. One day, we see the facts, and they are awful. The next, the very same facts don't seem so bad.

These moods happen to individuals on a day-to-day basis and to whole groups of people over long periods. One generation is bullish. The next is bearish. One generation wants war. The next wants peace. One generation is lost. The next is found.

As prices fall, our opinions fall too; we become gloomy. But sometimes, the opposite happens, opinions make markets. Gloominess sets in, for no particular or apparent reason, and then prices fall. Moods and facts, sometimes in harmony, but often in opposition, struggle to dominate our generation's zeitgeist.

Currently, both are in harmony. The public's mood is ridiculous. But so are the "facts." Never before have people been expected to believe so many impossible things. But perhaps, never before have so many impossible things seemed, at least for now, true. All we know is that they will change.

IV

THE ESSENTIAL INVESTOR

What is prudence in the conduct of every private family, can scarce be folly in that of a great kingdom.

—Adam Smith

13

Welcome to Squanderville

The citizens of Squanderville, as Warren Buffett calls the United States, are a happy bunch. They believe happy things; it doesn't bother them that the things they believe are impossible.

After 20 years of mostly falling interest rates, mostly falling inflation rates, and mostly rising asset prices (stocks and real estate), people have come to believe that this is the way the world works: Interest rates mostly go down, and house prices mostly go up; it goes on forever.

Even the professionals in Squanderville have never been more certain: A 2005 poll of economists working for major brokerage houses found that 100 percent of them expected rising stock prices over the next 12 months. And real estate? Who believed house prices will fall? Almost no one.

While it is all very well to think happy thoughts and spend happy money, it is savings and investments that produce real jobs and real earnings.

As the years go by, Squandervillians make less and less that they can sell abroad, and consume more and more from overseas. So, when they spend money, much of it goes to buy products from Thriftville. (Buffett's term, perhaps he had Asia in mind.) The industrious people of Thriftville use the money to hire more workers, build more factories, import more technology, and improve their products. Thus, do the authorities in Squanderville find themselves in a remarkable position: they can still use monetary and fiscal policy to create a boom, but the boom happens in Thriftville!

The happy residents of Squanderville hardly know or care. The latest job numbers are celebrated; who bothers to notice that the new jobs are not quite as nice as the old ones? While companies lay off relatively highly paid people in the manufacturing sector, other companies hire relatively more cheap employees in the service sector. General Motors declines; Wal-Mart grows.

What would happen if real estate prices actually started to go down? They would wait, figuring the boom would soon resume. But what if it didn't? Soon, the homeowners of Squanderville might be faced with a brief interval of horrible sanity. They might be unhappy.

THE WAY WE LIVE NOW

As the year 2005 matured, the corpus of the world financial system became even more grotesque than it had been the day before. Connecting the thigh bone of bond yields . . . to the hip bone of Asian purchases of U.S. bonds . . . to the vertebra of credit expansion . . . we stood back in awe and wonder: What kind of monster was this? It looked like a creation of Frankenstein.

The world's richest, most powerful country, depends on the savings of the world's poorest. The world's foremost economy offers its money at negative real interest rates and is afraid to normalize them for fear the whole thing will collapse. Americans buy what they cannot afford, and the Chinese build factories to produce what their principal customers don't have the money to buy. The whole world economy advances—apparently—only so long as U.S. house prices continue to rise at three to five times nominal inflation and an infinite multiple of household income, which went backward in 2004.

Whatever it may be, this is no ordinary economy—it has a hunchback and two club feet. Jobs that ought to exist don't. Income that should be helping consumers to spend isn't there. Savings that are vitally important to economic growth have disappeared.

We look at the body parts—the Dow, the latest employment numbers, Consumer Price Index (CPI) rates, and so forth—every day. But most of what we read is "noise"—meaningless distractions. The news items only make sense when we connect them to the spine. The best way to understand America's economic predicament is to look at it as a system of imperial finance. The United States is an odd and reluctant empire. Its body parts fit together, but only in an absurd and comic way; it's the imperial backbone that gives it shape.

Only an empire can run such a trade deficit for many years. Only an empire can maintain so many expensive outposts all over the world. Only an empire's money will be accepted by so many people in so many different places. The American empire, circa 2005, still sets the trends in fashion, arts, style, and manners—but it neglects engineering, science, and homeland-bound industries. It depends on the periphery states for its savings and its consumer goods. As an empire matures, its center weakens and its backbone bends under the weight. Eventually it either passes off its imperial burden to a friendly power to which it becomes beholden—as England did to America between 1917 and 1950—or its back breaks. When it breaks, we don't know. How it breaks, we don't know either.

All we know, dear reader, is that it is a spine that invites a shiver.

BUBBLE MANIA

After investors have lost a lot of money in one bubble, they practically can't wait until the next one comes along. In the 1960s boom, anything with "onics" in the title sold for far more than it was worth. If you added "onics" to your company name, you were almost sure to be a rich man the next day.

In the boom of the 1990s, the magic syllables were "dot-com." Remember Dr. Koop.com? Furniture.com? Webvan? So many examples come to mind: It is like trying to select the dumbest member of Congress; we don't know where to start. The dot-coms were so popular with investors—and mining companies so unpopular—that at least one firm that supposedly had been mining gold switched to supposedly becoming a dot-com to take advantage of it.

Near the end of the tech bubble, an e-trading firm ran an arresting advertisement. It showed a doctor peering down at a trader on the operating table; the doctor says, "Why . . . he's got money coming out of the wazoo!"

Five years later, you could replace the e-trader with a house flipper. Whether they were trading houses or stocks, Americans enjoyed the new empire of debt. Coast to coast, money was coming out of wazoos all over the place.

In Paradise Cove, California, even people who lived in mobile homes were getting rich. Trailers doubled in price every year for the first five years of the twenty-first century. Some were selling for more than $1 million. And in another Paradise, this one in Nevada, house prices rose faster than anywhere else in the nation. By mid–2005, in Paradise, Nevada, they were rising at nearly a 50 percent annual rate.

"If you can fog a mirror, you can get a home loan," said a mortgage analyst to the *Los Angeles (LA) Times.* In the past, being able to fog a mirror was a necessary requirement for credit. Only now has it become sufficient. If the present trend continues, soon lenders will not even bother to hold up the mirror.

There was no particular reason why the dead should be denied mortgage credit; they would probably be at least as good risks as many of the living who are getting it. Maybe better. At least they don't skip town and don't put their feet on the furniture.

We are obviously on the cutting edge of new developments in the credit industry. But judging from the ads seen on the Internet, we are not far in the lead. "Borrow up to $250,000," says an advertisement. "Less than perfect credit is okay. . . . No income verification. . . . No Home Equity requirement. . . . 24-hour approval."

Between 2001 and 2005, the property bubble raised house prices in California by $1.7 trillion. That is equivalent to 35 percent of personal income. Now, the whole economy not only enjoys a rising real estate market, it depends on it. Coast to coast, people buy big houses they can't afford. They expect to sell them to someone else for more than they paid for them. What they do not expect is to pay for them themselves. How can they? What would they pay for them with?

No one seems interested in actually owning real estate. Houses have become like futures contracts. People trade on margin and never take delivery. Houses are financial assets to be actively managed, just as though they were stocks or a sailboat. When interest rates dip, new credit is unfurled; the house is refinanced at a lower rate with the borrower often taking out a little cash to spend. If rates seem to be going down, more sailcloth is hoisted at an adjustable rate to catch the favorable wind.

What if rates rise? What if the weather turns bad?

The California Association of Realtors reported that only one in five households in the state had enough money to buy the house that one in two of them lived in; in some areas, it was only one in ten.

There were thousands of million-dollar houses on the market. But there were few people with a million dollars. If you wanted to actually own a million-dollar house, you would have to earn enough so that you could *save* a million. Say you earned $200,000 a year, you might be stretching to buy a $1 million house, but people stretch much further. If you borrowed the money at 6 percent, you would spend $60,000 a year on interest alone. With other living expenses and taxes, you would have little left over to pay down the principal. Even if you saved like the Chinese do, you would be lucky to be able to pay down $20,000 in principal each year. At that rate, it would take you 50 years to pay off the house. If you saved at the current national savings rate—about 1 percent—you would have to make payments for the next 500 years.

The average American lives in a suburban house thought to be worth $188,800. Since stocks began to decline in January 2000, his net worth has not necessarily declined, but it has become less abstract; he now has to live in it. Even in Philadelphia.

A housing bubble in Philadelphia? It seemed almost impossible. Who would want to buy a house in Philadelphia, much less at a premium? But house prices rose in Philadelphia, and even in Baltimore. Parents and grandparents had been loath to spend more than 25 percent of their incomes on rent or a mortgage. Now, people are spending more than 50 percent. By mid-2005, it was reported that one in five new home buyers spent half their disposable income on housing.

In America, the average house went up 44 percent in real terms between 1995 and 2005. The increase was even greater in Britain and Australia. Americans have come to expect house price increases far beyond what the market is likely to give them. A survey by Shiller and Case found average annual expectations of 12 to 16 percent—three to four times likely increases in GDP and not much different from what investors had come to expect from stocks in the late 1990s. Since these gains were almost as good as money "in the bank," in the eyes of house buyers, many spent the money before it had been made. Equity withdrawal (borrowing against the increased price of the house) rose to 6 percent of personal disposable income in the United States in 2004, 8 percent in Britain.

There is disappointment built into this delightful show. We suspect it comes near the end. It is all very well that the world financial system matches up borrowers with lenders, but the matchmaking only works if it produces satisfying results. If you match a princess with a frog, when the poor girl bends down to give the amphibian a kiss something remarkable better happen or there will be regrets. Reproaches. Maybe lawsuits.

Just as a traveler is never really sure he's had a good trip until he gets home, you never know if a loan is a good one or a bad one until the money makes its way back to the lender. That is where the disappointment is likely to come. Are lenders too lenient? We will know when the money gets ready for the return portion of the trip. Our guess is that not as much will make it home as people expected.

The amount owed in home equity lines of credit soared 42 percent in 2004. And the median down payment slipped from 6 percent in 2003 to only 3 percent in 2004.

"The boom in interest-only loans—nearly half the state's home buyers used them last year, up from virtually none in 2001—is the engine behind California's surging home prices," said the *LA Times*.[1]

California house sales hit a new record in February 2005. And again in March. And again in April. Housing starts nationwide were at a 21-year high. All over the 50 states, people were buying, flipping, refinancing.

"It is as if you were paid to live in California," said a skeptic to the *LA Times*.[2] Prices rose 22 percent in 2004. It meant that an average homeowner, with an average $400,000 house, added $88,000 to his net worth. He did this without lifting a finger.

In the Bay Area, houses were selling for half again as much as people asked for them. The *LA Times* mentioned a house offered for $980,000 that sold almost immediately for $1.5 million. The *Times* told of a young woman who bought her first house with no money down and "interest only" payments. In 2001, fewer than 5 percent of new houses were purchased with "interest only" mortgages. By mid-2005, the total was nearly 50 percent. From the newspaper report, the woman appeared to be headed toward a financial crisis. Homeownership, she believed, would bail her out. She told the paper that she intended to use her equity to pay down her credit card debt! More of the *Times* article: "I have $40,000 in student loans from my master's degree," she said. "I have high credit card debt. I'm a typical American. And yet they wanted to give me more debt to buy a house."

"If you're like me, you're so incredulous that anyone would give you any money whatsoever, you just close your eyes and sign the papers. . . . I would have signed anything."[3]

On the East Coast, the situation was not much different:

An expert was interviewed by the *New York Times*. He remarked that in the past real estate investors expected annual rental returns of 8 percent to 10 percent of the purchase price. But such a "historical perspective" is wrong, he said. It causes investors to pass up good opportunities. What they need is a "fresh prospective": "They're not being foolish; they're looking at it differently than people who have been in the market for a long time."[4]

Forget the wisdom of the dead, in other words. This is a new era.

People buy property now as they bought tech stocks five years ago—without any regard for earnings. It is all a greater fool game—betting that someone will come along who is an even bigger numskull than you are. The game continues such a long time that people come to see it as eternal. And the more confidence people have in it, the more reasons they invent that it should go on. Most experts cite "demographic factors" as guaranteeing higher residential property prices. There are supposed to be many more people who will need a roof over their heads in the years ahead. According to the theory, there are so many new immigrants and baby boomer children that the homebuilders can't keep up with them. Prices will rise. Why the homebuilders can't build enough houses to keep up with the demand is a matter of debate. How the new buyers will be able to pay higher prices—when incomes are falling—is not clear either. And there is always the outside chance that these new households may rent. Rental yields are falling; relatively, rents are cheap.

A major reason given for why stock prices had to continue rising in 1999 was that so many people were putting so much money into stocks for their retirements. The logic was supposedly irrefutable: The baby boomers must save money. They had no choice but to put it into stocks. Stocks had to go up.

The reasoning was perfect—as long as stocks went up. But then something happened; stocks went down. Baby boomers felt little desire to buy stocks. But the "demographic factors" argument was still perfectly serviceable for the housing market. It will work fine—until houses go down in price.

On April 10, 2005, an article entitled "The Hunt, Becoming a Mogul Slowly" appeared in the *New York Times*. It told the story of a 25-year-old New Yorker, who had been making real estate deals ever since 2002. Drawing on this deep well of experience, the young Trump offered advice. "An apartment is more attractive to me when other people want it. While the price might seem expensive now, it might not be expensive six months to a year from now. We overbid to capture the opportunity." By some instinct, he had captured the gist of the efficient market hypothesis—and applied it to real estate (discussed in Chapter 15). Whatever price he paid was okay—because it was the price others were willing to pay.

The *Times* article told us that "his success has inspired six of his young, former-renter friends, to follow in his experienced footsteps," because "I made it seem like a very cool thing to do." Meanwhile the real Donald Trump said he was getting a million dollars a pop just to tell young mogul-hopefuls his secrets.[5]

In mid-2005, you only had to get in a cab to realize that the real estate boom has become a bubble. Cabdrivers would point out how much houses have gone up. While once they gave tips on tech stocks, now they told you which neighborhoods were likely to experience the greatest price inflation. Listen carefully, and you were likely to overhear drivers on their cell phones talking to real estate agents about their new condos.

"My daughter is only twenty-five," wrote a friend, "but she just bought a house in Northern Virginia. Of course, she mortgaged most of it. But can you believe that they lent her $275,000? Is that crazy, or what? She works as a bartender, part time. She's very responsible and is good for the money, I'm sure, but I can't believe they would lend her that much money. How do they think she will pay it back?"

The trick was to find a "fixer-upper," do a little cosmetic work on it, and put it right back on the market. So many people were looking for fixer-uppers that canny sellers were considering deliberately making a wreck of their houses—so prospective buyers could hallucinate about how much money they would make after fixing them up.

In the spring of 2005, the Federal Deposit Insurance Corporation identified 55 areas in the nation that it said were undergoing a boom in residential real estate. These were areas where prices rose 30 percent or more over the preceding three years. Not in 30 years had so many parts of the country experienced such a boom, said FDIC. Even in the last boom of the 1980s, only half as many areas met the test.

Nationwide, house prices rose 40 percent from January 2001 to January 2005. This increased household net worth by about $6 trillion. In 2004—the increase was 12.5 percent, adding approximately another $2 trillion to homeowners' worth.

THE SAGE OF THE PLAINS

"A lot of the psychological well-being of the American public comes from how well they've done with their house over the years. . . ." said the Sage of the Plains, Warren Buffett, in April 2005. "Certainly at the high end of the real estate market in some areas, you've seen extraordinary movement. . . . People go crazy in economics periodically, in all kinds of ways. Residential housing has different behavioral characteristics, simply because people live there. But when you get prices increasing faster than the underlying costs, sometimes there can be pretty serious consequences."

"You have a real asset-price bubble in places like parts of California and the suburbs of Washington, DC," added Charlie Munger.

Buffett: "I recently sold a house in Laguna for $3.5 million. It was on about 2,000 square feet of land, maybe a twentieth of an acre, and the house might cost about $500,000 if you wanted to replace it. So the land sold for something like $60 million an acre."

Munger: "I know someone who lives next door to what you would actually call a fairly modest house that just sold for $17 million. There are some very extreme housing price bubbles going on."[6]

"Flipping real estate . . . without getting burned," is a headline from the weekend *Seattle Times.*[7]

There's something about a bull market that weakens brains and permits senseless metaphors. The *Times* could have said, "Flipping houses without having them fall on your head" or "How not to get burned in a red-hot real estate market." But the hacks in Seattle didn't bother to think about it; who did? Everybody knew property was hot, and everyone knew you could get rich—fast. By April 2005, the press was beginning to report on people who had quit their jobs to get in on the house bubble before it went sour, we mean, before it popped.

The *Times* article referred to "30-something investors" who have left gainful employment to invest in real estate. What they were doing had little in common with real investment, but neither they nor the reporter seemed to realize it. The houses they bought rarely yielded any real, net income. What they were really doing was gambling on rising property prices.

It was much like the end of the 1990s when young investors were quitting their jobs to day-trade stocks. As long as stocks were rising, these traders were geniuses. When the stocks went down, they were idiots.

"I lost a ton of my portfolio in 2001," the *Times* quoted a rising property mogul. The man fired his financial planner and put his money in a self-directed IRA that he can use for speculating in houses, practically day-trading them. "By the end of the year we'll be doing two or three a month," says he.[8]

DELUSIONS OF MEDIOCRITY

Another similarity between the bubble in tech stocks at the end of the 1990s and the housing bubble in 2005 was the rise of "clubs" designed to help members speculate in the company of others. At the end of the 1990s, people joined investment clubs so they could yak about stocks with other people who didn't know anything either. In 2005, they joined real estate clubs. There were at least 177 of them by mid-year. Members get together to talk about "techniques" and "strategies." Four of these "strategies" are recorded for the benefit of future Donald Trumps, and perhaps history, in the *Times* article: (1) Buy a house, hold it, and sell it later, (2) buy a house, fix it up, and sell it, (3) flip the damn house before you actually have to pay for it, and (4) rent the house for more than it is worth, giving the tenant the right to buy it in the future.

We were tempted to add exclamation marks after each strategy. But the items scream such imbecility that amplification seems unnecessary. They reminded us of our own dictum about stock market speculators of the late 1990s: There is smart money; there is dumb money; and there is money so moronic it practically cries out for court-ordered sterilization.

They say on Wall Street that no one rings a bell at the top of the market, but so many bells were ringing in the spring of 2005 we thought we would go deaf—or mad. Playmate of the Month, Jamie Westenhiser, was abandoning a promising career as a model to take up real estate investing.

What would make a nice girl like her end up in place like that? Maybe it was the 12.5 percent gain in real estate nationwide in the previous 12 months? Or maybe it was the 50 percent increase in housing prices in five years? In hot markets—such as California, Florida, and Washington, DC—prices had gone up 60 percent in two years.

It was a "real estate gold rush," said the cover of *Fortune* magazine. Americans were suffering from delusions of mediocrity. They took for normal what is actually extraordinary.

Prices of American residential real estate, in real terms, rose 66 percent between 1890 and 2004. But all the increase happened in just two brief periods: right after World War II, and since 1998. Other than those two periods, the real price of housing was either flat or falling. The big difference between the period following World War II and the present era was that back then the U.S. economy was growing and healthy. America not only had a positive trade balance, but had the most positive one in the world. Wages were going up, so people could afford more expensive houses. Families were expanding faster than the economy—so they needed more houses.

But now, households are getting smaller. Incomes are stable or shrinking. The nation spends more than it earns; it desperately counts on rising house prices—and the savings of poor people in foreign countries—just so it can continue living beyond its means. Lenders come up with creative finance to permit themselves to lend money to people who can't pay it back. Houses in some areas are already so expensive that barely 1 buyer in 10 can afford a median-price house. And Playmates of the Month are giving up strutting their stuff to invest in real estate. This is not a normal situation.

Other news stories told of friends who were teaming up to buy houses—they had become too expensive for a single couple to afford on its own. The main cause of foreclosure is said to be couples who divorce, believe neither one wants or can afford to keep the marital home. Imagine two couples. You might think the risk would double. In fact, it probably quadruples—or more. Either couple might break up. Even more likely, the two couples might decide they can't stand each other. A lender would have to be brain-dead to agree to such a sale. But in 2005, many did.

This is the great comedy of the financial markets. They put a fool together with his money just so they can get a good laugh by taking it away from him. These "investors" think they are geniuses. They think their techniques and strategies are making them rich. Of course, tech stock speculators also thought they were getting rich. Then, they lost "a ton" of their portfolios. It is amazing that they have a ton left. But that is going soon, too, we imagine.

As prices rose in 2005, Congress wanted to know if the Fed might raise rates faster than anticipated. It looked as though the bubble in real estate was getting out of hand. Don't worry about it, said the world's most famous economist, inflation was no problem.

"The economy seems to have entered 2005 expanding at a reasonably good pace, with inflation and inflation expectations well anchored," Alan Greenspan told the nodding heads on the Senate Banking Committee. "The evidence broadly supports the view that economic fundamentals have steadied."[9]

He must not have looked out the window that day. For the very same day, as headlines made clear, inflation and inflation expectations—notably in the housing market—were under full sail in hurricane-force winds.

The cost of housing, in many areas of the country, was not just inflating—it was blowing up like a front-seat air bag. In Alan Greenspan's hometown, Washington, DC, prices were rising six times faster than GDP growth. Buyers were not looking for a place to live; they were speculating—betting that their neighbor, the Fed chairman, would continue giving away enough money to make them rich.

As we write, in the summer of 2005, the house flippers are driving around in new Mercedes, making big money by buying and selling each other's houses. One genius buys a condo before it is built. He flips it to another investor, who holds it until it is completed, making a bundle when he sells it to a professional couple who intend to stay for two years and then sell (at a huge profit) to other buyers. All of them are making the smart moves—buying with little money down and making minimum monthly payments on adjustable rate mortgages. And all of them are getting richer—or so they believe—as long as prices continue to rise. They talk about it at cocktail parties. They look at their balance sheets with pride and pleasure, and if they need cash, they "take out a little equity" as easily as calling for a pizza.

Pity the poor renter. He might just as well drive an old economy car and buy his clothes at Goodwill. He is the sort of man you wouldn't want your daughter to date, let alone marry. He is the poor loser who forgot to buy tech stocks in the late 1990s and now is missing the real estate bubble. He is the quiet, lonely dork who never gets invited to parties and has nothing to say—except an "I told you so" that he has been holding onto for years waiting for the right moment.

AMERICANS GET POORER . . .

"This is the greatest crisis facing the country that people can do something about," writes Ben Stein in *Forbes*. Stein is talking about people who fail to save enough for retirement.

"With less than 20 percent of U.S. workers now in employer pension plans (many of those plans are on shaky financial footing) and with Social Security typically replacing less than 40 percent of pre-retirement income, personal saving has never been more important," continues Stein. And yet, few people save any money.

"Savings rates have never been lower," Stein explains. "In 1999, the national savings rate dipped below 3 percent for the first time since 1959, according to the U.S. Commerce Department. It has been declining further since then, and in 2004 it was at a mere 1 percent. The low savings rate, coupled with large deficit financing by Asian banks, is dangerous for the U.S. But it's more dangerous for individuals."

People are forever crying alarm about this or that. There is a crisis in health . . . a crisis in moral values . . . a crisis in the Middle East . . . or in the newspaper trade. For all the whining, there is usually little that can be done about the emergency, and if it is left alone, it generally takes care of itself in its own way.

"Nearly 28 million U.S. households—37 percent of the total—do not own a retirement savings account of any kind," continues the *Forbes* article, "Among the households who owned a retirement savings account of any kind as of 2001, according to a 2004 report by the Congressional Research Service (CRS), the average value of all such accounts was $95,943. That number was distorted by the relatively few large accounts, and the median value of all accounts was just $27,000.

"The median value of the retirement accounts held by households headed by a worker between the ages of 55 and 64 was $55,000 in 2001," the CRS says. To that, Stein adds that "just 11 percent of all Americans have retirement savings of $250,000 or more."[10]

You can jabber to people about saving money until your jaw falls off; they're not going to put an extra dime in a savings account—not when property prices are going up at 10 percent per year and the Fed is still giving away money. Eventually, however, the things that must happen sooner or later do happen. Of course, that's when people wish they had saved money. That's when they'll really need it. That's when the whining really begins.

Saving—like manufacturing—is one of those early-empire virtues that was once an important part of the American economy . . . but seems to have gotten exported. The Chinese now make our products and do our saving for us. They save more than 25 percent of their income. According to Ben Bernanke, they now have so much of savings, they are thankful to us for taking it off their hands.

As a percentage of GDP, consumer spending in China is only half what it is in the United States. Americans, for example, consume 25 percent of the world's oil. China, with four times as many people, uses just 7 percent.

But what goes around comes around. When the U.S. real estate bubble pops . . . some of that old virtue is likely to make its way back home. Americans will save again. Whereas they put aside only a penny on the dollar now . . . they are likely to set aside 10 cents or more. The savings crisis will be over. A new crisis can then begin: a depression.

In traditional economic theory, people save. Their savings are borrowed by entrepreneurs and businesspeople to build new enterprises, new factories, and new consumer items. This new output is then sold at a profit, which creates new jobs—and higher incomes—that give people more purchasing power, more savings, and so forth.

But in modern America's fabulous twenty-first century economy, things happen so much differently that we wonder: Is the theory mistaken . . . or are Americans? Hardly a dime is saved today. We have not seen a new factory put up in the past 20 years, though we don't deny there must have been a few. (We've seen dozens of shopping centers built.) Per hour, jobs pay little more—in real terms—than they did 30 years ago. Yet, Americans seem to have more purchasing power than ever.

Something is wrong. The picture is grotesque, unnatural . . . like a pretty wife who rotates her own tires—it is almost too good to be true. We suspect we're going to find out later that she sets fire to her cat.

The problem with not saving money is that you won't have any. If you want to do anything beyond what you're already doing, you have nothing saved up to do it with. Even current levels of consumption cannot be maintained. Factories wear out and need to be rebuilt. Competitors race ahead. There is no standing still. You are either going forward . . . or falling behind. "Day by day, all the earth ages, drooping unto death," saith the old Anglo-Saxon poets. You need a reserve of "energy"—savings—to give it life again.

Even the mainstream media has begun to notice how odd things have become. "If current trends continue, the United States will borrow an unprecedented $1 trillion this year alone, mostly from abroad, a sum that is reflected in huge U.S. budget and trade deficits. Any sane analyst has to wonder how long it can last. . . ." The quotation comes from the *International Herald Tribune*'s editorial page. "The most powerful way to increase national savings it to cut the budget deficit," continues the *IHT*.

"To do that, Bush and his allies in Congress must defer the gratification they would derive from showering more tax cuts on the affluent."

How then can Americans live so well—without savings? The *IHT* explains: "Some argue that the amount of personal savings is understated because it does not take into account the increase in housing values, which has many homeowners feeling flush. But elevated home values do not add to national savings [or to national wealth, we add].

"Such wealth is not converted into cold hard cash until a house is sold, and at that point the money flowing into the seller's pocket is simply money that is flowing out of the buyer's pocket. No new wealth is created, unless the seller saves the windfall—which is generally not the case in today's consumer economy. Instead, sellers increase their purchasing power, while the saving rate declines and the United States as a whole becomes poorer."

The old theory is right after all—it works. People do save, they do invest, and they do get richer—just as they're supposed to. They just don't happen to live in the United States of America. The world economy has been globalized. In the new, international division of labor some people save and get rich. Others consume and get poorer.

China, as we all know, is on the opposite side of the planet. Over there, people make the things that we buy and don't buy the things we make. American households are rich and buy a lot. Chinese households are poor and buy little. Americans save little; the Chinese save a lot. Only 42 percent of Chinese GDP is domestic consumption. Another 35 percent is devoted to exports. And nearly half of all the money spent in China, according to Stephen Roach, is for fixed investment.

The truth is that we are becoming a nation of sharecroppers—but only a rich old man like Warren Buffett has the courage to say so. We do not earn enough to pay our way, so we borrow from our suppliers. Asia has become the company store to which we owe our souls.

THE COMING CORRECTION

Tout passé, tout casse say the French. Everything goes away. Everything breaks down. Nothing is born that does not die. Nothing begins that does not end. There is no morning without an evening, and no silver lining without a cloud. Empires come. Empires go.

In the financial markets, the "going" phase is called a *correction*. It is intended to correct the excesses and mistakes of the expansion phase. In a bull market, there are corrections that bring extraordinary gains down to more modest ones. In a bear market, corrections—which soften extraordinary losses into more ordinary ones—are known as *rallies*.

Generally, the force of a correction is equal and opposite to the trend that precedes it. And the pain it causes is directly proportional to the pleasant deception that went before it.

As a practical formula, this does little to help us. We still do not know when or how the correction will come. And, to borrow an idea from Lord Keynes, the deception can last a lot longer than you can remain solvent betting against it. And yet, it is even more dangerous to bet on it.

America's empire of debt rests on many huge deceptions that we have described in this book:

- That one generation can consume—and stick the next with the bill.
- That you can get something for nothing.
- That the rest of the world will take American IOUs forever—no questions asked.
- That house prices will forever go up.
- That American labor is inherently more valuable than foreign labor.
- That the American capitalist system is freer, more dynamic, and more productive than other systems.
- That other countries want to be more like America, even if it is forced on them.
- That the virtues that made America rich and powerful are no longer required to keep it rich and powerful.
- That domestic savings and capital investment are no longer necessary.
- That the United States no longer needs to make things for export.

The deception that sent credit expansion soaring between 2001 and 2005 came eagerly from America's own central bank. By setting its key lending rate below the current inflation rate, the Fed misled almost everyone.

Throughout the boom years of 2002 to 2005, the Great Deceiver, Alan Greenspan, appeared before the U.S. Senate and dissembled. Not only did inflation present no clear and present danger, neither did Americans' debt loads, nor did the negative numbers in the current account. Mr. Greenspan, who surely must have known better, found nothing to dislike and nothing to worry about.

So, we stop, draw breath, and wonder.

The deception is so large, we wonder how it could ever be fully corrected. We speak not merely of Mr. Greenspan's perjury before Congress, but of the larger deception, in which Mr. Greenspan plays a leading role.

The promise of American capitalism is that it makes people richer, freer, and more independent. But since the introduction of the Fed and the rise of the empire, the currency in which Americans keep score has so addled the figures, we scarcely know if we are winning or losing. The dollar we knew as a child—in the 1950s—is only worth a tenth as much today. The average household today has far more of them than we did. In 1950, U.S. household debt to disposable income, which is basically after-tax income, was 34 percent (if disposable income was $10,000, households had $3,400 in outstanding debt). Today, the average American household has learned to live large—on an imperial scale. Its house is worth more dollars. It has a bigger car. It eats out more often. It has a wider TV screen with a clearer picture. It has more employment insurance. More health insurance. More Social Security Insurance. More protection offered by more government employees than ever before. It has many more credit cards, with much larger lines of credit. It has more clothes. More toys. More gadgets, gizmos, and whatchmacallits. It has more debt. More obligations. More chains.

Almost every American believes he is richer. Certainly, compared with the Old World, Americans have no doubt that the rise of their empire improved every subject's life. Is it true?

We pause to deliver a shocking update.

People love myth, fraud, and claptrap—especially when it flatters them. Maybe their food, life expectancy, crime rates, transportation, liquor, women, and architecture are nothing to brag about, say Americans to each other, but when they grub for money, they grub good. "Old Europe," they say, making a comparison, "is too rigid, fossilized, hidebound . . . a museum."

And yet, even this is a fraud. Despite Laffer's curve, Greenspan's Bubbles and Reagan's revolution, the U.S. economy has done no better than Europe.

The *Economist* examined the evidence.

Everybody believes that America grew a lot faster than Europe over the past 10 years. But the figures, in terms of GDP/person are very close—2.1 percent per year for America against 1.8 percent for Europe. Take out Germany—which has struggled with absorbing its formerly communist cousins from the East—and the two regions are exactly the same.

And productivity? A study by Kevin Daly, an economist at Goldman Sachs, finds that, after adjusting for differences in their economic cycles, trend productivity growth in the euro area has been slightly faster than that in America over the past 10 years.

What about jobs? America is the greatest jobs machine on the planet, right? Again, excluding Germany, jobs in the rest of Europe grew at the same pace as in America. And more jobs have been created in the euro.

It's true that Americans earn more and spend more than Europeans . . . but they work a lot more hours.

Europeans simply enjoy leisure more.

But what about the post-2001 "recovery?" Hasn't it been much more vigorous in America than in Europe?

Well, only on the surface. Spiked up by the biggest dose of fiscal and monetary juice in history, America's economy has slightly outpaced Europe's. But the figures are hard to compare. Europe calculates GDP growth more conservatively than America . . . and understates the truth, rather than overstates it, as they do at the Labor Department. More importantly, America's jolt of growth has come at great cost. While Europe got no net stimulus, America has gotten enough to give it the shakes.

"Super-lax policies of the past few years have left behind large economic and financial imbalances that cast doubt on the sustainability of America's growth," says the *Economist*. "From a position of surplus before 2000, the structural budget deficit (including state and local governments) now stands at almost 5 percent of GDP, three times as big as that in the euro area. America has a current-account deficit of 5 percent of GDP, while the euro area has a small surplus. American households now save less than 2 percent of their disposable income; the savings rate in the euro area stands at a comfortable 12 percent. Total household debt in America mounts to 84 percent of GDP, compared with only 50 percent in the euro zone."

Barely has the twenty-first century begun and America finds itself in a remarkable position. It has, what it believes is, the world's most powerful economy . . . and the world's most powerful military force. Like the defunct Soviet Union, it has a sickle in one hand and a hammer in the other. The sickle, alas, has an awkward bend in it.

Since 1990, income for the average American household has risen only 11 percent while average household spending has jumped 30 percent.

How could people spend so much more money without earning more? Outstanding household debt doubled to more than $10 trillion between 1992 and 2004, even adjusted for inflation. And in Utah last year, 28 of every 1,000 households declared bankruptcy, almost three times the rate of a decade earlier.

People are determined to live large and live better than they can afford. They do this by what economists call *smoothing* income. Anticipating higher incomes in the future, young families spend the money now (e.g., buying bigger houses than they can afford). Nationwide, house sizes have grown 30 percent since 1980, says Cornell economist Robert Frank. And now even people in their 50s and 60s look forward to either higher incomes or miracles.

Some economists refer to the whole phenomenon as the "democratization of credit." "Innovation and deregulation have vastly expanded credit availability to virtually all income classes," says the Fed chief.[11] He did not mention his own role in this democratic revolution. He is too modest. He is a Danton and Robespierre put together. The Fed chairman accomplished more than all the nation's innovators and deregulators put together. Dropping the price of credit below the inflation rate, he offered the entire world something for nothing. Now, everyman could get himself into financial trouble, not just kings, speculators, and financiers. He made it possible for lending institutions to extend such a long rope of credit to the common man that millions are sure to hang themselves.

We don't know what to make of it, so we turn to the dead for an opinion. But it is hopeless, the corpses know even less than we do. They can't even imagine what is happening. Borrow against your house when you don't have to? Buy a house as an "investment?" Take out "equity?" "Depend on foreigners to balance your budget?" "Live beyond your means and expect Third World wage earners to make up the difference?" The ideas that Americans once took for absurd, they now take for granted.

What was wrong with our parents, grandparents, and long-dead ancestors? Why weren't they smart enough to realize that they could have a brand-new house with all the modern conveniences without paying for it? Why didn't they figure out that they could all get rich by buying each others' houses. But now, thank God, we are all geniuses.

The baby born when the empire began in 1913 came into the world with nothing. But he owed nothing. Now, he comes into the world owing his share of 37 trillion; that's about $128,560 with his name on it. Is he richer? Is he better off? What would the dead say? That doesn't include his share of Federal obligations and commitments that he'll have to pay, which could add $100,000 more.

WHAT WILL HAPPEN TO AMERICANS' DEBTS?

"He that dies pays all debts," said Shakespeare.[12] Who pays these debts? And how?

The total value of all assets in America is only about $50 trillion. Current U.S. debt is about $37 trillion. Add to it the present value of Federal government liabilities and America is broke. Busted. Bankrupt. No bread. Like nothing. It couldn't pay its debts even if it wanted to.

When people cannot pay their debts, they do not pay them. But the debts do not cease to exist. They are merely "paid" by someone else—the creditor. In the case of America's debts to foreign nations, this can be achieved in three ways: the currency in which the debt is denominated can be devalued against other currencies; the currency can be made less valuable through inflation; or the debt can be repudiated. One of these things—or all of them—is likely to happen.

Repudiation has a long and squalid history. If a man can get away without paying his debts, he will generally figure out why he shouldn't have to pay them. In public life, the reasons are often very good ones. When a new political regime takes over, why should it be stuck with the bills of the old one? When the Bolsheviks took over Russia in 1917, they made Tsarist bonds worthless. Why should they pay bills that they never agreed to? Why should they honor commitments of one capitalist to another? They didn't pay. And why, after 1919, should the new German republic have to pay the Kaiser's bills? France, Britain, and the United States had defeated the Kaiser; let them pay his debts!

The idea of public debt is an attractive nuisance. A father would not have dinner in a fine restaurant and send the bill to his son. Nor would he say to the restaurateur: Hold the bill for my unborn grandson. But such is the state of faith in democracy, that a relatively small group is not only willing to stick its heirs or enemies with costs to which they would never consent—but is happy to do so. Politics is a pernicious and barbarous occupation. There is nothing quite so satisfying in politics as, say, forcing the Religious Right to pay for an abortion clinic or making taxpaying pacifists pay for a bomb so you can blow up some poor foreigner on the other side of the earth.

Generally, the public has only the dimmest, most remote idea of the kind of obligations that are being contracted on its behalf. If asked about them directly, many—if not most—would surely object. But who asks? Besides, the unborn don't vote. And neither do foreigners. Or even out-of-staters.

In America, several states—Michigan, Mississippi, Arkansas, Louisiana, and Florida—totally and permanently repudiated their debts in the panics of the 1840s. In the 1880s, many Southern states repudiated the debts that had been run up by illegitimate carpetbagger governments. But the United States doesn't have to repudiate. All its debts are denominated in its own currency—the value of which it can control. Having the world's reserve currency means you can stiff your creditors without ever having to say you're sorry.

THE DEMISE OF THE DOLLAR

Among the many remarkable stories that appeared in the press in the years from 2000 to 2005, the story of Mr. Asakawa stood out.

The United States economy has been so strong for so long, people all over the world have come to accept the imperial currency. By 2005, no one had more of it than poor Mr. Asakawa in Tokyo. The man controlled the biggest stash of U.S. paper in the world. His life had come to imitate a popular joke. "A man who owes his banker $100,000 can't sleep at night," the joke begins. "But when a man owes his banker $1 million, it's the banker who can't sleep." Mr. Asakawa is the central bank's banker. At the end of 2004, he held an estimated $700 billion worth of U.S. dollar-denominated paper assets in his vault at the Finance Ministry. Beside his bed was a blue plastic monitoring device that would go off like an alarm clock when the dollar fell out of a given trading channel. Mr. Asakawa, needless to say, did not often sleep soundly.

A relatively modest drop in the dollar's value would mean huge losses to Japan's central bank and other dollar holders. But what can Mr. Asakawa do? His infernal alarm alerts him to drops in the dollar/yen exchange rate. But he merely aggravates himself and his wife. He can do nothing about it. The Asians own so many U.S. dollar assets that any attempt to sell would cause the very thing they most worry about—a drop in the value of their single biggest asset. Even if they were to buy General Motors shares—all of them—it would represent only 3.1 percent of Japan's holdings. They would have to buy the whole state of Michigan and Wisconsin, too. We don't know, but we would guess that all the assets in both those states together would not equal the pile of dollar cash now held by Asian central banks.

We understood why Mr. Asakawa would be alarmed. What bothered us was why no one else seemed to be. With as much as $100 trillion of the world's wealth denominated in dollars, how did the world watch so complacently as the value of its main asset was marked down? In 2002, the dollar went down against the euro by 10 percent. Then 20 percent. And then 30 percent. When Warren Buffett began putting his money in euros, he could buy one for just 86 cents. By early 2005, the euro cost nearly $1.36. In Europe, the dollar had lost about 40 percent of its purchasing power.

14

Still Turning Japanese

When people approach retirement, something happens to them: They become risk averse. A young man—with 60 years of life expectation—will do the damnedest things. He'll drink a half bottle of good scotch and drive down a mountain road as if he thought he was making a moonshine run. Or, he'll jump out of a perfectly good airplane. Or enlist in the army just when war has been announced.

An older man has less to lose, but like a shipwrecked sailor down to his last pack of cigarettes, he guards it carefully. He won't cross against the light and won't even have a cup of coffee before going to bed for fear it will disturb his sleep.

Imagine what happens to an economy when millions of people grow old at the same time. Well, you don't have to imagine. You have only to look at what has happened in Japan since 1989. In our previous book, *Financial Reckoning Day* (John Wiley, 2003), we argued that the American economy was following Japan with a 10-year delay. We still believe it—with a reservation (that we explain later). Now we see that as the empire matures, so does the imperial race. America's population is growing old—just like Japan's. But its baby boom came about 10 years later. The average American is 45 years old, has $68,000 in his 401(k) and owes $69,227 in mortgage and $8,000 in consumer debt. He has effectively 10 to 15 years to save enough money to retire. If he wants a retirement income of two-thirds of his salary, then he needs to save something like $500,000 over the next 15 years.

How will he do it? He can't.

He will have to retire poor or live poor until retirement. Neither of these is particularly encouraging for real estate prices, consumer spending, growth of gross domestic product (GDP), or the stock market.

Biology and actuary science converge at around 50 years of age. They soften up a man's brain and his stomach, and turn him from a dynamic risk taker into a fretful old coot who won't part with a penny without a court order.

A man over 50 doesn't want to wait a quarter of a century for stocks to come back to where he bought them. Rather than take the chance, he typically shifts his portfolio from capital gains to income. His risk tolerance also shifts, from return on investment to return of investment; and his savings strategy drifts, too, from just-in-time to just-in-case.

Everything important happens at the margin, as the economists say. The marginal grumpy old man of the 1990s entered the stock market along with everyone else. Who could resist such a party? So, along he came, dressed for a funeral but hoping for a good time. If he got into stocks in 1997, his portfolio in 2005 is now worth about what it was when he bought the stocks. But in the meantime, his debts increased, his savings went down, and the cost of living rose 12 percent over the past five years.

Amos Tversky, a Stanford University psychologist, found that people would rather not lose money than make it. This confirmed something that did not need confirmation, a self-evident insight from the economics profession known as the *marginal utility* hypothesis. As people get more and more of something—whatever it is—each additional unit is of less and less value. (In the case of calories, information, and heroin—after a certain point, additions are not only worthless, they are less than worthless.) An extra dollar means less to a billionaire than it does to a pauper. This is another way of saying that the loss of an additional dollar is of lesser consequence than the loss of a man's last dollar. This is obvious when it is reduced to the extreme situation—where a man only has a single dollar. If he loses it, he will go hungry. But if a billionaire fails to make an additional dollar, it will not even be noticed. This means that a speculation with 50/50 odds is inherently senseless—but people make worse speculations all the time.

Tversky also noticed what he called the *prospect theory*—that investors are more ready to gamble with "house money" than their own. Investors took the fall of the Nasdaq and the decline of the Dow with good grace. But in 2005, they are five years older—closer to retirement age—and taking losses, not just of house money, but of real money: savings that were intended to cosset gray heads and wrinkled brows.

That these marginal, 50-something investors will panic out of stocks seems a foregone conclusion. Will they panic out of houses, too, and out of the habit of consumption?

When Americans begin saving like the Japanese, should it surprise us if the U.S. economy also turns a little Japanese?

Who would believe it? Japan's problem is that its people do not consume enough. America's problem is just the opposite. We are too good at it. We consume with our eyes shut. We're the best consumers in the entire world. When it comes to buying things we don't need with money we don't have—no other nation comes close.

If only consumption could make you rich! Who wants to hear it? Don't waste your time telling your neighbor that rising house prices won't make him rich. You might as well tell him that his wife is fat; he's probably already noticed and won't appreciate the observation in any case.

Besides, property prices are still rising. Who's going to believe he is getting poorer when his house is rising at 20 percent per year? And when he gets so much money without working for it, it is hardly surprising that he spends it. Easy come; easy go. Americans flock to luxury.

But there are signs that the trend is nearing an end. Rental vacancies reached 10 percent in April 2005—a record high. This has cut rental income to the point where the price-earnings ratio (P/E) of houses (average selling price divided by 12-month rental income) has risen to 34, higher than the P/E of stocks at the bubble peak in 2000. Another way to look at it is that rental income averaged about 5 percent of house prices in the 1990s. By 2004, the number had dropped to 3.5 percent.

WHAT ABOUT INFLATION?

In the early 2000s, the U.S. monetary base expanded at the fastest rate in 30 years; it rose 20 percent or more in 2003 and 2004. Why was the money supply increasing so rapidly? It was the work of the U.S. central bank, which was desperate to avoid a long, deflationary Japan-style slump. So far, it has avoided the slump, but at the price of creating a bubble in the entire U.S. economy—centered around residential real estate. Guess how much prices of houses rose in California during the same two years? Twenty percent per year—equal to the increase in the money supply.

The phenomenon is not limited to the United States. Real estate bubbles have been spotted all over the world. And money supplies also are bubbling up—particularly in Asia. What happens is this: U.S. consumers spend more than they can afford buying Asian-made goods. This leaves billions of extra dollars in the hands of Asian exporters. They deposit the money in their central banks, who convert it to local currency—thus raising their own money supply. The U.S. is exporting inflation, say economists, and importing deflation (low-priced goods).

If this news had come out in the 1970s, things would have been different. The "bond vigilantes" would have seen the rising money supply figures and panicked. They would have dumped bonds. Yields would have soared. All of a sudden, mortgage rates would have spiked up and the housing bubble would have been over. But now, no one pays much attention to the money supply figures. Now, everyone knows what no one knew or would have believed 30 years ago—that central banks can create as much money as they want without causing consumer price inflation.

We understand the mechanics of how the Fed's inflation of the money supply ends up in central banks in Asia. We also understand how this works to suppress consumer prices in America and reduces its long-term competitiveness. The unbalanced trade between the United States and Asia leaves huge amounts of money in Asian hands. Much of it is invested in new factories and plants in Asia, which is inherently deflationary, since this policy increases production capacity and the quantity of goods that money chases. Low consumer price increases in the United States permitted the Fed to hold down lending rates lower and longer than would have otherwise been possible. This, in turn, gave speculators and house buyers the credit they needed for the residential real estate boom.

In our previous book, we argued that Japan-style deflation was a greater risk than consumer price inflation. Prices have been falling, off and on, for the past 10 years in Japan. Not that the government and the central bank have not tried to stop it. But prices are harder to control than economists pretend. Prices typically rise when the Fed reduces interest rates. Credit is more affordable, so people buy more. On the other hand, buying decreases when the Fed raises rates, for the obvious and inverse reason that things financed on credit are more expensive. But prices and Fed policy do not always work hand in glove. Occasionally, the hand comes out of the glove and smacks us in the face. This is what happened in Japan. Despite a heroic effort by the Bank of Japan to destroy its own currency, from 1995 to 2005 the yen became more valuable. Domestic prices fell in Japan. The central bank cut rates down to zero. Still, who would want to borrow when prices were falling? Each year, the currency became more valuable; borrowers would have to pay back loans with more expensive money. Who would want to buy anything when he knew he could get it cheaper in a few months? And who would want to invest in new plant and equipment when the prices of his product were actually falling? The Bank of Japan could offer all the credit it wanted. There were few takers.

Could that happen in America? Yes, it could. Could the United States suffer a long, slow, soft slump like the Japanese—as we forecast in our last book? Yes, but there is a big difference between the United States and Japan. The United States is an empire of debt. Japan was a republic of credit. The Japanese never stopped saving. They never stopped making things. If they had a fault, it was the same fault that the Chinese have now—they made too much. While Americans underinvest in productive capacity, the Japanese overinvested. They had so much capacity, the world's consumers could not keep up with it.

The Japanese went bust with the rest of the world owing them a lot of money. And every year since, even through the darkest years of their recession, the Japanese trade balance was positive.

The United States is a very different story. We have elaborated it in this book—the story of an empire of self-delusion and flattery. America can have a soft, slow slump, but not a long one. It can't afford it.

Let us imagine for a moment that the U.S. stock market did fall as much as Japan's—not just the Nasdaq, which has tracked the Nikkei Dow rather closely—but all U.S. stocks. At its peak in 1989, the Nikkei was at 38,915.87. On June 1, 2005, the index stood at only 11,329, a 70 percent loss. And imagine that residential real estate were to fall in the United States as it did in Japan: After 1989, Japanese house prices dropped for 13 years. And imagine that consumers would stop shopping as they did in Japan and that prices would fall for nearly 10 years in a row. To put that last item in perspective, remember that consumer spending is 71 percent of the U.S. economy; in Japan it was never more than 55 percent. Now, ask yourself . . . how many U.S. households would still be solvent (see Figure 14.1)?

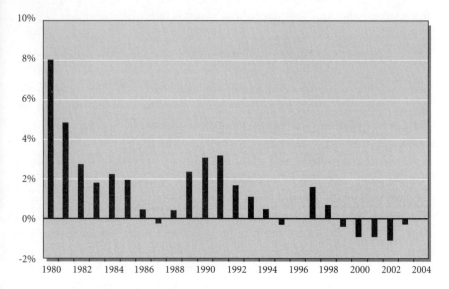

Figure 14.1 **Japanese Inflation Rate, 1980–2004**
After the Japanese stock market bubble burst in 1989, consumers stopped spending and prices fell for 10 years. Imagine what would happen if a collapsing credit bubble set in motion a similar trend in the United States. Consumer spending is now 71 percent of the U.S. economy; in Japan it was never more than 55 percent. How many U.S. households would remain solvent?
Source: Statistics Bureau (Japan).

The answer, of course, is that we don't know. Mortgage refinancing would cease; it would be replaced by mortgage foreclosure. The home-building industry would collapse. So would most other industries. Jobs would become scarce. Credit card payments would go into arrears, then into collection, and then into workout and bankruptcy.

But people who have expected something for nothing for so long do not go gently into that good night. They rant and rail against the failing of the light—and demand action from their imperial representatives. "We want inflation," they will say. "We will not be crucified on a cross of strong paper dollars," they will add, as a theatrical flourish.

Inflation would be an obvious way of reducing the value of America's debts. This is how Germany reduced her debts after World War I. The Reich was left with a bill for $33 billion in reparations to be paid to the Entente powers. But Germany was worn out by the war and had no way of making such large payments. Out of desperation, she resorted to the printing press.

If you are a foreign holder of dollars, and you suspect that the U.S. Treasury may be warming up the printing presses, you will probably not wait until inflation reduces the purchasing power of your money. A 50 percent fall in the value of the dollar would wipe out half the real value of the U.S. overseas debt—an amount greater than the entire dollar currency reserve holdings of all Asian central banks put together.

At some point, America's debts will probably be incinerated by inflation. When the howls from consumers and voters grow loud enough, the Feds will panic. In desperation, Ben "Printing Press" Bernanke will point south, toward Argentina. "There . . . that is our only way out," he will say.

15

The Wall Street Fandango

If a man wants to drive a nail through a 2 × 4, he does so without pretense or illusion. Unless he knows what he is doing, he probably will split the wood or bend the nail and make a mess of it. But as soon as he goes beyond the stretch of his own arms and the reach of his own eyes—beyond his own private world—he is in a public world where he can imagine the most extravagant things. Nothing is ever clear or certain in public, and every error is someone else's fault. That is why so many men prefer it. The public world is so surrounded in fog that he thinks he sees half-naked nymphs hiding behind every tree and $100 bills under every cushion.

Many industries have arisen and thriven on these illusions. Here, we take a look at one of them: Wall Street.

What is Wall Street's purpose? "To allocate capital efficiently," a traditional economist might say. But economists are merely victims of their own theories. A communist economist would snarl and spit; Wall Street's function is merely to aid the capitalist as a lackey aids a knight—he would say—to help the greedy bastard onto the backs of the working class.

One might just as well ask the question: Why are there giraffes? To which, we can honestly answer: because they have not been exterminated yet. All animals—including humans—exist only because they have not yet become extinct. Wall Street exists because it has not yet disappeared.

This sort of reductionism is not very useful, except that it provides a solid footing on which to begin our climb. We need to get down before

305

we can get up. Down at the bedrock essentials of what really is happening, we can build and work our way up out of the mist, to the heights where the air is clear and we might actually see something. For the problem that most investors face is that they do not see Wall Street for what it really is, but as a mirage that changes shape depending on what theory you use to look at it.

"Where you stand depends on where you sit," it is said. If you sit on the board of General Motors or another major cash-hungry corporation, your stand on Wall Street is fairly obvious: It is a worthy and necessary ally. If you sit in an office of Goldman Sachs or Merrill Lynch, or in any other office of the financial industry, you are sure to view Wall Street as a generous and benevolent employer; it puts your children through private school and pays for your house in the Hamptons. And if you are the typical investor, you are likely to look on your Wall Street professional as though he were the family doctor; he provides a necessary and helpful service. Like a doctor, he is a phone call away, ready to fly to your aid and comfort. He even wears a tie and drives a nice car. He is a professional. He is there to help.

You are not wrong; he provides a valuable service. But before you send a thank-you note, you should realize: The man is probably a quack.

Medicine is a science, of sorts. Progress is cumulative. Over the years, doctors have learned what works and, more often, what doesn't. Give a patient enough strychnine and he is unlikely to pay his bill. Gradually, doctors learned not to do it. Even a bad doctor has at his fingertips the results of thousands of years of trial and error, including a few years of real scientific research and observation. He can still make a mess of things; but there is no reason why he should, except for simple incompetence or a diabolical urge.

But the financial industry is not the same as the medical industry. It is not science. Progress is not cumulative, but cyclical. One generation learns. The next forgets. One makes money; the next loses it. One adores Wall Street; the next wants nothing so much as to get away from it. Both medical science and the financial industry claim positive results. As to medical science, we have no reason to doubt it; we have seen some of its wonders firsthand. But the claims of the financial industry are mostly a swindle.

If you are to make money from your Wall Street placements, you must ask yourself: Whence cometh the lucre? Apart from taking it from each other—after the financial industry has had its cut—the only possible way for investors to make money in stocks is for the companies they buy to become more valuable. The value of a share of a business is nothing more than the value represented by that share's portion of the profits; The share would only become more valuable if profits were to rise. But how could the profits of American businesses be expected to go up?

To make more money, U.S. businesses would have to sell more or increase their margins. To whom would they sell more products? Not to Americans. Real discretionary purchasing power is falling in the homeland. Americans have a mountain of debt to service. And in the rest of the empire, the competition is too fierce.

As for increasing margins, there are only two ways to do it. You can increase prices or lower costs. Either way will widen the margin between revenues and expenses. Either way will increase profits. But in the globalized economy of the twenty-first century, anything that can be shipped across borders or communicated electronically is subject to Asian competition, which is cutting prices, not raising them. What about cutting costs? When you cut costs anywhere, you run into a problem that economists refer to as the *fallacy of composition.* An individual company can increase its margins by cutting costs. It can lay off workers or cut expenses. In this way, it can increase its profit margin. But one business's expenses are another's revenues. The laid-off employee can no longer afford to buy as much. Or, perhaps it is the supplier that feels the blade. Either way, gradually or suddenly, revenues shrink throughout the system. Generally, profit margins remain unchanged—or fall for everyone.

We have no way of knowing what the future holds for corporate profits, we merely note that investors have no reason to think they will go up. The U.S. economy has just experienced the biggest rush of stimulus ever, including a quarter century of falling interest rates, three years of a "prime" rate below the CPI level, and an additional $700 billion jolt of federal spending. Corporate profits should be at epic highs, and there is no reason to anticipate more.

The other possible source of gains for investors is other investors' money. If some other investor's pile were to go down, yours might go up. Wall Street promises as much; practically every advertisement for a mutual fund claims that it does better than its peers. Even if they all went down in actual, real value, they nevertheless crow that their "relative performance" beat out just about everyone else. A doctor might similarly advertise that his patients died in less agony than the patients of his competitors; generally, he has the good sense to refrain from mentioning it. Nor is he likely to bring it up. For medicine is not a zero-sum game. No one has to die at the age of 20 so another can live to be 80. They can all live longer.

Wall Street insists that investing is like health care; it is not a zero sum game either. One investor does not have to die so that another can make above-market gains. We can all get rich. This is like saying we can all be above average. "Rich" is a relative measure, not an absolute one. Compared with most of the world, almost all Americans are already rich. But most of the world doesn't live next door or drive by in a new Mercedes on his way to work. We compare ourselves with our neighbors, who also invest on Wall Street and who insist that their investments go up more than yours. Suppose that one year everyone's investments doubled in value—except for one poor fellow whose portfolio rose only 10 percent. Ten percent is still a very good return. But the poor man would feel like a total failure nonetheless. He would be lucky if his wife didn't leave him for her tennis coach.

Obviously, relative performance is guaranteed to disappoint at least half the players, even under the best conditions. Al Gore was shocked that half of all students performed below the average. Investors are alarmed when—in good times—half of them don't keep up with the average gains and they are disgusted in bad times, when all of them lose money.

Over time, all investors are destined to lose money (compared with the general market), for the cost of the Wall Street casino must be paid. Brokers, analysts, deal-makers, financiers, fund managers, account managers—all the financial intermediaries who make up the Wall Street industry—draw salaries and pensions as long as they draw breath. That money, too, must come out of investors' pockets, so that over the long run, the average investor's real return must be lower than the actual return from the investments. And many, including most of the little guys, will actually lose money.

Not only is investing not a science, it is not even an art. It is more like holding up liquor stores. Sometimes you get away with it. Sometimes you don't. But you are generally better off if you don't; for there's nothing like success to set up failure. As soon as you get the idea that you are such a smooth operator that you can pull off a job like that, you'll be planning the next one when the cops pull up.

The typical investor in public markets has no idea what he is doing. Putting his money into a stock or a mutual fund brings him a temporary happiness. He sees himself as Kirk Kerkorian making a bid for General Motors or Warren Buffett shrewdly moving on an insurance company. "I bought Google," he tells his wife. His chest expands. He feels a crown of authority on his head and imagines his most private part growing. For he has mastered the most sacred and all-powerful rite of our time; with a single gesture he has joined the Knights Templar, the Freemasons, and the local country club. He is in. He is with it. He gets it. He is one with all the other swells who make up this wondrous modern economy. He has gone to Wall Street like Sir Galahad to Camelot.

He does not realize the misery awaiting him. Only later, much later, does he discover that he is not a hero, but just a chump—an insignificant speck of dust on Wall Street's white shoes.

The scene would be depressing if there weren't something gloriously comic in it. Wall Street is doing nothing evil; it is merely doing its job— separating fools from their money.

The root of the misconception is the nature of investing, at least, the public form of it. The idea of it is that a man can get rich without actually working. All he has to do is put his money "in the market" by handing it over to Wall Street, and through some magic never fully described, it comes back to him 10-fold. He must see his broker as Christians see Jesus at the wedding feast. He casts his dough on the water of the lower Hudson and the East River, and it comes back multiplied into really big money.

There must be some science to it, he imagines, some wisdom that investment geniuses came up with years ago that—like penicillin or quinine—is now available to him. But it is not so. Instead, the whole edifice of Wall Street is built on a hollow wish: that you can get something for nothing.

That is not to say you can't make money on Wall Street. You can even make money on Wall Street as a simple investor. But for that, you will have to do a lot more than just be "in the market." You will have to treat your investments as though you were driving a nail through a 2 × 4. You will have look on it not as a public investment, but as a private one. You will have to look at the company, not the stock. You will have to do a lot of serious research and thinking or pay attention to someone who does. In short, you will have to earn it.

One of the great myths of late, degenerate capitalism is that everyone can be a capitalist. It is easy, the brokers tell you in the ads; all you have to do is buy some stocks. Of course, Wall Street is eager to sell stocks to you. And, presto, you're just like Warren Buffett. See how easy it is to get rich!

But you don't get rich by buying stocks; you get rich by buying companies at good prices, holding them for a long time, and not spending your money. In this regard, Wall Street is not a friend, it is an enemy. And so is, by the way, the Securities and Exchange Commission (SEC). The fraud perpetrated by Wall Street and the SEC is that mom-and-pop investors are on the same level playing field as real investors. It is just not true. The insiders know vastly more than the average investor and so does Wall Street. Do you think Wall Street's insiders would sell a stock if they thought it was going up? Of course not; they sell stock because they know they make more money on commissions—buying and selling for customers—than they are likely to make from the stocks. They are like the owners of casinos. The owners of any Las Vegas glitter-hole could pull the levers on their slot machines if they wanted to do so. They don't. Because they know they will make more money by letting the customers win from time to time so they will keep playing and hoping that they will turn out to be big winners. Ultimately, it's the House that wins, not the players.

AN INSIDER'S GAME

A corporate insider has a huge advantage. Like Warren Buffett, he invests in public markets, but with the close, detailed information of someone running a private business. He doesn't get his information from the newspaper—but from his own eyes and ears, his own balance sheets and inventory reports, and his own sales numbers. He is someone who really knows something. He is not out to improve the world. He is only interested in improving his own world. He is sometimes right and sometimes wrong, but at least he acts on the basis of real information, not public babble.

Wall Street's great pretense is aided and abetted by academic economists who maintain that the market is always correct. The market always knows all there is to know about a stock, they say. This delightful con is known as the *efficient market hypothesis* (EMH). Whatever price the market sets, they say, is the right one. So whether you are Warren Buffett or a bus driver, you will always buy at the "perfect" price. And since the price will be correct—no matter what it is—you don't have to worry about how high prices go. Just buy! And then buy some more! Wall Street loves it. The SEC encourages it—with the preposterous insight that all investors are created equal and endowed with the same right to buy stocks at the market price!

Here again, the comparative conceits of modern democracy and modern investment markets are too amusing not to point out. In the short run, says Warren Buffett, the stock market is a voting machine. In the long run, it is a weighing machine. In the short run, the "voters" decide how much to pay for a stock. The price they choose is perfect say EMH dreamers, because they know all there is to know. There is no other means of valuing a stock. There is no higher authority than Mr. Market. So, the bus driver or public prosecutor can buy any stock he pleases, at any price Mr. Market sets, convinced that he is as smart as Warren Buffett.

Back in the days when royal families ruled Europe, a monarch might do a good job of ruling his kingdom or a bad one. If he bungled the job, he would have to face his nobles, his people, and ultimately, his God. If his mistakes were egregious enough, he could lose his kingdom, his head, or his soul.

The lumpen democrat, like the lumpen investor, faces no such check. He believes he can make no mistake, because there is no higher authority. Whatever he wants, whatever he thinks, whatever crosses his mind—there is nothing and no one to tell him he is a fool. If 51 percent of voters want something, who can say they are "wrong," even if what they want is sordid and revolting? If the majority of stock buyers decide to pay 200 times earnings for a tech stock, that, too, must be the correct price, right?

Both concepts—democracy and the efficient market hypothesis—are empty. They only tell us that the mob gets what it wants—in the near term. Longer term, the mob gets what it has coming.

Real capitalists are not mob investors. They do not buy stock in the public market based on public information. They buy companies. And they buy them only when they understand what the companies do and how their investment will pay off.

If you want to make money, you must reject the lunkheadedness of the masses. You should invest like an insider, on the basis of private information—even if it comes from public sources—and direct, personal experience (though not necessarily your own). Merely putting your money at play with the rest of the lumpeninvestoriat, on the other hand, will give you no greater gains than anyone else which, at this stage of the empire, are not likely to be good.

Many investors believe they can improve their investment return by watching insiders; after all, who wants to buy a stock when its own managers are dumping it? During the entire period—from the final years of the great tech bubble through the bear market and recession—followed by the rally in the stock market and economic recovery, people who knew what they were doing were selling stocks.

Insiders sometimes buy and sometimes sell. They have a tendency to sell. Corporate shares are often a form of compensation, which must be sold to be realized. And insiders often simply need to diversify their holdings, convert them to other forms of wealth such as houses in the Hamptons, or pay off divorced spouses, and so forth. But though the figures have a bias toward the short side, trackers had rarely seen such an eagerness on the part of corporate insiders to get rid of their shares, nor such a reluctance to buy more, as they saw in 2004 and 2005. And by January 2005, insiders practically stopped buying altogether. The total of insider purchases was only $34.1 million—the lowest number in 12 years.

AMPLIFIED SENTIMENTS

There are two ways to try to make the world better, dear reader. And two ways to invest. But only one of them really works.

You can read the papers, watch the news, look at the whole public spectacle and try to form an opinion about what is going on. If you are a world improver or an empire builder, you might come to the conclusion that outsourcing needs to be stopped, or that China needs to revalue its yuan, or the architecture in Ireland needs to improve, or that the women of west Texas need to lose weight, or that Pakistan needs a regime change. If you are an investor, you might think China stocks will be a big success in the years ahead, or that Bush is bringing down the deficit, or that 2006 will be a good year for stocks.

But if you put down the papers and turn off the TV, you could study the things closer to you. If you wanted to make the world a better place, you could plant flowers in your front yard or flirt with the homely girl down the street. As an investor, you could study the company you work for or visit one that is looking for investors.

Public information is little more than the amplified sentiments of the crowd. In broad terms, the crowd of investors is either fearful or greedy. Actual news items are interpreted to give the lumpen the interpretation they want. At the crescendo of a bubble, almost every cursed event is bullish, as was the war against Iraq in 2003, and the hurricanes that hit Florida in 2004. Bullish sentiment ran so high for so long, even the impact of a giant meteor would have been taken as a good omen. In January 2005, investment advisors were still bullish by a two-to-one margin after the longest stretch of bullishness ever recorded. During the same period, insiders—private investors, with private and independent knowledge—had been extremely bearish on their shares. Not only did the insiders buy little of their own stock, they sold a lot of it—$1.9 billion worth. For every share they bought, in other words, they sold 55. We don't know if that is a record, but it must be close to one.

In bull markets, your stocks will go up. In bear markets, they will go down. Every transaction will be clipped by brokers and intermediaries. If you put your money in a mutual fund, a hedge fund, or with professional managers, you will pay additional fees. Some poor souls pay stockbrokers and managers to help them place their money in funds of funds . . . or even funds of funds of funds. This style of investing almost guarantees losses. It makes time work against you, like staying at the slot machines long after being ahead. Over time, you are practically guaranteed to give back any gains—either in the next bear market or simply in management fees and other charges.

'TIL DEATH DO US PART

Don't ever get married to your investments, say the experts. When they don't work out, dump them.

But a real investor is not a cad. We were looking over some of our investments recently. We found some stocks we have been married to for years. We hadn't seen them in so long, we had forgotten what they looked like. We have held WR Grace, for example, through boom, bust, bankruptcy, and boom again. We only married the stock in the first place because we felt sorry for it. WR Grace was being hit with lawsuits for asbestos, as we recall; we figured the poor girl needed a little support. Then, she went Chapter 11. But it has worked out. The company came out of bankruptcy, and the stock went back up. We have no regrets.

We only bring this up to compare our own antique style of investing with today's one-night-stand investment world. People don't seem to believe in marriage anymore. When the going gets rough, investors get going somewhere else. Or, people merely think they can have more fun by fooling around. Nobody buys a house expecting to live with it forever. Nor do they buy stocks and houses with the intention of having them and holding them until they are parted by death. Instead, they flip them—changing assets nearly as often as they change their pants.

Almost nobody buys a stock for the dividends—few stocks have any to speak of. Nor do they buy a house merely as a place to live. Instead, they keep moving from one thing to the next hoping to get rich on capital gains.

If only it were true! If only making money were as easy as "wham, bam, thank you ma'am."

Alas, you do not, generally, make money overnight. Instead, you make money by investing patiently and faithfully. Your money needs time to work; it must get together with resources, expertise, and opportunity. They have to get to know each other. They have to make plans and execute them. If you're lucky, the project will eventually work out and you'll get a decent return on your investment. But it can take years. Warren Buffett says the ideal holding period for a stock is forever. That sounds like an exaggeration to us. Forever is a long time. And since everything degrades, everything dies, everything goes away—including the best companies ever created—forever might be a tad too long. But this is only a theoretical problem. In practice, you will expire, or your investments will, long before forever comes.

Even houses take a long time to pay off. The stream of revenue from a house is the utility of living in it over time. That is why it makes sense to buy a house that you will want to live in for a very long time. You will be able to afford to fix it up, plant trees and a garden, and amortize the house and improvements over many years.

You may say, yes, but house prices are soaring. And, yes, you are right. As near as we can tell, the fastest, surest way to make money in the United States today is to buy an expensive house in a bubbly market with a zero-down mortgage. You have no capital at risk and you stand to make a fortune.

But don't confuse this with investing. It is pure speculation, a series of one-night stands that could be very enjoyable. The trouble is that most people don't know the difference. They begin to think there is something magic about real estate that makes it always go up. They begin to think they can't lose. Then, when the bubble pops, they become the biggest losers of all.

16

Subversive Investing

"Dere's dem dat's smart . . . an' dere's dem dat's good," said Uncle Remus. Many young people today can't even identify Uncle Remus. Some of their elders might want to arrest you for quoting him in the original dialect. But the man was a genius.

When we were young, we were a lot smarter. But as the years go by, many of the things we thought were smart don't seem so smart anymore. And now we realize that no matter how smart we think we are, we are never quite smart enough. We think stocks are going up, we think we can build a better world in Mesopotamia, we think we can tell the fellow down the street how to discipline his children or decorate his house. But what do we know?

It is easier to be smart than to be good; that's why there are so many smart people, and so few good ones. Smart men get elected to high office. They run major corporations. They write editorials for the newspaper. Pity the poor good man; he goes to parties and has nothing to say that is not mocking and cynical. Others talk about their smart deals, their smart ideas, their smart plans and successes. Women crowd around them; a smart man grows taller as he speaks. The good man shrinks.

We bring it up here just to argue with it. Because we think it is virtue, not brainpower, that really pays off. "All the world is moral," said Emerson. It is moral in the sense that if you are careless enough to step on a hoe, the handle will hit you in the face.

One generation takes the virtuous path. The next is likely to slip off, honoring the old virtues in speech, but not in act. The oldest generation of Americans remembers the Great Depression. They borrowed reluctantly,

saved eagerly, and made the United States the greatest power on earth.
Their children still talked their parents' talk, but didn't mind walking off
in a different direction when the wind was at their backs. And their grandchildren? The newest generation seems to have no regard whatever for the
virtues of their grandparents or the futures of their grandchildren. They
disregard the wisdom of the dead, and load up the unborn with debt.

THE ESSENTIAL INVESTOR

The word *essentialism* has been used to describe other crackpot strains of
philosophy. But no one had a good grip on it, so we took it for ourselves.
Although it is a creed derived from studying the markets, it applies to the
rest of life.

At the foundation of essentialism is ignorance, not knowledge. Ignorance rules the world of finance. It also rules the rest of the world. You can
never know whether a given action will produce beneficial results; you can
never know whether a stock will go up or down. You don't know what the
price of oil will be in the next hour, let alone the next 10 years. You do not
know whether General Motors will be in business in 10 years' time. You
do not know much about the past, little about the present, and nothing
about the future.

What do you do when you know so little? You become very modest.
You turn to the essentials. You focus on what you do know and what you
can control. You follow the rules.

Essentialism venerates humility as its highest virtue. Your authors are
so humble, we are practically arrogant about it. No one is more humble
than we are.

But the humble recognition of your own ignorance still leaves you
with decisions to make. How do you make them?

Well, you turn to the essential rules—the traditions, the lessons of history, the distilled wisdom of generations of dead people. In the investment
world, you "buy low, sell high." That is what has always worked for investors. Buying high and hoping to sell higher is another game—speculation. If you think you might enjoy it, do go ahead, dear reader. But it is
not really investing.

Warren Buffett, an essentialist investor, says you should buy "great
companies at fair prices." We don't disagree. Of course, it is hard work to

find them. But there you are: another essential insight—you don't get something for nothing.

You generally get what you deserve from the markets, not what you expect. Following the rules, working hard with patience and discipline will usually get you a decent result. Reckless speculation, overspending, and frenetic trading, on the other hand, generally give investors what they have coming—good and hard.

Somewhere in the still-unwritten *Essentialist's Handbook,* it warns readers that they "cannot be too trusting in private or too cynical in public." Essentialists make private life paramount. They "sweep their own doorsteps," as Goethe put it, hoping to make the whole world clean. They are not empire builders, at least, not public empire builders. Instead, they build their own private little empires, constructed with the voluntary help of others and a great deal of luck. Essentialists do not take themselves too seriously. They mind their own business; they do their best. They read the newspapers only to gawk and giggle. They do not particularly care if their investments go down. For, if they do the right thing—if they do their best—they recognize that the outcome is not up to them.

In business and investment, essentialists operate on the basis of private knowledge, not public knowledge. They buy companies, not stocks. They trade on the basis of insider information, not public information. They buy assets at good prices, not outrageous ones. They purchase stocks at low p/e ratios (price to earnings)—between 5 and 10. Let the public investor buy stocks over 15 p/e. Essentialists turn off the TV, they trust their own eyes and ears, their own experiences, and the reasoning power of their own brains. But they trust even their own brains only so far. They know that they are just like everyone else—easily swayed by emotion and easily influenced by mass sentiments.

It is not grandiose. It is not messianic. Nor is it guaranteed to work miracles. But at least it doesn't make things worse, and it will leave your money and dignity intact.

THE MYTH OF CAPITAL GAINS

Capital gains in housing and stocks is a fraud. A house produces no more "income" just because it is more expensive. Instead, the utility remains exactly the same. You could double the price of all the houses in the

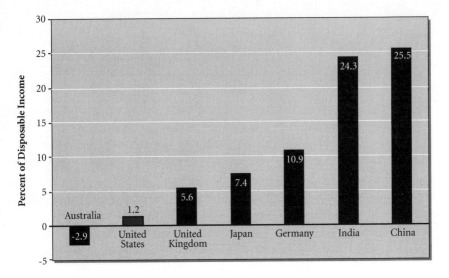

Figure 16.1   **Personal Saving Rates around the World**
The virtues that made U.S. stocks and property investments pay off can still be found overseas. It is as if they have been outsourced. You can still see them, but they now travel with a Chinese, Japanese, or Indonesian passport and speak with an accent.
Source: OECD.

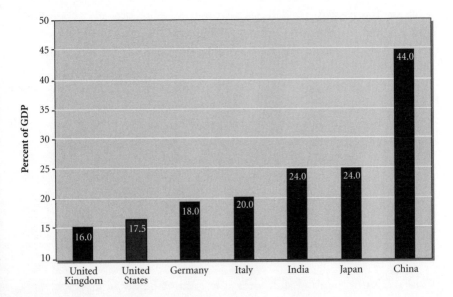

Figure 16.2   **Capital Investment Rates around the World**
Source: World Bank, BEA.

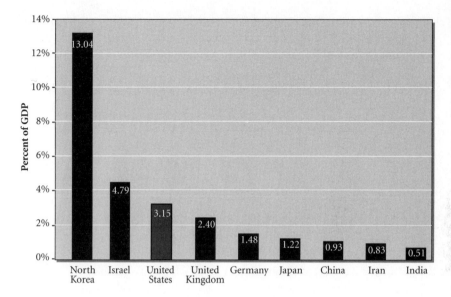

Figure 16.3 **Military Spending as a Percentage of GDP around the World**
Source: CIA World Factbook.

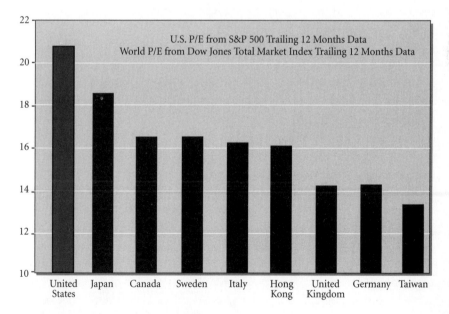

Figure 16.4 **P/E Ratios around the World**
Source: Dow Jones, Standard & Poor's.

United States, and Americans would still not be a penny richer—unless they could sell their houses to foreigners.

A house cannot go up in value. It can only go up in price.

But what about other investments? Suppose stocks doubled in value? Or bonds? Or gold coins? What difference would it make? Here again, we look into the mists and fog that surround the extraordinary popular delusions of our time—and we find the most remarkable shapes! Millions of investors, fund managers, analysts, brokers, strategists, speculators, and gamblers all over the world sweat and strain, day after day, to try to find investments that will go up in price. But what difference does it make? None. Of course, it makes a difference individually, privately, and personally. If you have a collection of rag dolls and then have the good fortune to find that rag dolls have become all the rage, with rag doll prices doubling every year, well bravo for you. People give you more money for your rag dolls. Money has moved from someone else's hands to yours.

You are richer. The person who bought the rag dolls figures he is no poorer—he has merely exchanged one form of wealth for another. But so have you. Now he owns rag dolls instead of dollars. He even believes the rag dolls will bring him more wealth, for they are going up in price. You on the other hand, have given up the wealth-building rag dolls in return for the paper dollars.

Taken as a group, buyers and sellers included, nothing has changed. People still have exactly the same number of rag dolls and the same amount of money. All that has happened on a macroeconomic level is that preferences have changed; people now prefer rag dolls to the other things money can buy. Overall, they are not a penny richer. They have merely moved money from one pocket to another.

Bonds, gold, real estate. All are about the same. An increase in the price does not make people, generally, richer. It makes a few people relatively richer—which is all they care about. But all these transactions involve nothing more than moving money around; a people as a whole—or the average investor—cannot expect to get rich by investing in them. They are only means of saving money or putting it to use. A bond is nothing more than a loan that should come back with interest. The interest is a real gain; it makes the lender richer. He has the original capital, plus something. Real estate, too, may pay dividends to the holder—in terms of rent money or actual personal use. These, too make him richer, without capital gains. Gold is a different thing altogether. It can never make people richer for it produces no dividends. As a means of holding and preserving wealth, on the other hand, it has no rival. We will look at it separately in a moment.

Stocks also are different. They are a claim on a share of a company's income. If the company's income goes up, so does the real value of the stock. What happens, though, when the company does not earn more money? What happens when stocks go up anyway? What happens when the stock market rises, when investors "vote" for higher share prices? Don't they all get richer, as the stock market rises? Well, yes and no. They are richer, compared with nonholders of stock. Society has merely switched its preferences, just as it did in the case of rag dolls. On a macrolevel taking everyone together, they have gained not a single sou.

Since stocks and real estate are so widely held, an increase in prices spreads throughout the entire society, like consumer price inflation, so the average home owner or stockholder is not much better off. He can sell his stocks at a profit, but he has to buy others back at higher prices. Likewise, he can sell his house for more than he paid for it, but he still will need a place to live. And it will cost him more money.

There is no particular reason why one generation would want to pay $5 for $1 worth of earnings and the next pay as much as $30. These preferences shift—just as voter preferences shift. Sometimes, voters are expansive and bullish. Other times, they are fearful and gloomy. The history of the stock market is one of long shifts in sentiment that run up capital gains over a period of 15 to 20 years and then run them down again. In the 1930s and 1940s, investors could have bought a stock for 5 to 10 times earnings. In the 1960s, they would have paid twice to three times the price. Then, in the 1970s, sentiment shifted again. Investors weighed the risks and rewards and voted for lower prices. By the late 1980s, stocks were selling for 5 to 10 times earnings again. Then, they shifted again. Capital gains were back in style, with prices rising over the next 18 years, to the point where investors paid 20 to 30 times earnings and believed that capital gains were forever, not for just a cycle.

Capital gains come. And go. They do not make society richer, only the people who happen to get them, and then only if they are smart enough to sell at the very moment when they have become most convinced that the gains will go on eternally.

SUBVERSIVE INVESTING

An investor who follows the crowd and gives in to the collective mood of the market cannot expect to make any money. For he will only get what everyone else gets. Only the contrarian who subverts the will of the mob and goes against the prevailing mood can hope to make any money.

Somehow, the markets always have to surprise us. If they did not, what would be the point of having them? People trade assets because one believes they will go up, the other believes they will go down. At least half of the traders must be surprised. Besides, if they all knew what would happen, they would never have to trade, bargain, or take a risk.

The more people all come to believe the same thing, the more they must all be surprised, because as they become more and more sure of themselves, they tilt the odds against themselves. The person on the other side then has an edge. It is a bit like pari-mutuel betting at a horse race. Whatever horse is going to win is going to win. You can't know which. So the payoff, over time, is not in the horse—it is in the odds. The favorite pays off most handsomely when he is least favored; that is, when the most people are surprised to see him in the winner's circle. When he is favored out of proportion to his real chances of winning, you are better off putting your money on another nag even if you believe the favorite will win.

The more people stand to be surprised by a given turn in the market, the more the contrarian investor stands to make money. Not that he has a copy of tomorrow's *Wall Street Journal* under his arm. Nor can he read the future in the stars. He is merely a better judge of his fellow man. He knows that when men get together they tend to amplify and reinforce each other's sentiments and tilt the odds.

The polls show that both the pros and the amateur investors are currently overwhelmingly bullish. This is a feeling, not a thought. They can give you all the reasons stocks should go up. On the other hand, the man with a bearish feeling will have his own reasons—just as good and just as many. The reasons balance themselves out; it is feelings that move the market. Like bilgewater, they tend to slosh from starboard to port and back, in short cycles and in long ones. In the end, they give us the averages—the normal, the ordinary, the balance that keeps the boat from sinking altogether.

The same is true in all areas of collective action. The crowd can do no real thinking or real analysis. It has no private, insider information. It is not because of logical, objective reasoning that the mob of investors deems a stock worth 10 times earnings one day and 20 times earnings two years later. Nor does logical reasoning lead one generation to favor a republican form of government while the next happily consents to a dictator or an empire.

The natural inclination is to simplify and exaggerate the prevailing mood by pressuring people to conform to it. This creates circumstances in which the favorite horse, favorite stock, or preferred political outcome is greatly overbought. The opportunity then, lies disproportionately on the other side of the trade, where only subversive contrarians can take advantage of it.

In no field of human activity is contrarian thinking less welcome or more subversive as in warfare. When a troop of cavalry attacks, it must do so in unison. Every man must give up his own thoughts—even thoughts of his own survival—to lend weight to the collective action and give it a hope of success. If he malingers or holds back, he may increase his own chance of survival, but he weakens the force of the assault. This is why cowardice or dereliction is so severely punished in wartime. At Stalingrad, in World War II, when Marshal Chuikov came to take charge of the defenses, one of his first actions (at least so it has been reported) was to line up a company of soldiers who had performed badly in a recent battle and have every tenth man shot. The ancient tradition of "decimation" had not been used since the Roman era.

In a letter to his family, a French soldier in World War I told how his group had been ordered "over the top" in what they all realized was a hopeless mission. They were to attack German trenches, across a "No man's land." Between them and the Germans was a stout emplacement of barbed wire. From bitter experience, the French knew they wouldn't make it beyond the barbed wire.

The officers sent desperate messages to their commanders, informing them of the hopelessness of their situation. They asked for clarification and confirmation: Did they really mean for them to attack? But the answer came back in the affirmative. The men did not protest. They did not mutiny. Instead, they wrote farewell letters to their families—and went to their deaths as ordered.

The contrarian solider would have tried to save himself. He would have feigned a wound. He might have lingered in the trenches. He might have given himself a real wound—but not a deadly one—to avoid combat. Relatively few did so—even though it was the only choice rational self-interest might have offered him.

In World War I, bullet wounds to the hand became popular. "You've got a ticket home," soldiers said to their friends who were lucky enough to get shot in the hand. Everyone was jealous of the man who got to go back to his private life with his honor, his wits, and his body more or less intact. But after a while, anyone with a wounded hand was suspected of doing it to himself. Doctors inspected for powder burns. If they found evidence of a self-administered wound, the poor man would be executed. Then, inventive soldiers found they could get the enemy to inflict the wound simply by holding a lit cigarette above the trench at night.

Wars are tragic examples of collective action: Defection is considered disgraceful and dishonorable; the punishment is death. Markets, on the other hand, are comedies; you can say goodbye to the trenches any time.

The greater the commitment of the group to itself and its own purpose—the greater the advantage to the person who subverts it. In war, he might live while his comrades die. In markets taking the other side of a crowded trade, he might make money while the large group of investors loses it.

THE POWER OF GOLD

Mr. James Surowiecki wrote a wise and moronic piece on gold in the *New Yorker*. His wisdom is centered on the insight that neither gold, nor paper money are true wealth, but only relative measures, subject to adjustment.

"Gold or not, we're always just running on air," he wrote. "You can't be rich unless everyone agrees you're rich."[1]

In other words, there is no law that guarantees gold at $450 an ounce. It might just as well be priced at $266 an ounce, as it was when George W. Bush took office for the first time. Since then, a man who counted his wealth in Kruggerands has become 70 percent richer.

But gold wasn't born yesterday, or four years ago. Mr. Surowiecki noticed that the metal has a past, just as it has a present. He turned his head around and looked back a quarter of a century. The yellow metal was not a great way to preserve wealth during that period, he notes. As a result, he sees no difference between a paper dollar and a gold doubloon, or between a bull market in gold and a bubble in technology shares.

"In the end, our trust in gold is no different from our trust in a piece of paper with 'one dollar' written on it," he believes. And when you buy gold, "you're buying into a collective hallucination—exactly what those dot-com investors did in the late nineties."

Pity he did not bother to look back a little further. This is the moronic part. While Mr. Surowiecki looked at a bit of gold's past, he did not see enough of it. Both gold and paper dollars have histories, but gold has far more. Both gold and dollars have a future. But, and this is the important part, gold is likely to have more of that, too.

The expression, "as rich as Croesus," is of ancient origin. The king of historic Lydia is remembered, even today, for his great wealth. Croesus was not rich because he had stacks of dollar bills. Instead, he measured his richness in gold. No one says "as poor as Croesus." We have also heard the expression, "not worth a Continental," referring to America's paper money during the Revolutionary War era. We have never heard the expression, "not worth a Kruggerand."

Likewise, when Jesus said, "Render unto Caesar that which is Caesar's," he referred to a denarius, a coin of gold or silver, not a paper currency. The coin had Caesar's image on it, just as today's American money has a picture of Lincoln, Washington, or Jackson on it. Dead presidents were golden back then. Even today, a gold denarius is still about as valuable as it was when Caesar conquered Gaul. America's dead presidents, whose images are printed in green ink on special paper, lose 2 percent to 5 percent of their purchasing power every year. What do you think they will be worth 2,000 years from now?

A few years before Jesus, Crassus, who had made his fortune on real estate speculation in Rome, decided to put together an army to hustle the east. Alas, such projects almost always meet with disaster; the attempt by Crassus was no exception. He was captured by the Parthians and was put to death in an unusually cruel and costly way. He did not end his days with paper money stuffed down his throat, and certainly not dollar bills. No, they poured molten gold down his gullet—or so the story has it.

Gold has a long history. And during its history, many was the time that humans were tempted to replace it with other forms of money— which they believed would be more convenient, more modern, and most importantly, more accommodating. Gold is hard to find and hard to bring up out of the earth. By its nature, the quantity of gold is always limited.

Paper money, by contrast, offers irresistible possibilities. The list of bright paper rivals is long and colorful. You will find hundreds of examples, from assignats to zlotys, and from imperial purple to beer suds brown. But the story of paper money is short and predictable. Since the invention of the printing press, a new paper dollar or franc can be brought out at negligible cost. Nor does it cost much to increase the money supply by a factor of 10 or 100—simply add zeros. It may seem obvious, but adding zeros does not add value.

Still, the attraction of being able to get something for nothing has always been too great to resist. That is what makes goldbugs so irritating: They are always pointing it out. Even worse, they seem to enjoy saying "There ain't no such thing as a free lunch," which comes as a big disappointment to most people.

Once people were able to create money at virtually no expense, no one ever resisted doing it to excess. No paper currency has ever held its value for very long. Most are ruined within a few years. Some take longer. Even the world's two most successful paper currencies—the American dollar and the British pound—have each lost more than 95 percent of their value in the past century, which is especially remarkable since both were linked by law and custom to gold for most of those years. For the dollar, the final link to gold was severed only 34 years ago.

Some paper currencies are destroyed almost absentmindedly. Others are ruined intentionally. But all go away eventually. By contrast, every gold coin that was ever struck is still valuable today, most have more real value than when they first came out of the mint.

Central bankers reported in early 2005 that 70 percent of them were increasing their reserves of euros. As for the world's erstwhile and present reserve currency, the dollar, they seemed to have, not growing reserves, but growing reservations. We also have reservations about the dollar. Whatever it is worth today or tomorrow, we are sure it will have less worth eventually. That it is not regarded as worthless already is remarkable. The average dollar is nothing more than electronic information. It exists thanks only to the ability of digital technology to keep track of it. Relatively few dollars ever make it to paper, and many of them end up in the pockets of Russian drug dealers and African politicians. Most dollars in most people's accounts are not even graced with the image of a dead president; when the end comes, they won't even be useful for starting fires.

It is imperial vanity that keeps the dollar in business. And it is vanity that will make it worthless. Economists want money they can control. Central bankers want money they can debase. And politicians want money they might get their mug on.

The trouble with gold is that it turns its back on world improvers, empire builders, and do-gooders. It is money that no central bank promotes and none destroys. It is money that exists only in a tangible form, a real metal—a number on the periodic table. "Gold goes up and down, just like other kinds of money," say economists. Which is true. "You can protect yourself from inflation in other ways," say the speculators. True again. "Gold pays no dividends or interest," say the investors. True.

Nor will gold cure baldness or add inches to your most private part. Even as money, gold may not be perfect. But it is better money than anything else.

Gold was around millions of years before the U.S. dollar was invented. It will probably be around a billion years after. This longevity is not in itself a great recommendation. It is like buying a suit that will last longer than you do; there is no point to it. But the reason for gold's longevity is also the reason for its great virtue as money: It is inert; it yields neither to technology nor to vanity.

The world improvers will always be with us. They will spend more than they have, boss other people around, and generally make the world a worse place to live. They will offer proposals like those of Thomas L. Friedman. The nice thing about gold is that it is so unresponsive. It neither laughs nor applauds. Gold is money that no central bank promotes and none destroys.

Paper money is a handy tool for the world improvers. They use it like politicians use civil service jobs and generals use heavy bombers—to get their way. Whatever the vapid ideal *du jour,* it takes money to pursue it. Given enough money, the poor can be fed and housed. The middle classes can be given free medical care and low-cost loans for houses. The upper classes can be given contracts and favors. Enemies can be summoned up, bombed, and reconstructed. Bread, circuses, war—the imperial program costs money.

How to get more money for these great new programs, these marvelously worthwhile ideals, these fabulous public spectacles? Gold flatly refuses to cooperate. It doesn't even give a reason. Instead, it stays as mute and reticent as a dead man in front of a television. No matter how persuasive the advertising, the man is not going to go for it.

Paper money, on the other hand, barely needs encouragement. Start up the presses! Lower the interest rate! Relax reserve requirements and lending standards! Sell more bonds! Create more paper! Paper money is ready to go along with anything. Like George W. Bush, it never met a boondoggle it didn't like. Sooner or later, it ends up as worthless as the projects it was meant to pay for.

Gold is merely the subversive investor's way of protecting himself.

SPECULATIONS

Is. Was. Will be again. If things remained the same, there would be no need for verb tenses. But things do not remain the same, they change.

After a long while of remaining the same, investors begin to under-price change. A speculator can make money by betting against the present tense. But not always, not when the present tense only came into being recently. For that case, investors still price things based on the past. But after a long spell, investors begin to believe that that which is will be forever. They make their bets on a false premise by underpricing risk, underpricing change, and overpricing stability.

Everything in life has a beginning, a middle, and an end. Each day that passes in which present trends do not come to an end brings us a day closer to the day when they will.

"Stability leads to instability," said economist Hyman Minsky. The longer things remain stable, the more people become convinced that they will never change. As long as the camel's back doesn't break, why not heap more straw on it?

Today's house flippers are taking riskier and riskier positions—because they are sure that present trends will not come to an end anytime soon. Instead of buying a house with 20 percent down, they buy one with 10 percent or nothing down. Instead of buying one, they buy two. Instead of buying a modest house, they buy an extravagant one. Instead of living modestly, they live large, on an imperial scale.

But as more and more people make such risky bets, it actually hastens the arrival of what all of them forgot to fear: that something will happen.

Rising prices put pressure on the financial system. Interest on loans must be paid. The greater the loans, the greater will be the interest payments. Unless incomes rise, the straw piles on until the camel's knees begin to wobble and then break.

This tendency to overprice the present tense is another way of looking at what Amos Tversky had observed: that investors' perceptions of risk are overinfluenced by recent history. This leads to a speculative opportunity, for the average investor has come to believe something that isn't true. He has placed his bet inappropriately, unwisely paying too much for stocks and houses in the mistaken assumption that they pose little risk to him. The shrewd speculator has no more idea of whether stocks will go up or down than the naive punter. But he knows that the lumpen have miscalculated the odds, so he will take the other side of the trade. Naive players may be right—maybe prices usually go up. But that is like saying the favorite horse usually wins at the racetrack. It is perhaps true, but not helpful. For as likely as it is that the favorite horse will win, the odds are still less than 100 percent.

Here is another, related error that people make: they look for meaning in things where there is none. We have seen how the homeland people flatter themselves. Why do they rule the earth? They must be better than others. How do they know they are better? Because they are the rulers, they are not the ruled. The group seeks reasons, beyond mere chance, to explain its good fortune. It is smarter. It is racially superior. Its religion, its civilization, its culture—all are thought to be more advanced or more conducive to progress. The climate in the homeland is either favorably soft or rigorously harsh.

People misapprehend the randomness of events. They see a fund manager who has done very well for five years in a row and they buy his fund. They don't realize that his performance may be a feature of randomness—pure chance, in other words. Out of a group of thousands of funds, some are going to produce spectacular results. Most likely, the results are nothing more than chance, but investors' misperceptions create a speculative opportunity.

It is as if they had watched a group of men flip a coin. Out of a group of 10 flippers, one gets heads 10 times in a row. Normally, the odds of getting heads would be only 50/50. But this man, they believe, has a talent for flipping heads. So, they bet on heads again—not at 50/50 odds, but at 60/40 odds. To win a dollar, they must pony up 60 cents.

The shrewd speculator spots his opportunity. He realizes that the man has flipped heads 10 times in row purely by chance and that his odds of getting heads again are still only 50/50. No one has any idea whether heads will come up, but the clever speculator knows that he must bet against it—because the odds favor him.

Over the broad sweep of stock market history, prices have gone up. From barely 100 following the crash of 1929, the Dow is now over 10,000. Who can doubt that the tendency is up? Yet, adjusted for consumer price inflation, the Dow is only about 500, and most of that increase is merely cyclical. A dollar of stock market earnings is sometimes judged to be worth only $5 or $6 of capital investment. Other times, investors are willing to pay more than $20. At any particular time, a speculator may have no idea whether stocks are headed up or down. But he knows that they are likely to overprice the present tense. He knows also that things in nature tend to regress to the mean. After having marched from under 1,000 to over 10,000, from 1982 to 2005, investors have come to believe the tendency is definitely up. Over time, the likelihood that stocks will be relatively cheap or relatively expensive is about 50/50. But today's naive buyers think they have come across someone who flips heads every time; they expect stocks will become even more expensive than they are now. They have made their bets accordingly, and they are reflected in stocks' current prices.

Over the past 100 years, the mean price that investors were willing to pay for $1 of stock market earnings was about $12. Today, investors pay $20 on the S&P 500. They believe prices will go up. They are not wrong. Sometime, prices will go up, but investors pay too much for the opportunity to find out when.

A real fat tail event, however, would be more than just a stock market decline. Prices decline all the time. What happens so rarely that investors tend to forget all about it is a crash. What are the odds of a crash on Wall Street? No one knows, but they are probably greater than most investors realize. A crash in the stock market would be accompanied by the usual complaints. But a crash in the residential property market would be much worse. Households have come to rely on equity buildup to keep themselves solvent. Without it, they would have to cut back, reducing consumption. This would produce all the negative things the Fed has worked so dishonorably to avoid: recession, job loss, personal bankruptcies, mortgage foreclosures, and falling prices.

We know the past tense—how America's empire of debt was built. What we don't know is the future tense—how and when it will end. It is like our own death; we know it will happen, but we don't want to think about it. Still, it is the sort of thing you want to be prepared for all the time. A sensible man may not know the hour or the place of his demise, but he does not doubt that it is coming. If he is smart, he is ready for death any day of the week. So is a sensible investor ready for the day a great empire peaks out. He doesn't know when it will happen. And the longer it doesn't happen, the more he believes it may never happen at all. But nature smiles neither on vacuums nor monopolies. Empires are a monopoly on force; they don't last forever. What is peculiar and promises to be entertaining about the U.S. debt empire is that it is more absurd than most; which is to say it is less likely to last very long. That does not mean that the United States will disappear. But you should be prepared for a write-down of its debt at any moment.

You do not want to go to your grave after saying an unkind word to your mother. Neither do you want to wake up to a market crash with a portfolio of junk bonds, tech stocks, and U.S. dollars.

There is never a good time to die. Nor is there a good time for a crash or a slump. Still, death happens. Be prepared. Say something nice to your mother. Offer a bum a drink. And buy gold.

Appendix

The Essentialist Glossary

Alan Greenspan: God, or the Maestro, take your pick.

Bear Market: A 6- to 18-month period when the kids get no allowance, the wife gets no jewelry, and investor gets what's coming to him.

Bed and Breakfast Stage: This is a new phase in the life cycle of humans wedged in between the career phase and traditional retirement. It usually kicks in when children have left home, careers have run their course, and a man's balance sheet begins to look better than he does.

Bill Gates: Where God goes for a loan.

Bonner's Law: This one is eponymous. It describes the interaction of Moore, Metcalfe, and the process of creative destruction. Moore and Metcalfe are used by technology investors to justify high prices. Why not pay a lot, they say, when the whole industry is evolving at an exponential rate? Bonner's Law predicts that the revved-up speed of creative evolution in the technology marketplace will produce revved-up rate of destruction. Moore + Metcalfe = Creative Destruction squared. Investors may want to gamble on Internet companies. But they should pay very low prices, not high ones. Low prices recognize the truth—that the company is most likely to fail. (See also Metcalfe's Law; Moore's Law.)

Broker: What my broker has made me.

Buffett versus Gates: This is shorthand for the conflict between the older Graham and Dodd investment approach and the younger, Bill Gates/Jeff Bezos wealth creation formula. The eminent Graham and Dodd investor, Warren Buffett, won't buy Internet stocks or even

Microsoft, though he knows the company and plays bridge with Bill Gates. Technology investors, on the other hand, who tend to be younger, believe that Moore and Metcalfe trump Graham and Dodd. New technology is exploding so fast, they say, that the old standards no longer apply. The old guys just don't get it. Who will "get it" in the end remains to be seen. (See also Graham and Dodd.)

Bull Market: A random market movement causing an investor to mistake himself for a financial genius.

The "C" Spot: A dangerous little corner of the brain where collective thinking occurs. It is useful in sporting events, cavalry charges, and political campaigns, and is essential for reading the editorial pages without laughing; but otherwise it is an impediment to the human race and should be surgically removed.

Call Option: Something people used to do with a telephone in ancient times before e-mail.

Cash Flow: The movement your money makes as it disappears down the toilet.

Chateau: This French word might be translated as "money pit" or "place for people who don't like tech stocks to lose their money." By way of introduction, Bill is the founder and CEO of a group of investment services, called Agora Financial. We have offices in Paris, London, and Baltimore. Bill chose to live in France and bought a *chateau* not far from the late David Ogilvy's much larger pile. *Chateaux* are the only investments that have lasted for a very long run, a period of 1,000 years or more . . . and lost money every year.

Cisco: Sidekick of Pancho.

Creative Destruction: The economist Schumpeter came up with this expression. It describes the natural process of open markets—where new companies destroy old companies and old technologies. Dirigisme tries to block the forces of creative destruction. By contrast, laissez-faire, another French term, lets the chips fall where they may. Bill Gates, America's Last Great Capitalist, built his company on the dirigiste model. Linux is an example of the laissez-faire approach. Gates created vast wealth. Linux, or the process of Creative Destruction, will destroy it.

Day Trader: Someone who is disloyal from nine to five.

Dirigisme: This is also a French term. It is the modern French version of Plato's ideal form of government—where you get smart people together and they tell everyone else what to do.

Dollar: More valuable than gold, the dollar has nevertheless been going down in value since the Federal Reserve system was set up more than eight decades ago to protect it.

Erfahrung: Things you know from personal experience. For example, if you slam your fingers in the door of a *Deux Cheveaux* (the French answer to the Volkswagen, without the power or the comfort), the next time you close the door, you move your hand out of the way. Why? "*Erfahrung.*"

Esperanto Money: This is the term we apply to the euro. Esperanto was a made-up language designed to make it easier for people to communicate. It flopped. The euro will flop, too.

Financial Planner: A guy who actually remembers his wallet when he runs to the 7-Eleven for toilet paper and cigarettes.

Fin de Bubble: The spirit of our age. We live in a world that is waiting for something to happen. In the meantime, people are all very optimistic about the future—especially the financial future. Like people during the *fin de siecle* period of the Gay Nineties and pre-World War I, they are impressed by technological progress and see few clouds on the horizon. World War I ended the *fin de siecle* sentiment. What Archduke waits to be assassinated so our *fin de Bubble* can be entered in the history books?

Gambling: What you do with your excess money when you are too lazy to invest the way Buffett does.

Gold: A heavy, yellow metal, rarely seen or spoken of. It is a barbaric relic that went down in dollar terms for the past 20 years of the twentieth century. It is about the only thing you can leave on the seat of your car in Baltimore without worrying about the windows being smashed.

Graham and Dodd: These are the guys who wrote the book on investing; Warren Buffett—their most brilliant student.

Head and Shoulders Pattern: Not to be confused with the dandruff shampoo, a head and shoulders pattern on a chart vaguely resembles the head and shoulders of a very strangely shaped man. It is thought to be a precursor of a decline. But if the market doesn't go down, the technicians take another look and tell you that it didn't look like a head and shoulders after all. It was really a horse's rear end.

Heart of Darkness: Where Internet investors go—the horrors.

Homo Analogiens: People who have trouble setting their alarm clocks and believe the new economy is mostly hype.

Homo Digitaliens: Ed Yardeni, Al Gore, Bill Gates, Jeff Bezos, and a few others. They walk among us.

The Information Age: The handle given to today's postindustrial, postmodern economy. The successor to the Age of Ignorance, the Age of Information is characterized by such an abundance of useless facts and senseless data that, now, everyone knows everything, and almost no one knows anything.

Institutional Investor: Investor who is now locked up in a nuthouse.

Investing: This is the activity that many people say they do but few understand. It involves studying the likely stream of income from an investment, anticipating its growth or decline, and adjusting for risk. Most of today's investors wouldn't know a balance sheet if it bit them on the derriere—which, we predict, it will.

Leicht Denken: *Schwer uberlegen*'s distant cousin. The kind of superficial reasoning a person does when he only has gross generalities or someone else's money to work with. The source of much misguided action in government, politics, finance, and romance. (See also Schwer Uberlegen.)

Market Correction: The day after you buy stocks.

Metcalfe's Law: Metcalfe noticed that a system like the Internet becomes more valuable the more people use it. For example, the first telephone was virtually useless by itself. The millionth, by contrast, is exceptionally useful. Thus, the value of the system itself increases exponentially as its use becomes more widespread. Metcalfe's Law helps explain why the dollar has been such a hit all over the world. Investment Biker, Jim Rogers, driving around the world with his then-girlfriend, Paige Parker, reported that he could use dollars almost everywhere—and in many places where even the government won't accept its own currency. Dollars have become a worldwide medium of exchange—made more valuable simply because they are so ubiquitous.

Momentum Investing: Find a trend and stick with it until you go broke.

Moore's Law: A key to understanding tech investing. Moore said that computer power would double every 18 months. Interestingly, statisticians use this device to ramp up the gross domestic product (GDP) figures arguing that a computer purchase today is worth more than the actual dollars exchanged. They never applied this logic to autos or any other sector, but some $300 billion of these fictitious "chained dollars" have been added to the nation's GDP.

P/E Ratio: The percentage of investors wetting their pants as the market keeps crashing.

Sand, Small Towns, and Old Towns: Where people go to have their mid-life crises.

Schwer Uberlegen: Either the kind of reasoning one does based on firsthand experience or the winner of the Gold Medal in the luge in Nagano 1998. We don't speak German, so we're not sure.

Sensation Mongers: People think the news media just reports the facts. Yet, a zillion things happen every day, and the news media doesn't mention any of them. Instead, the media confines itself to amplifying the madness of crowds and reporting all the news that fits its groupthink agenda.

Significant Base Formation: This is what you get when you sit around and eat too many donuts while reading the financial news.

Speculating: This is what you call gambling when your wife asks what you doing.

Stock Analyst: Idiot who just downgraded your stock.

Stock Split: When your ex-wife and her lawyer split all your assets equally between them.

Triffin Paradox: The trouble with making a currency the world's leading brand is that to do so, you have to print a lot of them and export them vigorously. Each dollar is an IOU from the government. The more dollars outstanding, the weaker the issuer's balance sheet, and the less each one is worth. Eventually, Triffin and Metcalfe will have to come to terms.

Unified Theory of Greed (UTG): The insight that we are all greedy SOBs, but the real SOB is the guy whose greed—whether for power, money, or love—is not held in check by his wife, the market, or the law.

Value Investing: The art of buying low and selling lower.

Wissen: Things you think you know—but usually have no direct experience of and couldn't pick out of a police lineup if your life depended on it. Most "isms" fall into this category—capitalism, communism, antidisestablishmentarianism—the kind of thing that is reported in the paper and discussed with pompous gravity on the editorial pages.

Yahoo!: What you yell after selling your tech stocks to some poor sucker for more than you paid for them.

Notes

Introduction   Slouching toward Empire

1. Claes G. Ryn, "Appetite for Destruction: Neoconservatives Have More in Common with French Revolutionaries Than American Traditionalists," *American Conservative,* January 19, 2004.
2. John Chuckman, "America's Imperial Wizard Visits Canada," December 6, 2004, http://www.countercurrents.org/us-chuckman061204.htm.
3. Ramsay MacMullen, *Corruption and the Decline of Rome,* Yale University Press, 1990.
4. John Markoff, "China Joins Global Race for Fastest Computers; Beijing and Tokyo Aim at a New Barrier to Overtake U.S. Lead," *International Herald Tribune,* August 18, 2005.

Chapter 1   Dead Men Talking

1. Margaret Wilson Oliphant, *The Makers of Venice, Doges, Conquerors, Painters and Men of Letters,* Burt, 1897.
2. Ibid.
3. Edward Gibbon, *The Decline and Fall of the Roman Empire,* Everyman's Library, 1993.
4. See note 1.
5. Edmund Randolph, 1787 Constitutional Convention.
6. James Madison, "The Federalist No. 10: The Utility of the Union as a Safeguard Against Domestic Faction and Insurrection (continued)," *Daily Advertiser,* November 22, 1787.
7. Constatino Bresciani-Turoni, *The Economics of Inflation: A Study of Currency Depreciation in Post-War Germany,* Routledge reprint ed., 2003.
8. Karl Theodor Helfferich, *Das Geld,* Adelphi English ed., 1927, p. 650.
9. See note 7.
10. http://chinese-school.netfirms.com/abacus-Sir-John-Templeton-interview.html.
11. Nassim Nicholas Taleb, *Fooled by Randomness: The Hidden Role of Chance in Life and in the Markets,* 2nd ed., Texere, 2004.

12. Ibid.
13. Ibid.

Chapter 2   Empires of Dirt

1. Paul Ratchnevsky (Thomas Nivison Haining, trans.), *Genghis Khan: His Life and Legacy,* Blackwell reprint ed., 1993.
2. "Changing Perceptions of Genghis Khan in Mongolia: An Interview with Dr. Ts. Tsetsenbileg by Yuan Wang," *Harvard Asia Pacific Review,* http://hcs.harvard.edu /~hapr/winter00_millenium/Genghis.html.
3. http://khubilai.tripod.com/mongolia/id3.html.
4. http://en.wikipedia.org/wiki/Genghis_Khan.
5. Francis Fukuyama, *The End of History and the Last Man,* Free Press, 1992.
6. http://www.rain.org/~karpeles/armadadis.html.
7. http://www.angelfire.com/ok3/chester/maindir/armarda.htm.
8. Alfred Thayer Mahan, *The Influence of Sea Power upon History, 1660–1783,* Dover Publications, 1987.

Chapter 3   How Empires Work

1. Emily Eakin, "Ideas and Trends; All Roads Lead to D.C.," *New York Times,* March 31, 2002.
2. Robert Kaplan, *Warrior Politics: Why Leadership Demands a Pagan Ethos,* Vintage, 2003.
3. Roger Cohen, "Globalist: Rumsfeld's Blunt Style May Backfire in China," *International Herald Tribune,* June 11, 2005.
4. Paul Kennedy, "The Greatest Superpower Ever," *New Perspectives Quarterly,* Washington, winter 2002.
5. Thomas Cahill, *How the Irish Saved Civilization,* Anchor, 1996.
6. Ibid.
7. Deepak Lal, *In Praise of Empires: Globalization and Order,* Palgrave Macmillan, 2004.
8. Ibid.
9. Rudyard Kipling, *The White Man's Burden,* 1899.
10. Stephen Howe, *Empire: A Very Short Introduction.* Oxford University Press, 2002.
11. Ramsay MacMullen, *Corruption and the Decline of Rome,* Yale University Press, reprint ed., 1990.
12. Ibid.
13. Ibid.
14. http://www.antiwar.com/justin/j112299.html.

15. Aristotle, *Politics,* Nuvison Publications, 2004.
16. John Perkins, *Confessions of an Economic Hit Man,* Berrett-Koehler Publishers, 2004.
17. Niall Ferguson, *Colossus: The Rise and Fall of the American Empire,* Penguin, reprint ed., 2005.
18. John Quincy Adams' Address, July 4, 1821.
19. Floyd Norris, "Floyd Norris: Will China Be Setting U.S. Rates?" *International Herald Tribune,* May 13, 2005.
20. Grandfather Economic Report Series, http://home.att.net/~mwhodges/debt.htm.
21. *China Daily,* http://www2.chinadaily.com.cn/english/doc/2004-12/15/content _400251.htm.
22. See note 19.
23. CIA: *The World Factbook,* http://www.odci.gov/cia/publications/factbook/geos /us.html#Econ.
24. Institute for International Economics, http://www.iie.com/publications/papers /paper.cfm?researchid=26.
25. See note 23.
26. Niall Ferguson, "The End of Power: Without American Hegemony the World Would Likely Return to the Dark Ages," *Wall Street Journal,* June 21, 2004.

Chapter 4   As We Go Marching

1. John T. Flynn, *As We Go Marching,* Ayer Company, reprint ed., 1972.
2. Ibid.
3. Ibid.
4. Ibid.
5. Ibid.
6. Ibid.
7. Jose Ortega y Gasset, *The Revolt of the Masses,* W.W. Norton & Company, reissue ed., 1994, Chapter 7.
8. See note 1.
9. Ibid.
10. Ibid.
11. Ibid.
12. Sol Bloom, Chairman of the House Foreign Relations Committee, 1926, to colleagues.
13. "Arming for Peace," *New York Times,* October 31, 1951, p. 27.
14. Finance and Development, http://www.worldbank.org/fandd/english/0696/articles /0100696.htm.
15. Garet Garrett, in his pamphlet "Rise of Empire," 1952.
16. Ibid.

17. Garet Garrett, *The People's Pottage,* Truth Seeker Co. Inc.; TS ed ed., 1992.
18. Ibid.
19. Ibid.

Chapter 5   The Road to Hell

1. Malcolm Gladwell, *Blink: The Power of Thinking without Thinking,* Little Brown, 2005.
2. Ibid.
3. Ibid.
4. Ibid.
5. Warren Harding, Inaugural Address, 1921.
6. H. L. Mencken, 1880–1956.
7. Judge Learned Hand, speech at "I Am an American Day" ceremony in Central Park, 1944.
8. Sigmund Freud, William C. Bullitt, *Thomas Woodrow Wilson: A Psychological Study,* Transaction Publishers, 1999.
9. Woodrow Wilson, *Address to Congress Asking for a Declaration of War,* April 2, 1917.
10. The Raab Collection, http://raabcollection.com/detail.aspx?cat=0&subcat=34 &man=344.
11. http://www.ieru.ugent.be/palo.html.
12. See note 9.
13. Ibid.
14. Adam Gopnik, "The Big One: Critics Rethink the War to End All Wars," *The New Yorker,* August 23, 2004.
15. Viscount Esher, 1852–1930.
16. Winston Churchill, MIT's "Mid-Century Convocation," April 1949.
17. Ibid.
18. See note 8.
19. See note 9.
20. Hew Strachan, *The First World War,* Viking Adult, 2004.
21. Winston Churchill, letter to his wife, July 28, 1914.
22. Stefan Zweig, *The World of Yesterday,* Viking Press, 1970.
23. Randolph Bourne in his essay, "The State," http://www.bigeye.com/rbquotes.htm.
24. The International School of Toulhouse, http://194.3.120.243/humanities/ibhist /war/wwi/europe_1914/germany/germany_before_1914.htm.
25. See note 9.
26. John F. Kennedy, Inaugural Address, January 20, 1961.
27. Richard Nixon, Inaugural Address, January 20, 1973.
28. David Lloyd George, *War Memoirs,* 1934.

29. Ludwig von Mises Institute, http://www.mises.org/fullstory.aspx?control=224 &id=74.
30. History News Network, http://hnn.us/articles/10108.html.
31. Edward Chancellor, *Devil Take the Hindmost: A History of Financial Speculation,* Plume, reissue ed., 2000.
32. Rod Mickleburgh, "He Did the Best He Could That Day . . . He Survived," The Memory Project, *Toronto Globe and Mail,* http://www.theglobeandmail.com/special /memoryproject/features/fox.html.
33. See note 29.

Chapter 6   The Revolution of 1913 and the Great Depression

1. John T. Flynn, *The Decline of the American Republic and How to Rebuild It,* Devin-Adair Publishers, 1955.
2. Civil War Currency Facts, http://www.civil-war-token.com/civil-war-currency-facts.htm.
3. The Ludwig von Mises Institute, http://www.mises.org/etexts/rootofevilb.asp.
4. Ibid.
5. Representative Robert Adams, January 26, 1894.
6. See note 3.
7. President William H. Taft's Message to Congress, June 16, 1909.
8. Amendment XVI, 1913.
9. Article V of the Constitution in its original form.
10. John Dickinson, June 7, 1787, Constitutional Convention.
11. James Madison, "The Federalist No. 63, The Senate (continued)," *Independent Journal,* Saturday, March 1, 1788.
12. C. H. Hoebeke, "Democratizing the Constitution: The Failure of the Seventeenth Amendment," *Humanitas,* Volume IX, No. 2, 1996.
13. John Kenneth Galbraith, *A Short History of Financial Euphoria,* Penguin Books, 1990.
14. United States Constitution, Tenth Amendment.
15. Franklin Delano Roosevelt, "Fireside Chat," March 9, 1937.
16. Ibid.
17. See note 1.

Chapter 7   MacNamara's War

1. Ken Hagler's Radio Weblog, Recitation of the Battle of Camerone, April 30, 2003.
2. *Le Figaro,* May 7, 2004.

3. Ibid.
4. Ibid.
5. William J. Duiker, "Ho Chi Minh," *Theia,* September 27, 2000.
6. Ibid.
7. Vo Nguyen Giap, "When a Nation Was Born," *Vietnam News Agency,* 2000.
8. Charles W. Eliot, *The Congressional Record.*
9. Oliver Cromwell, letter to the synod of the Church of Scotland, August 5, 1650.
10. Robert S. MacNamara, James Blight, Robert Brigham, Thomas Biersteker, and Herbert Y. Schandler, *Argument without End: In Search of Answers to the Vietnam Tragedy,* Public Affairs Press, 2000.
11. The infamous domino theory: "You have a row of dominoes set up; you knock over the first one, and what will happen to the last one is that it will go over very quickly," President Eisenhower, April 7, 1954.
12. Lyndon B. Johnson, speech, October 21, 1964.
13. Memorandum from the President's Special Assistant for National Security Affairs (Bundy) to President Johnson, en route from Saigon to Washington, February 7, 1965.
14. See note 10.
15. Lyndon B. Johnson, *Public Papers, 1963–1964,* p. 952.
16. Walter Heller Oral History, 1965, in the Johnson Library.
17. "Tell the Vietnamese they've got to draw in their horns or we're going to bomb them back into the Stone Age," General Curtis LeMay, May 1964.
18. See note 10.
19. Bruce Palmer, *The Twenty-five Year War: America's Military Role in Vietnam,* University Press of Kentucky, 2001.
20. See note 10.
21. Ibid.
22. Martin Luther King, speech, New York City, April 4, 1967.
23. Lyndon B. Johnson, conversation with McGeorge Bundy, May 27, 1964.
24. See note 10.

Chapter 8   Nixon's the One

1. Richard Duncan, *The Dollar Crisis: Causes, Consequences, Cures,* John Wiley & Sons, 2003.
2. Gardner Ackley, memo to Lyndon B. Johnson, July 30, 1965.
3. Lyndon B. Johnson, State of the Union Address, January 12, 1966.
4. Joseph Califano, *The Triumph and Tragedy of Lyndon Johnson,* Touchstone Books, 1992.
5. Ibid.
6. Ibid.

7. Ibid.

8. *The Columbia Electronic Encyclopedia,* copyright © 2005, Columbia University Press.

Chapter 9   Reagan's Legacy

1. Claes G. Ryn, "Appetite for Destruction: Neoconservatives Have More in Common with French Revolutionaries Than American Traditionalists," *American Conservative,* January 19, 2004.

2. Ross MacKenzie, "The Reagan Legacy: He Led a Revolution. Will It Survive?" *Economist,* June 10, 2004.

3. Ronald Reagan, Inaugural Address, January 20, 1981.

4. Murray N. Rothbard, "Repudiating the National Debt," Ludwig von Mises Institute, posted Friday, January 16, 2004, http://www.mises.org/fullstory.aspx?control =1423&id=74.

5. Rod Martin, *Thank You, President Bush: Reflections on the War on Terror, Defense of the Family, and Revival of the Economy.* World Ahead Publishing, August 30, 2004.

6. Ibid.

7. Jude Wanniski, "A Chinese/Asian Currency Zone?" http://www.wanniski.com /showarticle.asp?articleid=4529.

Chapter 10   America's Glorious Empire of Debt

1. David H. Levey and Stuart S. Brown, "The Overstretch Myth," *Foreign Affairs,* March/April 2005.

2. H. A. Scott Trask, "Perpetual Debt: From the British Empire to the American Hegemon," Ludwig von Mises Institute, posted January 27, 2004.

3. Thomas Jefferson to James Madison, September 6, 1789.

4. Ron Suskind, *The Price of Loyalty: George W. Bush, the White House, and the Education of Paul O'Neill,* Simon & Schuster, 2004.

5. Alan Greenspan at the Adam Smith Memorial Lecture, Kirkcaldy, Scotland, February 6, 2005.

6. George Orwell, "The Lion and the Unicorn: Socialism and the English Genius," essay, 1941.

7. James Surowiecki, *The Wisdom of Crowds,* Anchor, 2005.

8. F. A. Von Hayek, "The Pretence of Knowledge," Nobel Memorial Lecture, December 11, 1974.

9. Richard Duncan, "How Japan Financed Global Reflation," ANDONGKIM, May 20, 2005.

10. Ibid.

11. See note 1.
12. Ibid.

Chapter 11   Modern Imperial Finance

1. http://www.princeton.edu/pr/news/03/q2/0612-brain.htm.
2. "Dennis Kucinich on Free Trade" On the Issues, http://www.issues2000.org /2004/Dennis_Kucinich_Free_Trade.htm.
3. Alan Greenspan at the Adam Smith Memorial Lecture, Kirkcaldy, Scotland, February 6, 2005.
4. Robert McTeer, Dallas, 2001.
5. Edmund L. Andrews, "Greenspan Shifts View on Deficits," New York Times, March 16, 2004, section A, column 1, page 1.
6. http://www.census.gov/prod/www/abs/decennial.html.
7. See note 3.
8. Ibid.
9. Stephen Roach, "Global: Confession Time." Global Economic Forum, Morgan Stanley, February 7, 2005, http://www.morganstanley.com/GEFdata/digests /20050207-mon.html.

Chapter 12   Something Wicked This Way Comes

1. Thomas Friedman, New York Times, March 8, 2004.
2. Ibid.
3. Ibid.
4. "Outrage and Silence," Thomas L. Friedman, New York Times, May 20, 2005.
5. Paul Craig Roberts, Counter Punch, March 16, 2005, http://www.counterpunch .org/roberts03162005.html.

Chapter 13   Welcome to Squanderville

1. David Streitfeld, "They're In—But Not Home Free," Los Angeles Times staff writer, published April 2, 2005.
2. Ibid.
3. Ibid.
4. Joyce Cohen, "The Hunt: Becoming a Mogul, Slowly," New York Times, April 10, 2005, late edition—final, section 11, column 1, page 12.
5. Ibid.
6. Warren Buffett and Charlie Munger, Berkshire Hathaway shareholders meeting, April 30, 2005.

7. Jane Hodges, "Flipping Real Estate . . . Without Getting Burned," *Seattle Times,* May 3, 2005.

8. Ibid.

9. Testimony of Chairman Alan Greenspan, Federal Reserve Board's semiannual Monetary Policy Report to the Congress before the Committee on Banking, Housing, and Urban Affairs, U.S. Senate, February 16, 2005.

10. Dan Ackman, "Retirement Doomsday," *Forbes,* May 4, 2005.

11. Alan Greenspan, at the Federal Reserve System's Fourth Annual Community Affairs Research Conference, Washington, DC, April 8, 2005.

12. William Shakespeare, *The Tempest,* Act iii, Scene 2.

Chapter 16   Subversive Investing

1. James Surowiekci, "Why Gold," *New Yorker,* November 29, 2004.

Index

Ackley, Gardner, 164–165
Adams, John, 1
Adams, John Quincy, 1
Afghanistan, 43, 52, 89, 198
Africa, 5, 11, 50, 57, 66, 71, 105,
    159
Agora Financial,
Agricultural Adjustment Act (1933),
    145
Aid to Dependent Children (ADC),
    141
Aid to Families with Dependent
    Children (AFDC), 141
Airplanes, 108
Alaric, 62, 76
Alaska, 95
Albright, Madeleine, 25
Alcibiades, 58
Aldrich, Nelson, 139
Alexander the Great, 13, 42
al-Qaida, 52
America/Americans:
    assets, total value of, 294
    difference, today versus 1776, 3
    economic body parts, 276
    getting poorer not richer, 25, 213,
        215, 224, 268, 286, 299
    having history, versus the French,
        159

parody of itself, 192
present position compared to
    Britain's World War I
    position, 125
present situation summed up, 214
self deception, 67, 77
American empire, 74–80, 219–246
    absurdity of, 39, 55, 77, 265
    belief in, 18
    of debt, 219–246
American military:
    budget/spending, 17, 80, 82, 85,
        87, 183, 191
    four regional commands, 74
    number of actions since World War
        II, 74
    power of, 14, 292
    Reagan and, 197
American Revolution, 131, 227
Angell, Norman (*The Great Illusion*),
    107
Anglo-Saxons, 223–224
Annamite Patriots league, 153
Arabs, 264
Argentina, 303
Aristotle (*Politics*), 71
Aron, Raymond, 251
Arthur, Chester A., 94, 97
Asakawa, Mr., 295–296

Asia/Asians, 4, 8, 14–16, 29, 40,
    42–44, 52, 56, 59, 65–67, 73,
    78, 127, 151, 161–163, 166,
    171, 177, 211, 222–224, 265,
    269, 275–276, 287, 289, 296,
    300, 303, 307. *See also specific*
    countries
Assets, total value of American, 294
Athenian empire, 58
Auden, W. H., 248
Auerback, Marshall, 242
Augustus, 50–51, 61, 71, 222
Austro-Hungarian Empire, 67, 106
Automobiles:
    buying decisions and limbic system,
        247
    financing debt, 245

Babar, 42
Baby boomers, 281
Baghdad, 45–46, 50, 76, 80, 195. *See*
    also Iraq, invasion of (2003)
Baltimore, 93, 124, 262, 270, 279
Bangalore, 261–262, 266
Bank of England, 223
Bank of Japan, 237, 301
Bankruptcy, 36, 60, 146, 217–218,
    293, 302, 313–314
Beer-Wine Revenue Act (1933), 143
Begin, Menachim, 87
Belgium/Belgians, 18, 93, 104,
    118–119
Bell curve, extreme edges, 251
Berlin Wall, fall of, 48, 234, 259
Bernanke, Ben, 31, 214, 236, 248,
    254, 287
Bethmann-Hollweg, Theobald von,
    115
Bill of Rights, 12, 209

Bin Laden, Osama, 210
Biology and actuary science,
    convergence of, 298
Bismarck, 83, 114–115
Bloom, Soldier, 85
Bolsheviks, 100, 153, 294
Bonaparte, 150, 155, 161
Bonds, 19, 300, 330
Booms, real versus phony, 205
Boot, Max, 59
Brain, two centers of decision making
    in, 247–248
Brazil, 53, 267
"Bread and circuses," 14–15, 142,
    180–181, 185, 202
Bresciani-Turoni, 30, 31
BRICS (Brazil, Russia, India, and
    China), 267
Britain/United Kingdom:
    economy, 60, 268
    empire, 55, 211, 226, 250
    English Pirates, 52
    government debt, 227
    pound, 60, 328
    war with France, 150
    World War I, 58, 84, 105, 108,
        109, 111, 119, 125, 129
    World War II, 109
Brooke, Rupert, 121
Brown, Stuart S., 240
Bryan, William Jennings, 104, 132,
    136
Bubbles:
    confidence, 197
    credit, of pax dollarium age, 178
    economic, 258, 300
    empire as, 60
    housing (*see* Real estate)
    Japanese, 177, 242

mania, 277–278
markets, 46, 62
Spanish economy, early sixteenth
    century, 51
tech stocks, 284
Buckley, William F., 192
Buffett, Warren, 25, 33, 240, 275,
    283, 289, 296, 309–311, 314,
    318
Bundy, McGeorge, 161
Burns, Arthur, 178
Bush, George W.:
  boondoggles, 330
  comparisons with other presidents,
    97
    Harding, 97
    Reagan, 215
    Washington, 27
  denouncing spending of predecessor
    and spending even more, 84
  fiscal policy, 25, 31, 79, 98, 222,
    227, 260
  foreign policy, 182, 194, 234
  gold price on taking office, 326
  lessons of the Fourth Crusade for,
    24, 25
  liberal politicians in 1960s
    compared to, 182
  Martin's ode, 210
  Medicare Drug Benefit program,
    245
  neocons and, 194
  ownership society, 244–245
  positivism of, 261
  reelection, 256
  Second Reich officials in same
    situation as, 30
  State of the Union address (2004),
    "time set apart," 192
  vote in a democracy, 30
  War on Terror, 52, 59
  among Wilson's accomplices, 98
Bush administration:
  China and, 38
  Iraq, 222, 264, 265
  perspective on actions of, 265
  public debt and, 256

Caesar, 39, 50, 65, 69, 71, 76, 120,
    135, 161, 219, 327
Cahill, Thomas (*How the Irish Saved
    Civilization*), 61
California Association of Realtors, 278
California housing boom, 216, 220,
    277–278, 280, 299, 300
Caligula, 61, 219
Cambodia, 166, 170
Camerone, Battle of, 150
Canada, 2, 122
Capital gains, myth of, 319–323
Capitalism, 46, 211, 234, 265, 291,
    310
Carranza, Venustiano, 101
Carter, Jimmy, 200, 213
Central African Empire, 71
Central bankers/banks, 32, 36, 126,
    234–235, 257, 328–329
Central planning, 195, 234, 259
CEO pay, 4
Chamberlain, Neville, 48, 197
Chancellor, Edward (*Devil Take the
    Hindmost*), 121
Chase, Stuart, 141
Cheney, Dick, 35
Chiang Kai Shek, 155
China:
  capitalism/investment rate, 211
  central bank, 37

China *(Continued)*
  Clinton's trip (1998), 1–2
  competition from, 4, 16, 211–212, 223, 254
  currency/yuan, 37, 42, 45, 265, 312
  democracy and, 110
  economic history, 8, 211–212
  GDP per capita, 60, 211, 268
  Italy and, 82
  jobs going to, 249
  lending to U.S., 19, 29, 36–37, 78, 253
  military, 59
  Mongol invasion, 42, 44, 63, 64
  rising power/economy, 125, 128, 267–268
  Roman era, 59
  savings rate (versus Americans), 10–11, 15, 38, 212, 248, 266, 268–269, 287–288, 289
  selling to U.S./trade deficit, 19, 57, 269, 276, 287
  Vietnam and, 155, 160
  vulnerability of U.S. economy to, 128, 242
  Yuan dynasty, 42
Chodorov, Frank, 131
Christ/Christians, 26, 51, 203
Churchill, Winston, 107–108, 113, 157
Church of England, 52
Citibank, 139
Civilian Conservation Corps (1933), 144
Civil War. *See* War between the States
Civil Works Administration, 144–145

Clemenceau, 118, 120
Clinton, Bill, 1–2, 87, 256
Clovis, King of the Francs, 173
Cobb, Ty, 117
Cockburn, Alexander, 160
Cohen, Roger, 59
Cold War, 79, 87, 157, 171, 184, 187, 193–194, 196, 206, 227
Communism, 196. *See also* Cold War; Domino theory; Soviet Union
Competitive Enterprise Institute, 147
Congress:
  election of Senators, 135–137
  meeting in deceit, 25
  nature of not what it was meant to be, 72
  and war, 89–90
Conservatives, traditional, 193, 195–196, 199
Consiglio Maggiore, 24, 25
Constantinople, 26–27, 46
Constitutional Convention in Philadelphia in 1789, 29–30
Constitutionalist party, 101
Constitution of the United States, 3–4, 6, 89, 99, 131
Consumer debt. *See* Household debt
Consumer Price Index (CPI), 208–209
Contrarians, 324–326
Coolidge, Calvin, 191
Corporate insiders, 310–312
Corrections, 289–294
Cost of Living Council, 179
Courts, Roosevelt and, 145–147
Crain, Mark, 148
Crassus, 327
Credit card debt. *See* Household debt

Credit cycle, 255
Credit industry, 277
Crews, Clyde Wayne, Jr., 147
Croesus, 327
Cromwell, Oliver, 160
Ctesiphon, 45, 50
Currency, 14, 37–38, 60, 138, 139,
 177–179, 249, 265, 312, 328.
 See also Gold standard; Paper
 money/dollars
Cycles, 10, 17, 33, 216, 271

Daily Reckoning, 3, 16, 244
Daly, Kevin, 292
Dandoli, 27
Darrow, Clarence, 104
Daugherty, Harry, 95–96
D'az, Porfirio, 101
Debt(s):
 government:
  federal (*see* Public debt)
  private (*see* Household debt)
 repudiation of, 294–295
De Castries, Christian, 151, 152
Deceit/deceptions:
 America's empire of debt resting
  on, 220–223, 290–291
 great public movements and
  empires beginning in, 120
 Iraq war, 222
 market, by central planners,
  236–238
 Oliphant's dictum (easy to deceive
  the multitudes), 24–25
 self, 25, 67, 77, 221
 Senate, 25
 something-for-nothing, 32, 203,
  302
 statistics, abuse of, 221

Vietnam, 163
Wall Street and SEC, 310
Decision making, brain and, 124,
 125, 247–248
Declaration of the Rights of Man,
 155
Deficits:
 federal (*see* Federal deficits)
 trade, 6, 32, 51, 253–254, 277
De Gaulle, Charles, 37, 174
Degenerate stage of empire, 18
Democracy(ies):
 American style, 110
 ease of stirring masses to absurdity
  in modern, 164
 empty concept of, 311
 extending World War I, 111, 112
 Greeks invention, 110
 making the world "safe" for, 120,
  123–126
 not "God's choice" or universal
  constant, 110
 versus republics, 30
 thievery tolerated by, 182
 using military forces to build, 264
Democratic/Republican economists,
 2004 campaign, 266–267
Democratization of credit, 293
Dickinson, John, 136
Diem brothers, 164
Dien Bien Phu, Battle of, 151, 158
Diocletian, 90, 179
Dividends, 314
Dollar:
 China pegging its currency to, 38
 demise of, 295–296
 extra, marked to unforgiving
  market, 187
 marginal utility hypothesis, 298

Dollar *(Continued)*
  paper, 8, 17, 56, 187, 249, 295–296
  pax dollarium, 77, 178, 185–187,
      214, 222–223, 265
  post-Nixon plunge in value of,
      185
  value of today:
    in comparison to 1913, 186
    in comparison to 1950s, 291
Domino theory, 162, 170, 171
Dot-coms, 277
Douglas, Paul, 182
Dow Jones Industrial Average, 185,
    298, 332
Drayton, William, 75
Dual monarchy, 67
Duiker, William J., 152
Duncan, Richard, 236

Economic Opportunity Act (1964),
    183–184
Economy Act (1933), 143
Edict of Prices, 90
Efficient market hypothesis (EMH),
    310–311
Einstein, Albert, 119
Eisenhower, Dwight, 162, 170, 192,
    214, 215, 255
élan, 242
Election of 2004, 25
Eliot, Charles W., 159
Elizabethan Poor Laws, 142–143
Elizabeth I, 52
Emergency Banking Act (1933), 143
Emergency Railroad Transportation
    Act, 144
Empires, 39–53, 55–80. *See also*
    American empire
  Austro-Hungarians, 67–69
  bankruptcy of, 15

characteristics/common elements,
    18, 39, 73–74, 85–86
Genghis Khan, 42–46
history, 57–60
how they work, 55–80
Huns, 40–42
life cycle/stages of, 18, 48, 60–63,
    270
making of, 69–73
as monopoly on force, 7
in praise of, 63–67
Roman, 49–51 (*see also*
    Rome/Roman Empire)
Spanish, 51–53
End of History, 10, 46, 251
England. *See* Britain/United
    Kingdom
Escoffier, Auguste, 154
Esher, Lord, 107
Espionage and Seditions Acts, 116
Essentialism, 318–319
Euro, 296, 328
Europe. *See also specific countries*
  barbarian invasions of, 40–42
  colonial empires in the New
      World, 66, 67
  globalization, 250–251
  relative standard of living (1700), 8
  worst ideas of twentieth century
      coming from, 192
Evolutionary biology, 76–77

Fallacy of composition, 307
Farm Credit Act, 144
Fat tails, 251, 342
Federal Deposit Insurance
    Corporation, 282
Federal Emergency Relief Act (1933),
    144
Federal debt. *See* Public debt

Federal deficits:
  creating disorder on purpose with,
    265–266
  no-matter attitude toward, 199,
    200, 214
  Reagan tax cuts and, 206
  Templeton on, 32
Federalist Papers, 131
Federal Reserve System, 99,
    139–140, 146, 178, 186, 235,
    238, 293–294. *See also*
    Greenspan, Alan
Federal Securities Act, 144
Federal Unemployment Insurance Act
    (FUTA), 141
Feldstein, Martin, 147
Field, Stephen J., 133
Fillmore, Millard, 95, 97
Finance, modern imperial, 78,
    247–260
  globalization and its discontents,
    248–254
  Greenspan, 255–260 (*see also*
    Federal Reserve System;
    Greenspan, Alan)
  limbic system, 247–248
Financial industry compared with
    medical industry, 306–307
Financial Reckoning Day, 19, 297
First Bank of the United States, 137
Flanders, Ralph E., 88
Flynn, John T.:
  As We Go Marching, 81–85, 147
  *Decline of the American Republic,
    The,* 131
Ford, Gerald, 182
Foreign ownership of U.S. assets, 14,
    215, 217
Foreign workers cutting into
    American salaries for years, 266

Founding Fathers, 13, 105, 111, 116,
    135
Fourteen Points, 120, 123
Fourth Crusade, 24–27
France:
  economy:
    GDP growth expected, 267–268
    maximizing leisure versus
      income, 11
    policy deficits (2004), 224
    thriving in post war era "les
      trente glorieuses," 223
  élan, 241
  empire, 11–12, 25, 57, 66
  "isms," 192
  Revolution (1791), 155
  Rights of Man, 12
  security differences (versus United
    States) for public figures, 1
  Vietnam, 13, 149–150, 152, 155,
    156, 158–159, 167, 174
  wars:
    financing, 109, 111, 127, 128
    Franco-Prussian War (1870),
      105, 120, 241
    Napoleonic, 60
    World War I, 121, 122, 123, 325
Franklin, Benjamin, 30, 135
Franks, 155
Franks, Tommy, 50
Franz Ferdinand, Archduke, 68, 106
Franz Josef, Emperor, 68
Fraud. *See* Deceit/deceptions
Freedom, extending, 3, 182, 196, 210
Free market paradigm, 195, 234
Freud, Sigmund, 99, 108, 114, 126
Friedman, Milton, 196, 200, 204
Friedman, Thomas L. (of the *New
    York Times*), 261–266, 329
Fukuyama, Francis, 10, 46, 48

Galbraith, John Kenneth, 138
Galerius, 46
Galieni (French general), 121
Gardner, Gilson, 118
Garfield, James A., 94, 95
Garrett, Garet, 87–89
Gates, Bill, 3
General Motors, 4, 214, 223, 276, 296, 306, 309, 318
George, Lloyd, 119
George V, 112, 125–126
Germany:
  East/West, 170
  economy:
    government debt, 227
    relative economic health, 250, 268
  empire, 57
  fall of Berlin Wall, 48, 234, 259
  Second Reich, 30–32
  Wilson's attack on Vera Cruz and, 101
  World War I, 81, 104–107, 111–117, 121, 124, 159, 325
    debts after, 294–295, 302
    lost overseas colonies after, 57
  World War II, 74, 81
Gettysburg Address, 116
Geyl, Pieter, 125
Giap, Vo Nguyen, 151–152, 156, 166, 170, 174
Gibbon, Edward, 26–27
Gladwell, Malcolm (*Blink*), 95–96
Glass-Steagall Banking Act, 144
Globalization, 14–17, 248–254
Gold:
  amount mined since 1971, 187
  buying as investment, 19, 20, 322–323, 326–330, 333

  permanence of, versus paper dollar, 56
  power of, 326–330
  price of, 36, 186, 215, 326
  purchase price of Dow in (1982 versus now), 215
  reserves depleted (1968), 182
  trouble with, 329
Gold standard:
  Federal Securities Act (1933) removing U.S. from, 144
  globalized commerce backed by, 185–186
  Greenspan's changing position on, 256
  Nixon abandoning, 14, 177–179
  trade deficits and, 36
  World War I, 126–129, 131
Google, 309
Gore, Al, 308
Government debt:
  federal (*see* Public debt)
Grant's Interest Rate Observer, 238, 243
Gravelines, Battle of, 53
Great Depression, 33, 141, 227, 317–318
Great Society, 180, 183, 186
Great War. *See* World War I
Greeks, 57, 58, 66, 110
Greene, Graham, 151
Greenspan, Alan, 255–260. *See also* Federal Reserve System
  bubbles, 260
  deception of, 221, 290–291
  easy money policies, 15, 16, 31
  Federal Reserve, 14, 235–239
  on job losses (productivity versus outsourcing), 254–255, 266

Open Market Committee, 234–235
pact with Devil, 257
paper dollar and, 15, 17
Pontius Pilate comparison, 257
positivism of, 38, 215, 261, 286
on Smith (Adam), 234–235
speech in Scotland (February 2005), 234, 258
among Wilson's accomplices, 98
Groups:
smarter than individuals, 235
subverting, 326

Hadrian, 45
Haiti, 100
Hamilton, Alexander, 131, 137
Hamilton-Grace, R. S., 126
Hand, Learned, 99
Hanoi, 151, 152, 156, 165, 171
Hansen, Alvin, 146
Harding, Warren Gamaliel, 94, 95–97, 227
Harrison, William Henry, 95
Hayek, Friedrich A., 218, 235
Head Start, 184
Hegel, 10
Helferrich, 31
Heller, Walter, 164
Hemingway, Ernest, 93
Henry VIII, 52
Heraclius, 46
Herzog, Buck, 117
Hill, Vernon W., 238–242
History:
as an argument without end, 125
end of, 10, 46, 251
ranking/rating of presidents, 94
Hitler, Adolph, 48, 76, 160, 183

Ho Chi Minh, 152–158, 165, 166, 169
Hoebeke, C. H., 136
Holland's Tulip Bubble, 47
"Hollow dummies," 6, 48
Holy Roman Empire. *See* Rome/Roman Empire
Homeland Security, 137
Home Owners Refinancing Act (1933), 144
Hoover, Herbert, 140, 227
Hopkins, Thomas, 148
Household debt:
as a consumer choice, 269–270
credit card debt, 227
Greenspan commenting on housing prices and, 17
home equity lines of credit, 280
mortgages, 28, 220, 227, 258–259, 277
soaring, 35–36, 260
Housing boom. *See* Real estate
Howe, Stephen (*Empire*), 67–68
Hue, Robert, 1
Huerta, Victoriano, 100, 101, 102
Humphrey, Hubert, 183
Hundred Days, 143
Huns, 40–42, 76, 104, 117, 118, 122, 194
Hussein, Saddam (ancestors), 26

Ideologies, 33
Immigration, 29
Imperial finance. *See* Finance, modern imperial
Income(s):
Americans versus French; maximizing, 11
average American households, 293

Income(s) *(Continued)*
  increasing, 252
  regressing to mean, 8–9
  smoothing, 300
Income tax system, 131–135, 137
India:
  BRICS, 270
  competition from, 211
  incomes, 8–9
  Mogul Empire, 65
  Mongol Empire and, 42, 63
  rising economy of, 210–211, 267
  scientists from, 57
Indirect elections, 136
Indochina, 153, 154, 158
Industrial revolution, 8
Inflation, 37, 178, 202, 204,
  299–303
Information, distilled/undistilled, 34,
  35
Innovations, 33
Institutions evolving over time, 3
Interest-only loans, 280
Internal Revenue Code, complexity
  of, 134–135
International Herald Tribune, 59, 78,
  149, 240
International Monetary Fund, 217
Investing/investors. *See also* Wall
  Street
  art/science, 308
  capital gains myth, 319–323
  compared to "holding up liquor
    stores," 308
  confidence of, 285
  dumping investments, 313–314
  essentialism, 318–319
  gold, 19, 20, 322–323, 326–330,
    333

  past/present/future, 326–330
  private versus public knowledge,
    309, 319
  versus speculation, 315
  subversive, 324–326
  U.S. Treasury bonds, 185
  zero sum game, 308
Invisible hand, 234, 259
Iran, 12
Iraq, invasion of (2003):
  Congress authorization, 89
  as costly blunder, 6, 11, 79, 80
  debate surrounding, 12, 13, 265,
    313
  Giap on, 175
  historical context, 45–46
  as imperial interest versus national
    interest, 13
  lies told to stir up support for, 222
  political gimcrackery of, 186
Iron curtain, 157
"Irrationally exuberant," 256
Isms, "awful," 192
Italy/Italians, 81–85, 113, 227, 267

Jackson, Andrew, 138
James, Ollie, 117
Japan, 297–303
  automobiles from, 57, 241
  baby boom, 297
  Bernanke appeal to (2003), 236
  bubble of late 1980s, 47, 177
  central bank, 37, 295–296
  competition from, 222
  deflation, 299, 300–301
  dollar, 249, 295–296
  economy went bust with rest of
    world owing them a lot of
    money, 301

GDP per head, 267–268
liberals perception of economic management (1973), 252
monetary policy (2003–2004), 236
selling to U.S., 57, 241
U.S. economy following that of, 297–303
Vietnam and, 155, 156, 167
vulnerability of dollar to, 128
Westernized, 211
World War II, 74
Jefferson, Thomas, 1, 6, 73, 110, 226
Jerusalem, 25
Jews, 66, 79, 81, 114, 170, 173
Job Corps, 184
Jobs/labor markets, 212, 249, 266, 267, 299. *See also* Outsourcing
Johnson, Andrew, 95
Johnson, Harold K., 179
Johnson, Lyndon, 79, 159–167, 174, 180, 182–183, 200, 237
private comments on Vietnam War, 173–174
State of Union Address (1966) on Great Society funding versus financing war, 149
among Wilson's accomplices, 98
Johnson, Paul, 103
Julius Caesar. *See* Caesar

Kaiser Wilhelm, 115, 118, 294
Kaplan, Robert (*Warrior Politics: Why Leadership Demands a Pagan Ethos*), 59
Kennedy, John F., 72, 79, 116, 160, 161, 162, 165, 174
Kennedy, Paul, 59
Kenyon, William Squire, 117

Kerensky government, Russia, 100, 109, 112
Kerkorian, Kirk, 309
Kerry, John, 149
Keynes, John Maynard/Keynesian economics, 182, 199, 201, 203, 206, 290
Khan, Genghis, 42–46, 65, 125
Khan, Kublai, 45
Khan, Mongka, 45
Khan, Ogedei, 44
King, Martin Luther, 172
Kipling, Rudyard, 66
Kissinger, Henry, 165–166, 210
Knowledge principle, 195
Korea/Korean War, 13–14, 42, 57, 72–73, 86, 87, 89
Kosztolanyi, Dezso, 114
Krauthammer, Charles, 58
Kucinich, Dennis, 249
Kuhn, Loeb Investment House, 139
Ku Klux Klan, 153–154

Labor markets/jobs, 212, 249, 266, 269, 292
Laffer, Arthur (Laffer Curve), 205, 213–214, 291
La Follette, Robert, 104–105, 117, 118, 119
Lal, Deepak (*In Praise of Empires*), 63–64
Lane, Harry, 117
Laos, 170, 174
Latin America, 101–103
Law, John, 32, 93
League of Nations, 93
Legionnaires, 150–151
Lerner, Abba, 199
Levey, David H., 221, 240, 241

Lewis, Syndham, 114
Liberty Loans, 128
Life/death, and reversion to mean, 9
Limbic system, 124, 247–248
Lincoln, Abraham:
  abolition of slavery, 197
  blockading South, 104
  Gettysburg Address, 116
  historians' rating of, 94, 95, 97
Long-Term Capital Management, 168
Louis IX, 25
Louis XIV (Sun King), 70
Lumpen democrat, 311
Lumpen investors, 177, 311
"Lusting after money is better than,"
  192–203

MacArthur, Douglas, 88
Macedonian empire, 58
Machiavelli, 85, 161
MacKenzie, Ross, 197
MacMullen, Ramsay (*Corruption and
  the Decline of Rome*), 5–6, 69
MacNamara, Robert S., 159–166,
  168–169, 174, 180, 182
Madero, Francisco, 101
Madison, James, 30, 110, 131, 136,
  137, 226
Madrid bombings (March 2004),
  149
"Magic economy," 252
Magna Carta, 124
Mahan, Alfred Thayer (*The Influence
  of Sea Power upon History,
  1660–1783*), 53
Malaysia, 57
Malpass, David, 269
Marburg, Theodore, 93
Marginal utility hypothesis, 298

Markets:
  bear/bull, 41, 62, 215, 313
  as comedies, 285, 326
  intelligence of, 235–236
  opinions made by, 3, 9, 47, 256
Martin, Rod, 209, 210
Martin, William McChesney, 214
Marx, 10, 154, 211–215
Mary Queen of Scots, 52
McCarthy, Joseph, 157
McTeer, Robert, 38, 255
Mean, reversions to, 7–9
Medicare/Medicaid, 35, 141, 183,
  184, 186, 217, 245
Mediocrity, delusions of, 284–286
Mencken, H. L. (*Gamalielese*), 97
Mesopotamia, 317
Mexico:
  American war, 159, 227
  Austro-Hungarian Empire and, 69
  competition in labor market, 266
  French foreign legion and Battle of
    Cameron, 150–151
  Spanish empire and, 53
  Wilson and, 99–102, 117
Michaels, Jason, 243
Microsoft, 3
Military:
  armies as blunt instruments, not
    precision tools, 264
  elevation of (characteristic of all
    empires), 85–86
  nation's economy and, 82–83
  support for government, and, 83
  United States (*see* American
    military)
Mills, Wilbur, 182
Minsky, Hyman, 330
Mogul Empire, India, 65

Mongol Empire, 42–46, 63, 64, 66, 88
Mongolia, 43, 44, 65
Monopoloy on force, empire as, 7
Monroe County Bank (Vernon W. Hill), 238–242
Mood, public, 272
Moore, Thomas Gale, 214
Morgan, J. P., 139
Morgan Bank, 139
Morning in America, 197, 207
  sunrise/sunset, 215–216
Mortgages, 28, 220, 221, 227, 258–259, 277
Mr. Market, 235, 259, 311
Munger, Charlie, 283
Muslims, 87, 194, 264
Mussolini, Benito, 23, 81, 84, 85, 160

Nader, Ralph, 249
Napoleon, 60, 76, 150, 159, 161, 258
Nasdaq, 298, 301
National Banking Act (1863), 138
National Council of Bishops, 255
National Employment System Act, 144
National Industrial Recovery Act, 144
National Youth Administration, 143
Naughton, Morning, 243–245
Neo-conservatism, 192, 193, 194, 198, 210
Nero, 51, 61, 90
New Deal, 139–140, 144, 148, 183, 186
Newfoundlanders, 122
New Frontier, 186
Newman, Dan and Frank, 271
New York Times, the, 58, 164

Nguyen Sinh Cung, 152–153
Nhu, Madame, 165
Nicaragua, 11, 100
Nicholas II, 112
Nikkei Dow, 301
9/11 attacks, 87, 233, 262–263
Nixon, Richard, 177–187, 200, 213
  on foreign policy (in 1973 inauguration speech), 116
  freezing prices, 90
  gold standard, and pax dollarium, 14, 177–179, 185–187, 252
  paying for Vietnam, 179–185
"Normal," 7, 56
Norris, Floyd, 78
Nye Committee, 113

Obituaries, 30
Octavian, 50–51, 71
Oliphant, Margaret Wilson (*The Makers of Venice, Doges, Conquerors, Painters & Men of Letters*), 24–25, 27
O'Neill, Paul, 194, 199, 233
Open Market Committee, 235
Oppenheimer, Franz, 251
Ortega y Gasset, Jose, 83
Orwell, George, 6, 48, 48, 109, 234
Ottoman Empire, 42, 63, 65, 129
Outsourcing, 249, 255, 263, 267, 312. *See also* Jobs/labor markets
Owen, Wilfred, 121–122
Owen-Glass Act, 139
Ownership society, 245–246

Pakistan, 312
Palestine, 263
Palmer, Bruce (*Twenty-five Year War*), 169

Panic of 1907, 133
Paper money/dollars, 15, 17, 56, 186, 249, 295–296, 303
  contrasted to gold, 327–330
  paperless (electronic registration), 55
  zero mean value, long-term, 8
Papini, Giovanni, 83
Path dependent, 207
Patriot Act, 137
Patti, Archimedes, 157
Pax Americana in Asia, 59
Pax dollarium, 38, 40, 77, 178, 184, 185–187, 214, 222–223, 265
Pax Romana, 5
"Peace in our time," 48
Pearl Harbor, 74
Peffer, William, 132
Peloponnesian War, 57
Pensions, 212, 213
Pericles, 58
Perkins, John (*Confessions of an Economic Hit Man*), 74–75
Pershing, John J. ("Black Jack"), 103, 159
Peru, 53
Peterson, Pete, 217
Philip II, King of Spain, 52, 53
Playmate of the Month, 284, 285
Political gimcrackery (list), 187
Politics, bubbles in, 47–48
Ponzi, Charles, 32
Pope Innocent III, 26
Portugal, 51, 53
Positivism, nabobs of, 263
Pound, Ezra, 23
Price freeze, 90
Princip, Gavrilo, 106–107, 123

Private knowledge. *See* Public versus private knowledge
Private sector debt:
  consumers (*see* Household debt)
Productivity, 202–203, 220, 255
Progressive Party, 117
Prospect theory, 298–299
Public debt:
  held by foreign investors, 56, 246
  increasing, 226–238
  intergenerational, 227
  no-problem attitude, 35, 37, 38, 146
  size of, 294–295
  statutory limits on, 199
  traditional conservative attitudes against, 29, 205
  what will happen to, 38, 294–295
Public versus private knowledge, 305, 309, 313, 319

Raffarin, Jean-Pierre, 1
Railroad Retirement Act of 1934, 144–145
Randolph, Edmund, 29
Randomness of events, 331
Reagan, Ronald Wilson, 191–218
  cornerstones of era of, 202
  death, 196, 209
  describing himself as conservative, 198
  economic policies/legacy:
    funny numbers, 207–208
    pensions, companies stopped offering fixed-benefit, 213, 214
    public debt, 217–218, 227
    Reaganomics, four key elements, 200

real booms versus the phony
variety, 205–207
savings/investment rates falling
during administration of,
248, 253, 254–255, 269
something-for-nothing, 213
sunrise/sunset, 215–216
supply-side economics, 201,
203–205, 213–214
tax cuts, 206–207
trade figures and job numbers
falling, 266
foreign policy stance, 195
inaugural address, 197–198
Martin's ode to, 209–210
Marx's revenge, 211–215
military spending, 197
Soviet Union, 194, 209–211, 271
Thatcher on, 196
wages, 212–213
what lusting after money is better
than, 192–203
among Wilson's accomplices, 98
Reagan Doctrine, 209
Reagan Revolution, 198, 211, 212,
291
Real estate:
flipping, 283, 330
Greenspan on rising home prices
and household debt, 17
home mortgages, 28, 220, 227,
258–259, 277
home values as inactive, 242
housing boom/bubble, 7, 46, 47,
216, 223, 260, 277–286,
314–315
California, 277–278, 299, 300
Philadelphia, 279
signs trend nearing end, 299

myth about, 4, 18
Templeton on house prices in
America, 32
world bubbles in, 299–300
Real Simple, 244–245
Recession, 254–255
Regulations:
cost of federal, 147–148
reducing, 200
Reich, 31, 302
Religion:
abortion funding and the Religious
Right, 295
War on Terror subtext of, 52
Wilson and God's mind, 99
Rental vacancies, 299
Republic, 30, 56, 135
Republicans, 29, 192, 253
Repudiation of debt, 294–295
Residential property bubble. *See* Real
estate
Retirement, 214, 245–246, 281, 297,
298. *See also* Social Security
Reversions to mean, 7–9
Revolutionary War, 110, 159, 327
Revolution in America (1913–1971),
72, 131–148
American Caesars, 135–137
bread and circuses, 142–144
New Deal, the, 140–142
new money, 137–139
Revolution of 1913, 131, 148
safety net, 139–140
stuffing the court, 144–146
Ten Thousand Commandments,
147–148
where the money comes from,
131–135
Reynolds, Alan, 203

Rilke, Rainer, 114
Roach, Stephen, 259, 268
Roberts, Paul Craig, 271
Robin, Corey, 192
Rolling Thunder, 167
Rome/Roman Empire, 5–8, 15–17,
     45–46, 49–51, 56–76, 87–88,
     90, 150, 155, 219, 325, 327
Roosevelt, Franklin Delano, 79, 84,
     94, 98, 139, 140, 141, 144–146,
     163, 184, 227. *See also* New
     Deal
Roosevelt, Theodore, 13, 74, 79, 93,
     97, 115, 133
Rothbard, Murray, 198
Royal "we," 20
Rusk, Dean, 162
Russia:
   Alaska purchase, 95
   Bolsheviks, 100, 210, 294
   competition from, 211
   empire, 57, 65
   living standards, 267
   Mongol invasion, 42
   Napoleon's campaign against, 150
   Reagan and, 209, 210
   socialism, 113
   Stalin, 112
   Vietnam, 160
   Wilson on, 100
   World War I, 111, 112, 127
   World War II, 57, 112

Sabines, 50, 57
Safety net, 139–140
Salan, Raoul, 169
Saracens, 46
Sarajevo, 68
Saudi Arabia, 267

Savings rates, 15, 202–203, 247–248,
     253, 268–269, 287
Savings of world's poorest, U.S.
     dependence on, 276
Scandinavia, 64
Scheler, Max, 114
Schlesinger, Arthur, Jr., 75
Schumpeter, Joseph, 261
Scopes Trial, 104
Second Bank of the United States,
     138
Secret Service, 2
Securities and Exchange Commission
     (SEC), 310
Self-deception, 25, 67, 77, 221
Senate:
   election of Senators, 135–137
   meeting in deceit, 25
September 11 attacks, 87, 234,
     262–263
Septimus Severus, 45
Seventeenth Amendment, 136
Shareholder Nation, 214
Sharpton, Al, 249
Sixteenth Amendment (income tax),
     134, 136
Slavery:
   Lincoln credited with abolishing,
     197
   Roman Empire, 50
Smith, Adam (*Wealth of Nations*),
     64, 195, 234, 235, 259
Smoothing income, 293
Snow, John, 37, 38
Social contract, 227
Social Security, 35, 140–142, 147,
     186, 217, 246, 291
Soule, George (of *The New Republic*),
     141

South Sea Bubble, 47
Soviet Union:
  actual tax rates, 206–207
  collapse of, 76, 86–87
  "Evil Empire," 86, 194, 210
  gulag system, 70
  Hitler attacking, 183
  Ho Chi Minh and, 157
  Mongolia and, 43
  as rival, 79
  totalitarian regime (taking
    resources from citizens), 110
  trade within, 252
Spain, 51–53, 58, 66, 149, 159
Spanish Armada, 51–53, 58
Sparta, 58
Speculators, 330, 331, 332
Squanderville, 275–296
Stagflation, 204
Stalin, 112
Stalingrad, 325
States that repudiated their debts in
  panics of 1840s, 295
Statistics, abuse of, 221
Stein, Ben, 286–287
Stocks/stock market, 18, 281, 323,
  332. *See also* Wall Street
Stone, William J., 119–120
Strachan, Hew, 109
Strong, Ben, 32
Student loans outstanding, federal
  (1979–2000), 233
Subversive investing, 324–326
Sullivan, Mark, 96
Sun King, Louis XIV, 70
Superpowers, 76
Supply siders, 203–207, 213
Surowiecki, James (*The Wisdom of
  Crowds*), 235, 327

Suskind, Ron (*The Price of Loyalty*),
  233
Switzerland/Swiss, 12, 13, 59–60,
  64, 170–171

Taft, Robert, 89
Taft, William Howard, 101
Taiwan, 57, 266
Taleb, Nassim Nicholas (*Fooled by
  Randomness*), 34
Tax, income, 131–135, 136, 252
Tax cuts, 200, 202, 205, 206, 207,
  213
Taylor, A. J. P., 106, 129
Taylor, Maxwell, 161, 162, 163
Tech bubble, 277
Templeton, John, 32–33
Tennessee Valley Authority Act, 144
Tenth Amendment, 143
Thailand, 171
Thatcher, Maggie, 196
Tiberius, 61
Tonkin Gulf, 165
Townsend, Francis, 141
Townsend Plan, 141
Trade deficit, 6, 32, 35–36, 51,
  253–254, 277
Trajan, 6, 45, 50
Tran Quang Co, 168–169, 174
Trask, H. A. Scott, 226
Treaty of Versailles, 46
Truman, Harry, 13, 72, 73, 79, 156,
  157
Trump, Donald, 281–282, 284
Tsetsenbileg, Professor, 43
Tulip Bubble, 47
Tullock, Gordon, 125
Turkey, 84
Tversky, Amos, 298, 331

Two ways:
  to get what you want, 172–173,
    251
  to invest, 312
  to make the world better, 312

Uncle Remus, 317
Unemployment, 185
United Kingdom. *See* Britain/United
    Kingdom
United States. *See*
    America/Americans
USSR, Hitler attacking, 183
Utility, 319

Vanity, 193
Venice, 23, 24–27, 46
Vera Cruz, battle of, 102
Versailles boxes, lemon trees, 250
Victoria, Queen, 112
Victory Loan, 128
Vienna, 271
Vietnam War, 159–166
  American troop levels, 165
  casualties, 13
  contemporaneous expenditures on
    Cold War, 87
  cost of, 13, 166–168, 179–185,
    186
  entertainment value of, 79
  as farce (versus crime/tragedy),
    169
  historical background (France/Ho
    Chi Minh), 149–159
  MIA and POWs, 166
  paying for, 179–185
  pointlessness of, 13–14, 170
  public sentiment following, 116,
    196, 213

Villa, Pancho, 102–103
Visigoths, 62, 76
Volcker, Paul, 200, 201, 214, 238,
    243, 253–254, 258
Volunteers in Service to America
    (VISTA), 184
Von Hotzendorf, Franz Conrad,
    115
Von Reininghaus, Gina, 115
Von Schlieffen, Alfred, 121
Voodoo economics, 203
Voting, 83

Wage increases, real, 202, 212–213,
    265
Wage/price controls, Nixon, 178
Walker, David M., 35
Wall Street, 305–315. *See also*
    Stocks/stock market
  Crash of 1929, 33, 141, 332
  deception, 310
  insider's game, 310–312
  in the 1990s, 28
  odds of crashing, 332
  Panic of 1907, 139
  purpose, 305–306
  quackery, 306
  separating fools from their money,
    309
  short-term/long-term investments,
    313–315
Wal-Mart, 16, 215, 270, 276
Walpole, Robert, 226
Wanniski, Jude, 217
War(s):
  as distraction from personal
    problems, 115
  as health of the state, 114
  as meaning in empty lives, 114

as tragic examples of collective action, 326

world (*see* World War I; World War II)

War between the States, 105, 109, 120, 132, 138, 161, 197, 227

War of 1812, 137, 227

War on Terror, 6, 52, 79, 87, 210, 233

Washington, George, 6, 27

Watergate, 177

Wealth illusion, 241

Welfare programs, 143, 252–253

Westenhiser, Jamie, 284

Westmoreland, William, 169

Wildcat banks, era of, 138

Wilhelm II, 112

William, Duke of Normandy, 52

Wilson, Thomas Woodrow:

criticism of, 77, 79, 94, 98, 99, 100, 115, 166, 197

death of first wife, 102, 103, 115

Freud describing, 99

guardians of foreign policy legacy of, 162

Latin America and, 101–103

League of Nations, 93, 160

limbic system, 124

in MacNamara's book, 166

madness of, 99

as national hero, 94, 197

reelection platform slogan ("He Kept Us out of War"), 163

stroke, 120

as world "improver," 97–100, 109, 155, 166, 197, 252

World War I, 13, 74, 103–115, 123, 153, 166, 227

Wolfe, Tom, 252

Wolff, Edward, 213

Works Progress Administration, 143

World Trade Organization, 249

World War I, 103–115

American involvement, 119, 166

Canadian veterans of, 122

combatants that were democracies, 108

cost of/paying for, 111–112, 113, 126–129, 234

democracy prolonging, 111, 112, 123

French casualties, 159

Germany using inflation to reduce debts after, 302

Ho Chi Minh, 153

Italy, 85

popularity of bullet wounds to the hand ("ticket home"), 326

Russia, 111, 112, 127

understanding of, as "bull market in death," 123

Wilson, 13, 74, 100, 103–115, 119, 123–126, 153, 166

World War II:

boom after, 252

"decimation" in, 325

federal debt at end of, 234

globalization of pax dollarium era after, 222–223

income tax rates at end of, 134

insights from book (*As We Go Marching*) written during, 81, 84

panzer divisions, 44

personal consumption spending expanding after, 185

World War II *(Continued)*
  Russia, 112–113, 325
  Templeton perspective, and dark
      days of, 33
  United States' entry into, 74, 159
  United States' military actions
      (number) since, 74
WR Grace, 313–314
Wright brothers (Orville and Wilbur),
    33, 108

"Yanqui go home," 103
Years 1982 and 2005 compared,
    215–216

Yuan:
  currency, 37–38, 265, 312
  dynasty, 45

Zara, city of, 26
Zero sum game:
  investing, 308
  politics and war, 40
Zweig, Stefan, 114